W9-CUN-280

THE MAKING
OF
URBAN HISTORY

THE MAKING OF URBAN HISTORY
Historiography Through Oral History

BRUCE M. STAVE

 **SAGE PUBLICATIONS, Inc.**   Beverly Hills   London

Copyright © 1977 by Sage Publications, Inc.

All rights reserved. No part of this book may be reproduced or utilized in any form or by any means, electronic or mechanical, including photocopying, recording, or by any information storage and retrieval system, without permission in writing from the publisher.

For information address:

SAGE PUBLICATIONS, INC.
275 South Beverly Drive
Beverly Hills, California 90212

SAGE PUBLICATIONS LTD
28 Banner Street
London EC1Y 8QE, England

Printed in the United States of America

Library of Congress Cataloging in Publication Data

State, Bruce M.
    The making of urban history.

    Includes bibliographies and index.
    1. Cities and towns—United States—History.

I. Title.
HT123.S76   301.36'3'0973   77-7245

ISBN 0-8039-0868-7
ISBN 0-8039-0869-5 pbk.

FIRST PRINTING

Contents

Other works by Bruce M. Stave:

THE NEW DEAL AND THE LAST HURRAH (1970)
URBAN BOSSES, MACHINES, AND PROGRESSIVE REFORMERS (1972)
THE DISCONTENTED SOCIETY (1972 with LeRoy Ashby)
SOCIALISM AND THE CITIES (1975)

Several Dedications:

For

My brother, HDS,
more versed in
oral argument than
oral history;

The good memories
of MSS and DGS;

The memory of
Constance McLaughlin
Green, pioneer and
a heck of an oral
history interview
one stormy day in
Bethel, Connecticut
shortly before she
died;

The growing number of
urban and oral historians,
whose enthusiasms are
gratifying.

ACKNOWLEDGEMENTS

Without the cooperation of the nine scholars whose conversations appear within, this volume would have been impossible. I especially appreciate their suggestions and the opportunity to share ideas about urban history with them for our readers. The conversations began as a series in the *Journal of Urban History,* and for the inception of that series I owe a great debt to the *Journal's* first Editor, Raymond A. Mohl. I have worked with Ray on several projects and believe he epitomizes the best qualities of urban historians discussed in this volume. His *JUH* successor, Blaine A. Brownell, has been equally encouraging and helpful.

The most arduous task in the oral history process is transcribing the tape recordings. Five of the conversations in this book were transcribed by Robert McMahon, a recent recipient of the doctorate from the University of Connecticut, whose talents in the history of American foreign policy will, I anticipate, surpass even his exceptional abilities as a transcriber. Other students who aided in transcribing are Charles Connerly, Patrick Hayes, Alison Roth, and John Benson; their efforts are greatly appreciated. I also owe thanks to Allan Bossoli and Robert Cooper for assistance with footnotes, and to the latter for his typing. The anonymous typists of the University of Connecticut Research Foundation typing pool are equally thanked. A grant from the Foundation has generously assisted this project from its beginning, and I am indebted to its director, Dean Hugh Clark, for his encouragement to research generally. That task is made easier at Storrs by the University of Connecticut reference Librarians, who have been particularly helpful in answering my many calls about bibliography and references; it is pleasant working with true professionals, even if they are not in a faculty collective bargaining unit. Bill Breadheft, of the University of Connecticut Photography Lab, graciously assisted with the photographs for this book, and my colleague R. Kent Newmyer applied his photographic talents to a difficult subject. The enthusiasm for these conversations on the part of my colleagues and students in History and Urban Studies at the University of Connecticut and the readers of the *Journal of Urban History* has been gratifying. Rhoda Blecker, Senior Editor, and Betsy Schmidt, Executive Serials Editor of Sage Publications have been patient, encouraging, and helpful in the completion of *The Making of Urban History*.

Finally, my wife, Sondra Astor Stave, appears as a questioner in only one of the conversations. However, she was present at several others, and her silence does not imply lack of creative participation. As Chairperson of the Conventry Connecticut Planning and Zoning Commission, who recently completed her work for a Masters Degree in Public Affairs, is teaching adult education classes in baking and cooking, has written restaurant reviews for magazines, indexed scholarly books, edited the town's Bicentennial Cookbook, served on its Democratic Town Committee, oversaw a household, and parented, she is worthy of an oral history project in herself. Our seven-year-old son Channing has been the subject of one since birth and we expect *The Making of Channing M.L. Stave* to appear about 2010. We'll be especially interested in hearing what he has to say when the interviewer asks him about his formative years.

B.M.S.
Conventry, Connecticut 1977

Photo by R. Kent Newmyer

Bruce M. Stave

BRUCE M. STAVE (1937-   ) is Professor of History at the University of Connecticut where he specializes in U.S. urban history, is a member of the interdisciplinary Committee on Urban Studies, and has directed several oral history projects. He has been a Fulbright Professor of American History in India, an NEH Fellow, and a Guest Fellow at Yale, and is currently Associate Editor of the *Journal of Urban History.* His works on U.S. urban politics and reform include *The New Deal and the Last Hurrah, Urban Bosses, Machines and Progressive Reformers,* and *Socialism and the Cities.* In 1977, he received the first Harvey Kantor Memorial Award for Significant Work in Oral History granted by the New England Association of Oral History.

INTRODUCTION

Ours is an age of duplication; we live in a time of instant replay. Copying machines, television and audio tapes permit men and women in modern society to replicate the past, whether it be distant or immediate. For historians, the duplication revolution brought not only a new means of taking research notes, and concomitantly potential infringement upon copyrighted printed materials, but also the opportunity of a new research technique—oral history, which has been used in a variety of ways for a variety of purposes. This book employs the oral history technique to explore the evolution of urban historiography and thereby combines two of the fastest growing and most significant developments in historical study to emerge since World War II.

During the past three decades since Allan Nevins fathered the oral history movement, the use of the tape recorder to make history has become commonplace. A recent directory of oral history collections identified 323 centers in the United States and 61 foreign oral history programs. More than 1200 individuals and institutions across five continents were affiliated with the Oral History Association in 1975. Books based substantially upon interviews have been the recipient of national awards. Subjects including *Hard Times* and *Good Times, Jewish Grandmothers,* suffrigists reminiscing about their experiences in *From Parlor to Prison,* labor's *Rank and File,* and a president's *Plain Speaking* demonstrate the wide range of published oral history.[1]

Oral history projects differ in the types of persons interviewed, the kind of historical material which is generated, and the way this material reaches publication. Interviews have been undertaken with both the famous and the anonymous, with elites and nonelites; they have provided narrative information as well as demographic data; and they have been published whole or have provided information to be synthesized with other historical source material. Oral history can probe the memory for a record of the past or record the present for the future.[2]

The interviews in this book represent explorations into the making of United States urban history. The proliferation of interest in that field has been at least as great as that shown in oral history. A quarter of a century ago, in an article on "American Urban History Today," Blake McKelvey pointed to only five historians, Arthur M. Schlesinger, Sr., Allan Nevins, W. Stull Holt, Bessie L. Pierce, and Bayrd Still, who were teaching or had taught seminars or lecture courses in American colleges or universities dealing with urban history. By 1969, nearly 150 institutions were offering or planning to offer courses in the history of the American city. Today, dissertations and sessions at national and international meetings of historians devoted to the subject of urban history have become more the rule than the exception.[3]

A recent bibliography of doctoral dissertations completed in the field of United States urban history since 1882 shows that degrees were granted by 119 universities, with the five most prolific, Columbia, Chicago, N.Y.U., Harvard, and Pennsylvania, awarding 30% of all urban history Ph.D.s. The studies undertaken investigated a total of 275 U.S. cities and, not unexpectedly, the nation's largest cities received most attention, with New York being the subject of 187 dissertations, Chicago, 118, and Philadelphia, 106; Boston, the subject of 83 doctorates, easily outdistanced St. Louis, the next most studied city, which was investigated by 44 scholars. A chronological arrangement of the number of urban history dissertations written testifies to the dramatic increase in interest during recent years. The 1930s produced twice as many dissertations as the entire period prior to 1930; the war-disrupted 1940s turned out only one more dissertation than the previous decade's 127; while the 1950s witnessed an increase of over 100 doctorates in the field for a total of 232, 453 urban history subjects served as degree topics between 1960 and 1969. Most significantly, during the period of 1970 to 1974, scholars produced 413 dissertations in urban history. Half of all the Ph.D.s listed in the bibliography, then, had been awarded since 1964.[4]

Even if not foreseen, this proliferation of urban historical scholarship would have been welcomed by the small gathering of approximately 15 who came together at the first meeting of the Urban History Group in the winter of 1953. The group, spearheaded by McKelvey and Bayrd Still, agreed to the desirability of exchanging information about research, sponsoring programs dealing with urban topics and issuing a newsletter, which within a year expanded from a meager two mimeographed pages to a slightly more promising four. One of the most popular features of the

Newsletter was the publication until fairly recently of course outlines for the teaching of urban history. The printing of these syllabi points to the classroom newness of the field. Since so few practitioners of urban history had taken courses in the subject they began to teach during the city-conscious 60s, the outlines were not simply interesting; they were essential. Except for Charles Glaab's documentary history, *The American City,* published in 1963, few texts were available to the teacher of urban history during the 1960s until the publication of his and A. Theodore Brown's *A History of Urban America* four years later.[5]

Shortly thereafter, however, a number of textbooks and anthologies answered the need raised by new courses in the subject and testified to its development in history curricula across the nation. Texts such as Sam Bass Warner, Jr.'s *The Urban Wilderness,* Zane L. Miller's *The Urbanization of Modern America,* Blake McKelvey's *American Urbanization: A Comparative History,* and Howard Chudacoff's *The Evolution of American Urban Society* synthesized and interpreted America's urban experience. Important articles, interpretive syntheses and documents were reprinted or appeared for the first time in anthologies such as Alexander Callow's *American Urban History,* Kenneth Jackson and Stanley Schultz's *Cities in American History,* Raymond Mohl and James Richardson's *The Urban Experience,* Allen Wakstein's *The Urbanization of America,* and Bayrd Still's *Urban America.* By the mid-1970s, teachers of the subject no longer had to look far for classroom materials.[6]

Increasingly, scholars found ready, willing, and even eager audiences for their research. In 1967, Oxford University Press began publishing its *Urban Life in America Series* under the general editorship of Richard C. Wade. It included approximately 25 titles by the time the series would end a decade later. Discussing its origins, the general editor noted the earlier state of the discipline. "We knew they'd almost all be first books. One of the reasons urban history was so weak in the 1960s was that there were few people and the topic was immense. We knew full well that urban history would depend on the next generation. We wanted to encourage those new scholars by the possibility of publication by a major firm. That was the idea—a first generation of monographic work, significantly different from what had been done before."[7]

In a similar vein, introducing its *Harvard Studies in Urban History* series during the early 1970s, Harvard University Press contended, "In the past few years, the field of urban history has suddenly come to life. Until now, however, the historical character of the urbanization process has not received the fundamental scholarly research necessary for placing it on solid intellectual foundations." Despite such claims concerning the paucity of fundamental research and, perhaps, in recognition of the field's emergence, the American Historical Association had already granted its prestigious Albert J. Beveridge Award for the best book in American History in 1969 to Sam Bass Warner, Jr.'s *The Private City: Philadelphia in Three Period's of its Growth;* subsequently, Stephan Therstrom's study in the Harvard series, *The Other Bostonians: Poverty and Progress in the American Metropolis, 1880-1970,* won the Bancroft Prize. The scholarly establishment recognized the importance of urban history and the quality of the work being produced.[8]

In 1974, the publication of the first issue of the *Journal of Urban History,* the original source for the conversations in this book, served as another indication of urban history's coming of age. Raymond Mohl, the *Journal's* first editor, pointed out the inclusiveness of the field, and how the *Journal* would be receptive to varied methodologies and concerned with the study of the history of cities and urbanization over wide areas of time and space. In its inclusiveness, "urban history is a big tent," in its approach, the *Journal* hoped "not only to reflect the current state of urban history, but chart new avenues of historical research." Not long afterward, the *Urban History Group Newsletter* changed its title to *Urbanism Past and Present,* welcomed nonhistorians to its editorial board, thereby emphasizing an interdisciplinary approach, and became "dedicated to the exchange of theories and techniques for uncovering the history and the social organization of cities." One of the primary reasons for this change could be traced to the disbanding of the Urban History Group. As A. Theodore Brown remarked, "The number of those teaching courses and doing research in this field had become simply too large to be considered a special group in any real sense." Thus, the exclusiveness of early decades disappeared by virtue of acceptance and popularity. The "big tent" grew increasingly crowded. Urban history had come of age.[9]

It would be misleading, however, to assume that United States historical scholarship had roots of little more than a decade or two. Compared to sociologists at Columbia University and the University of Chicago, who used the city as their laboratory in the early years of the 20th century, historians had paid little attention to things urban. However, as early as 1890, Albert Bushnell Hart pondered "The Rise of American Cities" in *The Quarterly Journal of Economics,* and devoted much attention to the "problem" of the foreign-born pouring into urban America. By 1921, Edward Channing devoted a chapter of the fifth volume of his *History of the United States* to the "The Urban Migration" of 1815-1848. In the interim, the practitioners of the "New History," historians such as James Harvey Robinson, Charles A. Beard and Frederick

Jackson Turner, moved to shift the craft's primary concern away from government and politics to emphasize social, economic, cultural and geographic forces. The city, however, received relatively little attention.[10]

Much of the emphasis of American history, in fact, was drawn in the opposite direction—to America's Great West—and the influence Frederick Jackson Turner and his followers claimed it had on the nation's development. For them, the city played little role and the "frontier thesis" set the tone for a generation or more of American historians and their students. Even Turner, however, was not entirely insensitive to urban development. Just as he asserted his famed thesis after the Census Bureau announced the closing of the frontier in 1890, he may have been following the 1920 census returns when he noted to himself in 1922, "Do a paper on significance of the city in American history." The "Jazz Age," the turbulent twenties, the era of normalcy, the period of good times for flappers and flivvers, of poor times for farmers and workers, with all of its contradictions, was the first decade in which the census classified the majority of Americans as being urban.[11]

It is hardly surprising that during the 1930s historians began to pay greater attention to the city. Arthur M. Schlesinger, Sr. played a leading role in this movement and *The Rise of the City* found urban growth to be a unifying theme for the period of 1878-1898. Moreover, Schlesinger chaired the American Historical Association's Committee on the Planning of Research, which in 1932 suggested areas of future study and gave priority to:

(1) Urban life and urbanization as a factor in the development of American civilization.

    (a) The effect of urbanization on political constituencies.

    (b) The history of suburban development.

By the time the Harvard professor published his 1940 essay, "The City in American History," he went far to shift emphasis away from Turner's frontier toward more urban themes, although not necessarily developing an urban interpretation of U.S. history. He saw the city as a safety valve, as a place of social reform, and one that encouraged collective responsibility contrasted to frontier individualism. He discussed national events in the context of the city, and pointed to topics such as the role of city merchants in the Revolution, the urban environment as hospitable to the growth of America's labor movement, and the urban roots of progressive reform. Schlesinger claimed that the city, no less than the frontier, was a major force in shaping American civilization—a theme that has won adherents, especially among urban politicians and urbanologists, to this day.[1 2]

The works that emerged during and after the 30s followed the lines laid out by Schlesinger. They emphasized national events within an urban framework and produced a large number of studies of individual cities. For urban biographers like Constance McLaughlin Green, Bessie Louise Pierce, Blake McKelvey, Bayrd Still, Thomas J. Wertenbaker, Gerald M. Capers, and Rollin G. Osterweis, cities were organic entities. A biographer of a human being might study the growth and development of an individual from birth; so, too, did the urban biographers investigate the growth and development of specific cities. While urban biography often represented "the tradition of local history at its best," it was sometimes difficult to "distinguish the 'scholarly' urban biography from the best works produced by the amateur local historian." These were primarily narrative histories, in many instances extremely useful upon close reading, but which frequently did not generalize about the process of urbanization.[1 3]

The professional historian of the city faced the same pressures as the antiquarian to polish the big or small apple and paint a community in the best possible light, to name as many local influentials as possible within a volume so that books would sell, and generally to do well by doing good. Topics would be chosen because of convenient location; the historian happened to be present in a city, but so were other citizens who knew the "true story." When Constance McLaughlin Green completed her study of Holyoke, Massachusetts, one local critic was instructed to go through the book and check for mistakes if he believed the book damaging to the city. He responded, "But that's just the trouble; it's all true." On the other hand, with slight pain, but a good deal of amusement, Mrs. Green overheard neighborhood women at a bridge party asking "How did she have the gall to think that she could write a history when we know so much better than she does?"[1 4]

Parallel to the popular period of urban biography, which roughly crossed the three decades of historical scholarship from the 1930s through the 1950s, urbanists also considered topics such as period studies, urban rivalry and transportation, municipal reform, and urban immigrants. Following Schlesinger's direction, but also breaking new ground, Richard C. Wade, at the end of the 1950s, published *The Urban Frontier*. In that study of pioneer life in early Pittsburgh, Cincinnati, Lexington, Louisville and St. Louis, Wade depicted cities and towns as the "spearhead of the frontier," class structure and imitation of the east, especially Philadelphia, marked these areas rather than Turnerian democracy and innovation. Wade's study is more a narrative of events in such areas than a foray into the general process of urban development, but he did offer an index to urbanization, which included the following variables: (1) urban growth and suburbanization; (2) division of labor and specialization; (3) the separation of work and residence; (4) the impersonalization of city life; and (5) the disappearance of grass and foliage.[15]

While such a framework inched toward a conceptual scheme that social scientists and some historians proposed, Charles N. Glaab, in 1965, could still conclude that, "Urban history is a relatively new and unestablished division of American history ... characterized by its lack of precise definition both in subject matter and method; much of the scholarship that falls within its vague limits cannot easily be disassociated from antiquarian local history." He did, however, note the possibility of an imminent and dramatic breakthrough in the field by a vanguard of younger scholars. That vanguard would move toward a *new urban history*.[16]

Its intellectual ancestry ranged back to several historians who proposed new conceptual frameworks for ths study of urbanization, but most immediately to the work of Eric E. Lampard. Synthesizing his ideas developed during the previous decade, Lampard, in a 1961 *American Historical Review* article, argued that while historians might study the history of cities in national and traditional terms and consider the roots of urban problems, they really were not studying the process of urbanization as a societal process. He suggested that urban must not merely signify subject matter alone, but also a scheme of conceptualization. The British native further elaborated that this scheme might take the form of an ecological complex, which conceived of community structure as the outcome of a changing balance between population and environment mediated by technology and organization—easily remembered by students by the acronym POET (population, organization, environment, and technology). Borrowing from sociologists such as Amos Hawley, Otis Duncan, Leo Schnore, and their "Chicago School" antecedents, Lampard urged that the ecological principle might aid historians in their attempt to understand interrelationships among currents of migration, territorial division of labor, and industrialization. He called for more measurement of social mobility in terms of career movements of individuals and in light of the composition of the population and structurally induced changes in the labor force; finally, he advocated more historical investigation of changes in income distribution and of the process of bureaucratization. The next decade and a half would prove that while the response was not immediate, Lampard's challenge did not go unheeded.[17]

Innovations in technology and the shifting currents of American politics prompted younger historians to move in such new directions. Manipulation of statistical data marked the ecological approach in sociology; and similarly, quantification emerged as a landmark of the new urban history. The computer simplified the task of "massaging" large masses of data relating to populations, economy, politics, and the interior spatial structure of cities. The new urbanists culled manuscript censuses, tax rolls, building permits, city directories, and other similar evidence which could be quantified, charted, graphed, tabularized. Aspirations to methodological rigor, model building, and the relating of historical materials to sociological theory gave rise to a preoccupation with a limited range of topics such as urban stratification, social mobility, and spatial patterns. The use of quantitative materials was not new to urban historians. As Blake McKelvey told this writer during our oral history conversation, "I'm a quantifier, if I may do a little boasting." He then pointed out how he dealt with the concept of mobility in Rochester, and later, how he gained an early appreciation of statistical tables. It was the style in which quantification was used, the methodological constructs employed, and the heavy emphasis on an amazing machine that separated the younger practitioners of urban history from their seniors.[18]

Perhaps, too, the younger scholars reflected their times, its politics, and their own heritages. The civil rights movement of the 60s placed emphasis on the nation's minorities; the decade's urban crisis with its smoldering ghettos set them into a city context; the New Left rhetoric which emerged during the Viet Nam era emphasized "power to the people" and "participatory democracy." Translated into historiographical terms, some of Clio's youthful practitioners advocated "history from the bottom up," the study of the "historically inarticulate" and "anonymous Americans" as opposed to the nation's elites. Since those to be studied were the unfamous who didn't leave manuscript collections and rarely bequeathed diaries to history, who weren't written about in the newspapers, the data most appropriate for their study were the same sources most compatible for computer usage. The new urban history, then, with its emphasis on subjects like social mobility and neighborhood structures, simultaneously dealt with topics of ordinary people and their everyday world as did other, perhaps more politicized, fields of history. Moreover, many of the urban historians who entered that field of study during the 1960s were themselves children or grandchildren of the city, in a symbolic sense at least. The flood of students to graduate schools during the 1960s and the expansion of higher education generally broadened the profession to include a larger number of Ph.D.s who may have had more than a passing interest in the development of cities and the humble origins of urban populations.[19]

Nevertheless, the questions asked and the issues considered reflected the fundamental problems of American society. Stephan Thernstrom, who played a leading role in shaping the new urban history, remarked that his work began with the question, "Why no socialism in America? What is distinctive about the American political system, the American social ethos?" He resolved to try to explore the question not through further study of ideology, but through the study of the social fabric, and he began his work on *Poverty and Progress,* tracing the lives of hundreds of obscure, unskilled manual laborers and their families in Newburyport, Massachusetts from 1850-1880. This thrust for the new urban history was, of course, not all that new. In the introduction to *Boston's Immigrants* in 1941, Thernstrom's adviser at Harvard, Oscar Handlin, wrote of the necessity to piece together the story, from widely diversified sources, of "the intimate lives and deepest feelings of humble men and women who leave behind few formal records." Accordingly, neither New Left nor new urban historians discovered the historically inarticulate and America's anonymous citizens.[20]

In fact, the entire issue of a new urban history has come into question. When Thernstrom was asked in our oral history interview whether the new urban history was really a facet of social history, he replied, "I've come pretty much to feel that myself, and have largely given up on the term; in fact, I've stopped labeling myself an urban historian at all." Earlier, he had begun his retreat from the phrase, and the subsequent bickering over methodology which greeted his 1973 book, *The Other Bostonians,* seemed to split the ranks of the new urbanists. As Zane L. Miller has observed, "By the latter half of the 1970s . . . the 'new' urban history looked neither so new nor so confident of its techniques and findings as some of its earlier proponents suggested we might expect."[21]

Yet, as Samuel P. Hays remarked, there was a new urban history in the sense that scholars were doing things in 1975 that they hadn't been doing ten years earlier. If the polish wore off the phrase and the concept tarnished, he preferred to consider a "systematic social history." For Hays, social history offered a distinctive way of looking at many different kinds of content. It focused on society, and society concerned relationships among people. The University of Pittsburgh professor pointed out that cities were cases of intensive human interaction which displayed patterns of organization, both horizontal and vertical; these patterns should guide the development of the subfield of urban history. The framework of thinking about urban history should reflect patterns of urban social organization.[22]

A major effort in this direction, both in name and concept, is the Philadelphia Social History Project, which has been labeled as the "most ambitious effort at the systematic study of urban history yet undertaken." Project Director Theodore Hershberg and his interdisciplinary colleagues at the University of Pennsylvania have established a block-by-block data base describing the 2.5 million persons who lived in the city in the years 1850, 1860, 1870, and 1880, as well as the city's housing, businesses, manufacturing firms, and transportation facilities. In its study of urbanization and industrialization, the Project emphasizes *process* rather than specific time and place. Much of its research attempts to make "systematic 'then' and 'now' comparisons to learn how relationships among demographic, spatial and socioeconomic factors have changed in the last century." Since the new urban history placed major emphasis on the nineteenth-century cities, to make a worthwhile contribution it should illuminate the differences and similarities between urban America in the nineteenth and twentieth centuries.[23]

Another historian who significantly contributed to the shaping of urban history, Sam Bass Warner, Jr., offered a scaffolding for its study. By systematically arranging "a few facts" about Philadelphia's population in 1774, 1860, and 1930, he attempted to generalize as "if all the world were Philadelphia." Basing his generalization on variables such as population growth, the course of industrialization, the changing locations of workplaces and homes, the shifting intensity of residential clusters, and the group organization of work, Warner offered his findings as a model for students of other cities seeking a descriptive framework relating changes in scale to changes in structure. If they arranged their data in the same way, comparisons would enable scholars to actually determine if all the world *really was* Philadelphia.[24]

Warner, who earlier had done much to influence the study of the spatial development of the city in his *Streetcar Suburbs,* added a new emphasis to his scaffolding concept when he elaborated upon it in his book, *The Private City.* To the barebone variables of "a few facts," he appended the enduring tradition of "privatism" as another and more normative framework for the study of American urban development. "What the private market could do well American cities have done well; what the private market did badly, or neglected, our cities have been unable to overcome," contended Warner, who believed that the American city ceased to be an effective community when the private search for wealth exceeded the bounds of municipality. The internalized values of capitalism led many individuals to seek their own interest and pushed America's cities toward crisis. In his 1972 book, *The Urban Wilderness,* he suggested that to the extent that the American city was rotten, it was rotten at the top, not the bottom. Vital neighborhoods suffered from unsound national policies; they needed the assistance of democratic national and regional planning.[25]

Following logically from his earlier work, in 1976, Warner, in conjunction with computer analyst Sylvia Fleisch, proposed a new framework. Characteristically, he considered a social history of America's metropolises, moving backwards in time from 1960 to 1860. The Boston University historian expressed concern that planners, social scientists and historians moved in diverse directions, causing national and local planning to be determined without much attention to recent scholarship, while scholars specialized without reference to the needs of planning or the insights of other disciplines. He especially noted that historians, once "generalists of the widest ambition," were engaging in detailed case studies of cities and towns that created knowledge gaps separating findings relating to community from those relating to nation. Thus, aiming at a usable past, Warner attempted to introduce historians and other social scientists to a modern planning system of social and economic accounting, "in the hope that historical case studies can be placed in the context of useful modern knowledge," and that the system could serve as a common point of departure for all social scientists concerned with planning and public policy. The issues of population growth, race, industrialization, urbanization, migration, and fertility considered within this framework rested "at the heart of all American social science and public policy."[26]

Thus, for Warner, more than most urban historians, the value of the field rests primarily in its worth as a policy science—a frame of reference to guide the making of public policy. While this view is certainly not universal, many of the subjects needing further exploration by urban historians may well have practical application. It has been suggested that more studies focus on real estate, planning and zoning, housing, mass transit, parks, public health, fire and police departments, neighborhood structures, suburbanization, cultural institutions, and urban cultural and ethnic conflict.[27]

Vast areas of research then, remain open to future scholars. Those that have been included in this book, however, have made major contributions to the field of urban history in several of these categories: by pioneering in its writing, developing important interpretations, publishing widely and significantly, establishing broad frameworks for its conceptualization, or training large numbers of doctoral students in the subject. The interviews have been arranged so that the first three represent pioneer scholars; the fourth, with Oscar Handlin, was undertaken both to illuminate his contributions to the field and because of his link to several of the following interviewees when they studied at Harvard; the members of the final quintet have all greatly influenced recent currents in the making of urban history. All interviews, conducted over a period ranging from the spring of 1974 through the summer of the 1976, were open-ended and not shaped by a specific questionnaire. This approach allowed for what should be a cardinal rule of oral history—the interviewer listening as much as possible, interrupting as little as possible, and permitting his or her subject to carry forth on a topic. If necessary, a leading question can bring things back into focus, but one should not cut off an interviewee and possibly lose an unexpected insight or relevant factual material.

While the interviews were open-ended, however, the published and sometimes unpublished work of each historian and criticism of it, was reviewed and questions were formulated prior to our conversations. My interests included learning about the major influences on each historian's work, whether they have modified their views since publication, their reaction to criticism, what they considered to be their impact on other scholars, their views concerning the general state of urban historical scholarship, and what they considered to be the future of the art (or science). At times, conversation ran to issues of current urban interest such as the effects of the energy crisis on cities, changing urban demography, and the significance of New York City's fiscal plight.

Informally, the interviewer and interviewees sometimes discussed by mail or in person the shape of the questions before our conversations; once the earlier interviews appeared in the *Journal of Urban History,* beginning in November, 1974, a pattern of questions emerged so that one of the scholars included in these pages formulated his own interview of himself, which set the basis for our taping. Once taped, the tapes were transcribed, minimally edited and then sent to the interviewee for final approval. The interviewee, except for Constance McLaughlin Green who died prior to the completion of the process, then had the opportunity to add to, delete from, or otherwise edit the transcript. Thus, the conversations included herein attempt to capture the flavor of the interview, but are not always verbatim. They reflect an interaction between interviewer and interviewee not only in actual conversation, but also in editing the work for publication.

No footnotes or bibliography accompanied publication of the earliest interviews with Warner and Thernstrom in the *Journal of Urban History;*

realizing that many scholars unfamiliar with United States urban history might be unacquainted with the work discussed, a select bibliography was added to the third in the series with Eric Lampard. Finally, footnotes appeared with the publication of the fourth conversation with Samuel P. Hays in November, 1975, and the addition of scholarly paraphernalia has since remained the style. For the purposes of this book, notes and bibliography have been appended to those interviews published originally without them in the belief that they do not lessen the conversation's readability; moreover, it is hoped that they increase the volume's work as a historiographical tool for scholars in the field and as a teaching aid in the classroom. Few other changes have been made in the originally published interviews.

In sum, the oral history technique has been employed to probe beyond the surface of publication, and to develop information for the historiography of a rapidly developing field of study. If the interviews offer a coherent basis to assist in understanding the diverse methodology and interpretations within urban history, if they suggest new directions of study and thereby influence the discipline's development, as well as providing scholars and students with enjoyable reading, the goals of this book will have been attained. As John Garraty remarked about his *Interpreting American History: Conversations with Historians,* "It is . . . a search for the *meaning* of American history to our own day."[28] This book searches for the *meaning* of the making of urban history.

NOTES

1. The Oral History Association Newsletter, 9 (Summer 1975), 2, describes Alan M. Meckler and Ruth McMullin, eds., *Oral History Collections* (New York, 1975), and it is reviewed in that issue on p. 4; also see Louis M. Starr, "Meditations on the New Bowker Guide," Oral History Review (1975), 76-81; Samuel Proctor, "Oral History Comes of Age," Oral History Review (1975), 1; award winning books include Robert A. Caro, *The Power Broker* (New York, 1974); T. Harry Williams, *Huey Long* (New York, 1969); and Theodore Rosengarten, *All God's Dangers: The Life of Nate Shaw* (New York, 1974); for titles mentioned see Studs Terkel, *Hard Times* (New York, 1970); Peter Joseph, *Good Times* (New York, 1974); Sherna Gluck, ed., *From Parlor to Prison* (New York, 1976); Merle Miller, *Plain Speaking: An Oral Biography of Harry S. Truman* (New York, 1973); Alice and Staughton Lynd, *Rank & File* (Boston, 1973); Sydelle Kramer and Jenny Masur, *Jewish Grandmothers* (Boston, 1976).

2. For a statement regarding different types of interviews, see Alice Hoffman, "Who are the Elite, and What is a Non-Elitist," Oral History Review (1976), 1-5. The various presidential libraries have made good use of elite interviews, collecting information from famous individuals, such as cabinet officers, about a presidential administration; in my own work, I have used oral history to explore the immigrant

past in the state of Connecticut as part of the Peoples of Connecticut Ethnic Heritage Project; I have also recorded the present for the future in an oral history project which explored the attempt by a Hartford business consortium, The Greater Hartford Process, to establish a new community in Coventry, Connecticut; some good oral history primers are Willa K. Baum, *Oral History for the Local Historical Society* (Nashville, 1969, 1971); Gary L. Shumway and William G. Hartley, *An Oral History Primer* (Salt Lake City, 1973); Richard D. Curtiss, Gary L. Shumway, S. E. Stephenson, *A Guide for Oral History Programs* (Fullerton, Cal., 1973); John J. Fox, *Oral History: Window to the Past* (mimeoed manual, Salem State College, Salem, Mass., 1976); Joseph Cash, et al., *The Practice of Oral History: A Handbook* (Glen Rock, N.J., 1975); Edward D. Ives, *A Manual for Field Workers* (Orono, Maine, 1974); and William W. Moss, *Oral History Program Manual* (New York, 1974).

3. Blake McKelvey, "American Urban History Today," American Historical Review, 57 (July 1952), 928-929; Bayrd Still and Diana Klebanow, "The Teaching of American Urban History," Journal of American History, 55 (March 1969), 844; the international interest in urban history has been reported in the Urban History Newsletter, founded by Professor H. J. Dyos of Leicester University, England, in 1963 and in the *Urban History Yearbook* which he has edited since 1974.

4. For a full listing of universities awarding degrees, and cities studied, see R. David Weber and Donna C. Belli, Dissertations in *Urban Studies: The Historical Dimension* (Ann Arbor, Mich., 1976), v-vii; the bibliographers noted that the listing for 1974 was partial and that a more complete list would indicate that the production of urban history Ph.D.s in the first half of the 1970s was greater than the entire 1960s. They also point out that the increase in urban history dissertations is part of a trend in proliferation of scholarship and, compared to other academic fields, urban history was actually lagging behind its level of several decades ago. This probably reflects the reflective status of history generally, rather than the status of urban history in particular.

5. Blake McKelvey and A. Theodore Brown, "The Urban History Group Newsletter," Urbanism Past & Present, 1 (Winter 1975-1976), 36-37; see interviews with McKelvey and Still within; Charles N. Glaab, *The American City: A Documentary History* (Homewood, Ill., 1963) and Charles N. Glaab and A. Theodore Brown, *A History of Urban America* (New York, 1967; revised edition, 1976); other available books during the period included Constance McLaughlin Green, *The Rise of Urban America* (New York, 1965) and *American Cities in the Growth of the Nation* (London, 1957; New York, 1965), and Christopher Tunnard and Henry Hope Reed, *American Skyline* (New York, 1956).

6. Sam Bass Warner, Jr., *The Urban Wilderness* (New York, 1972); Zane L. Miller, *The Urbanization of Modern America* (New York, 1973); Blake McKelvey, *American Urbanization: A Comparative Perspective* (Glenview, Ill., 1973); Howard P. Chudacoff, *The Evolution of American Urban Society* (Englewood Cliffs, N.J., 1975); Alexander B. Callow, ed., *American Urban History* (New York, 1969, 1973); Kenneth T. Jackson and Stanley K. Schultz, eds., *Cities in American History* (New York, 1972); Raymond A. Mohl and James F. Richardson, eds., *The Urban Experience* (Belmont, Cal., 1973); Allen M. Wakstein, ed., *The Urbanization of America* (Boston, 1970); Bayrd Still, *Urban American* (Boston, 1974); other works include James F. Richardson, ed., *The American City* (Waltham, Mass., 1972); Raymond A. Mohl and Neil Betten, eds., *Urban America in Historical Perspective* (New York, 1970); and William H. Wilson, *Coming of Age: Urban America, 1915-1945* (New York, 1974).

7. See "A Conversation with Richard C. Wade," within.

8. See the book jacket of Michael H. Frisch, *Town Into City* (Cambridge, Mass., 1972); the Harvard series, edited by Stephan Thernstrom and Charles Tilly, was not limited to U.S. urban history, nor to writings by historians only; Sam Bass Warner, Jr., *The Private City* (Philadelphia, 1968, 1972); Stephan Thernstrom, *The Other Bostonians* (Cambridge, Mass., 1973).

9. Raymond A. Mohl, "Editorial," Journal of Urban History, 1 (November 1974), 3-5; Urbanism Past & Present, 1 (Winter 1975-1976), iii-iv, 37; as noted in footnote 3, in Britain, the *Urban History Yearbook* began publishing in 1974.

10. Albert Bushnell Hart, "The Rise of American Cities," The Quarterly Journal of Economics, 4 (January 1890), 129-157; I would like to thank Bayrd Still for bringing this article to my attention. See "A Conversation with Bayrd Still," within; Edward Channing, *History of the United States, Volume V* (New York, 1921); Charles N. Glaab, "The Historian and the American City: A Bibliographic Survey," in Philip M. Hauser and Leo F. Schnore, *The Study of Urbanization* (New York, 1965), 53; Zane L. Miller, "Urban History, Urban Crises, and Public Policy," Urbanism Past & Present, 1 (Winter 1975-1976), 1.

11. See: Frederick Jackson Turner, "The Significance of the Frontier in American History," American Historical Association, *Annual Report for the Year 1893* (Washington, D.C., 1894), 199-227, reprinted in Ray Allen Billington, ed., *The Frontier Thesis: Valid Interpretation of American History?* (New York, 1966), 9-20; for Turner's note of 1922, see "A Conversation with Bayrd Still," within; while the census definition of urban is often more symbolic than real, the symbolic definition is significant.

12. Arthur M. Schlesinger, Sr., *The Rise of the City, 1878-1898* (New York, 1933); The Committee of the American Historical Association on the Planning of Research, *Historical Scholarship in America: Needs and Opportunities* (New York, 1932), 93; Arthur M. Schlesinger, Sr., "The City in American History," Mississippi Valley Historical Review, 27 (June 1940), revised and reprinted as "The City in American Civilization" in his *Paths to the Present* (New York, 1949), 210-233; a politician advocate of cities was New York City's Mayor John Lindsay, when he remarked, "In the last year I've begun to realize how little any of us have understood the meaning of cities and their role in American life. The cities are not the problem. They are the solution. They always have been the solution. And that's the reality we have lost sight of. The city is not the creator of social problems, and it doesn't spread them. It solves them, for the city is the machine of social change." New York *Times,* August 14, 1972, 27.

13. Weber & Belli, op. cit.; see within for works of Green, Still, and McKelvey; also see Bessie L. Pierce, *A History of Chicago* (3 Vols; New York, 1937-1957); Thomas J. Wertenbaker, *Norfolk* (rev. ed. by Marvin W. Schlegel, Durham, N.C., 1962); Gerald M. Capers, *The Biography of a River Town: Memphis, Its Heroic Age* (Chapel Hill, 1939), viii-ix; Rollin G. Osterweis, *Three Centuries of New Haven, 1638-1938* (New York, 1953); quote from Glaab, "The Historian and the American City," 60-61.

14. See conversations with McKelvey and Green within.

15. For a review of the appropriate literature on these themes, see Glaab, "The Historian and the American City," 66-72; some leading examples are Richard C. Wade, *The Urban Frontier, 1790-1830* (Cambridge, Mass., 1959) and Blake McKelvey, *The Urbanization of America, 1860-1915* (New Brunswick, N.J., 1963)

and *The Emergence of Metropolitan America, 1915-1966* (New Brunswick, N.J., 1968) as period studies; for urban rivalry and transportation, see Edward C. Kirkland, *Men, Cities, and Transportation: A Study in New England History, 1820-1900*, (2 Vols.; Cambridge, Mass., 1948), James W. Livingood, *The Philadelphia-Baltimore Trade Rivalry, 1780-1860* (Harrisburg, Pa., 1947) and Julius Rubin, *Canal or Railroad? Immigation & Innovation in the Response to the Erie Canal in Philadelphia, Baltimore and Boston* (Philadelphia, 1961); for municipal reform, see Arthur Mann, *Yankee Reformers in the Urban Age* (Cambridge, Mass., 1954) and Richard Hofstadter, *The Age of Reform* (New York, 1955); for urban immigrants, see Oscar Handlin, *Boston's Immigrants* (Cambridge, Mass., 1941; rev. ed., 1959) and *The Uprooted* (Boston, 1951, 2nd enlarged ed., 1973), Moses Rischin, *The Promised City: New York's Jews, 1870-1914* (Cambridge, Mass., 1962) and Robert Ernst, *Immigrant Life in New York City, 1825-1863* (New York, 1949); Wade, *The Urban Frontier;* his later *Slavery in the Cities* (New York, 1964) investigated a national phenomenon in the urban context and considered the difference between urban and plantation slavery.

16. Glaab, "The Historian and the American City," 72-73; the first major references to the *new urban history* can be found in Stephan Thernstrom and Richard Sennett, eds., *Nineteenth-Century Cities: Essays in the New Urban History* (New Haven, 1969); for a useful discussion of the subject and bibliographic references, see Michael H. Ebner, *The New Urban History: Bibliography on Methodology & Historiography* (Council of Planning Librarians, Exchange Bibliography 445, August, 1973).

17. Examples of historians seeking such new approaches were Ralph E. Turner, "The Industrial City: Center of Cultural Change," in Caroline F. Ware, ed., *The Cultural Approach to History* (New York, 1940), 228-242; W. Stull Holt, "Some Consequences of the Urban Movement," Pacific Historical Review, 22 (November 1953), 337-351 and R. Richard Wohl, "Urbanism, Urbanity and the Historian," University of Kansas Review, 22 (Autumn 1953), 53-61; see Eric E. Lampard, "American Historians and the Study of Urbanization," American Historical Review, 67 (October 1961), 49-61; for a brief summary of the ecological school, see Dwight W. Hoover, "The Diverging Paths of American Urban History," American Quarterly, (Summer 1968), 296-317, reprinted in Callow, *American Urban History,* 642-659, especially 646-649; also see Amos H. Hawley, *Human Ecology* (New York, 1950); Otis D. Duncan and Leo F. Schnore, "Cultural, Behavioral and Ecological Perspectives in the Study of Social Organization," American Journal of Sociology, LXV (September 1959), 132-146; Leo F. Schnore, *The Urban Scene: Human Ecology and Demography* (New York, 1965); Roy Lubove accepts Lampard's framework, but recognized the limits of the ecological approach. He underscores the relationship between technology and the city and stresses "the process of city building over time." See Roy Lubove, "The Urbanization Process: An Approach to Historical Research," Journal of American Institute of Planners, XXXIII (January 1967), 33-39, reprinted in Callow, *American Urban History,* 660-671.

18. For the *new urban history,* see Thernstrom and Sennett, *Nineteenth-Century Cities;* Stephan Thernstrom, "Reflections on the New Urban History," Daedalus, 100 (Spring 1971), 359-375, reprinted in Callow, *American Urban History,* 672-684; Leo F. Schnore, ed., *The New Urban History: Quantitative Explorations by American Historians* (Princeton, N.J., 1975), 3-9; Zane L. Miller, "Urban History, Urban Crises, and Public Policy," 3-4; for a statement on quantification, see Eric E. Lampard, "Two Cheers for Quantitative History: An Agnostic Foreword," in Schnore, *The New Urban History,* 12-48; for Blake McKelvey's view, see conversation within.

19. For a New Left view of U.S. history, see the essays which emphasize "history from the bottom up" in Barton J. Bernstein, ed., *Towards a New Past: Dissenting Essays in American History* (New York, 1969), which contains an essay by Stephan Thernstrom, "Urbanization, Migration, and Social Mobility in Late Nineteenth-Century America," 158-175; to study "anonymous Americans," see the essays in Tamara Hareven, *Anonymous Americans: Explorations in Nineteenth-Century Social History* (Englewood Cliffs, N.J., 1971); the reference to the personal backgrounds of the younger urban historians is a subjective observation of the author and is not based on empirical data. Such a study awaits further investigation.

20. See "A Conversation with Stephan Thernstrom," within; Oscar Handlin, *Boston Immigrants,* x.

21. See "A Conversation with Stephan Thernstrom," within; Thernstrom, "Reflections on the New Urban History,"; for criticism of *The Other Bostonians,* see the review by Richard S. Alcorn and Peter R. Knights, "Most Uncommon Bostonians: A Critique of Stephan Thernstrom's *The Other Bostonians,*" Historical Methods Newsletter, 8 (June 1975), 98-114 and Thernstrom's rejoinder, 115-120; Zane L. Miller, "Defining the City—and Urban History," a review of Blaine A. Brownell, *The Urban Ethos in the South* in Reviews in American History, 4 (September 1976), 437; Miller also identifies another reason for the declining glamor of the *new urban history.* This is the attraction to the cultural approach to urban history, which focuses on a city rather than a social or economic group. "It displayed a concern ... with the history of cities as cities and explored all facets of urban society as a means of understanding the development of American civilization."

22. Samuel P. Hays, "A Systematic Social History," in George A. Billias and Gerald N. Grob, eds., *American History: Retrospect & Prospect* (New York, 1971), 317-320; see "A Conversation with Samuel P. Hays," within.

23. The assessment of the Philadelphia Social History Project is by Jonathan Levine in the Historical Methods Newsletter, 9 (March-June 1976), 141; for information about the project, see Theodore Hershberg, "The Philadelphia Social History Project: An Introduction," Historical Methods Newsletter, 9 (March-June 1976), 43-58, quote from 43; the author is grateful for Hershberg's suggestion in informal conversation about the potential contribution of the *new urban history.*

24. Sam Bass Warner, Jr., "If All the World Were Philadelphia: A Scaffolding for Urban History, 1774-1930," American Historical Review, LXXIV (October 1968), 26-43.

25. Sam Bass Warner, Jr., *Streetcar Suburbs: The Process of Growth in Boston 1870-1900* (Cambridge, Mass., 1962; New York, 1973); Warner, *The Private City,* x; Warner, *The Urban Wilderness,* 267-276; for the internalization of capitalist values, see "A Conversation with Sam Bass Warner, Jr.," within.

26. Sam Bass Warner, Jr. and Sylvia Fleisch, "The Past of Today's Present: A Social History of America's Metropolises, 1960-1860," Journal of Urban History, 3 (November 1976), 3-118, see 3-4; the accounting system Warner employed was the BEA accounting system set forth during the 1960s by the U.S. Department of Commerce, Bureau of Economic Analysis. It rested upon four principles: national inclusiveness, stable small areas of account, functional grouping, and flexibility.

27. For a consideration of history as a policy science, see Richard Jensen's review of Hugh Davis Graham and Ted Robert Gurr, eds., *Violence in America, Vols. I & II,* in The Journal of American History, LVI (March 1970), 882-886; Zane L. Miller,

"Urban History, Urban Crises, and Public Policy," offers another good statement on the policy implications for urban history. He suggests several topics for future research as do the conversations within this volume. Some of these topics have already received attention. For example, urban education has been approached from the perspective of structural sociology in Michael B. Katz, *Class, Bureaucracy, & Schools: The Illusion of Educational Change in America* (New York, 1971; expanded ed., 1975); police departments have been studied by James F. Richardson, *The New York Police: Colonial Times to 1901* (New York, 1970) and *Urban Police in the United States* (Port Washington, N.Y., 1974), and Roger Lane, *Policing the City: Boston, 1822-1885* (Cambridge, Mass., 1967; New York, 1971); mass transit receives attention in Warner's *Streetcar Suburbs* and Clay McShane, *Technology and Reform: Street Railways and the Growth of Milwaukee, 1887-1900* (Madison, Wis., 1974) as well as in Glen E. Holt, "The Changing Perception of Urban Pathology: An Essay on the Development of Mass Transit in the United States," in Jackson and Schultz, *Cities in American History*, 324-343; housing has been considered in Roy Lubove, *The Progressives and the Slums: Tenement House Reform in New York City* (Pittsburgh, 1962) and Anthony Jackson, *A Place Called Home. A History of Low-Cost Housing in Manhattan* (Cambridge, Mass., 1976); John Duffy has offered *A History of Public Health in New York City, 1866-1966* (New York, 1968, 1974); for studies of planning and parks, see John W. Reps, *The Making of Urban America: A History of City Planning in the United States* (Princeton, N.J., 1965); Albert Fein, *Frederick Law Olmsted & the American Environmental Tradition* (New York, 1972); Laura Wood Roper, FLO: *A Biography of Frederick Law Olmsted* (Baltimore, 1973); Geoffrey Blodgett, "Frederick Law Olmsted: Landscape Architecture as Conservative Reform," Journal of American History, LXII (March 1976), 869-889; Thomas S. Hines, *Burnham of Chicago: Architect & Planner* (New York, 1974), and Mel Scott, *American City Planning* (Berkeley, Cal., 1969, 1971); on neighborhoods, see Henry D. Shapiro and Zane Miller, *Clifton: Neighborhood and Community in An Urban Setting: A Brief History* (Cincinnati, 1976); The *Boston 200 Neighborhood History Series* (Boston, 1975); Roger D. Simon, "Housing and Services in an Immigrant Neighborhood: Milwaukee's Ward 14," Journal of Urban History, 2 (August 1976), 435-458; on suburbanization, see Kenneth T. Jackson, "Urban Deconcentration in the Nineteenth Century: A Statistical Inquiry," in Schnore, eu., *The New Urban History*, 110-142, and his "The Crabgrass Frontier: 150 Years of Suburban Growth in America," in Mohl and Richardson, *The Urban Experience*, 196-221; Joel A. Tarr, "From City to Suburb: The 'Moral' Influence of Transportation Technology," in Callow, *American Urban History*, 202-212; and Richard O. Davies, *The Age of Asphalt: The Automobile, the Freeway, and the Condition of Modern America* (Philadelphia, 1975); for cultural conflict, see Kenneth T. Jackson, *The Ku Klux Klan in the City* (New York, 1967); John Higham, *Strangers in the Land: Patterns of American Nativism, 1860-1925* (New Brunswick, N.J., 1955; New York, 1963), and his *Send These to Me: Jews and Other Immigrants in Urban America* (New York, 1975); Paul Kleppner, *The Cross of Culture* (New York, 1970); and Michael Novak, *The Rise of the Unmeltable Ethnics* (New York, 1971, 1972).

28. John A. Garraty, *Interpreting American History: Conversations with Historians, Vol. I.* (London, 1970), vii.

Blake McKelvey

Blake McKelvey (1903-   ) was City Historian of
Rochester, New York, until his recent retirement, and he is
author of a multi-volume study of that community. His
other publications include a two-volume general study of
urban America. He played a leading role in establishing the
Urban History Group during the early 1950s.

A CONVERSATION WITH
BLAKE McKELVEY

STAVE: You are the first city historian that I've interviewed. I'd like to talk to you about your role as a city historian and as an early practitioner of American urban history. Could we start off with your family background, youth, education, and like matters?

McKELVEY: Surely. I suppose you'd like to have the aspects that might relate to the study of urban history. Well, my Dad was a Methodist minister in Pennsylvania and, thinking over the possibility that you might ask such a question, I recalled that at the age of 12 or 13 we moved, after living in a couple of small towns, into a larger community, to Huntingdon, Pennsylvania. I can remember a discussion we had about whether Huntingdon was a city; we had learned that the population was 8,000 and the question was whether 8,000 or 10,000 made a city. Since Dad was a minister we had to be pretty quiet on Sundays, but he would take us Sunday afternoons on a hike to a hill from which we could see the city. Of course, he was always pointing out the number of churches, and I remember looking down, identifying the churches and seeing the court house, the jail, the railroad station, and the high school. A couple of years later we moved to Williamsport, Pennsylvania, which is a much larger town, where I finished my high school work. I can remember when we first arrived that I got a bicycle and rode out to the edge of town to see the amusement center there, and then to the resort area at the other end. I rode across the bridge to where you could climb a hill and see the whole town. I remember this curiosity about cities. I began to get new experiences—city experiences—in the jobs I found in Huntingdon, Williamsport and later Syracuse.

STAVE: What kinds of jobs and how many?

McKELVEY: Oh, newsboy of course, errand boy for a fish market, taxidermist's assistant, book salesman one summer, machine tender—I counted them up once and recalled 19 or 20. The most dramatic and most profitable was coal mining, my last summer job; we went out on strike on September 1, and I went to graduate school. You don't usually evaluate such experiences until later, for example, my first job as extra boy in Huntingdon's only department store during Christmas week. I ran errands, delivered packages, and when the elevator man was out to lunch or something I ran the elevator. They put me there briefly on Christmas eve, but suddenly the manager took me off the elevator and shoved me under a counter. Soon he was back with my coat and gave me an extra $10 for being such a great help and ushered me quickly out the front door, not the service entrance I had been instructed to use. I thought Santa had got to him. Years later, when I read about child labor laws, I made a second guess. I was getting some urban experience in addition to savings for college.

After graduating from high school I went on to Syracuse University. I don't remember much curiosity about that place as a city until my junior year. At the end of my junior year, I signed up with a YMCA group which was being recruited nationally—a couple of chaps from each of several different universities to go down to New York and spend two months in a volunteer capacity in a program cooperating with the various settlement houses in New York. I had the good fortune to be assigned with a chap from Amherst to Henry Street Settlement. We moved into the settlement and did everything that they asked us to do. Once a week we would take a group of kids to one of the parks, and another day we would take another group to the beach; another day we would go by buses to a farm on the outskirts of New York, someplace where we could show the kids cattle and horses and so forth. Twice a week we would meet with the other college chaps who were stationed in similar settlement houses; we discussed our mutual problems and then went off to dinner in Chinatown or a Greek restaurant.

STAVE: What year was this?

McKELVEY: This was in 1924, the summer of 1924. For the first time I saw a big city. It was fascinating because we discussed the problems that a big city faced, many of them from the point of view of first-hand observation. When I went back to Syracuse the next fall for my last year, I remember that I took a new interest in some of the problems of Syracuse as a city. When I went on to Clark University for an M.A., I took a similar interest in Worcester, Massachusetts. From there I had an opportunity to teach in high school in Haverhill, Massachusetts and taught American history and ancient history for two years before I returned to graduate study. I went back to Clark, but the professor that I wanted to work with, James B. Hedges, was invited to Harvard and I followed him there. He was only there for one year so at this point I switched to Arthur Schlesinger in social history. But my curiosity about cities was stirred up again because I attended one lecture by Professor William Scott Ferguson on Greek history. It was such a delightful lecture that I decided to take a course under him as one of my fields. The course was really about the city of Athens and this was a fascinating study. Of course I studied under Schlesinger at that time. He was not an urban historian; his book, *The Rise of the City*,[1] hadn't come out yet—he was working on it but not imparting that to his graduate students. I did get to know him fairly well because he had a very, very delightful practice of inviting his graduate students out for tea. You were invited out very shortly after you arrived and he always said, "come again." We all tried to be sort of restrained because we did't want to seem to be polishing the apple, but we were invited there every week. There were only one or two, I think, who had the effrontery to go so often; the rest of us didn't go more than once or twice a month because he had so many students, the teas would have been too large. But that was a delightful experience with a scholar discussing anything that came up.

STAVE: At Syracuse did you have any courses that would touch on anything like urban history?

McKELVEY: No. I went there with other aspirations. I was going to be a medical missionary and I got into pre-med and had my nose to the grindstone until my third year, when I was admitted to medical school. But fortunately, thinking that as a medical missionary in a foreign country I ought to know about foreigners, I joined the Cosmopolitan

Club. One of the lads from China one day made a provocative comment: "you know, missionaries in China are very much like communists in America—they're selling a new society, a new philosophy, and the only people that you pick up as a Christian missionary are those that failed in anything else." This struck me as an interesting objective observation and I decided—not that I didn't want to go and help some failures—that if I was really representing a culture rather than a religion, which I'd inherited from my parents, I ought to know something about American culture. So I decided that I would take the fourth year and study history and philosophy. Those two courses turned me into the field of history rather than medicine.

STAVE: You also said that in your junior year you went to the settlement house. What kind of people did you work with at the Henry Street settlement? What kind of influence did this have on you?

McKELVEY: Well, that of course was an entirely Jewish area at the time. I don't know if it had any particular influence other than the new experience of a large city and the problems that it faced. I can remember the sanitary problems. My friend from Amherst and I would walk around on nights that we weren't out with the group. We learned to walk in the center of the streets because as soon as dusk came on, the windows would be opened and bags of garbage would come down, and if you were walking on the sidewalk you might have something to brush off. That was one experience. We went also to the Henry Street Settlement Playhouse and saw the acting and dances there. I can remember walking out on one of the bridges—I'm not sure which one of the bridges it was—a very hot night and we slept on one of the benches; the whole bridge across the East River was full of men like ourselves trying to get away from the heat of the tenements, sleeping on the benches and getting a little air. We went to Chinatown and walked through various parts of the city that were a complete eye-opener to a chap who'd been brought up in small towns in Pennsylvania.

STAVE: You went to Clark for your M.A. Why did you go there and what did you study? Was this in history?

McKELVEY: History, yes. I went there chiefly because one of the courses I took in history at Syracuse was with Professor Keenleyside, who had come from Clark. He inspired me to go on in history and got me a scholarship of some sort at Clark. I, incidentally, was very fortunate when I went to Clark because it was a very small institution with a small history group, four first-rate professors, and you had a chance to really get to know them. I had gotten to be a senior at Syracuse without a history course, and the two courses that I took then were not too substantive. But Keenleyside sent me on. James B. Hedges was the man in American history that I specialized under. Blakesley was there, and William Langer, who took one look at me, at one paper that I wrote, and sort of decided that I was as ignorant as I was, but Hedges at least gave me a chance to grow a bit that year. Later at Harvard I got better acquainted with Langer, but not as his student. But at that time, without any knowledge of European history, I can well understand his reaction to this upstart who had somehow gotten into the program. I dropped out with an M.A., and taught for two years but returned to Clark, as I said, and then went on to Harvard.

STAVE: Now you studied with Schlesinger. From looking over your bibliography my impression is that your dissertation must have been on American prisons.[2] How did you get on to that topic?

McKELVEY: Well, I decided I wanted to write my doctoral thesis under Schlesinger but didn't know exactly how to proceed. So I jotted down some topics. When I got to see him I was a little bit nervous and instead of waiting for him to say something I said, "I don't know just how you proceed—do I propose topics, or do you?" He looked at me with a quizzical smile. "Do you have some?" he asked and I showed him my list. He looked at it. "I'll mark this (1), this one (2), and this one (3). Now go out and see what sources there are." And I took the list and went out and looked at it. Number one was the history of the bicycle.

STAVE: This was your own idea?

McKELVEY: This was my own idea. I'd put down a number of topics that seemed related to his type of social history—an institution, a movement, a development that had technological and social aspects that could be studied in perspective. I forget what the third one was; the second one was the history of prisons. When I got outside and showed number one to my friends, they all laughed when they saw the bicycle topic. I decided that I really wasn't secure enough to take a subject that would be laughed at. So after looking at a couple of shelves on the bicycle, I looked at many more shelves on prisons and took that topic.

STAVE: And what kind of research and sources did you use?

McKELVEY: Of course there were quite a number of materials available at Widener on prisons, but I got into the State House in Boston where they had all of the state reports on all of the prisons in the country; this was a real find. The Massachusetts State Library had this collection in the stacks, and I got permission to spend months in there going through all the state documents down to the period that I picked for the end of my thesis. It ended in 1915. I selected that date because, as I read along, I discovered that it marked the period at which psychology and sociology and psychiatry to a certain extent were coming into prisons. The educational period I was dealing with was going to be transformed, and to proceed further I would have to go much more fully into some of those sciences. In any case, that date was acceptable for the termination of the thesis.

STAVE: Did you do much on the effect of city life on penal institutions or the interrelationship of city life and penal institutions, or were you working within the context of prisons as social history?

McKELVEY: Yes. Of course I did get into a few urban institutions, and it happened that, since you ask that point, my great hero in the thesis was a man by the name of Zebulon Brockway who was the first head of the work house in Rochester, New York. He started to study what could be done with prisons, the first time in America that anyone had made a thorough study, and he became the leader in the developments of the reformatory period. This was the one thing I knew about Rochester when it came time to apply for the job at Rochester.

STAVE: In what year did you become assistant city historian of Rochester?

McKELVEY: 1936.

STAVE: In the intervening period between writing the doctorate and going to Rochester were you in Washington or other places?

McKELVEY: I was in training for the job of city historian but I didn't know it. I got out of Harvard with a Ph.D. in 1933 in the depths of the depression and there wasn't a job in sight. And then I saw that they were establishing something down in Washington known as the CCC. I decided if they were going to get a bunch of boys together they must need to teach them some American history. So I wrote to the director of this newly-created project and offered him my services to set up an educational program. I got back a reply that they were turning that over to the Army, that the Army was taking over education. I wrote to a friend who had a scholarship to finish a research project in Washington and he wrote back inviting me down to look around since a large number of New Deal projects were starting up. I went down and got into a dozen lines of people applying for various New Deal jobs, only to discover that a Ph.D. from Harvard was not in demand. Finally, one guy who saw my disappointment put me in touch with the director of his particular project, who had been a governor in either Washington or Oregon. When the former governor heard that I had written my thesis on prisons he was very much interested because he had helped to reform the prisons in his state. With his interest aroused, he searched the inter-office memos and discovered that in Pennsylvania they were setting up a project to survey the historic documents in the various county seats. "Now if you go back to Pennsylvania, you're from Pennsylvania, and get on the relief rolls, you can perhaps get that assignment." To make a long story short, I was soon in Harrisburg and in the central office of the survey of historic documents in Pennsylvania. They paid about $50 a month, later $40 when the funds were reduced, but it was good training for somebody who was going to get into urban history. I had to check what the field people were finding in the various county seats, how their record of what was there jibed with the records that should have been there. I had to look those up, the laws and so forth. We made quite a study. This was a unique project in Pennsylvania, and I was lucky to have that experience in surveying the type of documents that you find in a community that had county as well as urban responsibilities.

STAVE: Now, you were there until 1934 and then you went to Chicago, is that it?

McKELVEY: Yes, the project in Pennsylvania was being phased out that spring when the possibility of becoming an assistant to Bessie Pierce on the History of Chicago project opened up.[3] I applied for and secured the position, scheduled to commence in the fall. A week after accepting that appointment I had an unexpected call from the CCC in Washington. The Army had gotten tired of the CCC and had decided to turn the educational responsibilities back to its staff; they had looked through their files and found my application. [laughs] How they located me, I'll never know. They called me up. This might have been a very interesting and complete turn in my career, but I had already signed up with Bessie and so I turned them down and reported at Chicago in September. I joined her staff which was a fairly good one. I happened to be the only one with a Ph.D. but the others were advanced graduate students and working on the history of Chicago.

STAVE: Was she located at the University of Chicago?

McKELVEY: Oh, yes, she belonged to the faculty there, but this was a major part of her responsibilities. The project was well backed with Rockefeller funds. There were three or four of us in the office working on research and submitting drafts of materials that she would rewrite. She had that enormous city to study, that large staff to direct but worst of all she had a big committee looking over her shoulder; every draft she finished had to go the rounds and satisfy all of the various interdisciplinary approaches. It may have some advantages but it can also have disadvantages. I worked on the last chapter of the third volume of the history of Chicago. The first volume was finished—she'd been on this project for a dozen years at that time, I believe, but the staff changed quite frequently. The first volume came out shortly after I got to Rochester; the second a few years later. The third volume came out about three years after I got my third volume on Rochester published. And that was not her fault.

STAVE: Now you worked with her as an assistant. Were you writing or researching?

McKELVEY: I was doing research on the period of Chicago during the World's Fair. I looked through the newspapers for two and a half years, I guess it was, and put together a 100-page version of a chapter which was of course completely torn apart until it was unrecognizable in the third volume. There are, I think, about ten pages in the final chapter, and most of what I had discussed had been rolled into the other chapters or left out.

STAVE: Was it subsequent to that that you left Chicago and went to Rochester?

McKELVEY: No, my wife had a job at Sarah Lawrence. After one year at Chicago, I went back to see what I could find in the New York area, and again I bumped into something which proved to be excellent training for Rochester. I decided to do some work in the central library, the New York Public. I went in the first day thinking I'll look at the sources available on either southern history or immigrant history. I wasn't an urban historian then.

STAVE: Well, why southern or immigrant history?

McKELVEY: These were just two topics that I felt merited further study. And as I walked into the card index room, I remembered walking through there once as a graduate student with an older scholar who had said, "every time you go through the card index room you should look around because you always see some historian who is stopping off here on the way someplace to look up a few things he has not been able to find elsewhere." Sure enough, my friend Philip Bauer from Harvard was poring over a tray of index cards. As it turned out, he had just started a new job for the Encyclopaedia Britannica, and better still, within a week I was invited to join him. This was a temporary job of three to four months, going through the Encyclopaedia, picking out every article that had a dated ending. For example, an article on the city of New York would end up with a paragraph on the present mayor, the present population, and we updated it; every state had the same ending. This held for states abroad as well; on India we had a problem trying to determine the boundaries as well as the populations of its divisions. We discovered one thing about the editor—he was a Democrat, and this was the first time in his long years—he was getting on in age, he had a long career—the first time he had taken care of a revision in which the Democrats had won many victories. We discovered that if we could work into the revision that the Democrats had swept the city, or the Democrats swept the state, it went through without a hitch!

STAVE: You mentioned, and before we go on to Rochester, your wife was teaching at Sarah Lawrence—was she an instructor there?

McKELVEY: In economics, labor relations. I met her in the Harvard Library. We both got our Ph.D.'s in the same year. She found a job at Sarah Lawrence just before she got her Ph.D. She had been there while I was in Chicago, incidentally, and we have been one of those modern professional families since the beginning. When I came to Rochester she continued to teach at Sarah Lawrence until we got into the war. At that point the military would bump her off the plane, so she decided to take a leave of absence. She completed some research and found a job in a Rochester plant on the production line. She took a day off when Mr. Ives came to Rochester to hold a hearing.

STAVE: The man who became the New York Senator?

McKELVEY: Yes. But he was then at Albany and conducting hearings around the state on minimum wage questions. My wife popped up and asked a question at the hearing in Rochester which happened to be the only intelligent question asked. He continued the discussion after the hearing and soon invited her to help establish the new School of Industrial and Labor Relations at Cornell. She was one of the first instructors there and she's still there; she has retired twice, but she can't quit!

STAVE: Now, I think we finally have you at the point of coming to Rochester. The Encyclopaedia Britannica job—did that end or did you leave?

McKELVEY: Oh yes, we finished the complete set and ended that job; it was a couple of months after that that I got the invitation to come up and see, look over, and be interviewed for the job at Rochester. Dexter Perkins was offered and had accepted the job of city historian with the idea that he would get some young man to help do the work. He wrote to Columbia and Harvard, to his friends Dixon Ryan Fox and Arthur Schlesinger, and I was one of two that applied for the job. My training happened to be ideal—the survey of historical documents, actual work in an urban setting on a city's history, and editorial work. I got the job.

STAVE: So Perkins was the city historian until you became the city historian in 1948. Rochester is one of the few cities in the country, that

I know of at least, that has a professional city historian. Can you go into the origins of that?

McKELVEY: Of course it had a historical origin. In the First World War, D.A.R. and S.A.R. representatives, throughout the country as a matter of fact, became concerned that service records should be kept properly, and in New York State they pressed for the creation of an office for the preservation of the records of the boys in the army. Well this produced a law requiring, directing, towns to appoint a local historian, and specifying a number of functions—keep war records, make sure the archives are in order, write and lecture, and so forth on the community's history. Another law said that they may pay you. The only city in the country that took up the second law happened to be Rochester.

STAVE: That was the only city in the country?

McKELVEY: Well, it was the only one that has done it over the years. It was the only one in the state. There is no other state that has this kind of law that I know of. In Rochester, Edward Foreman was appointed—a competent man, a lawyer who had become president of the historical society and had done quite a bit of interesting and scholarly work in the history of law and on the charter of the city. He said he'd undertake it if they set him up properly, and they did. And that persisted. He brought out the only really thorough-going study of a city's and county's participation in the World War. The only rival appeared in Minneapolis and St. Paul—Hennepin County. They have one volume. We have three fat volumes of over 5,000 pages of the records of the boys in the First World War. Meanwhile, to get materials on the city, Foreman started under the historical society a program of publishing historical papers. Rochester had a historical society that went back about 40 years at that time, and a number of scholarly papers had been given; he dug these out and edited annual volumes. This was the Rochester Historical Society Publication Fund Series. That was already in the ninth volume when he finished his three-volume history of Rochester in the War, and he was facing the possibility that this might be the end of the job. But three or four years ahead, the centennial of the city was coming up. So Foreman persuaded them to bring out a centennial history—four volumes. He got this started before the depression hit and managed to live through the depression, the first years of the depression, at least, although he was cut off as an independent office and put under the library. As he finished the centennial set the library was finally cut by about $90,000, and a citizens committee was created to get that back and support the library.

Dexter Perkins was on the committee and went in and pounded on the table: "You can't cut culture in Rochester," and they put back about $70,000 of it. At this point Foreman died and they decided to make Perkins the historian. They thought he would resign at the university, as chairman of the history department, and become the historian, as Foreman had made it his career. But he said he would be the historian and get a young man—it goes pretty far back to think of me as a young man, but that's the way I fitted in.

STAVE: Now, when you came to Rochester, what were your duties as the assistant city historian?

McKELVEY: Well, I was going to carry on the program Edward Foreman had developed—he was already bringing out another volume in the series, so I edited that volume. Most of the material was already available and I carried it through the printer, my first experience with a printer. It was in that same year that I finally got my doctoral thesis published in Chicago. Then we faced the problem of setting up a plan for the future. The first task, we decided, was to discover what had already been accomplished, so I prepared an index of the earlier volumes. We were moving into a new library at the time and my office has always been in the public library—the Rundel Library. We decided we would focus the next volume on the history of libraries in the area. That would enable us as newcomers to get a hold of one subject and not be editing miscellaneous articles about which we knew little. So I wrote two of the articles and got people to write the others and we produced a volume on the history of our libraries. For the next volume we decided to do the same thing on schools. I'd done some work at Harvard on travel journals and I thought this was a good source for material on a city's history—and so we edited a volume on travel journals. In other words, we specialized each year in order, partly, to be sure of our scholarship.

STAVE: Now was the journal *Rochester History* published at that time?

McKELVEY: No, we started it in our third year. The Director of the library offered to finance it as a library publication. I think he expected us to drop the society's publication, but we kept both going for a time. Eventually the historical society ran out of funds. I wasn't too upset. It had been a hard struggle finding contributors able to produce creditable articles. The books were distributed to all members and a few libraries subscribed or supplied exchanges. But I occasionally got a letter saying "thank you for your volume but please don't send me any more because I have no more shelf space." By this time I had started writing my own history of Rochester, and so with *Rochester History* and my own work, I finally closed down that series.

STAVE: You are well known for several books, but very well known for the four-volume study of Rochester, an urban biography.[4] How did you start this work, why four volumes, and what's your view of it now?

McKELVEY: Well, I was working on the publication of the pamphlets, which came out quarterly, and I was pressing my research into the history of the community. I focused most of the early issues of *Rochester History* on the period before the Civil War. In one or two issues I made a desperate attempt to summarize the whole history without knowing too much about the later period. I don't know just when I conceived the plan of writing my own history of Rochester, but I was fascinated by the opportunity to study this city, and at some point during the first couple of years I determined to write a new, independent, one-man history of Rochester to supplement or replace the compilations that had been made by Foreman. I wanted to make a complete study. I had read Bessie Pierce's volumes. I don't know to what extent that influenced me, but I also remember eagerly looking at the early histories of other towns as they came out. I don't recall the exact chronology of Constance Green's volume on Holyoke[5] and Gerald Capers' volume on Memphis[6] and some of the others, but I read them all. I especially wanted to know what was happening in other cities contemporary to the period of Rochester I was studying. I wanted to make anything I wrote as sound as possible, and I was looking at and developing a library of these other volumes and attending the American Historical Association meetings. It was in this period that we began to consider the possibility of meeting together. I think that the formation of the urban history group, perhaps, grew out of the fact that at one point I was asked to write a paper on the state of urban history.

STAVE: I'd like to get back to both of these things in a minute. Let's focus on the Rochester study, on the four volumes. It's often pointed to as the classic example of urban biography. Today it's come in for criticism from the so-called "new urban historians," the new urban-social historians, as perhaps being too narrative. One of the interesting things I noticed is that in *Rochester: An Emerging Metropolis*, the last volume, the advertising blurb mentioned that there were a thousand names, a thousand individuals, covered in the book. You've been criticized for too much detail. How do you take to this kind of criticism? Is it necessary for the kind of history you were writing to include so many names because you want to appeal to the local area?

McKELVEY: I think maybe in the last volume I did put in more names than I did in the others, partly because people were living who were part of the movements I discussed; if you don't at least mention the leaders, your account loses force. The blurb you refer to was of course promotional, but the charge that there was excessive use of names in order to appeal to a market is false. People have always been a part of my history—they make it! And I really don't believe that I appeal to the market. By this time I have become somewhat disillusioned on that possibility.

STAVE: [laughs] How many books did it sell, by the way?

McKELVEY: Well, [laughs] I think you better skip that.

STAVE: How many?

McKELVEY: Well, we published—I think it was 2,000 of the first volume, and 2,500 of the second, and 2,500 of the third, and 2,500 of the fourth. The first volume has long been out of print. I must admit that there are still some copies of volume four around, and 15 or 20 of volume three.

STAVE: In other words, the first three volumes pretty much sold the complete run of 2,500.

McKELVEY: I wouldn't say this was really appealing to the market.

STAVE: [laughs] The market apparently was limited.

McKELVEY: Going back to the earlier question, I have discovered that the positive tense makes a much more readable text. If you can show a person doing something, rather than just reporting that something happened for various causes, your account gains force. You have to know your facts and what you want to say, but there is something too in the way you write. The market is limited, but possibly the reporters who quote me with gratifying frequency in the papers reach a wider public. I think that the best way to respond to the criticism is to look at my interest in city history as compared with the majority of those interested in urban history. If you look at Connie Green's or Bayrd Still's[7] original volumes—you'll see that they were very comparable in approach. They didn't devote four volumes to one city, but no other scholar has had that assignment. It should be noted that my studies of Rochester particularly have been written not for scholars, but for the city. I've written them to be read by citizens in Rochester, and I have not been trying to prove a thesis; I've not been trying to demonstrate new insights into any subject. I've been trying to recreate the experiences of that community, growing into a modern city, and this is something which historians normally do chronologically. There is a question as to whether you take it topically, but even if you do take it topically you usually follow the topics chronologically. I decided early that there was a distinct advantage, within the periods that I took, in treating the multiple developments in their relationships at the time.

My main source of material was the newspapers. We were fortunate at Rochester; when I arrived a newspaper index was already underway—by one of the New Deal projects, the NYA, and I helped to direct that project. I went out and gave them a lecture about every two weeks because the staff was changing; I would talk to the newcomers, training them in what to look for, and we got a newspaper index that is unrivaled in the country outside of *The New York Times.* And this has been very, very valuable to many historians. It came down to 1897. I also read through those newspapers—one for every day in every year. I switched from one to another every six months or so because for many decades we had six newspapers, and I wanted to get the point of view of each one, though I didn't want to read all of them. I also had the index to check other sources on any topic that warranted further checking. So I was getting a mass of chronologically arranged notes, and looking at it from this point of view I was trying to restore, recreate, retell the story as it had been experienced by the million or so people who were involved in the development of Rochester.

I discovered—when I had a chance at the end of my career to go out to Michigan for one year and try to teach a full course in urban history—I discovered that my approach was not exactly the approach that practically everybody else in the field was making. They were looking for theses. If I had been directing Ph.D. dissertations all this time, I might have been looking for theses, and I might have adopted a different approach, but I probably would not have written as much urban history! I got fairly well set in this approach and carried through with a full four-volume study of the city's development in chronological periods. In each period I draw out special themes.

STAVE: Well, your themes, if I could state them from a review by Estelle Feinstein, of *Rochester on the Genesee*,[8] which you put out in 1973: she talks about the river location and access to the canal as being a guiding principle of the first era of Rochester and later the foresight of the industrial leaders like Eastman. She notes securing patent control, critical inventions, expanding production, and so on as having a major impact on the growth of the city; the emergence of elite figures willing to serve on the volunteer committees—that these are sort of organizing principles that you looked at in the chronological history. Is this correct?

McKELVEY: Reasonably correct for a short summary.

STAVE: You said that if you had been guiding theses you would have been looking, perhaps, for others kinds of themes. If you were starting your history of Rochester again in 1975, how would you go about it?

Do you think you would go about it the same way? What kinds of things might you look for?

McKELVEY: Well, perhaps if I were starting a history of Rochester as a university professor someplace, I might look at it differently. I'm not sure that if I were a city historian, working for the community, I would alter my approach very drastically. After all, I don't think that when you're serving a community you should devote much time to what might be called abstract research. If a sociological or demographical approach to a certain aspect of your city's development offers promise, pursue it; you ought to use any new techniques you can. As I've developed my subject, I've tried to be as aware as possible of every other scholar working in the field of urban history and urban sociology.

STAVE: One of the things that I'm very interested in is that in looking over your work, and especially things like your reminiscences, that came out in *Rochester History,*[9] you have a great awareness of what is going on in the new urban history, of the quantification. You point in this direction, I think, in several places. Also in turning over the city historianship to Mr. Joseph Barnes, you talk about his familiarity with certain kinds of records, the quantitative kinds of records. So there is this awareness.

McKELVEY: May I interrupt here for just a moment.

STAVE: Yes, sure.

McKELVEY: I'm a quantifier, if I may do a little boasting. If you look in volume one, which came out in 1945, you will find that there are three references to mobility there. It just happens that as I was writing one day, I got a request from somebody to look up his ancestor. I looked him up in the first directory, in 1827, and found him, and looked him up in the second directory, in 1834, and he wasn't there. The question suddenly occurred to me, "how many people did disappear from Rochester?" I made a quick check, taking the top names on every page—from the 1827 directory, a couple of hundred, and searching for them in the 1834 directory. I found an incredible disappearance of Rochesterians, in spite of the fact that the city had grown sevenfold or something like that in that period. This struck me right in the face, and so I carried that study along throughout my volumes before anybody else in the field had thought of mobility. They're hidden there as directional symbols and I think that only one scholar has ever referred to them.

STAVE: This is interesting. In 1952 you published an article called, "American Urban History Today" in the *American Historical Review.*[10] Some of the paths that you point to, the urban history that you talk about, in a sense, is the "old" urban history as younger scholars see it—urban biography, studies dealing with commercial rivalry, and such. Yet, you talk about the need for critical standards on the part of urban historians. When you conclude, you say, "the contours of the recently discovered historical valley begin to take form, but as the pioneers know and many reviewers have said, we need new efforts to see our subject whole in successive periods of development, new efforts to relate the growth of urbanism to other phases of American history, new efforts to appraise the role of cities as crucibles of culture, to borrow a Wertenbaker phrase, new efforts to understand the vital relationship between man's independent, free venturing spirit and the urban environmental setting." And that is July 1952. Now, what prompted the publication of that article and do you think the standards that you set out, the goals that you set out, have been met almost twenty-five years later?

McKELVEY: As to the article—I was asked to give a paper at one of the American Historical meetings. As a result, as I started to say before, we did organize the urban history group.

STAVE: But the request—why you and why request someone to do a paper on American urban history today? Why the need for someone to summarize what was going on?

McKELVEY: Well, there were a number of us, as that paper indicates, who were already working in this field. I do recall that I had made an earlier canvas of the field for a paper which was never published on the number of studies being made of cities. I had discovered that Rochester was almost unique as far as an official historian was concerned. There was a historiographer in Detroit and one or two state historical societies located in cities and interested in their history; there was Bessie Pierce's project and Connie Green's projects. I don't recall when I first heard of Bayrd Still. Meanwhile, my first book came out, as well as Still's and several of the others, and there was an increased interest in the subject. Just how that program was set up I don't recall.

STAVE: Now from this came the urban history group?

McKELVEY: When the article came out, I got some comments, generally favorable. In October 1953, I had some correspondence with Bayrd Still, and we decided to set up a luncheon at the next session of the American Historical Association. It was at that luncheon, which Bayrd Still chaired, that we decided to start an informal urban history group, as we called it, and issue a newsletter. Probably because I was the only one at that time who had an office with a secretary, I was asked to be the editor and to serve as chairman. There was no more structure to it than that. We would try to have an annual get together of some sort, for luncheon, or just to discuss our programs and our projects, and everybody would send in some information about what they were doing. Well, very few sent anything in; it became a problem to get something to put in the newsletter. We had another meeting, the first formal meeting, at which we held a discussion of Dick Wade's *The Urban Frontier.*[11] He had finished his thesis but hadn't published it yet. He wrote a paper which we all read and discussed; that was the one meeting of this sort that I chaired. We had Professor Green and two others—Bayrd Still and Joe Norris then at Detroit—three commentators; we decided to hold annual meetings and try to get out two issues of the *Urban History Newsletter.* But the problem of getting a response was increasing. I needed some method of getting a larger response. I prepared a questionnaire asking each one to provide some essential details on his projects and promised to publish it. I got out one list of those who replied; there were about 25 of us, and the next year when the next issue came out [laughs], I had 20 more who hastened to get into the list. So we had a number identified much more securely than we'd had before and we held several quite interesting annual discussions, luncheons. I can remember one in which Nelson Blake at Syracuse, who'd just brought out his book, *Water for the Cities,*[12] discussed the field of urban history. Two years later we had a very famous session in which Eric Lampard took up that same subject and threw some of us for a loop because it was much more theoretical, asking us to develop concepts on all sorts of things. Meanwhile, at each of these sessions, we were all debating William Diamond's critique of Schlesinger.[13] William Diamond never showed up. We lost track of him. I don't know where his career went to. But that was a very interesting article, and his professor, Stull Holt, was a member of our group. We never got him to take part in a session; but he contributed to the discussions a couple of times. We had Lampard's paper; we had a paper by Richard Wohl. He had a great deal to contribute. And Ted Brown, who was his assistant (I went out to Kansas City to look at their projects; I spent two days with the two of them and a couple of others). Tom Cochran was a member or at least attended some of our early meetings. We never got him on one of our programs; he was on several related programs. I went down to see his project in Philadelphia, Norristown.[14] We were trying to touch all bases in approaching our work, and I was specifically interested in developing all possible approaches to my study of Rochester. But I was, as I said before, concerned to make it something that would recreate the community's history for those in the community.

STAVE: You became much more general when you published your next two volumes—*The Urbanization of America, 1860-1915,* and *The Emergence of Metropolitan America, 1915-1966.*[15] In a review, Eric Lampard claimed that *The Urbanization of America* volume added little since Arthur Schlesinger's *Rise of the City, 1878-1898,* to the understanding of urbanization and its relation to other phases of history. He said: "no distinction is made between city growth and urbanization, nor recognition of the former as a result of the latter. When urbanization is identified with everything it can explain nothing." But yet he called the book almost definitive in light of the state of the art at the time.[16] What is your reaction to this?

McKELVEY: Well, you might throw in another critic of that book, the leader of the urban history group in England—H. J. Dyos. In commenting on numerous books in his *The Study of Urban History,*[17] he cites this book as the most ambitious failure. [laughs]

STAVE: [laughs] The most ambitious failure in the field. Well, how do you react to that?

McKELVEY: Well, again, I think most people in the field, with the exception of a few that started about when I did—are writing chiefly for scholars. I would say that Connie Green was writing for readers who were intelligent readers rather than scholars. I don't regard this as writing down. I think that this is writing for readers of history and not just students of history. I recognize that a good many historians are hoping that what they write will be read by other scholars; scholars are their "market," as you put it. My object has been to write something that is still in the old concept of history rather than history as a social science. *The Urbanization of America* went around to six or seven different publishers, who sent it out to various readers and it came back with the comment that this isn't good sociology.

STAVE: This *isn't* good sociology?

McKELVEY: And I would write again, "would you be interested in looking at a volume on urban history, not urban sociology?" This consumed a couple of years—it had taken a year or six months to go through a couple of the readers. Finally my wife happened to see that some foundation had given Rutgers University Press a fund to publish books that wouldn't pay, and so I wrote to the editor of Rutgers Press. They sent it on to somebody who wrote in and said, "this isn't even as good as that unsatisfactory book by A. M. Schlesinger, *The Rise of the City.*"

STAVE: [laughs] Well, I wonder who that was.

McKELVEY: Well, whoever said that did me a favor. I wrote back to the editor and said, "your critic has high standards; he wouldn't publish a book by the dean of American historians." And so he sent it to a couple of other readers and it was finally approved and published, and incidentally, I still receive some royalties on that volume. They didn't take quite that much time to decide to publish the second one. And curiously enough, both of these books were rather critically, in the sense of unfavorably, reviewed in a couple of historical journals; they were very favorably reviewed in sociology journals, in geography journals, and in planning journals.

STAVE: What meaning does that have for you?

McKELVEY: These other scholars were looking to history for some review of the experience of history, not for some new insights into sociology or geography. They could do that themselves. But the urban historians who reviewed it were thinking, "we really should take this whole field over and we should show these boys that we know an awful lot more than they do." Well, just the other day I read an article, pointing out that William James made the distinction many years ago between *knowledge of* and *knowledge about*. Knowledge of, as he pointed out, was knowledge of the experiences of life; knowledge about is pulling it apart scientifically, examining it, getting to know it synthetically, as a scientist tries to know the body. Well, I would say that my objective has been *knowledge of*. This particular, very simplified distinction might characterize me. I was thinking today and yesterday, as we were sitting through these various discussions here at the Brockport Institute, that practically all the papers are trying to develop themes, theses, in which they seek to detect and study aspects of urban history or ethnic history by developing a social science approach, rather than an historical approach. I still go back to history.

STAVE: Now, in the preface of *The Urbanization of America* you wrote that even if one could quantify the "strictly urban factor in human affairs . . . the historian of cities would remain more broadly interested in the interplay of that influence with other forces affecting man's response to his environment."[18] So I think essentially you were saying then what you were just saying now—you're looking for this kind of interaction; you're not concerned with some of these other social scientific interpretations. And I get the feeling that there's an implicit criticism in this, that it's a wandering from history. Do you think so?

McKELVEY: Well, I'm not criticising or saying that this is something they shouldn't do; but I am saying that this is not my approach to history, though I want to use any new insights that the other disciplines evolve in throwing light on my interpretation. But my view is simply that a number of people made decisions and I'd like to see why. I still think people made the decisions, made choices. But we've heard in the last couple of days of trying to get from the ground up and get all people into the picture. But there haven't been any people, there have just been numbers.

STAVE: I've just spoken to several people about this. Don't the numbers represent people?

McKELVEY: Well, I'd like to see people.

STAVE: Isn't it a matter of color not being present?

McKELVEY: I would like to think that I could identify one or two of these people.

STAVE: You mean to label them, to get a handle on them?

McKELVEY: And to have other people able to identify them. I'm sure that any readers, the average readers out in the street, wouldn't think that there were people in those papers. I mean you're talking about people as abstracts, as numbers, so many people as classes; and I'm not saying this isn't something that's perfectly legitimate and very desirable in understanding our society, but it isn't my historical approach. I'm not saying that mine is the only possible historical approach, but you were asking what mine was.

STAVE: Okay, fine. One of the interesting things, I think, in light of this conversation is that recently your book, *American Urbanization: A Comparative History,*[19] along with Zane Miller's *The Urbanization of Modern America* and Sam Warner's *The Urban Wilderness,* was reviewed by Leo Schnore in *Reviews in American History.*[20] Professor Schnore, who is a sociologist, talks about your book as being the most methodological, the most analytical, of the three. Of course, you are quantitative in this final book, not in the sense of correlation analyses and matrices and this kind of thing, but you have a lot of numbers in there; in fact, I have used some of your charts in my classes. And why in this final book do you take on a new periodization, do you use a little more statistics than you have in the past?

McKELVEY: Well, I read that review with some surprise that he regarded that as quantification. I took a course back at Harvard in economic history under Gay, which I didn't mention before, and he always had tables on the blackboard. I learned to appreciate the value of a table; it focuses and permits you to see many aspects of the subject; a student would write many paragraphs before he could exhaust the possibilities of a good table. And I've used tables before, perhaps not as many as in that volume—which was, after all, even a bit more ambitious than the one which failed [laughs]—because this book compared American urban development with urban development in the rest of the world. I was not really trying to complete that topic; I was making a preliminary venture into it, exploring growth trends, data about the size of cities. Those statistics are not really quantification in any scientific sense, and I was a little bit surprised that Schnore dignified me with the praise that he did give.

I would like to make one comment—if I can go back to my *Emergence of Metropolitan America* and your questions concerning the writing of *The Urbanization of America*. My effort to see American urban development as a whole was a result, in the course of a decade or more, of writing Rochester history but trying to keep abreast with everything else. I was queried once or twice by an editor or a publisher, "would you do something on cities in general?" I discussed it with Dick Wade and Bayrd Still at one time in terms of three volumes, and we actually outlined something, but they both became too busy with many other projects. I did get started on the second volume at that time. I tried to look at it, the urban developments in that period, in a new way. Connie Green's study somewhat followed Carl Bridenbaugh's work, in which he picked out five cities; she picked out ten or more cities.[21]

STAVE: Yes, her *American Cities in the Growth of the Nation.*

McKELVEY: And she followed them somewhat chronologically, picking her cities at different periods. That was one possible method. Wade's volume on *The Urban Frontier* had come out by that time, in which he took five cities. The problem was how do you organize a review of the entire American urban scene. And my resolution of that problem, as several have pointed out, didn't meet everybody's satisfaction. But, in any case, at its publication, one scholar who probably was a bit critical of *The Urbanization of America,* but somewhat tolerant, said, "well, now you've finished that subject since cities become half the population at that point"—between 1910 and 1920 cities had become half the population. "That means that we no longer have any urban history," he said. Well, I was a little bit stunned at that conclusion. I didn't argue it with him, but I did think about it. I thought to myself, there must have been some impact on American history directly resulting from the fact that cities have become increasingly larger proportionately. Somebody at Syracuse asked me to give a paper, and I focused on this question. It suddenly occurred to me that in that volume, I had practically never mentioned the federal government, and you can't think of cities today without thinking of the federal government. Suddenly I realized, there was a topic. So I wrote my second volume with this specifically as the theme.

STAVE: This is *The Emergence of Metropolitan America: 1915-1966*, which was published in 1968. I am particularly interested in this topic, having done some work on it myself. Some people, I think, felt that you overemphasized it in this volume, in this 1915-1966 period. Now, you say that you cannot conceive of the city without the framework of the federal government. Could you elaborate on this?

McKELVEY: Well, I didn't quite say that, but you can't discuss urban problems today without considering the impact of the federal government and the relationships that the federal government has developed with cities. Now, there is a certain individual—President Ford—who thinks that we can get back to some period before the great flood! I did, perhaps, assume at the end of my book that we were moving ahead a little more rapidly. As a matter of fact, I expected that maybe a former mayor, Hubert Humphrey, might be president by the time my book came out or something like that. [laughs] I could think of a mayor being president, you see, rather than a governor or a senator. I think I was a little too confident that we would not have a slowdown in the relationship between cities and the federal government. In this specific question of New York, for example, which is up today, the issue is here. I point out in that volume on comparative history and comparative urbanization that London, Rome, Berlin, Moscow—any major capital city which is also the large city—is on a federal or a national budget; and they're not treated as tax poor by a federal government running off with the money the way New York is; they're all facing the same problem. Look at what the cities in South America are experiencing as the whole population is moving in on these tremendously rapidly growing cities.

STAVE: Like São Paulo.

McKELVEY: They're urban problems, but they're national problems too, and New York is faced with this kind of problem in America. It isn't actually the political capital but in all other aspects it's the capital.

STAVE: I find it interesting that we don't talk about the urban crisis today as much as we did when *The Emergence of Metropolitan America* got published. That was the real take-off period of urban history courses in college; especially in the mid-sixties everyone becomes interested in city and it's because of social problems in the city. Today we talk about a financial crisis but it's not quite the same thing as the urban crisis, the race riots, the problems that seemed manifest in the sixties. Now, Rochester was the site of one of these race riots. What was your view of this: (a) as a person who studied the city very intensely, was this something that you expected? and (b) how about now, with a perspective of ten years since the riot? Could you elaborate on that?

McKELVEY: Well, that's an interesting challenge. I didn't expect it. However, I had reason to be a little more alert to it than some others. I had published my fourth book on Rochester before Connie Green's book on Washington came out,[22] and I can remember being astonished at the amount of space she gave to the blacks in Washington! I suddenly picked up my volumes to see how I had missed this subject. But, looking over the sources and so forth, I realized that Rochester hadn't experienced the invasion or the migration that Washington had had for many years and that this was a major aspect of the population there. I hadn't realized that it was becoming such a major population problem in Washington, and she had properly put it in perspective. Rochester's small Negro population at the beginning had stayed at about 300 through several decades, while the population of the city was zooming; the immigrants had completely snowed the blacks over. There was a very small Negro population which I had carried along, percentage-wise less than 1% for several decades. During the First World War, when the migration into other northern cities occurred, we didn't receive any. It wasn't until after the Second World War that we began to get an in-migration. I had helped to establish a new settlement house in one of the neighborhoods involved and we were concerned about this problem. This was something that was growing and I was aware of it, but I never expected the outbreak. But we were faced with a tremendous migration in the 1950s. We did not realize that we were growing at the rate that we were. Much of the growth in other cities had taken place in the First World War or during the Second World War. Rochester was enjoying the smallest unemployment figure of any other city in the country. We were down near one, two, 1.3% for a couple of years. This attracted many people to Rochester looking for jobs. As the blacks increased, many were unable to find jobs but saw jobs advertised all the time—technological jobs beyond their reach—and they became restless. Some who did find jobs were not satisfied. And we had one of the hot spells that we sometimes get, one of the very excessive hot spells. The police agreed to permit a group of Negro ladies to hold a bazaar and dance in one of the streets. It was held on a hot night in July; a couple of youths started to battle each other and the ladies called the police. The police arrived and tried to settle the disturbance. Unfortunately, a second police car arrived at this point with a dog and apparently this rekindled the fury and a riot erupted. I covered the riot and its repercussions in considerable detail in my last Rochester volume, the summary volume—too much in detail, some have said, and I am sure you don't want me to demonstrate here the folly of detail!

STAVE: I get the impression that if another history of Rochester would be written that the black experience would certainly be covered and I also have the impression that if you were to rewrite the four volumes they might have gotten more attention, or do you think that this is presentism?

McKELVEY: I don't believe so. Rather, yes, no, and yes to the three questions. I think that I gave them fully adequate attention at the end in both the final volume and in the summary volume, the last chapter in the summary volume.

STAVE: Well, let's go back to that *AHR* article of July 1952, for a minute. You did set out certain goals. How do you assess the progress of American urban history since the time you wrote in 1952?

McKELVEY: Well, I think it's been very remarkable, the developments that have taken place. There have been a number of very suggestive approaches developed. The Kansas City project was one of the projects that we looked to for some new approaches—the death of Wohl was very unfortunate. Both Ted Brown and Charlie Glaab brought out their individual books, but what was originally hoped for was a study, an ongoing study, and I guess that has completely been dropped.[23] But, meanwhile, the study of Washington, D.C. came in. I believe that the promise that we looked for from Cochran's study of Norristown never really developed into an urban history study. I don't know if it was designed for that, but in any case we looked to it for new ideas. Meanwhile, a number of new approaches have been made and they are stimulating ones. I think that the field mushroomed for a number of years, and along with black studies for a couple of years it was *the* field. It is true that some of the new approaches in urban history do strike me as plotting a new approach to social history with limited reference to urban history. This comment has been made and I think there's something to it, and listening to the papers here I again thought of that.

STAVE: You mentioned some stimulating approaches or books that have been written. Your favorite works in urban history—if you had to choose a few that you can think of that have really done a fine job? Would you commit yourself?

McKELVEY: Well, from the point of view of their influence on me, we have to go back quite a distance. Maybe some would say I got into sort of a rut—I would call it a groove—after I developed my approach. I remember looking with real and critical interest at Connie Green's first volume and Dick Wade's when they first came out. Incidentally, I had a nice little debate with Dick. He was at the University of Rochester for a time and he prepared that paper in which he referred to cities as "the spearheads of the frontier." But Rochester wasn't a spearhead. We had quite a debate on this. Suddenly I realized that you had to really pay attention to the facts. Just because Rochester started after Canandaigua and several nearby towns, but suddenly zoomed ahead, you couldn't assume that every other frontier would start the same way; nor could you assume that because Cleveland or Louisville started as the first settlements in their particular neighborhoods, that other frontiers would do the same. In other words, I again was encouraged to recall that history was something that happens in time and in place; this strengthened my conviction that it wasn't a pattern that you're looking for, but the experience.

STAVE: Are there any other books or works that were influential in your thinking?

McKELVEY: Well, when it came to deciding to write *The Urbanization of America,* I looked with interest at the other books that dealt with more than one city. But when you ask me to pick out a favorite—I have reviewed thirty or more over the years and with few exceptions I found merits of note in all of them, in Warner's *Streetcar Suburbs,* in Miller on Cincinnati, in Nelli's *Italians in Chicago,* in Frisch's Springfield, to name a few that come to mind. There were others—Hays' *The Response to Industrialism,* Dahl's *Who Governs?* Stein's *The Eclipse of Community,* in allied fields.[24] And there was a volume on Boston's architecture by Walter Muir Whitehill.[25] I was also very much interested in Handlin's volume, *Boston's Immigrants.*[26] It was an earlier book. It came out while I was finishing up my first volume I believe. I looked at it in reference to what I had covered in my first volume on immigrants and it offered a different pattern, a different experience in terms of what I had found.

STAVE: What about any of the other younger historians, the new urban historians—any work that you particularly think is worthwhile or has been useful? Is there anything in the past decade or so that you would point to?

McKELVEY: Well, I'm quite interested in the studies that have come out on mobility and I used several in a course I gave at Michigan, both Thernstrom's and Knights' studies.[27] The Dyos volume, mentioned earlier, and his newsletters are very interesting, and a volume of papers on Atlantic seaboard cities, *The Growth of the Seaport Cities,* edited by David T. Gilchrist.[28]

STAVE: Well, you've mentioned books that have influenced you. What do you think your influence has been as an urban historian?

McKELVEY: Well, you put a good light on that at the start by saying that my books are well known. I would qualify that by saying that I have met several here today and in the last few days who made the comment: "oh, you're McKelvey. Yes, I've read your book."

STAVE: Your *book*! [laughs]

McKELVEY: As to impact—I don't think that I have made the impact I expected to make when I wrote my first volume. I really thought that there would be a wave going around the world. [laughs] I've discovered since then that that doesn't really occur. Possibly in the urban history group, which I helped to get started, I may have helped to provide a forum for younger scholars who, of course, developed new approaches. I was invited a couple of years ago to take part in a session in Madison in which I was to be the spokesman for the old school looking at the new school, and that was interesting. I don't believe that I can claim to have had any real impact. I know that many have made complimentary remarks about some of my books, but nobody has credited me with making a conceptual breakthrough, which was never my hope or intent. I have been content, in the main, to write the history of one city and to write it for those who want to know its traditions and something of their origins. I would like to suggest that historians, in a period where there is lax employment for professors, might really explore the possibility of becoming city historians to supply the needs that every community has for a knowledge of its history. People want to know a lot of things. Some want to know when a certain building was built. Some want to know the traditions of a certain neighborhood, or of their own ethnic group. I've had a couple of flattering reviews but the response that I really got a big kick out of came a couple of months ago. We had a leaky faucet and called up a plumber's outfit; they sent a plumber around who had an accent, I didn't quite catch his name. He was working away and suddenly he stopped and he said: "your name is, I noticed, Blake McKelvey. Are you *the* Blake McKelvey?" Well, I said "I'm the only one I know of." He said: "well then I've been reading your books for about 15 years." It turned out that he had been a member of a Ukrainian group that I addressed about 15 years ago; I had handed out a few pamphlets and he picked up one, and he'd been picking them up ever since then. Well, here was a plumber—an audience that I don't think many of the urban historians write for—and if you're talking about history from the ground up, it would be a good thing to reach down to some people who live on *terra firma*.

STAVE: Okay, I think on this note of history from the bottom up, or from the faucet down, and on the advice to urban historians to be historians, I'll conclude. I'd like to thank you.

McKELVEY: Thank you.

NOTES

1. Arthur M. Schlesinger, *The Rise of the City, 1878-1898* (New York, 1933).

2. Blake McKelvey, *American Prisons: A Social History Prior to 1915* (Chicago, 1936).

3. Bessie L. Pierce, *A History of Chicago* (3 vols., New York, 1937-1957).

4. Blake McKelvey, *Rochester: The Water Power City, 1812-1854* (Cambridge, Mass., 1945); *Rochester: The Flower City, 1855-1890* (Cambridge, Mass., 1949); *Rochester: The Quest for Quality, 1890-1925* (Cambridge, Mass., 1956); *Rochester: An Emerging Metropolis, 1925-1961* (Rochester, N.Y., 1961).

5. Constance McLaughlin Green, *Holyoke, Massachusetts: A Case History of the Industrial Revolution in America* (New Haven, Conn., 1939).

6. Gerald M. Capers, *The Biography of a River Town: Memphis, Its Heroic Age* (Chapel Hill, N.C., 1939).

7. Bayrd Still, *Milwaukee: The History of City* (Madison, Wisc., 1948).

8. Review of McKelvey, *Rochester on the Genesee: The Growth of a City* (Syracuse, N.Y., 1973), by Estelle Feinstein, Journal of American History, 61 (December 1974), 804-805.

9. Blake McKelvey, "Errata and Addenda: Plus Some Thoughts on the Nature of History and the Rochester Story," Rochester History, 24 (April 1962), 1-22; Blake McKelvey, "A City Historian's Report," Rochester History, 35 (July 1973), 1-24.

10. Blake McKelvey, "American Urban History Today," American Historical Review, 57 (July 1952), 919-929.

11. Richard Wade, *The Urban Frontier: Pioneer Life in Early Pittsburgh, Cincinnati, Lexington, Louisville, and St. Louis* (Cambridge, Mass., 1959).

12. Nelson Blake, *Water for the Cities: A History of the Urban Water Supply Problem in the United States* (Syracuse, N.Y., 1956).

13. William Diamond, "On the Dangers of an Urban Interpretation of History," in Eric F. Goldman, ed., *Historiography and Urbanization* (Baltimore, 1941), 67-108.

14. Sidney Goldstein, *The Norristown Study: An Experiment in Interdisciplinary Research Training*, Foreword by Thomas C. Cochran (Philadelphia, 1961).

15. Blake McKelvey, *The Urbanization of America, 1860-1915* (New Brunswick, N.J., 1963) and *The Emergence of Metropolitan America, 1915-1966* (New Brunswick, N.J., 1968).

16. Review of McKelvey, *The Urbanization of America*, by Eric E. Lampard, American Historical Review, 69 (July 1964), 1086-1087.

17. H. J. Dyos, ed., *The Study of Urban History* (London, 1968).

18. McKelvey, *Urbanization of America*, viii.

19. Blake McKelvey, *American Urbanization: A Comparative History* (Glenview, Ill., 1973).

20. Leo Schnore, "Beyond the Veil of Urban History: Three Glimpses," Reviews in American History, 3 (March 1975), 129-136.

21. Carl Bridenbaugh, *Cities in the Wilderness: Urban Life in America, 1625-1742* (New York, 1938) and *Cities in Revolt: Urban Life in America,*

1743-1776 (New York, 1955); Constance McLaughlin Green, *American Cities in the Growth of the Nation* (New York, 1957).

22. Constance McLaughlin Green, *Washington: Village and Capital, 1800-1878* (Princeton, N.J., 1962); *Washington: Capital City, 1879-1950* (Princeton, N.J., 1963); *The Secret City: A History of Race Relations in the Nation's Capital* (Princeton, N.J., 1967).

23. A. Theodore Brown, *Frontier Community: A History of Kansas City to 1870* (Columbia, Mo., 1964); Charles N. Glaab, *Kansas City and the Railroads* (Madison, Wisc., 1962).

24. Sam Bass Warner, Jr., *Streetcar Suburbs: The Process of Growth in Boston, 1870-1900* (Cambridge, Mass., 1962); Zane L. Miller, *Boss Cox's Cincinnati: Urban Politics in the Progressive Era* (New York, 1968); Humbert S. Nelli, *The Italians in Chicago, 1880-1930: A Study in Ethnic Mobility* (New York, 1970); Michael H. Frisch, *Town into City: Springfield, Massachusetts, and the Meaning of Community, 1840-1880* (Cambridge, Mass., 1972); Samuel P. Hays, *The Response to Industrialism, 1885-1914* (Chicago, 1957); Robert A. Dahl, *Who Governs: Democracy and Power in an American City* (New Haven, Conn., 1961); Maurice R. Stein, *The Eclipse of Community* (Expanded ed., Princeton, N.J., 1972).

25. Walter Muir Whitehill, *Boston, A Topographical History* (Cambridge, Mass., 1959).

26. Oscar Handlin, *Boston's Immigrants: A Study in Acculturation* (Revised and enlarged edition, Cambridge, Mass., 1959).

27. Stephan Thernstrom, *Poverty and Progress: Social Mobility in a Nineteenth Century City* (New York, 1964) and *The Other Bostonians: Poverty and Progress in the American Metropolis, 1880-1970* (Cambridge, Mass., 1973); Peter R. Knights, *The Plain People of Boston, 1830-1860: A Study in City Growth* (New York, 1971).

28. David T. Gilchrist, ed., *The Growth of the Seaport Cities, 1790-1825* (Charlottesville, Va., 1967).

SELECT BIBLIOGRAPHY OF WORKS
BY BLAKE McKELVEY

American Prisons: A Social History Prior to 1915 (Chicago, 1936).

Rochester: The Water Power City, 1812-1854 (Cambridge, Mass., 1945).

Rochester: The Flower City, 1855-1890 (Cambridge, Mass., 1949).

Rochester: The Quest for Quality, 1890-1925 (Cambridge, Mass., 1956).

Rochester: An Emerging Metropolis, 1925-1961 (Rochester, N.Y., 1961).

The Urbanization of America, 1860-1915 (New Brunswick, N.J., 1963).

The Emergence of Metropolitan America, 1915-1966 (New Brunswick, N.J., 1968).

The City in American History (London, 1969).

American Urbanization: A Comparative History (Glenview, Ill., 1973).

Rochester on the Genesee: The Growth of a City (Syracuse, N.Y., 1973).

American Prisons: A History of Good Intentions (Montclair, N.J., 1976).

"American Urban History Today," *American Historical Review,* 57 (1952), 919-929.

"Errata and Addenda: Plus Some Thoughts on the Nature of History and the Rochester Story," *Rochester History,* 24 (1962), 1-22.

"A City Historian's Report," *Rochester History,* 35 (1973), 1-24.

"The Urban History Group Newsletter," *Urbanism Past & Present,* 1 (1975-1976), 36-37.

Bayrd Still

Bayrd Still (1906-   ) was Professor of History at New York University between 1947 and 1974 and Head of the Department of History during the years 1955-1970. He was instrumental in establishing the Urban History Group in the early 1950s. His one-volume study of Milwaukee is considered a major achievement in the field of urban biography.

A CONVERSATION WITH
BAYRD STILL

STAVE: You've been quoted in print as saying, "I've always thought it a
sign of either senility or self-delusion when one allows himself to
become autobiographical in public." I would still like to get some of
your autobiography. You were born, I believe, in 1906, in Woodstock,
Illinois. Could you describe this town and what it was like living there?

STILL: Well, Woodstock, Illinois—it's a county seat town—is located
about sixty miles from Chicago. It had a population of five or six
thousand when I was going to grade school and high school there.
Actually it is at the outer limit of the Chicago metropolitan area as it
was proposed or planned by Daniel Burnham in 1909. However, I think
the people of Woodstock always have thought of themselves as living in
a self-contained small town, although many now commute to Chicago
and a few people worked in Chicago even in those days. Today, of
course, the metropolitan outreach of Chicago has come pretty near to
what Burnham envisioned in 1909. I would say that the aggressive push
of metropolitan population is within about ten miles of Woodstock
today.

STAVE: Well, when you were younger did you have much connection
with Chicago, did you go back and forth?

STILL: Yes, there was an interesting connection. As far as my family and I were concerned, Chicago was a kind of Mecca. We went in there two or three times a year. We went in to see a play; we were taken in to the Art Institute, to the opera; now and then my mother shopped, not frequently, but she made several pilgrimages for shopping purposes to Chicago. And the interesting thing to me about the attitude of my family is that when they referred to going to Chicago, they always referred to going to *"the city."* They never said, "I'm going to Chicago to shop," or "We're going to go to a play in Chicago." They would say, "We're going to the city," because Chicago connoted something big and glamorous. It had the image of a place that one admired—of course, the side of Chicago that I saw when I went to this Mecca was only the good side.

STAVE: Did you have any contact with the "bad side"—the slums? Were there any in Woodstock? Did you ever have any contact with settlement houses or anything like that?

STILL: No, I doubt that I knew anything about Hull House or Halsted Street. Our contact with Chicago was confined to the Loop, where Marshall Field was the outstanding department store, and Michigan Avenue, where one could go to the Art Institute and the Auditorium Theatre.

STAVE: What was your father's occupation?

STILL: He was a politician—well, public official is a better word. Actually, he was the vice president and cashier of the State Bank of Woodstock. He also held elective political office for the major part of his life. He was the county clerk of McHenry County, an elected position he held for many terms. He was a much-admired citizen. And in the rather generalized nature of the community, you could hold an elective office and also have a kind of part-time connection with a bank, which he ultimately made a full-time connection.

STAVE: So he was involved in politics. Did your mother work at all?

STILL: No, my mother was a housewife and never—perhaps my attitude here dates me—but I just can't conceive of my mother ever being employed or wanting to be employed. That doesn't mean that she didn't work hard as a housekeeper and housewife.

STAVE: You went to the University of Wisconsin, didn't you? What was your early education like?

STILL: Yes, I went through the public schools there in Woodstock, and my primary interest in high school was in student newspaper activities. I think that made me want a journalistic career and the University of

Wisconsin was regarded in those days as having about the best school of journalism in the United States. That's how I happened to go to Wisconsin. I enrolled as a Freshman in 1924, because of the acclaim of its School of Journalism; but by the time I was a Junior I had been won over to history, and the possibility of becoming a college teacher of history. In this decision I probably was influenced most by the skill and showmanship of Carl Russell Fish as a teacher. But there were other outstanding people in a department that always has had a tradition of distinction.

STAVE: Was Frederick Jackson Turner still a member of the Department?

STILL: No. He had left Wisconsin for Harvard in 1910 and was to go to the Huntington Library in 1927. But the identification of the History Department with Turner's "frontier hypothesis" was still strong because of the presence of Frederic L. Paxson, who had completed his Pulitzer Prize book on the *History of the American Frontier* in the Spring of 1924.[1] Paxson had come to Wisconsin in 1910. By the time I was granted a Ph.D. degree in History in 1933, other American historians in the History Department, in addition to the late Carl Russell Fish, included Curtis Nettels, with whom I studied American Colonial history, and John D. Hicks, who came to Wisconsin when Paxson left for California.

STAVE: To what extent did the History program at the University of Wisconsin prepare you for research in city history?

STILL: Very little. The emphasis of the American historians in the Department was strongly political, constitutional, and economic. I cannot recall any course in the American field that could be described as social history or intellectual history. The University of Wisconsin was strong in Sociology in those days, but I was never encouraged to explore that field. Most American history majors seem to have minored in political science. I did benefit from auditing Selig Perlman's course in labor history. I was drawn to the field of the American frontier because of my admiration for the substance and interpretive quality of Professor Paxson's lectures in his course on the history of the American West. I wrote my B.A. thesis under his supervision on the settlement of the German counties of Pennsylvania to 1755, a study descriptive rather than demographic in nature. Lancaster was in this area, and I know now that it was recognized by 1754 to be a "growing town," but I do not recall that Professor Paxson ever raised any questions as to the role of urbanism in the settlement of that region—as a nodal point for commerce in Philadelphia's hinterland, for example.

Paxson, however inadvertently, nevertheless was responsible for turning my interest momentarily in the direction of urban research when I was working for the M.A. degree. For my seminar paper he assigned me the task of studying the early history of Chicago—from about 1830 to 1850. This does not mean that Professor Paxson was interested in urban development as such. At the moment he was trying to delineate stages in the advance of settlement across the Continent, and he was playing with the idea of identifying a stage that might be labeled the "post-frontier period." He was attempting to establish criteria by which the "post-frontier stage" could be identified. He had this in mind, I think, when he assigned me the topic of exploring the early history of Chicago and St. Louis on the assumption that the emergence of cities would denote the onset of a "post-frontier" stage.

The exploration of this topic led me to what I think was an original interpretation—if I ever have given birth to one, and that is that there was a society with urban characteristics on the cutting edge of the frontier, even beyond the outer edge of the farmer frontier, in some instances. As I began to look at the early experience of Chicago, I saw evidence, in the very early days there, of cultural amenities and economic pursuits that one associates with an urban rather than a rural society. Chicago in this frontier era seemed to me to be more urban than rural, so far as its society was concerned. It thus appeared that urbanism was not only a clue to the presence of a post-frontier stage in the settlement process, the thing that Paxson was looking for; urbanization also was a development correlative with the expansion of the frontier, often an integral part of it. This idea is implicit in an article I published in 1935, based on that seminar paper. I called it "Evidences of the Higher Life on the Frontier, as Illustrated in the History of Cultural Matters in Chicago, 1830 to 1850."[2]

I later expanded the theme in a paper I read in 1940 at a meeting of the Mississippi Valley Historical Association and which shortly thereafter was published as "Patterns of Mid-Nineteenth Century Urbanization in the Middle West."[3] In this paper I asserted that town-making as well as farming constituted an important lure to westward migration and made the point that "on many a frontier the town builder was as conspicuous as the farmer pioneer." Nearly ten years later, Richard Wade more fully documented this suggestion in his book *The Urban Frontier.*[4] Here he went so far as to assert that "towns were the spearheads of the frontier." I'm a great admirer of Wade's work, but I am inclined to think that this is possibly an overstatement.

But without question, towns and urban development constituted *one* of the spearheads of the frontier.

STAVE: Could you explain how you think that he might have overstated?

STILL: I think that it is an overstatement only in the sense that urban development was just one of the spearheads. Wade has written, and he has been quoted so often as saying, that towns were *the* spearheads of the frontier. I agree that towns—that urbanism constituted a significant spearhead activity in the westward advance of settlement. But farms and forts in many instances were created beyond the towns, and we know that in many instances the towns which did spring up in advance of the farmer frontier couldn't flourish until there was an agricultural hinterland around them to support them. That was true of Milwaukee, actually. Even though Milwaukee was out on the edge to begin with, it ultimately went into the economic doldrums until there was an agricultural hinterland to support it. I think it's important to see the role of urbanism in connection with the westward movement, but to imply that urbanism was the only spearhead of the frontier advance is an exaggeration.

STAVE: Did Turner understand the relationship of urban development to the westward movement?

STILL: I doubt that he did. He thought of settlement as progressing according to stages and implied that the frontier experience concluded with the arrival of the farmer pioneer. I recall his referring to the procession of civilization westward in his famous essay on the significance of the frontier.[5] First came the buffalo, he said, then the Indian, then the fur trader and hunter, the cattle-raiser, the pioneer farmer—"and the frontier has passed by." He talked about differentiating the trader's frontier, the rancher's frontier, the miner's frontier, and the farmer's frontier. Nowhere does he talk about urbanism as an aspect of society on the edge or frontier of settlement. He does of course refer to the fact that early trading posts, built on the sites of Indian villages, ultimately became large cities such as Detroit, Chicago, St. Louis, and Kansas City. But the implication is that this urban development occurred once the frontier was gone.

This is not to say that Turner was insensitive to the significance of urban development in American history. I recall finding some of his comments on city growth in the Turner Papers in the Huntington Library. In a folder dated October, 1922, he wrote a note, presumably to himself, saying, "Do a paper on significance of the city in American history." Amplifying this reminder he wrote: "Use data on city growth in relation to developing section and extension of frontier; show how sectional rivalry for extending frontier, new settled regions, and new resources affected urban society." This suggests that he thought of the growth of cities as influenced by the development of the frontier, rather than thinking of urban development as an integral part of the westward movement "process." I think Turner saw the city as a *product* of the nation's frontier expansion. He never seems to stress or even allude to the fact that urban impulses often encouraged westward expansion.

Turner might have been more sensitive to the role of urbanism on the frontier if city life had been more congenial to him. Turner was an outdoor man and didn't like cities. Moreover, he probably blamed urban development for the changes in American society which led him to feel by the 1890s that a period significant in the nation's history was over.

STAVE: As I understand Turner, he talks about the orderly procession of civilization, and he starts off with the pioneers, etc., and he has the city as the last factor, I think of seven. Now is this what you mean when you're saying that he thought of urban development as occurring when the frontier was gone?

STILL: I think that description of Turner's progression of settlement constitutes a misunderstanding. Some people have interpreted him as saying, and perhaps at some points in his career he did refer to the fact, that the last stage of settlement was the urban community. After all, at the time he wrote the hypothesis he was triggered into doing this in part because he saw this last stage of urban development around him. But I looked at the essay just the other day, and he says specifically, first came the buffalo, then the Indian, then the fur-trader and hunter, the cattle-raiser, the pioneer farmer, and the frontier has passed by; he says it just that way. From everything that I have seen of his writing, both published and otherwise, I feel that he always thought of urbanism as a sequential development, not a correlative aspect of the westward advance; to him the last stage of social development was urban, but he didn't think of that urban stage as part of the frontier advance; nor so far as I know did he suggest that urban development attracted settlement to the frontier or that the urban community was a part of the frontier society.

STAVE: Did you continue to explore the interrelationship of urbanism and the westward movement as you went on to get the Ph.D. degree?

STILL: Unfortunately, no. After I earned the M.A. I taught for a year at Ohio Wesleyan University and when I returned to Wisconsin in 1930 to work for the doctorate, Paxson turned me toward a constitutional topic—state-making on the frontier between 1829 and 1854. I was not smart enough to realize that the urban topic would be more exciting and more professionally rewarding.

STAVE: How much attention, up to 1930, had the historical profession given to the growth, nature, and influence of cities?

STILL: Not very much. Egal Feldman explored this topic in an M.A. thesis that he wrote under my supervision.[6] He found that historians like Bancroft, Schouler, Rhodes, and McMaster gave some space, in their works, though not much, to describing the growth of cities; Channing and Beard show more evidence of attempting to elucidate the meaning of urban growth.[7] As early as 1890, Albert Bushnell Hart produced a thoughtful essay for the *Quarterly Journal of Economics* in which he attempted to explain the reasons for the phenomenal growth of cities in the United States.[8] This essay seems to have escaped the attention of students of the historiography of the city. Hart's interest apparently was triggered by the contemporaneous problem of municipal misgovernment and by concern over the long-term implications of the large number of foreign-born then pouring into the nation's cities. This led Hart to his rather innovative attempt to explain the rise of American cities. And he couldn't separate this from the contemporary problem of the city in his day. I think this is why historians actually came late to the study of the city. American historians of this period simply couldn't think of the city as being an historical phenomenon, it was so young and new and developing at this juncture.

STAVE: You say it's so young and new. New York had almost a million population in 1860. When you're saying that they're new, what do you mean by this?

STILL: I didn't mean that they were new in the sense that they hadn't existed. I think that the apparent newness of them simply was a factor of their continuing growth into very large cities. They had been growing for a long time, but the phenomenon of the 1880s and 1890s was the continuing and increasingly abundant growth of large cities. They were such an ongoing and developing aspect of the American scene that they were regarded as something that a *historian* would not be concerning himself with. If they had begun to decline, to decrease in size, then historians might have thought of this as something they ought to try to explain. But since cities were pushing outward and getting bigger all the time, they had a contemporaneity about them. The velocity of growth gave them a contemporaneity that kept people focused upon their existing problems. And even in the case of Hart's essay, he wasn't doing what the typical historian would do, simply explaining how these cities came to be; he went on to project what the implications for the future would be because of this new ingredient, the foreign-born, coming in. The combination of the contemporaneous with the historical changes the picture there a little bit. He discussed the causes and sources of city growth, topics Adna Weber was to deal with more fully in his essentially statistical historical study, *The Growth of Cities in the Nineteenth Century,* which he wrote as a doctoral dissertation at Columbia University in 1898 or 1899.[9]

Early in the 1920s Edward Channing called for study of the history of the nation's urban development. In volume 5 of his multivolume *History of the United States* he included a chapter on "The Urban Migration" of the pre-Civil War period which, he noted, was less well understood than the westward movement.[10] This volume was published in the early 1920s. About this time Lewis Mumford wrote an essay entitled "The City" for a symposium on *Civilization in the United States,* published in 1922.[11] In this essay he periodized the urbanization of the United States. He later contended that this was the "first historic analysis of its kind to be published in the United States." This augmented attention to the history of the city may well have been prompted by the disclosure, after the Census of 1920, that for the first time the United States was predominantly urban. In this connection, it seems significant that it was in 1922 that Turner wrote the note to himself suggesting writing on the significance of the city in American history.

STAVE: Hadn't a good many histories of individual cities been written before 1920?

STILL: Yes, but before the late 1920s the output of city history had been virtually confined to a kind of commercialized local history—multivolume works written or edited by newspapermen or librarians with an interest in local history and an eye to sales. These multivolume works appeared in two waves—one wave during the 1880s and early 1890s, the other and less abundant wave around 1910 to 1912. The pattern was becoming established by 1880, when Justin Winsor's *Memorial History of Boston* (a four-volume work) was published.[12] During the 1880s, J. T. Scharf edited similar voluminous works on Baltimore, Philadelphia, and St. Louis.[13] James Grant Wilson's four-volume *Memorial Historial of New York* appeared in 1892-93.[14] Winsor was a librarian; Scharf and Wilson had newspaper experience. Works of this kind were produced for virtually every major city, and states and counties as well.

These were cooperative ventures, made up of a running account of the history of the city and chapters dealing topically with the professions, merchants, education, women's activities, etc. The authors of such chapters sometimes were local professors, clergymen, and journalists of some capability, as in Winsor's work on Boston; sometimes the authorship was anonymous. Much emphasis was placed on the role and achievements of local citizens, past and present, for many of whom portraits were included. In most of the multivolume works of this kind that were published in the early 20th century, one or more volumes were devoted exclusively to biographies. Often the publisher was the prime mover in these ventures. These works often have been called "mug" histories because of the ingredient of biographies of locally prominent people, many of whom subscribed to the enterprise for the sake of seeing themselves pictured and praised in print. In these undocumented and often anonymously written histories, the biography of the city often was overshadowed by, if not lost in, the biographies of its prominent citizens.

STAVE: Do works of this kind have any value for today's urban historians?

STILL: I think they do. Their proliferation in the 1880s tells us something about popular awareness of the city in the 1880s. They often reveal popular perceptions of the nature of urban society. In the topical chapters on the church, schools, merchants' organizations, and bench and bar (a popular topic), information is preserved that otherwise might be lost, and this certainly is true of the biographical data. Almost always there was a chapter on women's activities, the activities of leading women. One of the areas of life in the late nineteenth century that social and urban historians have tended to overlook is the activity of women in cities and civic affairs. The people now working to expand women's place in the community may not be as conscious as they might of how active in leadership women were. Who they were, whether they were the wives of the elite male figures, is an interesting question. Certainly they were not being overlooked in these local histories. These histories give a useful indication of who was prominent or could afford to be treated as if he were. The chief trouble with these works as histories is that in most instances they are not the product of professionally trained historians. However, for all their shortcomings, I made very considerable use of works of this kind written on Milwaukee when I began serious work on that city.

STAVE: This brings us to the question as to how you became involved with the history of Milwaukee.

STILL: This, like my original involvement with city history, was accidental and in this instance a matter of environment. My interest in research on the history of Milwaukee coincided with a new wave of writing of city history—this one the work of professional historians whose attention had been turned toward the city in the late 1920s and 1930s, some in connection with their graduate training. Arthur Schlesinger, Sr., was extremely influential in this, I think, as well as was a rising interest in social history. Schlesinger was one of the editors of the *History of American Life* series which began to appear in 1927. In planning this series the editors stressed the need for historical studies of urban communities and urban life. Schlesinger was a member, I think, of a committee of the American Historical Association on the planning of research, which, in 1932, pointed to the need for studies of urban life and urbanization. This report must have inspired professors in graduate schools to direct their students toward urban topics. Apparently even the frontier-minded History Department at the University of Wisconsin was affected. I recall that one of the questions given me in my written examinations for the doctorate in 1932 was: "Discuss urbanization as a process in the United States; sketch its progress; indicate its influence on economic, social, intellectual life." The concept of "process" was very big at Wisconsin in those days—patterns of behavior—possibly a heritage of Turner's influence in the department. The recapitulation of experience was implicit in the frontier hypothesis.

STAVE: Do you remember how you answered that and what kinds of materials you used?

STILL: I cannot recall. I am sure that my answer was couched in expository rather than conceptual terms. The importance of the incident is that the question reflected the rising interest of the profession in the urban theme.

As a result, during the 1930s a number of professional historians, mainly younger ones, began to look at the total experience of individal cities—or at least at considerable segments of that experience. I think especially of Constance Green, Bessie Pierce, Blake McKelvey, Joe Norris, Leland Baldwin, Charles Hirschfeld, Gerald Capers, Sidney Pomerantz, Harold Syrett, and Francis Weisenberger.[15] Oscar Handlin's work on *Boston's Immigrants,* R. G. Albion's on the New York port, and Carl Bridenbaugh's comparative study of colonial cities reflect this interest.[16] W. Stull Holt at Johns Hopkins already was interesting his graduate students in this theme.[17] Schlesinger's paper on the "City in

American History" was published in the *Mississippi Valley Historical Review* in 1940.[18] Incidentally, McKelvey refers in his survey volume to the fact that Schlesinger gave this paper at the Mississippi Valley Historical Association. Actually it was not. I checked on this. It was at the December 1938 meeting of the American Historical Association. They devoted an evening session in the Grand Ballroom to three papers on urbanization: "Urbanization in Antiquity," "The Medieval City," which was no new topic, of course, at that time, and "The City in American History." The paper on the city in American history was read by Arthur M. Schlesinger, Sr., and was published in 1940. But I think it is significant that it was the American Historical Association and as early as 1938.

This was the climate of professional activity when in 1932 I took a position at the State Teachers College in Milwaukee, ultimately the University of Wisconsin—Milwaukee. This was another of the accidental developments that turned me toward the history of cities. When I first went to Milwaukee, I continued to do some research in constitutional history—the field of my thesis; but the history of the local community intrigued me—possibly because of the awakening professional interest in the history of cities. I was especially impressed by the first product of Bessie Pierce's work on the history of Chicago, a book entitled *As Others See Chicago*.[19] This was published in 1933. In it, Professor Pierce presented a brief account of the life span of Chicago, amplified by excerpts from the accounts of eye witnesses to its growth. I think she used this device as a method of periodizing the growth of the city. At any rate, it occurred to me that I could do the same thing for Milwaukee, which started me on a kind of research—and an approach to urban history—that I have employed throughout my career. I soon turned out an article that I entitled "The Growth of Milwaukee as Recorded by Contemporaries."

Fortunately, the editors of the *Wisconsin Magazine of History* were willing to publish this article (in 1938) and others that I wrote on Milwaukee dealing with various periods in its growth.[20] This led Joseph Schafer, Superintendent of the State Historical Society of Wisconsin, to suggest, in 1938, that if I would undertake to write a full-dress history of Milwaukee, the State Historical Society would consider publishing it. Schafer insisted that the proposed history should be limited to a single volume. I began the task, and although I had to take four years out as an Air Force officer in World War II, the book ultimately appeared. The first edition of the book was published in 1948;[21] it sold out, and a second edition was published in 1965. It too sold out.

If there is anything unique about my Milwaukee book it is that I attempted to compress a well-rounded exposition of the city's history into one volume. Constance Green put the history of Washington, D.C., into two volumes; Blake McKelvey completed four on Rochester; and Bessie Pierce completed three of the four she intended to do on Chicago. These books are all basically narrative and expository. They represent the genre of urban history referred to, at times with derogation, as "city biography." In a sense, their "biographical" quality is one of their chief merits. They were written on the assumption that a city is an organic entity that experiences a "life span"—that cities, like human beings, experience phases in their growth and development. In the instance of Milwaukee there seemed to be a frontier-townsite promotion stage that lasted from settlement until the mid-1840s, when the community had recovered from the Panic of 1837; a period of commercial-preindustrial growth which lasted until about 1870, at which time the city began to sense its destiny as a large industrial city; a period of adjustment to big city problems, which lasted until about 1920; and finally a period of metropolitan growth, influenced in a significant way by the widespread use of the automobile.

STAVE: This periodization that you suggest for Milwaukee seems to belie the assertion that the "old" urban historians did not use an "urban-relevant" periodization—that they tended to use such traditional periodizations as "antebellum" and "progressive" as the time-frames for study.

STILL: Professional urban historians always have let the facts, as they saw them, dictate the periodization. Bessie Pierce periodized the Chicago story in segments from 1673 to 1848, 1848 to 1871, 1871 to 1893. She chose 1848 because it marked the date of initial travel on Chicago's first railroad; 1871 is the date of the Chicago fire. The life span of McKelvey's Rochester fell into segments, 1812 to 1854, 1855 to 1890, 1890 to 1925, 1925 to 1961. These phases were dictated basically by the predominant economic pursuits of the residents during these years. Carl Bridenbaugh established periods in the growth of colonial cities that reflect the social and economic behavior of the city dwellers of that era.

STAVE: Would this hold for the periodization of urban development in the nation as a whole?

STILL: Population movements in response to economic and technological factors and the popular perception of the movement seem to me to be the best criteria for arriving at benchmarks for viable periods in the

American urban experience. The chronological framework into which Lewis Mumford in 1922 placed the nation's urban development included a provincial period, extending through the close of the War of 1812; a commercial period, comprising the era of canal and railroad building; and an industrial period. In my opinion a periodization based on census figures and the popular reaction to them is more meaningful than Mumford's narrower economic periodization, though such bases of periodization reflect economic causes. The census of 1830 exhibits an acceleration of the number of urban dwellers and urban places that had taken place during the 1820s. The decade of the 1860s constitutes another turning point. By 1870 there was a pervasive popular awareness that there were to be very large cities in the pattern of American urbanism, a development affected by the cumulative influence of railroads and the development of urban amenities not available to rural dwellers.

The 1920s brought a new period, reflected in both population movement and technological change. The regional orientation of the national economy caused population to gravitate toward a limited number of focal points. This centripetal tendency was offset by technological development that had a centrifugal effect in individual cities. Electricity and the motor car were basically responsible for encouraging the movement of industry and population to the periphery of the metropolitan clusters. Moreover, by the 1920s, motion pictures, radio, and television made it possible to enjoy in the suburbs some of the entertainment that had encouraged residence in the central city. In his 1890 article, Albert Bushnell Hart wrote that one of the "greatest problems of modern times" was "how to get people out of the exhausting or despairing life of cities into the quiet and comfort of villages," in view of the appeal of "concerts, libraries, . . . theaters . . . excitement and stir and activity" of cities. Later developments change the picture. The census of 1970 revealed for the first time that more Americans were dwelling in suburbs than in central cities. These demographic benchmarks elicited popular comment that reinforces the census figures as a means of periodizing the nation's urban development as a whole. I used this periodization in my recently published survey, *Urban America.*[22] I was interested to note that Sam Warner, in his book *The Urban Wilderness,*[23] employed the same periodization—1820, 1870, and 1920—a chronological framework for the American urban experience that we arrived at independently.

STAVE: In your new book, *Urban America,* you make the comment in your introduction that "Occupational and ethnic diversity is often posited as a manifestation of urbanism, but the degree of urbanism this reflects depends upon the extent to which residents and outsiders view such occupations and such ethnic variety as contributing to an image of urbanism. Attitudes are often more significant than numbers as indices of urban status," and you try to use both in delineating what was happening. You seem to put as much emphasis on attitudes as on population data. Why is this?

STILL: I do this because I believe that population data are relative as proof of the extent of urbanism, and demographic criteria often are unduly arbitrary. At one time, the census authorities insisted that a community must have a population of 8,000 to qualify as urban; later they decreed a minimum of 2,500. Sociologists insist that for a community to be called urban there must be evidence of ethnic and occupational diversity. In colonial America contemporaries identified communities as urban when their population was much less than 2,500 and when there was not much ethnic diversity in their society. I tend to trust this contemporary evidence more than conformity to arbitrary criteria. That's what I meant in the passage you cited.

STAVE: But do you think that the contemporary perceptions are trustworthy? Do you think that the public really perceives what actually is happening when it is happening? And are you really talking about the public or are you talking about an elite group of observers? Is there any sort of time lag or misinterpretation of what is happening?

STILL: In the case of comment on population movements I tend to trust the contemporary observations. Under any circumstances, contemporary observations corroborate the demographic data; and the relative volume of the comment on change identifies the benchmarks. For example, during the decade of the 1860s contemporary comment on the current attraction of large cities is so abundant as to suggest that this decade represents a benchmark in the evolution of urbanism in the United States. This evidence is found not only in editorial comment but in popular literature, advertisements, sermons, etc. In England, contemporaries were identifying an age of great cities as early as the 1840s. In the United States, the cumulative observation of this change does not come until the turn of the 1870s. I am not talking about the causes of change. Here economic and technological factors are compelling considerations; but the popular reactions are useful in identifying the benchmarks of change.

STAVE: What is the status of the city biography approach to the writing of urban history today?

STILL: Individual authorship of a comprehensive history or "biography" of any major city has now become an unrealistic pursuit for at least two reasons. Most cities are too large, and scholars (economists, social historians, geographers, and political scientists) are asking too many questions. The city biographers attempted to comprehend the whole span of a city's history, but in the case of most cities this has become an insuperable task, especially if one cannot give undivided attention, for a long period of time, to the project. Blake McKelvey was able to do this for Rochester, a city that had a shorter life span than some (roughly since 1812) and that is less sizable than many. As City Historian of Rochester, McKelvey worked almost uninterruptedly on the project for at least fifteen years. Bessie Pierce told me that in the preparation of the first two volumes of her history of Chicago she had the assistance annually of from two to ten graduate students working from a third to full time over a period of about ten years. To write a comprehensive history of any of today's major cities, cooperative authorship would appear to be the only viable approach. However if a team of historians were to undertake a largescale narrative or expository history of New York City, Philadelphia, Detroit, St. Louis, or San Francisco, the writing would have to be very rigidly structured and controlled for consistency of treatment because of the many and varied approaches to the writing of urban history today.

STAVE: You raise some very important questions about individual authorship and comprehensive history. You say that most cities are too large and scholars are asking too many questions. With respect to that, which do you think is more significant, the size of the cities as they've grown or the kinds of questions that are being asked now? Which creates the inability to write comprehensive history?

STILL: I think that the problem of size became evident even before the social scientists began to ask new questions. For example, take Bessie Pierce's history of Chicago. She was not attempting to answer the kinds of questions that the so-called new urban historians are raising, but she was attempting to treat each aspect of the city's history as one would do in a doctoral dissertation, and then boil it all down to a comprehensible or manageable narrative, even in terms of four volumes. And the city was just too big and too complex to make that possible, even though she had many skilled professional people helping her. Thus she never completed the fourth volume. I think that Blake McKelvey had an easier job in that Rochester is smaller; since he could give virtually his whole attention to this, he was able within a lifetime to do the job. The fact that new questions are now being asked makes the work of providing a comprehensive biography of a city more difficult because they open additional areas of inquiry.

STAVE: Younger historians have been encouraged to try individually to do comparative history. You note that it is very difficult for the single author to do the comprehensive history. What about the historian who is trying to do a comparative study, say of three or four cities, on a specific topic, let's say social mobility of various ethnic groups in the city? Do you think that the possibility still exists for an individual historian to do this type of thing if he narrows the focus of his study from the comprehensive book?

STILL: Yes. I think that many worthwhile studies could be developed along these lines. To refer to townsite promotion again. If one is going to understand fully the relationship of urbanism to the westward movement of population, we ought to have careful studies of town-site promotion in ten sample cities, cities that ultimately grew and some that didn't grow. I think of urban services—Nelson Blake's *Water for the Cities*[24] is a good example of taking an individual urban service and seeing how a variety of cities have dealt with that and out of that kind of comparative approach you may see something about process.

STAVE: What you're advocating with respect to cooperative authorship is something that some of the new urban historians and social historians have been talking about. Are you familiar with the Philadelphia social history project of Ted Hershberg?[25]

STILL: Only slightly.

STAVE: This is very quantitative in its orientation, and yet is its cooperative aspect getting at the kind of thing you are referring to here?

STILL: Whether the approach is quantitative or expository, the magnitude of the problem presented in any comprehensive historical study of a large city makes the cooperative approach virtually essential. If the history were to be a chronological narrative, in the fashion of the city biography, it would have to be done by a team, the members of which would be assigned chronological segments with a carefully structured uniform approach to be applied in the writing of each segment. If I understand the Hershberg project, it represents a cooperative approach aiming to reveal the processes of urbanization. The city biography, designed to elucidate the experience of a given city, is directed toward a somewhat different audience—the general reader and local citizen as well as the scholar.

STAVE: Don't you think the processes of urbanization elucidate the history of a city?

STILL: Oh, they do. I believe that anyone writing a history of Philadelphia or a history of St. Louis now would have to be much more concerned with social mobility, physical mobility, spatial considerations in those cities than I was with Milwaukee, that Bessie was with Chicago, or that Blake was with Rochester. The questions that are now being asked are supplying a new frame of reference to the city biographer, which he can't fail to take into account, must not fail to take into account. But I still think that there is a specific difference between city biography and writing that falls under the rubric of conceptual urban history, and that both of those pursuits have their place. And I'm not sure but what the people who are working on problems of a conceptual character do not need to have a basic city history to work with as a frame of reference for their work just as the best kind of city biographer needs the conceptualist's frame of reference as a guide in writing city biography.

STAVE: Are you thinking of a conceptualization like Eric Lampard's and his criticism of urban biographers as not being sufficiently conceptual?[26]

STILL: Yes, in part. When Lampard in 1961 called for more conceptualization on the part of urban historians, I thought that the writing of city biographies could be accommodated to his challenge. I was present at the session, held at the AHA meeting in December 1961, when the so-called urban historians undertook to discuss Lampard's article, "American Historians and the Study of Urbanization," that was published in the *American Historical Review* in 1961. Actually, although Lampard criticized the urban biographers for lack of conceptualization, a degree of conceptualization had been implicit in the structure of the urban biographies that appeared in the 1940s and 1950s. For example, their authors all were concerned with the economic factors that underwrote city growth. They were concerned with the human components of the city and with the role of the city in their adjustment. They were concerned with the way the municipal government had or had not responded to the problems resulting from the concentration of people in an urban setting. In my work on Milwaukee, I had emphasized developments that were related to themes of broader conceptual character, namely the role of townsite speculation in the original recruitment of population, the relationship of the settlement of the agricultural hinterland to city growth, urban rivalry, the behavior of foreign-born residents, and the expansion of urban services.

I recall making the point at this 1961 session, that in my opinion the historical study of urbanization as a process and the writing of the history of individual cities are two different, though not unrelated, pursuits; but that city biographies could contribute to an understanding of the process of urbanization and other related developments if the biographers of cities would attempt to provide a common body of data for purposes of comparison. In my history of Milwaukee I included appendixes similar in content to those Bessie Pierce had provided in her *History of Chicago:* tables revealing growth of population, sex ratios, origins and percentages of foreignborn residents, occupational breakdowns, presidential election figures for city and state, annexation maps, etc. I suggested at this 1961 meeting that the biographers of cities should try to supply the data that the sociologically oriented or process-seeking students were interested in, and that this could be done if urban historians would settle upon a pilot history or if the social scientists would prepare a kind of checklist of types of data they would hope to find in studies of cities by students not trained in the techniques of sociological inquiry. Perhaps this was too simplistic an approach to the problem; at any rate, no such pilot urban biography or checklist of topics ever was developed by either the urban historians or the social scientists.

STAVE: Some references have been made to that meeting asserting that the historians who were there didn't understand what Lampard was talking about at this time. As one who was there, was this your feeling, was there an understanding of what Lampard was driving at?

STILL: I know that Charles Glaab in the book by Hauser and Schnore[27] says that the historians did not understand it and as a matter of fact apparently didn't attempt to. I don't know how to answer your question exactly. I think my reaction to it may reflect my somewhat limited understanding of what Eric was driving at. I was of the opinion that the urban biographers could supply data which the conceptualists could make use of. I think most of the people there understood that he was asking to have the writing of the history of cities lifted beyond simply the narrative of a given city's experience to elucidate questions of social mobility or social change, acculturation of foreign-born, the interrelationship of these things with the urban setting. I suggessted that each urban historian try to present for his city the kind of data that would make it possible for the social scientists to arrive at those generalizations. So I think maybe I understood a little about it anyway. And I didn't sense any feeling of resistance to what he was doing.

STAVE: But it was taken seriously . . .

STILL: I think definitely it was taken seriously.

STAVE: You talk about the notion of the pilot study, how urban historians would settle upon a pilot history, how the social scientists would prepare checklists. Do you think that the quantifiers are trying to do this today perhaps through social mobility studies? Is this one of their values? And then do you think that your idea of a pilot study or a checklist would lead to too much regimentation in terms of what historians do and have to do in their work?

STILL: No. My thought with respect to the pilot study was that perhaps a group of urban biographers would settle upon a workable format for dealing with the biography of a city and that that could be a kind of frame of reference for others who were writing histories of other cities. I see nothing wrong with that. The personality of the city would be different for different cities—that's one of the interesting things about cities, how their personalities differ and why. But to remind all city biographers that they ought to be concerned about elucidating the personality of the city seems to me an appropriate kind of frame of reference to have available for them. Now on the question of a checklist by the social scientists, I was thinking of rather broad generalizations along those lines simply to encourage the city biographer to be concerned with demographic developments, with ecological developments, with behavioral developments, the kind of things that the conceptualists are most interested in.

STAVE: Do you think that this could lead to regimentation, if we are going to set up checklists?

STILL: I don't see any harm in this kind of regimentation. To suggest what should be included would not prevent anyone from adding anything he thought was important or from putting any interpretation he saw fit upon his findings. Thus, local histories, presenting comparable data from varying urban environments, could supply the bases of broad hypotheses as to the nature of urban development.

STAVE: Is there a distinction between local history and urban history? I've seen a paraphrase of a quote by Asa Briggs talking about local history as urban history with the brains left out.[28] Do you think that's a fair statement?

STILL: To answer the latter question, I suppose this depends upon who is writing the local history. If my history of Milwaukee is local history, I don't think it was written with the brains left out. Cities, of course, have been the subject of histories of an anecdotal, antiquarian, or superficially journalistic type, written by persons who lack the professional sense of how to handle the materials they are using or who fail to ask the questions of the material that a trained historian would. Many histories of localities are written by people with historical insight, and Asa Briggs knows this.

I came to my study of the history of urban development in the United States—"Urban history," if you want to call it that—through research in the history of a locality, but I brought to my treatment of local developments an understanding of the national setting in which the city grew. My aim was produce a narrative but also expository reporting of events at the local level, with an eye to treating historical developments there in the same way that one would portray the history of the nation at large.

STAVE: Okay. This gives us some idea of your concept of the relationship between local history and urban history. Now what are your views on the nature of "urban history"?

STILL: In the case of both "urban" history and "local" history I regard the adjectives as primarily descriptive, used to refer to a scholar's specialization, such as "political" history, "diplomatic" history, "business" history, "agricultural" history, etc. I think of "urban" history as having the same connotation of specialization. I think of it as dealing with the history of the urban dimension of the American experience in the same way that "diplomatic" history deals with the history of American foreign policy.

Practitioners of the so-called "new urban history" appear to think of it as having a generic quality, providing answers to such large conceptual questions as modernization and social change. This approach to urban history makes it something more than the description and interpretation of one aspect of the American experience. It raises its sights to inquiries about the broader nature of social development. It demands in the practitioner a knowledge of anthropology, sociology, and economic theory, for example, that the early students of the history of American cities did not possess. For this reason, I prefer to think of myself as an historian of American urban development rather than as an "urban historian" in the more specialized sense. I hope that this is not an exercise in semantics.

STAVE: Let's return to the later development of urban historiography.

STILL: Yes. By the 1960s, students of urban development had begun to depart from the city biographers' practice of covering the life span of a single city. Their work can be typified, I think, in the research and writing of Richard C. Wade and Sam Bass Warner. Wade is a student of Arthur M. Schlesinger, Sr. In the late 1940s or early 1950s Schlesinger encouraged Wade to look at the "urban West" through a study of Pittsburgh, St. Louis, Cincinnati, Louisville, and Lexington, Kentucky, from 1790 to 1830. This approach to urban history entailed the study of a group of cities for a limited chronological period, somewhat as Carl Bridenbaugh had done for colonial cities for a more extended period.[29] Within this limited chronological range, Wade was handling the five cities much as "urban biographers" had done for single cities, and he was relying on similar sources. The well-known book embodying his findings, *The Urban Frontier,* was published in 1959. He used a similar technique with similarly suggestive findings in his *Slavery in the Cities,* which was published in 1964.[30]

Another variation on the urban biography is the intensive study of a segment of a single city's experience with an examination in depth and in far greater detail than the city biographer could achieve. An outstanding example of this type of urban history is Sam Bass Warner's *Streetcar Suburbs,* published in 1962—the result of his interest in finding out how a part of Boston (Roxbury and Dorchester) came into being.[31] Building permits were a major source of an investigation that had a bearing on concepts concerning spatial arrangements in cities. This detailed study of one aspect of a given city's experience has become the predominant practice in the writing of urban history in recent years, in either "letristic"—to use a Lampard term—or quantitative fashion. However, a number of students have employed the Bridenbaugh-Wade pattern. Good examples of the latter are Robert R. Dykstra's *The Cattle Towns,* dealing with Abilene, Ellsworth, Wichita, Dodge City, and Caldwell,[32] and Kenneth Wheeler's *To Wear a City's Crown* (San Antonio, Galveston, Houston, and Austin, Texas).[33]

The approach exemplified by Warner seems to reflect a change in the motivation of research in urban history. The urban biographers of the 1930s and 1940s undertook to study cities simply because of their existence and their increasing visibility—something that the findings of the Census of 1920 had helped to dramatize. By the 1950s and 1960s, historians were inspired to look at cities because of the problems they presented in contemporary society. The awareness of the contemporary problem encouraged students to explore the historical roots of the problem.

I can illustrate this in the experience of some of the younger specialists in city history. During the mid-1960s, Raymond Mohl undertook as a doctoral dissertation a study of poverty in New York City in the early national period, in part because of contemporary discussion of welfare costs in the mid-twentieth-century city.[34] The books that resulted from this and from the doctoral research of James F. Richardson on police protection in nineteenth-century New York City made contributions to an understanding of the larger question of public order in the city.[35] In an informative new book on New York City from 1664 to 1710, Thomas Archdeacon adduces evidence to show that ethnic tensions were a factor of importance in municipal elections in the early eighteenth century, as they have been in recent years.[36] Humbert Nelli's *Italians in Chicago, 1880-1930* deals with the relationship of city living to a sense of nationality on the part of a significant ethnic group.[37] Books by Seth Scheiner and Gilbert Osofsky are examples of studies of the early history of black communities prompted by the increasing visibility of these segments of the society of many cities.[38]

STAVE: You raise an interesting point about how the urban biographers of the 30s and 40s undertook to study cities because of their increasing visibility, essentially, and that those of the 50s and 60s really were problem oriented. And you give some references to some of the studies that have been done. But I've noticed that you haven't dealt with some of the quantitative history that has been done. In talking about the problems coming out of the 50s and 60s, the problems approach, it seems to me that the quantifiers have been trying to get away from the pathological view of the city, the city as a problem or many problems, and are really trying to look at the developmental view of the city. They say we don't care about the problems, we're not going to approach it as a pathology, we're going to approach it as a thing that concerns urban development and process. What do you think of the work that is being done by these quantifiers? Are there any works that you find particularly helpful or particularly unhelpful, in the sense that you don't think that they really added to the field?

STILL: Well, I suppose that the social mobility studies are the ones that come to mind most along these lines. I think it likely that the social mobility studies actually were prompted by the pathological problem of the city; however, they also exhibit a strong concern for the place of the city in developing societies, and this is one of the things that led the social scientists to try to determine the extent to which there actually was social mobility in the cities. The contemporary problem of minorities in cities has also tended to encourage the concern for social mobility, for family structure in the city. The studies of population movements in and out of cities also are related to problems of contemporary concern. There's probably no aspect of the urban problem of today that is more vital than the problem of its population, the dependency of the population, the ethnic conflicts in the population, the relationship of the family pattern to crime in the city. Contemporary interest in these problems must have had some bearing on the effort to delineate social patterns and measure social behavior in the past. The new involvement of persons with sociological training has had an influence. I regard these studies as very useful. I think of them as social history in an urban setting. As far as the overall history of urbanism is concerned, their greatest utility will be in revealing whether there was greater social mobility in the rural or in the urban setting and how the situation differed from city to city. Of course, they also illuminate the experience of individual cities.

STAVE: With respect to quantification and sociological approaches, how does your Milwaukee book differ from some of the more recent studies of Milwaukee?

STILL: The recent studies of Milwaukee, which have been greatly influenced by Eric Lampard and Leo Schnore, start with a sociological model and measure the extent to which the Milwaukee experience conformed to the model.[39] In doing so, of course, they contribute to an understanding of the city's past. Typical models have to do with the spatial arrangements of the city in given periods of its growth and with the nature of population distribution and housing stock in enclaves of foreign born in the city. These studies make use of such sources as manuscript census data and building permits. Facilities available for quantification that did not exist when I was working on Milwaukee make for much more specific findings than I was able to achieve, despite the fact that I used city directories and published census materials.

When I began my study of Milwaukee, I approached the problem as one would the biography of an individual person—birth and background, adolescence, maturity. Fortunately, death was not the expected culmination of this biography, although the atom bomb, conceived at about the time I was completing the book, made this an apprehended possibility for big cities. My concern was with Milwaukee as a social organism: child of the westward movement; magnet for immigrant stocks that affected its popular image and its economy, especially Germans, though the Poles were to be highly significant, too; and example of a municipality that had responded in some rather unique and forward-looking ways to the problems of the early twentieth-century city. My approach was essentially narrative and expository. I was trying to explain how Milwaukee grew, what it was like at various stages of its growth, what accounted for what might be called its "urban personality." I was of course mindful that its experience was somewhat like that of its urban neighbors on the Great Lakes, but the history of Milwaukee as such, was the focus of my attention.

Two students of Eric Lampard recently have made significant contributions to Milwaukee history based on the use of spatial models. Kathleen Neils Conzen, studying population distribution as of 1850, shows that in its high-status core and low-status periphery the community conformed to the spatial pattern of the preindustrial city. Her quantified study of the German wards show that there was an internal economic differentiation there that made the section different from the traditional model of the pathological ghetto. This suggests that the space available in a frontier city may have led to a kind of community development that retarded rather than accelerated acculturation, as the frontier environment has been alleged to do. Roger Simon completed a quantified study of housing stock and services in Milwaukee's Fourteenth Ward. In providing information in depth and putting the city's experience in a conceptual framework these studies offer a substantial amplification of parts of my Milwaukee work. In my opinion these studies are stronger in exhibiting the pattern of behavior than in explaining it. Both appear to have made very considerable use of my Milwaukee book as a basic reference.

STAVE: What are your present interests in terms of research and writing in the urban field?

STILL: At the local level I am working on the history of New York City. I have just completed a chapter on New York in 1976 for a book dealing with New York in the centennial years,[40] and I am continuing my long-term study of the mayoralty. My chief interest with respect to the broader aspects of urban development has been the popular responses and attitudes to urbanism as evidence of existence of an urban tradition in American society. I believe that urbanism is more deeply embedded in the American tradition in both actuality and aspiration than has been realized. Of course this depends in some measure on how one defines urban. Without having studied the colonial period too carefully, I am inclined to think that there was more aspiration to urbanism and more evidence of urbanism in that period than traditionally is recognized, despite the small populations in the urban clusters.

The nineteenth century saw much more praise and promotion of cities than we realize. Every western state wanted to have the "Queen City" within its borders. This was true of the South—among the causes of tension between North and South were the competitive ambitions of Charleston and New Orleans with New York. Even when contemporaries are deploring size and congestion they don't want to see central cities lose population. New York City's support for consolidation was prompted in part by the desire to remain more populous than Chicago.

The differential in cultural amenities between country and city was emphasized in popular media in the last half of the nineteenth century and was a reality that made people think society could accommodate to big cities by resorting to technological and political improvements. For all the criticism of cities, they then connoted economic opportunity and national political power. Though the movement to suburbia is cited as repudiation of the city, it is obvious that the periphery has appeal only because the central city exists. These attitudinal studies are important because they bear on the capacity of people to adjust to the basic problem of our society—the large city. This was a phenomenon of American society to which Americans really became sensitive for the first time in the 1860s and at the turn of the 1870s.

STAVE: What attracted your interest to these attitudinal considerations?

STILL: I think it stems from the interest I always have had in the comments of contemporaries, both native and foreign, on American society. It was sources of this kind that early supported my belief that urbanization was a significant ingredient in the early development of the American West. Many European visitors reported their surprise at finding cities springing up as if by magic in the allegedly rural West. Related to this development is a fascinating booster literature concerning the West. Observations of contemporaries also shed interest light on the question of the "image" or "personality" of American cities. After I came to New York, I undertook to analyze the reactions of commentators to New York City which I worked into a book entitled *Mirror for Gotham*.[41] This led me into a study of contemporaneous comment on urbanism in the nation in general.

STAVE: You mention the fascinating booster literature concerning the West and you talk about *Mirror for Gotham*. I'm interested in this in light of two writings, one by the Whites, *The Intellectual Versus the City*.[42] They talk about the antiurban feeling because they look at the literature of the intellectuals and the work of intellectuals. And then I think of the Charles Glaab essay which talks about the effect of popular culture, newspapers, real estate ads, boosterism.[43] Which do you think is more important in the sense of American attitudes toward the city? I think depending on the choice, you're saying that there's a greater antiurban bias or there's in a sense a prourban favoritism. Do you think that the antiurbanism talked about by the Whites is more significant as the "American attitude" than the prourbanism talked about by yourself?

STILL: To begin with, I think that intellectuals were less unqualifiedly critical of cities than the Whites would have us believe. For example, Emerson, though he criticized aspects of American life, realized that American society had to accommodate to cities; he wanted the best of both worlds; he wanted to live close enough to the city to enjoy its advantages. Michael Cowan has dealt very effectively with this theme in his *City of the West*.[44] Even Jefferson, whom the Whites cited as the primordial opponent of the city, so to speak, and who did see cities as antithetical to nature and virtue in the philosophical sense, was enough of an opportunist to realize that cities were essential to national prosperity. So I would say that they misrepresented the intellectuals to begin with. Glaab certainly didn't misrepresent the boosters, but boosters are very likely to give an exaggerated opinion of things. So to take the booster literature as an irrefutable proof of prourbanism doesn't necessarily work either.

I think you have to look at a wide range of attitudes, and that's what I've been doing over the years. I've collected hundreds of these commentaries by every kind of person in all walks of life. It's true that the so-called inarticulate aren't much represented in this collection, but the response in the popular media is one way of sensing the nature of their attitude to the city. One of my students, Adrienne Siegel, recently completed a thesis on the response to the city in American popular fiction from 1840 to 1870.[45] She dealt with pulp fiction only, as a means of getting at what the average type of reader was reading and perhaps accepting. And she found that pulp fiction presented an image of the city as a place of excitement, opportunity, innovation, upward mobility, a place where the action was, back there in the 1840s and 1850s. Another good illustration of popular attitudes is the theater. I recall reading a play by Clyde Fitch, *The City*, written in the early twentieth century, in which he has one of his characters say that she preferred the smell of gasoline on Fifth Avenue to the smell of new-mown hay. Even the reformers of the later nineteenth and twentieth centuries, though they deplored some aspects of city life, believed that they could be corrected. Over the years I've set a number of students on the reaction of different individuals to the city: Dorothea Muller studied Josiah Strong, Diana Klebanow studied E. L. Godkin, Paul Hughes studied Edward Everett Hale, Howard Zavin studied Franklin D. Roosevelt, and Barry Rosen is working on Henry George, to see how they responded to the rise of large cities in the later nineteenth century.[46] And they all seem not only to reflect an acceptance, even an admiration, for the big city, but always a desire to do something about coping with it.

The work of Al Fein and Tom Bender on Frederick Law Olmsted exhibits the attitude of another significant public figure toward the large city of the later nineteenth century, the effort to accommodate to the large city that became evident in the 1860s.[47] Olmsted saw large cities as having more advantages than small towns but he recognized that they took a psychological toll. This was to be overcome by parks, which not only would bring the benefits of the natural landscape into the city, but would provide a place for the sociability, neighborliness, mingling of classes that had been possible in small towns. He proposed to naturalize the city through parks, in order to create a counterpoise to the disadvantages of city life. In reading Olmsted recently, I was interested to see that he coupled Central Park with the Metropolitan Museum of Art and Columbia University as three things that would bring civilization to the city, a wedding of nature and culture; this is a side of Olmsted that has not been too fully elucidated. To Olmsted, suburbia was another means of achieving the desired counterpoise. In the late nineteenth and twentieth centuries contemporaries viewed suburbia not as a repudiation of the city, but as a manifestation of what could be achieved in the marriage of city and country. Ambivalence and the desire for the best of both worlds constitute a more appropriate characterization of American attitudes to the city than prourban or antiurban.

STAVE: Just one thing, backtracking for a minute. When you talk about Olmsted's views—the lumping together of Central Park, Columbia, and the Metropolitan Museum—would you elaborate upon his emphasis on culture in the city as opposed to the pastoral aspect.

STILL: Cultural amenities always have been one of the major attractions of city living. Urban historians probably have not paid as much attention as they should to the role of cultural facilities in accounting for the appeal of cities, especially in periods when one couldn't enjoy cultural amenities by way of radio and television or automobile connections with the city.

STAVE: We've talked about the writing of urban history; how about the teaching of it?

STILL: I suppose I could say something about the first courses in urban history. I don't say that I did it right, but I did pioneer, I think, in designing courses in the history of the city that attracted many undergraduate and graduate students to what in the 1940s was a new field. That I had the opportunity to do this was another of the accidental, environmental developments that have characterized my connection with the history of the American city.

This came about as a result of becoming acquainted, while I was in the Air Force in World War II, with W. F. Craven, the colonialist, then on leave from New York University. At the close of the war, I returned to Duke University where I had been teaching since 1938—no urban history, of course, but I had been working on my history of Milwaukee while I was at Duke in the years before the war. Shortly after my return to Duke in the Fall of 1946, Craven wrote me saying that in view of the location of New York University in New York City, the History Department there had concluded that the University ought to "undertake some serious development of the field of urban history," for both undergraduate and graduate students, in a program that would be "not merely of assistance to the major in history, but would supplement offerings in the general area of urban life, by the departments of Sociology, Economics, Government, etc." I think it is significant that New York University proposed this innovation as part of its commitment to the city before the urban crisis of the 1950s attracted widespread popular attention to the historical study of the city.

When this offer came, I couldn't resist the opportunity to live in New York City, despite my warm associations at Duke University and despite the fact that I would have to devise undergraduate and graduate courses in urban history "from scratch." There was no model to follow. For a number of years, Arthur Schlesinger, Sr., Bessie Pierce, Allan Nevins, and W. Stull Holt—perhaps others—had been assigning topics on urban themes to their graduate students; but so far as I know no History Department had ever offered a formal course, graduate or undergraduate, dealing exclusively with the history of the American city. Courses in Sociology departments, of course, had been concerned with the topic for some time. Thus, in developing my course I had no model; obviously there was no survey suitable as a textbook. I had completed my history of Milwaukee by this time, so I had the Milwaukee experience as a model for the nineteenth and twentieth centuries. Carl Bridenbaugh's *Cities in the Wilderness* had come out in 1939. I had that as guidance for the seventeenth and eighteenth centuries. It is a good thing that I had been forced to compress the Milwaukee story into one volume; otherwise I wouldn't have had the whole spectrum of urban development in mind.

The periodization of my course was "urban-relevant" from the beginning, since it was based on my research dealing with urban experience rather than on the periodization customarily used in college history texts. As a matter of fact it followed a periodization I had evolved as early as 1940, when I gave a week of lectures on the historical background of the contemporary American city in a summer session course in Milwaukee. My projected courses at New York University were to be year courses. In the first semester I carried the story to 1870, which I consider a major benchmark in the history of the American city. As far as the content was concerned, this is indicated in the course description I had to prepare before I ever had any experience teaching the course. It read: "A study of the rise and growth of cities in America from the colonial period to the present day, with emphasis on the evolution of municipal institutions and adminis-tration, the elaboration of urban life and culture, the interplay of occupational and nationality groups, and the effect of urban com-munities upon the economic, social, and political development of the United States." A large order—dealing with urban-oriented develop-ments within a framework of chronological periods. Incidentally, I always entitled this course "History of the American City"—not "Urban History."

In preparing the content of the course, the published Census of Population was my constant companion. My colleagues frequently twitted me about the charts and tables I was always making, based on census figures. This was the elementary quantification of urban research in the 1940s and 1950s. I could not take the time to go to the manuscript census; but these published summary figures said something about comparative growth, the ingredients of urban populations, sectional differences in the incidence of urbanism, and the reasons for the changing criteria employed by the Census Bureau in measuring urbanism, metropolitanism, and the like. Classroom analysis of these charts and tables was one of the teaching methods I used. I have reproduced most of these charts in my recently published book *Urban America.*

In the absence of an appropriate textbook, I used my Milwaukee book as required reading. The first text designed for urban history courses was Charles Glaab's *The American City: A Documentary History,* in which the author reproduced documents dealing with the American urban experience from colonial times to 1960.[48] In this work, published in 1963, Glaab disavowed any attempt to deal theoretically with urban development. In 1967 Glaab and his colleague at the University of Wisconsin-Milwaukee, A. Theodore Brown, produced the first substantial survey suitable for use as a textbook.[49] This book dealt primarily with developments in the nineteenth century, only briefly with the colonial period and the contemporary scene.

By this date, courses in urban history were flourishing throughout the country. Between 1966 and 1968 Diana Klebanow and I made a study of the teaching of American urban history in American colleges, predominantly of the four-year variety.[50] On the basis of some 350 replies to a questionnaire, we concluded that in nearly 150 institutions provisions existed or were in prospect for the study of the history of the American city. A similar interest in urban history also was evident in the many existing urban studies centers, where a course in urban history often was available in the program. In the 1950s, my classes in the history of the city often drew more than a hundred students. Many of the Ph.D.'s in history in this period had an urban history specialty. Because of the decline in student interest in history during the 1970s, I suspect that the history of the city draws fewer students now than it did five years ago.

My organization of the course always was chronological. However, as thinking about the history of the city has become more social science oriented, the tendency in recent years has been toward a topical presentation, embodying the historical discussion of a series of topics intrinsically urban in character, such as the causes of urban expansion, urban politics, urban technology, social mobility in the city, minority groups in the city, and so forth. Certainly, whatever the method employed, today's urban history courses pay more attention to the spatial and social structure of the city than was usual when the first courses in the history of the city were devised.

STAVE: You mention that it's significant that New York University proposed this urban course innovation as part of a commitment to the city before the urban crisis of the 1950s attracted widespread popular attention. Are you talking about the urban crisis of the 50s or the 60s?

STILL: Cities were beginning to present major problems by the middle 1950s, and they continued to be critical thereafter. It was in the middle 50s that you began to find the rise of urban studies institutes. The city of the 50s was beginning to present the kind of problems that were only aggravated in the 1960s.

STAVE: What about that article you did with Diana Klebanow on the survey of the teaching of urban history? What's the origin of that? The findings are interesting in themselves about the proliferation of courses and interest in urban history, but so is the timing. It was published in 1969 at the height of the birth of many new courses. Why did you undertake this study?

STILL: The 1960s saw a great proliferation of research in the history of the city, partly because the city was recognized as a problem and partly because of the increase in graduate students that was stimulated by the GI bill. The novelty of the subject gave it something of the same kind of appeal that the study of the American frontier had had in the early twentieth century. The interaction between sociologists and historians, resulting from new interdisciplinary thrusts, especially encouraged the historical study of the city. In the mid-1950s, the urban historians organized for better communication, and this gave stature to studies and course work in courses dealing with the history of the city.

STAVE: Concerning the article, though, was it commissioned by the journal or was it your own idea?

STILL: It was my own idea and Dr. Klebanow's. Inasmuch as New York University was a vigorous center of the study of the American city we felt that it was appropriate for us to make an inventory of the state of teaching in this area. I may have been thinking in part about the prospect of jobs for my Ph.D. students. Over the years more than fifty students completed doctoral dissertations under my supervision.

STAVE: This was over a span of how many years?

STILL: The first doctoral dissertation I directed was completed at Duke University in 1947. I averaged about two a year thereafter.

STAVE: What do you believe has been your major impact on your students and the way they have approached things?

STILL: I hope I gave them some enthusiasm for the historical study of the city in American life and helped them develop interpretive historical judgment. Supervision of the details of composition took a great deal of time. History graduate students do not write very well these days. I permitted students to select their own topics, but where possible I encouraged them to work around a few common themes: mayoral administrations in New York City, the history of individual

municipal services in New York, and the responses to urban development on the part of influential individuals or in various media. Many of
the topics understandably were related to New York City.

STAVE: Your reference to New York City raises a question. The
opportunity of working in New York City is not one that most urban
historians have. Is there anything about New York City that makes it
especially advantageous as a place for an urban historian or a historian
of the city?

STILL: I would want to answer this question in terms of the attractions
of New York City, first as a place to be studied, and second as a place
in which to carry on scholarly work. As a city to be studied, New York
has the advantage of presenting the whole span of the American urban
experience from colonial times to the present. This is not true of
midwestern cities. New York also has the advantage of exhibiting, on a
more extensive scale than other cities, the ethnic and racial mix that is
characteristic of large cities generally. And of course New York is the
American city that has influenced the nation (in economic and cultural
terms epspecially) more than any other. The history of virtually every
problem in the nation's urban development can be studied here. As to
the advantage of working in New York City, one has only to mention
the New York Public Library and the other libraries of the city and
their abundant resources. Perhaps there's a psychological advantage also
in being in New York City, because for all its problems New York
connotes the ultimate in urban development.

STAVE: Back to your teaching for a moment. Have you always taught
your course chronologically? If you were starting teaching and writing
today, do you think you would have a different approach or would you
pursue the same approach that you have over the years?

STILL: If I were to resume teaching the history of the American city I
would continue to treat the subject chronologically, as the best way of
revealing the background of today's urban society in the United States.
I have never found an exclusively topical approach congenial, because if
the topical treatment is going to be historically oriented it must involve
a great deal of repetition. Within a given chronological period, I would
of course deal with developments by topic, such, for example, as the
nature and impact of the foreign-born ingredient in American cities,
with consideration of the differences from city to city. I would want to
include in my discussion of urbanism in a given period the findings of
relevant quantitative studies. For example, the many social mobility
studies should be taken into account in the presentation of the pattern
of urbanization in a given period. As for my research and writing, with

which I continue to be occupied, I believe that an understanding of urban development still can be gained from the orderly expository presentation of developments; and I continue to proceed along these lines.

STAVE: Now a number of years ago, when you were speaking to a Milwaukee historical group, Frederick Olson asked you how you would amplify upon your Milwaukee book. What I'd like to know is, if you were to revise any of your works, is there anything that you would redo in terms of your writings, or is there anything that, from this perspective, you wish you hadn't published?

STILL: As far as the Milwaukee work is concerned, it must be remembered that it was designed as a one-volume comprehensive work and was written at a time when there was virtually no existing monographic material to rely on. If I were writing a one-volume history of Milwaukee today there could be more cogent interpretation and more accurate detail because of recent research and writing on topics which I dealt in relatively superficial fashion. I am sure that some of my analysis of political developments is subject to correction since I based my treatment almost exclusively on the newspaper. Conzen's work amplifies what I wrote on the German community. The major gap that I would want to fill even in another one-volume work would be more attention to the spatial distribution of population in the city. However, despite its limitations in terms of coverage, the book seems to have provided a useful and not too misleading starting point for later studies, or so the young Milwaukee scholars have acknowledged.

STAVE: I had the experience of commenting on a paper dealing with neighborhoods at Rochester, in a conference. One of the amazing things was that it did not refer at all to McKelvey's work. And this is a mistake. You can't avoid the other good studies that have gone before. I wanted to ask you about seminal books in your own thinking, either seminal books that have influenced you or books that are among your favorite works in urban history.

STILL: This is a hard question for me to answer. Perhaps the best I can do is to list some of the books that, for one reason or another, I admire. Blake McKelvey's two general works impress me for their comprehensiveness.[51] Constance Green's two volumes on Washington are written with interpretative insight and in a felicitous literary style. Richard Wade's *Slavery in the Cities* is a stimulating model for a comparative study that provides provocative interpretation. I like Sam Bass Warner's *Urban Wilderness* for its organization, its forthright style, and the author's mastery of a wide range of new research and writing. I think he slights the colonial period. The work of Eric Lampard reflects both the expertise of the social scientist and the methodology of the trained historian in a way that I find quite unique. This is exhibited in his article, "The Pursuit of Happiness in the City: Changing Opportunities and Options in America."[52] His essay on the evolving system of cities also is impressive.[53] I have found geographer Allen Pred's work useful for the history of cities.[54]

STAVE: Are there any questions that you would like to see studied by historians of the American city or by urban historians in the future?

STILL: I would like to see comprehensive histories written dealing with a number of cities, especially for what they would show about urbanism and urbanization in the sections in which they are located. I think, for example, of St. Louis, Minneapolis, Seattle, San Francisco, Atlanta, and Miami. These histories probably would have to be written by cooperative authorship; and the authors certainly should take into account the frames of reference emerging from the work of the so-called "new" urban historians. But they should be comprehensive and basically narrative and expository.

I would like to see a synthesis of the role of urbanism as an ingredient of the westward movement of population during the nineteenth century. This would deal with urbanism as a lure to expansion, as a factor in the economic and social maturation of the area, and as an ingredient of the legend of opportunity and abundance associated with the settlement of the West. There also is a need for a comprehensive study of the cities of the South, in both the antebellum and later periods. I understand that Blaine Brownell and David Goldfield are at work on this topic.[55]

I would like to see more work done on the place of the city in American thought, on the appeal of the city as a place of residence for ethnic and racial groups despite the difficulties they endure, on racial and ethnic tensions in the urban setting, and on institutions like hospitals, urban colleges, museums, intellectual institutes, opera and theater, organizations like the Salvation Army and the YWCA, all of which contribute to the positive side of the big city.

STAVE: On that positive note, let's conclude. Many thanks.

NOTES

1. Frederick L. Paxson, *History of the American Frontier, 1763-1893* (New York, 1924).

2. Bayrd Still, "Evidences of the Higher Life on the Frontier, as Illustrated in the History of Cultural Matters in Chicago," Journal of the Illinois Historical Society, 28 (July 1935), 71-99.

3. Bayrd Still, "Patterns of Mid-Nineteenth Century Urbanization in the Middle West," Mississippi Valley Historical Review, 28 (September 1941), 187-206.

4. Richard C. Wade, *The Urban Frontier: Pioneer Life in Early Pittsburgh, Cincinnati, Lexington, Louisville, and St. Louis* (Cambridge, Mass., 1959).

5. Frederick Jackson Turner, "The Significance of the Frontier in American History," American Historical Association, *Annual Report for the Year 1893* (Washington, 1894), 199-227, reprinted in Ray Allen Billington (ed.), *The Frontier Thesis: Valid Interpretation of American History?* (New York, 1966), 9-20.

6. Egal Feldman, "A Study of References to the Growth of Cities and Urbanization in the United States in the Writings of Selected General Historians, 1840-1930" (M.A. thesis, New York University, 1954); also see his article, "The American City: from George Bancroft to Charles A. Beard," Societas 2 (Spring 1972), 121-141.

7. See the following, some of which are multivolume works: George Bancroft, *History of the United States of America from the Discovery of the Continent* (New York, 1891); James Schouler, *History of the United States of America Under the Constitution* (New York, 1894); James Ford Rhodes, *History of the United States from the Compromise of 1850* (London, 1900); John Bach McMaster, *A History of the People of the United States from the Revolution to the Civil War* (New York, 1893); Edward Channing, *History of the United States* (New York, 1905-25); Charles A. Beard, *Rise of American Civilization* (New York, 1927).

8. Albert Bushnell Hart, "The Rise of American Cities," The Quarterly Journal of Economics, 4 (January 1890), 129-157.

9. Adna Weber, *The Growth of Cities in the Nineteenth Century: A Study in Statistics* (Ithaca, New York, 1963).

10. Edward Channing, *History of the United States,* 5, "The Urban Migration," (New York, 1921).

11. Lewis Mumford, "The City," in Harold E. Stearns (ed.), *Civilization in the United States: An Inquiry by 30 Americans* (New York, 1922).

12. Justin Winsor, *Memorial History of Boston,* 4 vols. (Boston, 1880-1881).

13. For example, see: J. T. Scharf, *History of Philadelphia* (Philadelphia, 1884); *History of Maryland* (Hatburo, Pa., 1879).

14. James Grant Wilson, *Memorial History of New York,* 4 vols. (New York, 1892-1893).

15. For examples, see: Constance McL. Green, *Holyoke: A Case History of the Massachusetts Industrial Revolution in America* (New Haven, 1939); Bessie L. Pierce, *A History of Chicago,* 3 vols. (New York, 1937-1957); Blake McKelvey, *Rochester,* 4 vols. (Cambridge, Mass., and Rochester, N.Y., 1945-1961); Leland Baldwin, *Pittsburgh: Story of a City, 1750-1865* (Pittsburgh, 1937); Charles Hirschfeld, *Baltimore, 1870-1900: Studies in Social History* (Baltimore, 1941); Gerald Capers, *The Biography of a River Town: Memphis, Its Heroic Age* (Chapel Hill, N.C., 1939); Sidney Pomerantz, *New York, An American City 1783-1803; A Study of Urban Life*

(New York, 1938); Harold Syrett, *The City of Brooklyn: A Political History* (New York, 1944); Francis Weisenburger, *The Passing of the Frontier, 1825-1850* (Columbus, Ohio, 1941).

16. Oscar Handlin, *Boston's Immigrants: A Study in Acculturation* (Cambridge, Mass., 1959).

17. For an example of Holt's thinking concerning cities, see: W. Stull Holt, "Some Consequences of the Urban Movement in American History," Pacific Historical Review, 22 (November 1953), 337-351.

18. Arthur M. Schlesinger, Sr. "The City in American History," Mississippi Valley Historical Review, 27 (June 1940), 43-66.

19. Bessie L. Pierce, *As Others See Chicago: Impressions of Visitors, 1673-1933* (Chicago, 1933), with the assistance of Joe L. Norris.

20. Bayrd Still, "The Growth of Milwaukee as Recorded by Contemporaries," Wisconsin Journal of History, 21 (September 1938), 262-292.

21. Bayrd Still, *Milwaukee: The History of a City* (Madison, Wisconsin, 1965).

22. Bayrd Still, *Urban America: A History with Documents* (Boston, 1974).

23. Sam Bass Warner, Jr., *The Urban Wilderness* (New York, 1972).

24. Nelson Blake, *Water for the Cities: A History of the Urban Water Supply Problem in the United States* (Syracuse, N.Y., 1956).

25. For a statement regarding the Philadelphia Social History Project, see Theodore Hershberg, "The Philadelphia Social History Project: An Introduction," Historical Methods Newsletter, 9 (March-June 1976), 43-58.

26. Eric E. Lampard, "American Historians and the Study of Urbanization," American Historical Review, 67 (October 1961), 49-61.

27. Charles N. Glaab, "The Historian and the American City: A Bibliographic Survey" in Philip M. Hauser and Leo F. Schnore (eds.), *The Study of Urbanization* (New York, 1969), 607.

28. Asa Briggs as paraphrased in Alexander B. Callow (ed.), *American Urban History* (New York, 1969), 607.

29. Carl Bridenbaugh, *Cities in the Wilderness: Urban Life in America, 1625-1742* (New York, 1938) and *Cities in Revolt: Urban Life in America, 1743-1776* (New York, 1955).

30. Richard C. Wade, *Slavery in the Cities: The South, 1820-1860* (New York, 1964).

31. Sam Bass Warner, Jr., *Streetcar Suburbs: The Process of Growth in Boston, 1870-1900* (Cambridge, Mass., 1962).

32. Robert Dykstra, *The Cattle Towns* (New York, 1968).

33. Kenneth Wheeler, *To Wear a City's Crown: The Beginnings of Urban Growth in Texas, 1836-1865* (Cambridge, Mass., 1968).

34. Raymond A. Mohl, *Poverty in New York, 1783-1825* (New York, 1971).

35. James F. Richardson, *The New York Police: Colonial Times to 1961* (New York, 1970).

36. Thomas Archdeacon, *New York City, 1664-1710: Conquest and Change* (Ithaca, N.Y., 1976).

37. Humbert Nelli, *Italians in Chicago, 1880-1930* (New York, 1970).

38. Seth Scheiner, *Negro Mecca* (New York, 1965); Gilbert Osofsky, *Harlem: The Making of a Ghetto* (New York, 1966).

39. See: Kathleen Neils Conzen, *Immigrant Milwaukee, 1836-1860: Accommodation and Community in a Frontier City* (Cambridge, Mass., 1976); Roger D. Simon,

"Housing and Services in an Immigrant Neighborhood: Milwaukee's Ward 14," Journal of Urban History, 2 (August 1976), 435-458.

40. Bayrd Still, "Bicentennial New York City (1976)," in Milton Klein (ed.), *New York City: The Centennial Years* (Port Washington, N.Y., 1976).

41. Bayrd Still, *Mirror for Gotham* (New York, 1953).

42. Morton and Lucia White, *The Intellectual Versus the City* (Cambridge, Mass., 1962).

43. Charles N. Glaab, "The Historian and the American Urban Tradition," Wisconsin Magazine of History 46 (Autumn 1963), 13-25, reprinted in A. S. Eisenstadt (ed.), *The Craft of American History* 1 (New York, 1966), 35-55.

44. Michael Cowan, *City of the West* (New Haven, 1967).

45. Adrienne Siegel, "The Image of the American City in Popular Literature" (Ph.D. Thesis, New York University, 1973); also see her "When Cities Were Fun: The Image of the American City in Popular Books, 1840-1870," Journal of Popular Culture 9 (1975), 573-582.

46. See the following unpublished Ph.D. Theses at New York University: Dorothea Muller, "Josiah Strong and the Challenge of the City" (1956); Diana Klebanow, "Edwin L. Godkin and the American City" (1965); Howard Zavin, "Forward to the Land: F.D.R. and the City, 1882-1933 (1972); Paul Hughes, "Edward Everett Hale and the American City" (1975).

47. Albert Fein, *Landscape into Cityscape* (New York, 1968) and *Frederick Law Olmsted and the American Environmental Tradition* (New York, 1972); Thomas Bender, *Toward an Urban Vision: Ideas and Institutions in Nineteenth-Century America* (Lexington, Ky., 1972).

48. Charles N. Glaab, ed., *The American City: A Documentary History* (Homewood, Ill., 1963).

49. Charles N. Glaab and A. Theodore Brown, *A History of Urban America* (New York, 1976).

50. Bayrd Still and Diana Klebanow, "The Teaching of American Urban History," Journal of American History, 55 (March 1969), 843-847.

51. Blake McKelvey, *The Urbanization of America, 1860-1915* (New Brunswick, N.J., 1963); *The Emergence of Metropolitan America, 1915-1966* (New Brunswick, 1968).

52. Eric E. Lampard, "The Pursuit of Happiness in the City: Changing Opportunities and Options in America," Transactions of the Royal Historical Society, 5th series, 23 (1973), 175-220.

53. Eric E. Lampard, "The Evolving System of Cities in the United States: Urbanization and Economic Development" in Harvey Perloff and Loudon Wingo, Jr. (eds.), *Issues in Urban Economics* (Baltimore, 1968), 81-139.

54. Allan R. Pred, *The Spatial Dynamics of U.S. Urban-Industrial Growth, 1800-1914* (Cambridge, Mass., 1966); *Urban Growth and the Circulation of Information: The United States System of Cities, 1790-1840* (Cambridge, Mass., 1973).

55. Blaine A. Brownell and David R. Goldfield (eds.), *The City in Southern History: The Growth of Urban Civilization in the South* (Port Washington, N.Y., 1977).

SELECT BIBLIOGRAPHY OF WORKS BY
BAYRD STILL

"Evidences of the Higher Life on the Frontier, as Illustrated in the History of Cultural Matters in Chicago," *Journal of the Illinois Historical Society,* 28 (July 1935), 81-99.

"The Growth of Milwaukee as Recorded by Contemporaries," *Wisconsin Magazine of History,* 21 (March, 1938), 262-300.

"Milwaukee, 1870-1900: the Emergence of the Metropolis," *Wisconsin Magazine of History,* 23 (December 1939), 138-162.

"Patterns of Mid-Nineteenth Century Urbanization in the Middle West," *Mississippi Valley Historical Review,* 28 (September 1941), 187-206.

"The Development of Milwaukee in the Early Metropolitan Period," *Wisconsin Magazine of History,* 25 (March 1942), 297-307.

Milwaukee: The History of a City (Madison, Wisconsin, 1948: rev. ed., 1965).

Mirror for Gotham: New York as Seen by Contemporaries from Dutch Days to the Present (New York, 1956).

"The Personality of New York City," *New York Folklore Quarterly,* 9 (Summer 1958), 83-92.

"The Essence of New York City," *New York Historical Society Quarterly,* 43 (October 1959), 401-423.

"The History of the City in American Life," *American Review,* 2 (May 1962), 20-37.

"New York's Mayoralty: the Formative Years," *New York Historical Society Quarterly,* 47 (July 1963), 239-255.

"The City and the Arts: 1860-1910," in *Needs and Opportunities for Re-evaluation in the Arts in America, 1860-1910* (Detroit: Archives of American Art, 1963), 129-148.

New York City, A Students' Guide to Localized History (New York, 1965).

"Problems of an Urban Biographer," *Historical Messenger of the Milwaukee County Historical Society,* 23 (June 1967), 34-43.

"The Teaching of American Urban History," *Journal of American History,* 55 (March 1969), 843-847; with Diana Klebanow.

Urban America: A History with Documents (Boston, 1974).

Greenwich Village: A Brief Architectural and Historical Guide (with Joseph J. Roberto, New York, 1976).

"Bicentennial New York City (1976)" in *New York City: The Centennial Years,* Milton Klein (ed.), (Port Washington, N.Y., 1976).

Harris and Ewing; Permission,
Historical Pictures Service, Inc.

Constance McLaughlin Green

Constance McLaughlin Green (1897-1975) earned her doctorate in the late 1930s. From that time until her death, she actively participated in the making of urban history. The daughter of the Constitutional historian Andrew Cunningham McLaughlin, who won the Pulitzer Prize in 1936, Mrs. Green repeated his accomplishment by securing the award for the first volume of her study of Washington, D.C.

A CONVERSATION WITH
CONSTANCE McLAUGHLIN GREEN

STAVE: In the first instance, I find it interesting talking to you because
of two very significant facts—that you were writing urban history
before many people were interested in this field, and also you were a
successful woman historian in a field that didn't have many women at
the time. I'd like to start with your youth, your family life, your early
education. Could you tell me where and when you were born and what
it was like as a child?

GREEN: Oh, certainly. It was academic from the start—to this exact
moment really. And I don't doubt that I idealized a great deal of it, and
still do. I think it's the most agreeable profession one could have. But
there was a period, and a rather critical period, when I thought at least I
didn't have to subject myself to the miseries of being a graduate student
because for years on end I had answered the door bell from time to
time, and some dreary looking creatures would arrive at the door step
to ask for my father, and I thought, mercy, I don't ever want to turn
into one of those. My father was a professor of history at the University
of Michigan and then at the University of Chicago, with a two year

---

*Constance McLaughlin Green died approximately two months after par-
ticipating in this interview and never had the opportunity of reading the
original transcript. It was much longer than the one which appears here
and had to be extensively edited for publication.*

interval in Washington where he was organizing the Bureau of Historical Research for the newly-instituted Carnegie Institution of Washington. I didn't really get started until I was close to 40 and that doesn't leave anything like as many working years as I would have liked. (laughs). I taught but it was kind of on a haphazard basis, figuring that I knew enough from my college courses and from listening to my colleagues to get by, and it had to be half-time anyway because of my husband and children. But if I had started as soon as I got out of college I think I could still have had the family and children and still perhaps have been 15 years to the good in actual productive historical research. But, I enjoyed the distinctly amateurish kind of thing that I did to begin with, and then for a long time after I got my degree in 1937, I think I was so impressed with all the fun of learning that it spoiled my teaching pretty much. I think there was much more freshness in my teaching when I knew less and I didn't know how to adapt it. (laughs)

STAVE: For how long did you live in Chicago, and what memories do you have of the city?

GREEN: That would be from 1906 until I went off East to college in the fall of 1917. Oh, it was infinitely exciting to live in. In the first place, those were years when the faculty felt itself dedicated to exploring the city and being of immediate help to it. I think not only historians—in fact less the historians than the sociologists and the members of the Religion department and so on, the Medical School, the whole works. You had a sense that here was a great aggregation of people, many of them in desperate need of help, and here was an institution ready and eager to help, and something new and experimental frequently was always in the works. I won't say that I knew any nuclear physicists as a small child, but they lived in the immediate neighborhood and came to be that.

STAVE: Did you live in the Hyde Park area?

GREEN: I lived on Woodlawn Avenue and our next door neighbor was Robert Millikan and two or three doors down was one of the great physicists of the next generation, one of the space boys. It was just an intensely interesting aggregation of people, including almost every field of learning that you could think of.

STAVE: Did you know at the time any of these people who were in the so-called "Chicago School of Sociology?" People like Park and Burgess?

GREEN: No, as it happened I didn't. In the first place, I had gone by the time that Park arrived. But, nevertheless, it was intellectually the most stimulating place that I could imagine.

STAVE: Now, your interest in history, aside from starting off in an academic world, came through your father, or seeing what he did?

GREEN: Yes, also in a sense through mother because these people were always coming and going at the house and mother was an extraordinarily good listener and a wonderful hostess.

STAVE: What was her background?

GREEN: Well, she was the daughter of first the president of the University of Vermont and then of the University of Michigan with a mother who thought it was unsuitable to have a daughter have any higher education herself beyond learning how to be a good hostess.

STAVE: Did she ever go to college at all?

GREEN: No, to her vast and bitter disappointment. Her mother thought it was unsuitable. And one of the points that she always made to my sisters and me was that no daughter of hers was ever going to grow up without being able to earn her own living, and that, in those days, meant some kind of professional training, and it never occurred to any of the three of us not to.

STAVE: You had two other siblings, both sisters?

GREEN: I had five siblings, three older brothers, none of whom are now living, and one living younger sister.

STAVE: What kind of work did they go into?

GREEN: Well, actually, when I say both sisters, my younger sister taught for many years in Cambridge and Wellesley and wound up at the Woodstock Country School in Vermont, teaching mostly history but other things by the way. The in-between sister did not because she was in ill health a good deal of her life and was busy raising four children. But my three brothers—one wanted to become an English teacher, though he was killed before he was 19 in a diving accident, the second brother was going into university administration but was killed in World War I, and my oldest brother wanted to teach physics and astronomy but was assured that there was no future there, that everybody knew everything there was to know about that, so he went into law and for many years was at the Harvard Law School.

STAVE: Was your mother alive to begin to see you publish or to become active in the historical profession?

GREEN: Mother was still living when my Holyoke book appeared.[1] But she was in too frail health to take very much pleasure out of it, I think. It gave enormous satisfaction to my father.

STAVE: In the early part of your career, though, I assume that she was quite encouraging about your becoming a college teacher.

GREEN: Oh, she just sort of took it for granted (laughs). It's like not praising a child for doing something because you do no more than you ought, and I don't know if my mother was pleased about it. She thought that I snapped at the kids a good deal because if they interrupted me just when I thought I was having an idea I would yowl at them, but that slid off their backs very easily, and, on the whole, I thought mother concluded that to have changed from the excitement of living at home in the Chicago atmosphere to life in Holyoke, Mass., was a good deal of an adjustment and if I found it eased by teaching at either Mt. Holyoke or Smith I'd better teach. So I did. Not because she said so, but because the opportunity came and I took it.

STAVE: In Chicago you lived on Woodlawn Ave. Again, what was the city, the neighborhood like?

GREEN: That part of Chicago had many vacant lots at the time. I think the vacant lot was characteristic of the American city of the early twentieth century. When we went to Washington to live in the fall of 1903, where I really began my schooling, the same thing was true. We walked by endless, vacant lots with signs boards advertising stove polish and other things, but it was just part of the expected scenery, and always rubbish of course piled up in part of it.

STAVE: It's interesting—the vacant lot as a symbol of the early twentieth century city.

GREEN: Nobody's ever spoken about it before but I found myself thinking about it the other day and realizing how rare it is these days to find a little nook in which you can build your own house and I thought, "Well, Chicago and certainly Washington were examples." In Washington we lived just above the black bear's den at the zoo, (laughs) but that had its good points too. But in the big city, even New York City I believe had some vacant lots around the turn of the century. I don't know if anyone's thought to inquire about how many.

STAVE: I think this is interesting for someone to pursue because of the whole notion of open space today and what it means to people outside of cities, the implications for people 75 years ago and what it meant at that time.

GREEN: To be able to say, "Come on, let's do this," and there was the vacant lot in which you could do it. Sometimes you'd have to be thrusting aside the rubbish, but it had lots of possibilities.

STAVE: Do you remember at all attempts to build playgrounds which were popular at the time, to make use of those lots?

GREEN: Oh, I think so. I don't ever remember being robbed of a choice vacant lot by a playground going in there, usually it was a new house. But I think playgrounds almost always went in vacant lots.

STAVE: In Chicago do you have any recollection at all of Hull House?

GREEN: I never went there in my life until two years ago, although mother and father went there fairly often.

STAVE: What did they do there?

GREEN: They had dinner with Jane Addams. And then at the Chicago Settlement down on the West Side. But Hull House was just one of the interesting things that mother and father did that I never succeeded in tagging along on, and when I went back in later years there was no reason on God's earth why I shouldn't have made an expedition out there except that I never did. Another thing about Chicago in those days was that it was quite literally the jumping off point for your next point of departure. You always had trains in Chicago and so when an old friend would call up, mother would say, "Oh, good, come right along, what time do you have to leave?" and that became sort of the standard. There was just a constant flow of the intinerant academic that was very interesting and covered a great many more fields than history.

STAVE: Had you in Chicago had any sort of relationship with non-academic people, or, again, was it an academic colony?

GREEN: Well, it was mostly an academic colony, but with the university elementary and the university high school both affiliated with the university and its School of Education.

STAVE: Is that where you went to school?

GREEN: Yes.

STAVE: That's the famous laboratory school.

GREEN: Yes. It wasn't as famous then and everybody of that era objects like mad to being called a graduate of a laboratory school. We say we were not; it was a perfectly good school and everybody adored it and everybody hated to miss a single day. I do think that this is an amusing story about that school. My father leaned over my shoulder one night when I was preparing my homework in the sixth grade and looked with great disbelief and said, "Did I read the title of the paper that you're writing correctly?" And I said, "Why, I think so. It's how to feed a cow to make good manure." And he said, "Oh, well I'm sure you'll find that of great use to you in all your later life." (laughs)

STAVE: Did you ever find this useful?

GREEN: (laughing) No, one of the few things that I didn't.

STAVE: Your move from Chicago to Smith—what was it like? First, why did you choose Northampton? Why did you move there and what were your impressions?

GREEN: I went there, as I say, because I wanted to see whether I had anything to offer on my own, quite literally. That sounds a little silly. And I had some very good friends who were going to Smith, also some who were going to Vassar, and I just thought it would be kind of fun. And I realized that it was being extremely selfish because the family wasn't exactly floating in money and this was an expensive venture.

STAVE: What was your father's salary at the time, approximately? He was a professor at that time?

GREEN: Well, when he went—I know exactly what it was when we first went to Chicago; it was $5,000 as the chairman of the department, with an extra $1,000 for taking on the responsibility for the Church History department. That was 1906. And that was considered affluent.

STAVE: What was the tuition at Smith when you went there? Do you have any idea?

GREEN: I think it was $500. I think room and board where I lived off-campus came to about $1,000. But by that time not only had father's salary gone up, but he always contended that McLaughlin's *History of the United States* had put six children through college. (laughs) So he saw no objection to saying, "Yes, he'd written pot boilers, but the pot had boiled well."

STAVE: (laughs) That says something for textbook writing. Now at Smith, what was it like? What kind of classes did you take? What were your favorite classes? Was there anything that in the colloquialism of today, "turned you on," anything that you really found interesting?

GREEN: Well, I'm kind of ashamed to say, not very much. I thought it was pretty third rate stuff, (laughs), but don't forget that I had come fresh from classrooms at Chicago. I took a course early on in Municipal Government that Everett Kimball gave and it was rather sprightly because he had a rather sprightly turn of phrase, but it was intrinsically boring. I took two courses in European History with Sidney Fay that I thought were pretty slow moving and not very sprightly, and why my classmates sat around taking down every word he said baffled me because I figured anybody could remember that much for at least six months not to mention a year. (laughs) And I took a course in Logic which was required, which I considered an insult to human intelligence, and it was not very well taught, and a required course in Bible, which in retrospect I think I ought to have found interesting but thought that it was pretty dreary because it was only a couple of years before that my across-the-street neighbor and I had raced to see who could read the Bible through the fastest, this being the daughter of Ginn and Co. (laughs)

STAVE: So these are the kinds of courses that your were taking there At the time that you were in school, the United States was just moving towards suffrage for women, the war had just broken out. Did the Smith girls do anything special for the war effort? Was there much interest in suffrage? Was there much intellectual interest?

GREEN: This is what my mother's cousin's husband asked me when I went for spring vacation of my senior year to spend a week in New York with him; he wanted to know what Smith girls were interested in and whether they were reading things like *The Masses,* and I said, "Heavens no, most of them never would have heard of such a thing and if they had they would think that this is almost indecent."

STAVE: After Smith, you taught briefly at Chicago and then were married and moved to Holyoke. What followed?

GREEN: I went back to Holyoke to live there and found myself incredulous at the provincialism of the place, which was naive of me of course, but managed to wrangle the promise of a job in the History Department at Smith for the next fall, and meantime fell heir to pinch-hitting in and teaching English when one of the Freshman English teachers was taken ill. So I didn't have a very long interval of twiddling my thumbs. And then as it happened and summer grew nearer I discovered a baby was on the way, and in those days, believe it or not, every doctor in Holyoke felt it would be practically committing mayhem of some order to try to teach, particularly if it involved a trolley ride ten miles to get back and forth, and to my rage the medics just said, "Well, this wouldn't be appropriate or wise at all." And with great reluctance and a good deal of anger I threw in the sponge.

STAVE: And you didn't teach?

GREEN: And I didn't teach in the History Department. What I did do was to again pinch-hit in the English Department so that for the first semester there I was, and (laughs) I must say I was astonished to discover how many of my students didn't realize even to the point of mid-year examinations that I was great with child and wanted to know why I wasn't coming back for the next semester.

STAVE: And how long then did you not work? How long did you stay away?

GREEN: Well, then I found that the History Department had filled my place. And suddenly the English Department seemed well supplied. So,

I said, "All right, very well, if I can't teach I'll study." So I took myself out to Mount Holyoke and enrolled in graduate work in history there. I was considered very unusual because of my child, but the regime was that there were high school students who were delighted to come to the rescue for an afternoon, or every afternoon, but the arrangement was that you got a high school youngster who pushed the baby around for two or three hours and she'd shovel in the cereal or whatever, and three or four hours was plenty to get on your bike or trolley to South Hadley and back and attend class.

STAVE: You mentioned the trolley twice and we know how significant it was for transportation in the early part of the century. What were the trolleys like in New England at that time?

GREEN: Oh, they were fun, and reasonably clean and quite expeditious. After all, it was by no means everybody who expected to have an automobile then. Anyway, the trolleys were perfectly convenient. They took about half an hour to either Smith or Mount Holyoke, but since Smith had nothing in the way to offer for teaching for me and didn't look to me to have any courses that I was specially interested in the obvious thing to do was to turn to Mount Holyoke.

STAVE: Did your husband encourage you in this effort?

GREEN: Yes, bless him, he always encouraged me in doing anything that he thought would ease the shock of Holyoke for me. (laughs) And then to wind up writing a history of the city had its ironies. (laughs)

STAVE: When did you get the degree? How long did it take you?

GREEN: You see I always, always, until my husband's death, had half-time jobs, and I had two courses for two years of study and took the third year to write the thesis. And the thesis on The Condederation of New England was so good, according to some of my teachers, that they wanted me to take it to Charlie Andrews at Yale and get him to say that he would take me on as a graduate student. Well, I did go down to talk with him about it and we came to a meeting of the minds, but it was quite different from what I had intended. He said, "Do you like the Puritans?" and I said, "No." He said, "Don't you?" and I said, "No, I find them stiff and rather forbidding and I can't imagine spending very much time on them." And he said, "Well, that's the answer to pursuing this topic any further. Drop it. It's too bad because I've seen many a worse doctoral dissertation, but I don't think you can expand this without just plain padding it and what's the use?" So that was the end of that except that Albert Bushnell Hart asked me to do a chapter in the first volume of the Commonwealth History of Massachusetts, which was my first publication, and that gave me a lot of pleasure and nobody on God's earth has ever looked at it since then as far as I know. (laughs)[2]

STAVE: When would that be, the middle of the 1920s?

GREEN: It didn't come out until 1929 or thereabouts. But, meanwhile, an opening in the History Department at Mount Holyoke cropped up and they needed a junior member to carry a couple of sections of the required history that was Renaissance and Reformation and European, and which I must say I enjoyed a good deal and I just copied what everybody else was saying and doing, (laughs) and it went reasonably well although I was sometimes kind of ashamed of myself for sliding off so easily. And then the time came in 1932 when the college was in acute financial difficulty and somebody just had to be dropped and there was no question about who it had to be from the History Department. By this time the whole kit and caboodle were bosom friends of mine and I said, "Well, there just isn't any question about it; I'm the least well qualified and the youngest and I'm not completely dependent on this job," for which, incidentally, $80 a month was lucky.

STAVE: (laughs) That was the salary?

GREEN: And so I dropped out and I felt desperate. I knew perfectly well that there were plenty of things to do around Holyoke in the way of volunteer jobs that I had always had before the excuse that I had such professional commitments that I couldn't serve on the YMCA board or this or that, but now I was not only going to be prey to all of the volunteer organizations but I was going to just miss the interest of the academic community, which at Mount Holyoke was quite a distinguished aggregation. And so I wound up fussing around and finally wound up deciding that one way or another, if Don and I could scrape up the cash I would take myself off to Harvard to take what I think in those days was known as a "thirty course." Is there any such thing going now?

STAVE: Thirty courses or thirty hours?

GREEN: Well, it was a special regime whereby you had individual appointments with a professor while he was directing you in some special research undertaking, intended to turn into a doctoral dissertation. Well, anyway, I went armed with the proper notes of introduction and then I talked to Arthur Schlesinger Sr. and Fred Merk, and one of my favorite characters at the Business School. Mr. Merk, unintentionally I discovered, absolutely shut me off completely. He kept telling me that I couldn't have any idea what an assignment I was undertaking or I wouldn't even dream of proposing it and kept telling me how hard it would be.

STAVE: What was the project?

GREEN: To embark on graduate work.

STAVE: Oh, just graduate work, not any specific project.

GREEN: Commuting from Holyoke to Cambridge and to get anything done; he asked me if I knew some female scholar and I said no, not really, but I knew her work, and he said, "Well, it took her five years you know and that's a magnificent job. You couldn't hope to equal that with this kind of arrangement." And poor Mr. Schlesinger had a terrible bellyache, so he sat there sort of dismally saying that he admired my courage but he didn't know exactly what to say. (laughs) And the fellow at the Business School was, on the contrary, specifically helpful. He said, "I'll tell you what we really need, and what I want you to tackle, a history of the machine tool industry in New England. It's within reach and nobody has touched it, and it's one of the most important things." Well, to tell you the truth, I didn't know what a machine tool was and I wasn't going to admit it. I had gone in with the proposition of doing a history of specialized cotton textiles because my husband was in the business.

STAVE: Did he run a mill?

GREEN: He had an executive job, but being half the age of the other directors, they wouldn't pay any attention to him. He developed these fabrics more or less by experiment—he made the most beautiful cotton flannel I've ever seen in my life. But, anyway, that was another tale. At Harvard, I said I would supply the social history and my husband the technology and I don't see how this isn't feasible. And Edmond Gay, Mr. Gay, said, "It would be feasible, but I don't know that it would be awfully interesting to you or to your readers because there's been too much done in that particular area. But the machine tool business is something else." And I said, "Well, I will go home and think about it," and he said, "Think about it hard." Well, the first thing that I did, of course, was to find out what a machine tool was. (laughs) And then I was scared stiff. I could've wished that I'd followed it up because later on I realized that I could have done it and it would have been interesting, and if it had been really well done, it would have led into all sorts of new things as we approached the war and all this experimental business—the miniaturization, for example, and that kind of thing, all the preliminaries to the space program and so on. But I didn't and I taught one additional year at Mount Holyoke because someone was due for a sabbatical.

I didn't know just what I wanted to do but I was not going to enroll at Harvard, where I would have both had to buck Mr. Merk and placate Ed Gay and console Arthur Schlesinger if his bellyache continued (laughs). Even though it was further away, in addition to everything else, I decided to try Yale and went down and encountered Howard Phillips and Ralph Gabriel in the library and they both looked at me sort of askance. I said, "I just wanted to study in order to train myself to carry on college teaching with some kind of distinction," and whether he believed me or not I don't know. But, in any event, Ralph said, "What's your idea for a main line of study?" and I said, "Well, I want to pursue this whole business of what I suppose you'd call social Darwinism. How did it happen to hit Americans so hard and what was its actual social influence?" I wanted to do a study of Herbert Spencer. And Gabriel promptly said, "Well, how much of Sumner have you read?" and I said none. How much did I know about *The Golden Bough*? Nothing. And so on. And as I got dumber he got brighter (laughs) and he finally said, "Well, you know without a large library at your disposal I don't think you'd get very far with a topic like this. It would take you forever and ever just to accumulate the background." And that was very discouraging, but "Do you have any other ideas?" "Well, what kind of city, what kind of town, do you live in?" I said, "Oh, yes, I'm going to do that next." And he said, "Well, whatever it is, I think you'd better do it first." And so he questioned me a little bit about Holyoke and I said it was one of these dreary prefabricated industrial cities; it wasn't an old New England town at all and that it had all the humiliations and weaknesses of a place that was flooded with immigrants at an early stage and didn't know how to manage the hostilities that arose and are still going strong between Catholic and Protestant. He said, "Good, this sounds like just the thing."

STAVE: When you told him that you were going to do it next, were you serious or were you being facetious?

GREEN: Yes, I was thinking about it.

STAVE: You had thought about doing it?

GREEN: Yes, but I wanted to do something that was more in the run of intellectual history, and in many ways was exactly the thing that what's-his-name at Columbia did.

STAVE: Hofstadter?[3]

GREEN: Yes, Hofstadter. And I found myself reading Hofstadter wondering whether I would have done it that way, concluding that I wouldn't have, but that this was perfectly satisfactory. And so that was the way that that began. And so the illusion that I was one of the original perceivers of the importance of urban history is just sheer wrong. It was a thing which was available and which I could do on the scene. I could, for example, take home files of the only local newspaper that had begun its existence with the town in 1849. Take them home a few volumes at a time, peruse them, have interviews with people still living, poke around in the mill records, sometimes with not quite as free a hand as I had imagined would be possible because the head of the Holyoke Water Co. was the first to decide that he wasn't going to be the first who was going to have anybody like that looking at his records (laughs). But it was at my doorstep.

STAVE: So it was a matter of convenience?

GREEN: Yes.

STAVE: And Mr. Gabriel was interested in this sort of topic. Was anyone else doing this sort of thing at Yale while you were there with Gabriel or anyone else?

GREEN: No.

STAVE: Any town histories or histories of cities?

GREEN: No. Now, wait a minute, yes. Not doing it specifically at that time but the guy who did the history of Memphis who's now teaching at Tulane.[4] Well, again, that's another name that I can think of easily enough. I'm sure he's retired by now. Of course I was always older than the kids.

STAVE: The people you were working with. You were 40 by the time you finished your degree, right?

GREEN: I got my degree two months before I was 40.

STAVE: Now you already had several children?

GREEN: Well, I had my quota; I had three.

STAVE: You had your quota of three. How did this work out in terms of your working on your dissertation. Did you have to take courses at Yale as well?

GREEN: Oh, that was one of the benefits of the depression. Yale was so hard up for graduate students that they were willing to make all sorts of concessions, and the same thing would have been true at Harvard had I pursued it. But by the summer of 1932–I guess I actually started doing my commuting in the fall of '33–they were kind of scarce, and that first seminar that I took with Ralph Gabriel included two of my students from Mount Holyoke the year before, (laughs) which was not without its humor of course. But they gave me credit for a year and a half of graduate work for my teaching and that reduced the class work I had to do to one seminar and one supervised reading course.

STAVE: So then having a family really wasn't affected?

GREEN: I went down one day a week for the first year, collected my reading lists, brought home books if need be, did my work at home, went down the next Monday on the 6:30 train from Springfield, to which my spouse drove me on winter mornings when it was 30 degrees below zero, and if you don't think that was heroism. And I'd get the 6:00 o'clock train back. So it was one day a week out and the vacation time and examination periods and so on that were out, so that it was a minimum of time actually in New Haven.

STAVE: You mentioned that there were two of your students from Holyoke in the same class. Were there many women taking degrees at that time because of the depression?

GREEN: No. No, women had to work very hard to be accepted as graduate students at Yale. One reason was that the dean, Woodbury I think his name was, said to one of my professors, "You know, I'm not at all sure that we can afford to take any more of your students, no matter how capable they are, because they all get married and then it's just that much money thrown away," which I thought was a fine gentlemen's point of view. (laughs) But as it happened I don't think more than one or two of the Mount Holyoke girls that went did carry on after they got married. That was still, believe it or not, considered a daring thing to do. It's hard to believe now that it would have changed so profoundly in so few years. But that was the prevailing view and you might very well have to buck your in-laws, whereas, on the contrary, my mother-in-law, once Don was in my life, said, "If you want to do this I would be delighted to pay your tuition fees." Well, how's that for a mother-in-law? And she always took that point of view about my professional interests. She was interested, wished that she could have done it.

STAVE: Now, in doing your study of Holyoke, you mentioned that you used newspapers and that the head of the water company became a little suspicious. How long did it take you to write and what approach did you take in looking at this kind of material? Did you start out with any set notions that you were going to look for certain kinds of changes?

GREEN: No, I don't think I was that systematic. I simply began with the rather dramatic story of these rich birds in Boston sending out agents to look for a good water power site that they could use to develop into the Manchester of the west, and the sixty foot fall at Holyoke was it. They went in surreptitiously, more or less, buying up the land around about Chicopee, which was farther down the line and had proved to be quite a bonanza to Springfield and developing freight for the B&A Railroad. Further upstream, this really terrific power promised even more. Well, the first ten years brought a full-fledged disaster. The first dam was washed out, wasn't able to withstand the sheer spring freshet of power that came pouring down. They had to pay a good deal more for some of the land than they had expected to and they only had one cotton mill erected and operating when the Panic of 1857 came along and practically wiped that out. Although it survived, there wasn't any rush to buy mill sites, as the founders of the company had imagined. But what they did find was that someone with a discerning eye realized that the chemical qualities of the Connecticut River were peculiarly well suited to paper-making, and so you had half a dozen small paper companies coming into being while the intended cotton mills failed to materialize. What was to have been a cotton textile city became a paper-makers' abode within the course of fifteen years. The difference besides that was that paper-making didn't require a very large force of hands whereas textiles did, and so the investment that the Hadley Falls Company had made in not only mill sites but housing for the help was threatened with a good deal of a loss. These things turned up bit by bit. But the first stroke of luck was again out of being my husband's wife and my father-in-law's daughter-in-law and my mother-in-law's daughter-in-law, which opened up sources scattered around Holyoke that nobody had imagined were there. For example, the books of the Hadley Falls Company were sitting on the bottom shelf in the library of William Whiting, the parent of the Whiting Paper Company. And I said, "Mercy, Mr. Whiting, how did you happen to have these here?" and he said, "Oh, well you know we bought the old Lyman Mills to turn it into part of our paper-making establishment. These were in the office and I thought they looked kind of interesting so I just brought them along. Would you like to have them?" I said I would certainly like to. (laughs) There it was and there this really dramatic story was spelled out in what were four director's records, the best of any I've ever seen before or since. It was fine flowing handwriting and interesting narrative and who thought we should do what about what and so on. In any case, getting the city started and the first ten years of disaster was a good start right there, you see. Then came the question of picking up the pieces and plunging into the Civil War and what that meant, and at each point the inundation, the substitution for native farm labor of immigrants—Irish early on, resented and resentful, the French Canadians brought from French Canada and hated by the Irish and not exactly loved by the Yankees but still a lot better off than the Irish, and so on. So that you began to build up this mosaic of immigrant, native, and intra-immigrant conflict into an increasingly confused pattern, but one that then began to get some illumination from the fact that in 1869 the Massachusetts Bureau of Labor Statistics came into being and began making these detailed reports on conditions in town after town and industry after industry, and that then supplied a good deal of comparative information and that was interesting. And so I can't say that I had drawn an outline and stuck to it. I simply let the stuff sort of carry me on the tide, realizing that there were questions all the way along the line about the sheer mechanics of life—what did they do about their vittles? Did they have gardens or did they have grocers come in? Or what was the relationship with the railroad as it crept up the valley, to the growth of the town?

STAVE: All of these questions—did you have any model to work from?

GREEN: No.

STAVE: This was all developed as you went along? There was no book that you had read previously that might have influenced you in your thinking about this?

GREEN: No. The only thing that came closest to it was Vera Shlakman's history of *The Economic History of a Factory Town,* Chicopee, but that didn't come along until I had been working on Holyoke for a while, I mean in published form.[5] I think that came out in 1937 [sic] and by that time I was about through. And if there was anything that I could look at that would have been helpful I didn't find it. Books on mill architecture of Lowell and so on—that didn't help. And nothing in the field of sheer technology—Coughlin's history of cotton manufacturing, for example—was of any use. And I think it was the statistics of labor that were useful in time but I had to wait until I got to 1869 for that.

STAVE: In the Naugatuck book, and we'll get to the genesis of it fully, I think you mentioned the census records, the manuscript census, as being very helpful.[6]

GREEN: Yes.

STAVE: Did you use that in Holyoke too, the Holyoke study?

GREEN: What I did use was the Massachusetts Census.

STAVE: The state census?

GREEN: The state census, which was very helpful indeed. They were little skinny volumes you know, but beginning in 1837 and 1845, 1855, 1865, 1875, 1885—that was enormously helpful. I don't think that I found any—I can't remember finding any of the original census schedules for Holyoke. But, as I say, the state census was sufficiently detailed for small places and it did pretty well, and of course the federal census wasn't of any use at all until about 1885 because Holyoke wasn't big enough. But it was just a matter of picking these up.

STAVE: And thinking the questions out. Was Gabriel much of a formative influence or were you doing this to a great extent on your own?

GREEN: Yes, but I only saw him about twice while the thing was in process. It had occurred to me, though, that he might be perfectly willing to have it be more, but I only took a piece or a chapter to him when I thought it was as nearly complete as I could make it. But early on he taught me two things. In the first place, to take a good, hard look at the wider implications. When I started out on my chapter that began with after the collapse of 1857, I had some long-winded title and he said, "Well, what you're getting at in this chapter really is the rise of industrial nativism." And I said, of course. And I should have called the chapter that. I didn't. I called it the beginnings of local enterprise. But industrial nativism was what it was, and the rise of paper versus cotton. That was the first extremely useful and illuminating clue. The other was much further along when I was talking about the beginnings of machinery making, the Holyoke . . . what was the name of that company? Well, anyway, they made the water wheels. And I said a company was organized to do thus and so and he said, "Do you know who organized it?" and I said, "Of course," and he said, "Who?" and I said, "Oh, these birds who had been working on the upkeep maintenance of the Lyman mills. They were familiar with the kind of water dynamos and so on and after all the whole engineering system of the canals was very ingenious and very well-executed." And he said, "Well, if you know who they are why don't you say so." And I said, "Oh, you mean name them by name," and he said, "Yes, if you know." I said, "Well, they weren't very interesting guys; they just happened to know a good thing when they saw it and to know that they had the skills to carry it on." And he said, "Well, say that." And from that point on I learned something that I've never forgotten: never use the passive voice if you can possibly avoid it. Who did it and why and how well or how badly? And that's the way Holyoke came along, and you know I looked at it, the book, for the first time in about 30 years only about three weeks ago, and I thought, "Gee, there's really quite a lot of interesting stuff here."

STAVE: I'll tell you, I have it out of the University of Connecticut's library and I got a note the other day that somebody wanted it. So (laughs) somebody's using it besides me and you.

GREEN: (laughs)

STAVE: What was the immediate response to the book, both locally and nationally?

GREEN: The immediate response to the book locally was hostility, very distilled or. . . . In the first place, as I say, Mr. Barrett of the Holyoke Water Power Co. was wild with rage and he talked to the young woman who was trying to organize Pioneer Valley Enterprise and she said to him, "Well, if this is so troublesome, why don't you engage somebody to go through and check every mistake?" He said, "But that's just the trouble; it's all true." (laughs) And that was the kind of thing that I met with within Holyoke, and I overheard, with slight pain but a good deal of amusement, at my next door neighbor's bridge party a woman saying, "How did she have the gall to think that she could write a history when we know so much better than she does?"

STAVE: Because you were a stranger or an outsider?

GREEN: Well, because they just didn't like the comments that I had to make about a good many of the attitudes and so on. And her then ten-year-old son who was a great admirer of my husband, and he told me this himself not very long after, said, "You just try writing a book like that yourself and see if you think that you could do better." But the great indignation at what was considered my very cavalier treatment of the Roman Catholic Church conflict—I thought I'd handled it with kid gloves—indignation from people who weren't mentioned at all, and, well, even the gentle wife of the Episcopal Church minister said to me "I guess, you know, until I read your book I didn't realize how unimportant the Episcopal Church was." (laughs) And so on. I did not get any accolade within the city.

STAVE: What about the national or the academic reaction?

GREEN: There it went surprisingly well. A critic for the *Saturday Review,* in a rather long review, made rather a stinging remark from my point of view about my having no feeling about the workers in the field, as she entitled her piece, that I was writing this from the high-and-mighty point of view. And I was so indignant about this that I sat down and wrote her a letter care of the *Saturday Review* and said I realized that there were lots of weak spots in that book, but I want to call to your attention to one misapprehension that you speak of in what I consider an ornery fashion: that I had no feeling for the working people for this town. I happen to live here, and this is the community in which my children are growing up, and if you think for one moment that I don't have their interests at heart and am aware of them every day of my life—this was during the height of the depression, you know—you couldn't be more mistaken. And she wrote back one of the worst-typed, but kind of one of the most fascinating letters I've ever received: "Gee, I wished I'd had sense enough to write some of my critics; (laughs) I see what you mean." But it created somewhat of an impression almost exactly after it came out. And then World War II came along. This came out in 1939. I got my first copy in late May, so it didn't really hit until the summer of 1939, and then nothing like something that had to do with a small, New England mill town occupied the attention of the literary world very hard. Later on there was a kind of a revival, but at that particular moment everything that seemed to be giving it a big push just came to a complete stop.

STAVE: In explaining the reaction of local people you're talking about the hazards of local history, so to speak. You wrote an essay I think in Caroline Ware's *The Cultural Approach to History*. [7]

GREEN: Yes.

STAVE: It was about the value of local history. Not what you said then, but what do you see as the value of local history?

GREEN: I haven't looked at that for so long that I don't know what I did say, but I know that I was satisfied with it then and I'm sure I still would be. I don't see how you can arrive at a sound larger presentation without having a lot of pretty nearly foolproof pieces to fit into it, and that's where your local history fits in. I spoke of the book that I had to give up on a year ago when I realized that I haven't the physical strength to do it. This was a book for the Dial Press of the Bicentennial series that they were getting out, and I was undertaking 200 years of urban life in America. I found that to keep anything like an even pace of discussion, to treat given topics for each of a number of different places, contemporaneous places, and where there were gaps in the available material, the whole strength of the fabric began to weaken. There were just great big holes in it, and that was where I kept thinking, "Oh, if only I could get at this spot or that spot," and it's one reason why I'm throwing up my hands in delight at one of the undertakings that the National Endowment of the Humanities I'm sure is going to sponsor for New York City, filling in what's been missing for so many years, does seem to me a godsend and I thought, "Mercy, if I'd had this a year and a half ago maybe I would have felt that I could have finished." (laughs)

STAVE: What is your attitude toward the computer? While you never learned to use it, do you see . . . ?

GREEN: Because it came too late.

STAVE: In your career. But you seem to think that it's a worthwhile tool?

GREEN: Oh, to some extent I think it's ridiculous, but I think a lot of it is of enormous importance. For example, I am thrilled with excitement over one of the jobs that my daughter is pursuing in seventeenth century Maryland and the St. Mary's City project, and they are succeeding partly by computer techniques in figuring out how many families endured how long and had how many children and how many had a cow and how many of them did this—all the everyday aspects of a colony that was singularly poor in a good many ways, undistinguished as far as its settlers went, just run of the mill people, but filling in all of the stuff that we've guessed about. In Maryland, it was the men that kept dying off and "steppapa" was likely to swipe stepson's inheritance if there wasn't some formal arrangement with mother to supervise. The study that I speak of particularly, that I found of absorbing interest, is a collaborative job with one of Loy's assistants called, *The Role of Women in Seventeenth Century Maryland.*[8] The women generally outlived their husbands, but the immigrant women, that is the indentured servants, rarely married before they were 26, or so, so they lost 10 years of childbearing. Therefore they had smaller families and therefore since they died earlier there was that much less time, and all these factors entered in. Think of all the misconceptions we've sailed along with on the basis of what you read on the gravestones. They begin to pile up, and a totally different picture emerges.

STAVE: So the value of quantification and the computer is a new social history?

GREEN: Yes, social history of a very important order that I don't see how you could have done without what would have taken 400 hours now taking 4, that opening comment of one of Thernstrom's pieces I've always remembered.

STAVE: Well, talking about Thernstrom's pieces and this kind of history—in general, then, if you were, say, starting now would you think that you would probably end up being one of the quantifiers?

GREEN: I doubt it because I can't count well enough. I've been counting words for the last five days for an 800-word piece for the *Dictionary of Southern History,* which they say you cannot exceed 800 words. (laughs) I certainly wouldn't want to rely upon it exclusively because I think you also very much need the sentiment of what people at the time thought was the situation, and that you have to get out of letters and, if not out of correspondence, at least sermons and newspaper pieces.

STAVE: So what we call the impressionistic evidence is necessary to supplement?

GREEN: Yes, because almost as important as what was the fact is what people thought was the fact, and that's my view of it.

STAVE: Perception of the situation is often different.

GREEN: Yes. So I would like to be able to collaborate on a quantitative thing sometime, except that at the age of 78 I'm not going to embark upon another book or even another serious article anyway, and I would just find that it would require too much intensive hard work and I haven't got the physical strength to do it. You may not think that having heart failure takes any strength but it does, and so I have to be extremely careful about what I set out for myself to do, and while I might kick against the pricks at least I'm glad to have something to kick with. (laughs)

STAVE: The field of women's history has had increasing popularity in recent years for obvious reasons. You did a study in the 1940s of the women . . .

GREEN: I didn't know anybody had ever heard of it.

STAVE: Yes. I was just looking at it in fact. The women in industrial work in the Connecticut Valley.[9]

GREEN: In the wartime.

STAVE: Yes, World War II. Could you tell me—you went to work for the ordinance department, right?

GREEN: Yes. That study came out not because I was overwhelmingly interested in women as such, but because here was part of the whole industrial production business that was screaming for resolution. Here was a possible way and how well did it work and how many complications did it produce and was it worth pursuing further or is it something to be used only in the most dire emergencies? That was the point of view from which I wrote that piece.

STAVE: And looking back on it today, what value do you think it has for the people who are becoming increasingly interested in women's history?

GREEN: To tell you the truth, I haven't looked at it in 30 years. I haven't any idea whether it's really of any use or not.

STAVE: Well, you mentioned what happened to women in World War I as opposed to what happened to them in World War II in terms of how they were welcomed into the shops.

GREEN: Oh, yes.

STAVE: Do you think there's any social significance to that kind of thing?

GREEN: Possibly. I hadn't thought of that until you brought it up just now. I don't know. I think the circumstances were the determining factor then. Don't you?

STAVE: In what sense? How would you see the continuity or is there any continuity between, say, from the 1917 period to the present in industrial work? Have you followed this forward?

GREEN: No, I haven't at all since World War II. And I think the reason that it was of interest was that it did mean a higher standard of living for a good many families and that was an idea that hadn't occurred to me on any scale in the World War I situation. The World War I situation was because certain companies were in a spot and anything to get help was welcome. In World War II this became practically announced public policy, and that was something else again.

STAVE: Yourself as a woman who was active in the so-called war effort of the time by serving as a historian—were there many women who evolved as historians at the time?

GREEN: No.

STAVE: Or doing the kind of thing you were doing?

GREEN: No, not that I know of.

STAVE: Were you the only one to your knowledge?

GREEN: Oh, I think there were one or two others, though I don't remember. Of course these were things that I found kind of enjoyable, to go to these occasional sessions where I'd be the only woman. (laughs)

STAVE: How were you treated? Were these military people or . . . ?

GREEN: Military people and industrial people. Well, the red carpet, and it was flattering and I enjoyed the company of the men. And I'd find it a great relief, often found it an enormous relief, after struggling with some of the young ones at Smith College, to be thrown into a completely male setting. And when I went to the job in Washington for the Office of the Chief of Military History after working for the Red Cross, it was pure heaven. Here I was surrounded by extremely knowledgeable, quick-witted guys with whom it was the most wonderful fun to hobnob and to . . .

STAVE: Well, was there a special treatment because you were a woman do you think? A certain element of politeness, chivalry, deference?

GREEN: You mean they would laugh at my jokes? No, I was simply a peer, one among my peers, and the fact that they were male peers made them sturdier than most. (laughs)

STAVE: Do you think the women's libbers of today would challenge you on this kind of thing?

GREEN: Oh, I'm sure they would. They would think this is nonsense. But I just never wanted to eliminate the male under any circumstances. (laughs)

STAVE: How did you get into the whole role of a military historian?

GREEN: Oh, it seems to me that my entire professional career was a series of accidents, quite literally. The job at the Springfield Armory came about because I had a graduate student, a top-notch intelligence, who was the daughter of the head of the New School for years and years. She knew her stuff from way back and wrote a top-notch study of arms makers in the Connecticut Valley for one of the Smith College studies in history and while she was desperately hurrying through the stuff at the Springfield Armory, I went down to lend her a hand because it was about to be transferred. And then I felt, and I think rightly, that we may never lay hands on it again so easily. So for several months I went two or three days a week just to transcribe notes and speed the job up, and consequently when the time came for the ordinance department to act upon Roosevelt's demand that every unit of everything have a historian, they turned to her and she said that she couldn't and why didn't they tackle me, and they did and I did. So I went to the Springfield Armory as a historian and was having a fine time beginning at the beginning of the Armory and coming down to the 1830s and the beginnings of precision manufacture when along came a letter from some nitwit who was headquartered in Washington saying, "Well, this is all nice but where does World War II come in?" And I said, "You mean to say you don't want any background?" They said, "Well, we don't want that far back." So I dropped out a whole century reluctantly and began with World War I and moved on from there, and having then been the official historian for the Springfield Armory, when I then went to see Bob Greenfield about helping me get out of the Red Cross job which I was finding extremely uncomfortable. . . .

STAVE: What were you doing there, at the Red Cross?

GREEN: Oh, theoretically I was riding herd on a whole staff of historians who then would turn over their monographs to what's-his-name. Dulles?

STAVE: Allen?

GREEN: No.

STAVE: Foster Rhea Dulles?

GREEN: Foster Rhea Dulles. To put together into a finished volume. Well, you know writing stuff for someone else to use is not my idea of a favorite way of pouring out one's best efforts, and I couldn't wait to get out of there. But I felt that I had to have a job to move into. So I went to see Bob Greenfield and he asked me about my work and he said, "Oh dear, this is really such a pity, we really need somebody terribly for that job on ordinance, but of course the only thing is that they're just adamant about having a man." And I said, "Well, they didn't seem to feel that way when I took charge of the Springfield Armory," and he said, "What?" and he said, "Well, that's a different story." (laughs) So I was promptly engaged at the level of my associates. I was redoing the signal corps. I was writing on—well, I was a notch above the guy writing a transportation study because he didn't know enough to throw sand down a rat hole and he was almost ready to admit that he didn't. But in any event, I moved into a very agreeable, highly qualified male setting that was made into pleasurable work for me. It was a distraction that I would regret in that it headed me off the kind of social history that I had really wanted to pursue.

STAVE: I was going to ask you—you did this full-time then?

GREEN: Yes.

STAVE: You weren't teaching or you weren't commuting to Holyoke at this time?

GREEN: No, I had moved to Washington to live after my husband Don's death in the late fall of 1946. The Red Cross had announced to me that they would give me the salary I demanded but only if I were on the scene full-time. So I moved down in January of 1947. But by the summer of 1948 I was more than fed up and it was a pity.

STAVE: Before we go a little further, I just want to get back to the *History of Naugatuck,* which was published in 1948. First question— why did you move to Washington? Was it because of the possibility of a job there?

GREEN: Yes, you see at the end of the war, and I'd done the Naugatuck piece while I was living in Northampton, I had gotten the Armory to agree to my putting in only half-time on that job. I was getting down into the present and the thing was becoming kind of routine and I was frankly bored with it, and so I had half-time spent at the Armory and the other half-time spent on Naugatuck. And that came to me via Leonard Labarree.

STAVE: It was published in the Yale . . .

GREEN: Yes, and the town fathers, or rather the Board of Trade, the Chamber of Commerce, had turned to him and wanted him to do it but he said no and said that they could try me. So I took that on.

STAVE: I see. So there again, in a sense, it's accidental, that you had done your first study and he knew you were in this field so he referred it to you.

GREEN: And it was a field that I found very interesting indeed because it had any number of human elements with tentacles reaching out in any number of directions. But at the end of the war, just about the time I'd finished up the Naugatuck job, Smith College was reorganizing and people who'd had jobs were coming back and I went to see the president, who was about to retire and go back to England, and I asked him what the prospects were and he said frankly he thought they were virtually nil for my getting a permanent full-time job at Smith College. By this time, you see, I was a recent widow and felt great urgency. My son was just back from the war but he was still in college and he needed the G.I. Bill of Rights, that wasn't everything to be desired, and a younger daughter who was not yet through college, and I just didn't see how I could make the grade without a full-time job. It didn't augur well to stay there. And the year (1939-1940) I taught in the History Department, I taught very badly. I just started off with whooping cough and the family situation was very precious in a great many ways and I was just too wound up in anxieties to do the kind of job I should have done, and I knew that I had made a mess of it and had no quarrel with their decision to take on Foster Rhea Dulles as my substitute. (laughs) But I still felt badly about it and realized that I just had to start all over again. It's one thing to start as a wife with a husband's support and another to start as a widow not knowing what next. And so the Red Cross people with whom I'd done some work during the summer before wanted me and, as I say, provided I would come to Washington to live, were willing to offer me what seemed at the time a very handsome salary—$5,000. That was what a GS-13 in the Government would be getting.

STAVE: That was what your father was getting back in 1903.

GREEN: Yes. But, in any event, those were the circumstances. I was just saying that I have regretted that somehow or other I did not work out a method of keeping to the urban field and the American social history, rather than the technological business that I did get into, not that that wasn't interesting, but it lacked the continuity that I would have preferred, although Eli acted as my bridge.

STAVE: Eli Whitney? Is that who you mean?

GREEN: Yes. The work I'd done on Eli came in on the job I'd done for the Springfield Armory.[10]

STAVE: I see. I was going to ask you how you got interested in Eli Whitney.

GREEN: Yes. And so when Oscar Handlin asked me which of these famous Americans I would want to choose to write about for his series and gave me a choice of six or seven I chose Eli. And that was kind of fun. But that, you see, again, was somewhat of a diversion. And I don't think at that time that Oscar had any individual in the layout of what he was then calling, "The New American Statesmen Series," who could have been listed as falling into the pattern of city planner or city booster.

STAVE: The only urban thing in there was his own book on—this is the same series I believe—on Al Smith.[11]

GREEN: Well, naturally he wasn't going to offer me that one. But hindsight is something else again. Getting back to a return to social history, I'd taught one year of class at American University. I found it exhausting to put in a full day's work at the Pentagon and then try to do that, and I decided that I wasn't going to do that and I had to give up one if I was going to do the other. I wasn't at all sure of a job in American's graduate school and I figured I had just better hang on at the Pentagon until along came the offer from the Rockefeller Foundation.

STAVE: Was this for the Washington study?[12]

GREEN: Well, I chose Washington.

STAVE: I see. I'd like to get into the genesis of this. Now the Rockefeller Foundation made what kind of offer?

GREEN: They wanted me to write a pilot study of American urban history, really for the job that the guy from the University of Kansas . . .

STAVE: Glaab?

GREEN: Yes, Charles Glaab and A. Theodore Brown did.[13] But I didn't feel free to go roaming all over the United States at that point. This proposition came along about 1953, and while my youngest was married and living in Paris, my son was in graduate school and working himself almost to death trying to earn a living and go through school—he was out in California—and somehow or other I felt that it was kind of precarious to undertake something that would require intensive cerebration to begin with and then probably a good deal of traveling. Now maybe I'm wrong, maybe that wouldn't have been necessary, what they did I don't think required any travel at all, but I wouldn't have written that particular kind of book anyway. In any event, I turned it down and asked to be allowed to do the history of Washington, admitting that it was partly because it was now my home and that made life simpler.

STAVE: This is the way it seems a lot of urban histories get written—people are there.

GREEN: Oh, I'm sure. The urban biography is now rather despised, you know. It comes under fire as being . . .

STAVE: The old history.

GREEN: It's old history and it's out of date and it isn't very illuminating. The attack that who did—I admire the guy who said we've got to work out a technique of principles of urbanization.

STAVE: Eric Lampard.[14]

GREEN: Lampard. Lampard wrote some 50 typescript pages about this for the *American Historical Review,* citing some of my books as an example of what not to do, and so when it came for me to decide whether or not the *Review* should publish his piece, what I did was write to him and say: "Eric, I've been asked to pass upon your piece. I'm not very happy about some of the things you said about me, but I wanted to reassure you that I think that you're simply flogging a dead horse because you've already pointed that up half a dozen times, and why don't you just cut that and shorten the piece by this much and I'd take this out."

STAVE: Did he?

GREEN: He did and it came out; and it made an enormous impression as it should. Well, I admire him very much and I agreed with his criticisms of what I had done, which didn't make it any easier to have them publicized you know. (laughs) But I never have reached the point of wanting to depersonalize to the point that his every production seems to me to do. And even Thernstrom, who falls into another category of depersonalization I think, carries it too far, it strikes me in a good many instances.[15]

STAVE: Do you think, then, that this is the danger of the so-called new urban history—the dehumanization or depersonalization?

GREEN: I think that ideally it ought to be an admixture. Now that's hard to come by and hard to do.

STAVE: Well, when you say depersonalized or dehumanized—I've heard . . .

GREEN: I've never heard anybody else say that.

STAVE: I have heard that. This has been a basic criticism of the quantifiers and the new urban history. But I've heard people answer this by saying, "Well look, all of those numbers represent people," and that they're telling you what people did as you were describing before about the St. Mary's project. In a sense, you're learning by numbers; you're learning about social history. In this perspective, would you accept this kind of reply?

GREEN: Yes, I think so.

STAVE: I think what you're saying is that you're removing the color from the writing of history?

GREEN: Yes.

STAVE: Maybe this is it.

GREEN: Yes, I expect you're exactly right. And I'm afraid that I kind of lack color also.

STAVE: Well this is what makes it interesting.

GREEN: Well, it's what attracts the reader who might otherwise never read any history at all. And I think the world needs colorful history and I would very much regret to see the tendency to cancel college courses in history go any further.

STAVE: Well, it's a very bad tendency. Enrollments are generally falling since a few years ago because of the cultural revolution or the counter-cultural revolution that believed that history was irrelevant. Now it's because of the economy. A lot of places are suffering for students. They're saying, "We just can't afford to take history." I've had many students in my classes, in my office the past few weeks, saying, "I'd love to be a history major but I just can't afford to do it; I'm going to business school," or "I'm going to urban studies," which I happen to teach and from which they think they can get jobs. But I can't say honestly, "Stay in history and you'll get a job."

GREEN: I know. Well, you're quite right in saying it's not dehumanization. I find myself quoting father's quotation from Abraham Lincoln every now and again, saying "God must have loved the plain people, he made so many of them." (laughs)

STAVE: Yes, well this is exactly what they're trying to get at. But it is the color aspect which I think is one facet that's left out of the new urban history.

GREEN: And it does make a good deal of it kind of dreary, and that I think is a great failing. Now, I haven't looked very carefully at Peter Knights' book.

STAVE: *The Plain People of Boston?*[16]

GREEN: Wasn't there a later one?

STAVE: I haven't seen a more recent one.

GREEN: Well, *The Plain People of Boston* I found just plain dull, and that I think is enough to make one weep.

STAVE: Yes, well this is the attitude. This has been referred to as "bare foot empiricism," that in a sense it's a very dry kind of study. Well, the notion of the methodology becomes as important as the substance sometimes, and the emphasis is on methodology.

GREEN: Well, I was thinking about the pieces that I cut so reluctantly for my 800 words in order to have space for the last 50 years. (laughs)

STAVE: The last fifty years of Southern history or was it Washington or what?

GREEN: An 800-word piece on Washington. I hated to cut out the 138 members of the Sixth Congress, who arrived in a snowstorm in Washington to begin their first tour of duty in the new location. But to picture 138 members as the whole of the Congress just was a detail that seemed to me a little short of criminal to omit, but by the time I had gotten through the rest of the sentence I was going to save six words.

Well, anyway, I found myself reading your interview with Sam (Bass Warner) with enormous interest. He'd had a much more checkered career than I'd realized and I admire his work very much indeed except that I haven't been able to go for *The Urban Wilderness.*[17]

STAVE: You don't like the book?

GREEN: I haven't really tried. It came at a moment when I was being very ill and breathless enough that it was an effort to hold up the book, and I didn't really try to read it. But then I began to get a series of appeals from the editors saying, "Can't you do something about seeing that this *very* important book gets a big play?" And I just didn't answer because I couldn't say that I hadn't read it yet and I hadn't read it yet.

STAVE: It's an important book. It's also this period—but then of course most books are—in his view of the city. He starts off with the notion that the city is rotten from the top down. I think it's really tied in with the late 1960s and early 1970s. But it is an important book as comparative material and it's a significant work. My students like it.

GREEN: Well, that's very important. Furthermore, anybody who has the physical energy and the intellectual acumen to work in a good deal of the comparative material fills me with admiration because I found myself thinking: "Well, this is like trying to make myself into an encyclopedia, writing a monograph on a thousand topics," but the older I get the lazier I get. And when I get home I shall take *The Urban Wilderness* and take a good crack at it, just for my own delectation, not because I will ever be able to air my opinions to anybody who'd want to hear them.

STAVE: Okay, I'd like to get back to the Rockefeller offer to you and your counter-proposal to do Washington. And you were in Washington at the time and one reason you chose it, I guess, was because you lived there.

GREEN: I said for one thing they wanted something that would be a typical city. So I chose the most atypical, figuring that the atypical can be as illuminating as the typical of typicality. That was one argument I put forward—a little specious perhaps, but still. The second one was that the abundance of materials and the well-organized character of them was such that it was a feasible task to do almost single-handed, whereas practically no other big city that could rank as a fair sample. I said it would be atypical but it would be illuminating. The materials are here in abundance and this is my locality, and I think, in addition to that, it would have the advantage of being a book that would interest a great many people who weren't particularly interested in a model study of the American urban scene. And somewhat to my surprise, but greatly to my relief, they went along with it, and then said the only thing we need now is a sponsor. And I said, "Oh, I though you were going to be the sponsor," and they said, "Oh, no, we have to have an institution to make a grant to an individual."

STAVE: This is the Rockefeller Foundation?

GREEN: So that took another little while.

STAVE: American University?

GREEN: American University. And I might have fared better in some ways if I had written back to Yale and said, "Do you want to or would you be willing to sponsor? I shall be here and not a member of the faculty." It would have kept me in touch, for example, with some of the history department whose critical advice would have come in very handy at a good many points.

STAVE: Who would you have contacted particularly?

GREEN: Well, Gabriel I think was just about winding up then and I don't know exactly who else at the moment.

STAVE: This would be in the 1950s?

GREEN: Yes, it would be early 1950s. George Pearson would not have been ideal perhaps, but he would have had his points too. Anyway, I considered it vaguely but not very hard because I thought of all the correspondence (laughs) and I was lazy about that. Furthermore, I felt under considerable indebtedness to the people at American because it was they who had called my attention to the intensely interesting features of Washington. I was asked to speak to a seminar at some point and to choose any topic and I said, "Oh mercy, what do you want here?" and they said, "Well, what we would like would be something that would tie in and show how important the archives are to the writing of any competent study." I had to bring in the factor of the importance of the National Archives; that was what the seminar was all about, and how it could be used to advantage in the writing of history—the very thing that they've been continuing to do. And very useful they've been, I think, on the whole. In any event, well, I said, "Well, what would you say if I just talked about the problems of writing a competent history of Washington?" "Fine." And so I set out from there and what I did was in a way rather shabby, but it made a great hit I will say because all I did was to ask questions.

STAVE: What are the problems?

GREEN: Yes. What is this one; how do you discuss this; how much emphasis do you put on that; can you handle that, and so on—everything from the role of religion on up and down the line. And how did you find out about it if you decided that this was an important topic, then what were you going to do to find archival materials or others to discuss it. Well, I had I suppose about 40 people in the room and they sat without moving for two hours, and I don't consider myself a spellbinder by any manner or means, but they were just as much interested in thinking about the questions that I was raising as I was.

STAVE: This was what year?

GREEN: This was early 1949.

STAVE: In other words, this is what gave you the idea of Washington?

GREEN: Yes. Of course I couldn't talk about it without finding out something about it myself.

STAVE: What were the types of questions that were raised? What kinds of issues did you raise?

GREEN: Well, for one thing, a job of this dimension better be a collaboration than a one man job, and if it were going to be a collaboration how were you going to do it, and why did I think it was important to know how people thought about the descriptions of foreigners or what they had to say about the city. I said, "Well, in the first place, when you think of how dingy and sort of rotten ridden Washington really was during much of the nineteenth century, wouldn't you think Washingtonians would not have resented that kind of comment and would have done their utmost to correct it rather than feeling that they were being put upon, and isn't it important to know the extent to which they felt pride rather than grievances about the city and so on?" I honestly don't remember—I spoke from a list of about 12 questions that I'd jotted down on the back of a card and then let it carry itself. But it did waken my interest in realizing how much I had not known about the city. The absence of foreign-born in any numbers in a time when they were flooding into other cities was one element. And I found that questions that I had raised for that occasion I was able to use on frequent occasions later.

STAVE: Well, were other people helping you do this work? How was this project set up?

GREEN: It was set up that I was to do it and I was to have some money set aside for research assistants. And I said I didn't want an assistant until I'd been at the job for at least three months because I wouldn't know what to put him to work on. I thought that I could do the job in four years. Well, of course, it took me six, and for three years I had an absolute top-notch research assistant. And he always raised the right question and nine times out of ten had as good an answer as anybody, and when the grant money ran out and I had to pay for help myself, I couldn't manage it, so he went to the Washington Center for Metropolitan Studies and has made a very real name for himself and I went to work with a part-time assistant, who worked eight hours a week. That's one reason why volume two is more diffuse and less readable than volume one. I just got too hurried, didn't cut sufficiently or perceptively enough.

STAVE: The interesting parts, I think, of the first volume especially of the series—the two volumes plus *The Secret City*. *The Secret City* is a little different. Do you consider that as sort of the third volume of the series?

GREEN: In a way. And it's a pretty feeble reason. I enriched the story told in the earlier accounts, the earlier volumes. And then I added ten years taking it through the 1950s, added almost a third to the book, and it was extremely hard work dealing with all these law suits that were piling up and piling up. And one reason that I think it got less appreciation than it might have is that it's got the worst index in the world.

STAVE: You're talking about *The Secret City?*

GREEN: *The Secret City.* I didn't do it myself and I should have.

STAVE: It's interesting, you were doing some work on women, you were doing some work in urban history, you sort of stumbled into it, and you were right at the tip of the iceberg when black history emerged as an exploding field. Do you think being white and writing *The Secret City* had an adverse effect in terms of perception? You mention in your preface, I believe, that there could be . . .

GREEN: Well, I felt that I couldn't do the whole job of writing the history of black Washington; it had to be race relations because . . .

STAVE: Right, it's an interracial thing and you used the term—I have it here . . .

GREEN: Well, that was a criticism for that statement.

STAVE: Presumptuousness. "For a white person to attempt to describe the past of any Negro community smacks of presumptuousness." And this was picked up by some of the reviewers, Arvarh Strickland especially, implying that maybe this is so.[18] Now, do you think that writing in 1965—or, it was published in 1967?

GREEN: Yes.

STAVE: I guess you had pulled together material from the other books?

GREEN: Yes, that was one of the things that makes it not quite fair to call it a third volume. But there is a lot that was left out.

STAVE: Of the others, right. Well, do you think it made a difference writing as a white person the way you viewed Washington or "the secret city" part of Washington?

GREEN: Made a difference to whom?

STAVE: Well, to blacks and the perspective that you obtained. I think there was criticism that you were looking too much at the lack of unifying forces rather than at the unifying forces in *The Secret City.*

GREEN: Of "the secret city" or of the city as a whole?

STAVE: Of the city as a whole. Well, of the black community I think too.

GREEN: Nobody ever said that to me, nor have I perceived it in any of the reviews that I received. Two things I learned from the group of faculty to whom I spoke at Howard just after the book appeared were interesting. One man said that he thought I had given far too little attention to the Negro church. And I said, "Well, I thought I had pursued it as far as there were records to pursue." And he said, "Oh, no, there were a lot of things in addition." And I said, "Well, that's where my ignorance came in. But you think I underestimated the role of the church all the way along the line?" He said yes, he did, but that he thought that I could have gotten more understanding of the Negro community if I had read more widely in church materials; and I said, "Well, I found that an interesting comment, but I hadn't known where to find them." So maybe this was where my whiteness was at fault and that he didn't take too kindly to. So he made no comment, and that was that. The other criticism was the outcry about contending that the 1920s, the late 1920s, was almost the nadir of black fight was perfect nonsense because the whole group there had been young men at this point and they had thought that they had all rolled up their sleeves and were fighting like mad and for me to say that this was the absolute bottom and they had all given up was a personal insult. It was a personal insult. And I said, "Gee willicky, I really hadn't thought of it this way, but the odds were so heavily against you at that time that I would have thought that you'd all wanted to give up, and, after all, you were still young enough so that by the time the early 1930s rolled around you were all rolling up your sleeves again with a vengeance and going to it." Well, that assuaged them a little bit, but not very much.

STAVE: If you were writing that book again today, at least ten years later, would you change your title, would you think your synthesis, your view, would be changed?

GREEN: Oh yes, I'm sorry to say I do. I was writing it from a distinctly optimistic point of view and I think Washington is a very discouraging and discouraged black city today.

STAVE: Have you thought of leaving—you still live there—have you thought of leaving the city?

GREEN: Oh, I very reluctantly have left the city as of this month and am now enjoying quarters with my daughter and her family in Annapolis, because I can't live alone any longer. I have agreed to that limitation and short of paying out nine-tenths of my income, I can't get anybody to come in and take care of and live with me, and so I'm putting my house on the market and pulling out. But not because of the discomforts of social antagonism.

STAVE: This is a personal thing that is leading you out of the city.

GREEN: It's my health, that's all.

STAVE: But it's not the matter of the situation, as you put it, the discomforts of the city.

GREEN: No, but it is nevertheless uncomfortable, and I always thought that the stories of street crime were exaggerated and still do think so though my own house has been broken into three times over. That's uncomfortable and so on, but, no, to walk into a department store where you've traded and always had pleasant, efficient service and find that you can stand around for ten minutes and can't persuade one of the clerks to pay any attention to you because she or they are all engaged in anecdotes of their own private lives. You find that kind of thing.

STAVE: Well, as an historian of the city, as *the* historian of the city essentially, was this something that, well, historians don't predict, but how predictable do you think this situation was?

GREEN: Well, I think it was more predictable than I was willing to admit.

STAVE: Now, two questions: what do you think accounts for this and why do you think you were more optimistic back in 1965?

GREEN: Well, because this had not become so apparent. I was optimistic because for one thing the March on Washington in the summer of 1963 . . .

STAVE: I was there.

GREEN: Didn't that seem to you to be a landmark?

STAVE: Oh yes, it did at the time. It seems like ancient history right now.

GREEN: Exactly. Well, I kept thinking there was going to be a recurrence, a resurgence, of that kind of spirit. Instead, it's been a drop the other way.

STAVE: Why? What is there about the American city or the American life?

GREEN: I think for one thing, probably—I'm guessing—there's disappointment at things not moving faster, and the physical rewards of achieving full citizenship, so to speak, have been so far fewer than blacks have expected.

STAVE: Do you think that—well, Washington, as you point out, has never had large immigrant groups coming in . . .

GREEN: Of course now it has.

STAVE: Yes, but in the past. What of the situation of the blacks in historical perspective in Washington? Now you have two factors here: the factor of race and the factor that they are the majority in the city. But do you think that this is sort of the newness of the experience or do you think that your own work shows that the experience isn't that new, that there is a heritage and a history so that they aren't newcomers? Is it the immigrant who's coming in, or the in-migrant in this case, and adjusting to an urban life that they're not used to or is there another factor there? Am I making myself clear?

GREEN: I think maybe you're making yourself clear but I've gotten side-tracked a little by thinking of Dick Wade's insistence that one of the things that had gone wrong with the handling of black problems was that historians have taken it for granted that they were going to follow the pattern of the European.[19]

STAVE: Okay, but are you arguing that blacks vis-à-vis foreign born immigrants would be having much different experiences? Or am I reading this correctly?

GREEN: No, I think Dick's main point was that it wasn't the same.

STAVE: Yes. This has been written—Allan Spear has done this, others have done it too.[20] I'm asking you your view. Nathan Glazer has set forth the view that, really it's not a matter of racism that has made the difference, that the experiences are the same, and it's a matter of newness in a sense, a nostalgia on the part of the whites, saying that, "Well, we weren't like that," but they really were.[21] And the blacks, as far as coming to cities, are still relatively new in the context of foreigners, Europeans, coming to American cities. On the other hand, you have the people who say that the experience is really keyed to racism and this is the real element that's made a difference in the black experience.

GREEN: Well, I'm afraid that I agree with the latter. And I can't pin it down exactly, but after all, it's been a great many years that there's been a very solid portion of Washington that's been solid black, and the fact that, say, from the late 1890s on Washington was practically split into two independent cities, mutually dependent but nevertheless, and to say, therefore, that this is a new experience isn't quite true. They had power, they lost it, it slipped through their fingers. To say that this is a new experience isn't just, because one could hardly ask for anything more dramatic than the degree of progress they had made by 1870. And, all right, you can say that the City Council vote didn't count, that nobody paid any attention to it, but nevertheless there it was, and then to have those civil rights laws revived, not passed again starting from scratch but revived starting in the early 1950s is testimony to the fact that there is a long experience behind Black Washington, and to say that it is new is . . .

STAVE: What about the people, in a sense? What about in-migration and the massive increase of population: *When* Blacks moved to the city—does this make a difference?

GREEN: All right, yes, of course it does. It's the dilution of the old by the inexperienced new, not a small proportion of which I fear is still filled with a good deal of hate, but it's the newcomers that are primarily responsible, I think. That seems sort of shabby and exploratory but I can't see any other way of understanding it.

STAVE: One of the points in your study of Washington is the counterpoint between the local and the federal that was pointed to as a very successful aspect of your work, and one of the problems that urban historians have to deal with in their local studies is to try to get this balance. Someone has written that urban history is not national history writ small and national history is not urban history writ large. How do you go about achieving the balance as successfully as you tried to do? I mean you had a city that fits right into this pattern because, of course, it is Washington. What kinds of things did you do or should a historian do to try to achieve such balance?

GREEN: Heaven only knows. I hadn't realized that I had achieved it. In fact, in retrospect, perhaps except apart from Holyoke itself or even Naugatuck I think, heavens, what a shabby piece of work this is.

STAVE: Which?

GREEN: The books I've written.

STAVE: (laughs) Why would you say that?

GREEN: Well, because there are so many things that seem to me aren't discussed adequately or are overrated, individual leadership very rarely emerges. I long, for example, to take, say, the present City Council, which I think has two white members, and have a thumbnail sketch of each member as well as Walter Washington as mayor, and I have a strong suspicion that neither would anybody want to read it, but neither would I have had the insights that would have made it worth reading. That's partly growing old, you know, that you no longer have the drive to pick up all the loose ends and gather them together and see.

STAVE: Most people don't have it to start with. (laughs) So if you lose a little of it when you get old. . . . Well, two more books we haven't covered: your synthesis, *The Rise of Urban America* and *American Cities in the Growth of the Nation*.[22] The origins of those two? How did they come about? These were broader studies. *The Rise of Urban America* is a synthesis, the other select studies I guess.

GREEN: Yes, those were based on lectures for the Commonwealth Fund in London and H. Hale Bellot wrote and said choose any topic you like but preferably involving municipal history, and so I got the invitation some three months late because he had written care of Smith College and they had written "address unknown," which was not very flattering. (laughs) Anyway, I had to make up my mind hurriedly whether I was going to do them. And then I said, you know, the English hate generalizations, make it as specific as you can. So I took particular places to illustrate the westward movement and the importance of transportation of each and then the two exceptions as the last. In a way that was as much fun to write as any book I've done, partly because I didn't have any footnotes and that meant I could rely upon my judgments without pinpointing my source every few minutes. *The Rise of Urban America*—I was told they wanted 60,000 words. Now that's not very much. And I was mad as hops at the reviewers who never once took into consideration that this was by publisher's instructions to do not more than 60,000 words. And a number of things that I passed over lightly or didn't mention at all, of course, made it look like a very superficial job indeed, except that a 60,000-word book is bound to be superficial if you've got that much ground to cover. So I was really awfully put out at the editor when the first time we met we had breakfast together, she coming in her role as editor and I as what I thought successful author, and she said, "Well, what do you yourself think of the book?" And I said, "I think it's a damn good book, all things considered." She didn't say anything, and I thought, "Well, this is cold water and then some." And I said, "I gather you don't," and she said, "Well, there are some criticisms." Well, I suppose the most basic, and I don't know who told me this—it wasn't she—from the many-faceted guy at the University of Michigan, John . . .

STAVE: John Higham?

GREEN: Yes. He said that it had no conceptualization.

STAVE: And your answer to this?

GREEN: My answer to it was: "Well, I think it has conceptualization, mainly that urban life has been infinitely varied and you can't tell all in 60,000 words." (laughs)

STAVE: Well, here's an example where I was talking about the counterpoint between the local and the national, is that there you seem to follow more of a national kind of synthesis, chronologically following a national thing, rather than looking at. . . . Well, following the conceptualization that we were talking about with Lampard, the urbanization notion. By putting it in that framework, it looks like a book that's dealing with the city in the context of the nation as opposed to the rise of the city. These are criticisms. Do you have any reaction to that?

GREEN: No, I suppose that's just. But it struck me that for a 60,000-word treatment of the rise of a city, or of a nation of cities, you had to take it in these broad sweeps.

STAVE: With the Pulitzer Prize—did you anticipate that?[23]

GREEN: Oh, certainly not. In fact, somebody said, "Is there any possibility?" I said, "Not a chance." My real grievance about that business was that the New York *Times* didn't give me right credit for writing the book that won the prize. They confused me with a Woodward.

STAVE: Now wait a minute, you're not talking about C. Vann Woodward are you?

GREEN: No, some theology student, who was writing on the conflict of Catholicism and Protestantism in Holyoke, and that was why it was assigned to me to review by the *Times* some years earlier. The guy writing up the piece on the Pulitzer Prize winners in 1963 said Constance McLaughlin, author of *Protestant and Catholic*. And I wrote back and said I don't think Mr. Woodward would be any better pleased than I am at having his book attributed to me and will you please correct this mistake, whereupon they wrote an apology to him which appeared two days later and never mentioned me again. That ought to have taught me to brag hard when you get the chance. (laughs)

STAVE: Finally, do you have any advice for younger historians who are working in the field of urban America?

GREEN: Well, my advice is to maintain enthusiasm and keep going, and that means lots of patience and hard work, unlike the students who say, "We'd like to be history majors but . . . " I don't know how they're going to manage but I hope they will.

STAVE: On that note of optimism, I think we'll stop.

NOTES

1. Constance McLaughlin Green, *Holyoke, Massachusetts: A Case History of the Industrial Revolution in America* (New Haven, 1939).

2. Constance McLaughlin Green, "New England Confederation," Chapter 9 in Albert Bushnell Hart, *Commonwealth History of Massachusetts,* Vol. 1 (New York, 1927, 1966), 226-258.

3. Richard Hofstadter, *Social Darwinism in American Thought* (Rev. ed., Boston, 1955).

4. Gerald M. Capers, *The Biography of a River Town: Memphis, Its Heroic Age* (Chapel Hill, N.C., 1939).

5. Vera Shlakman, *Economic History of a Factory Town* (Northhampton, Mass., 1935).

6. Constance McLaughlin Green, *History of Naugatuck, Connecticut* (Naugatuck, Conn., 1948).

7. Constance McLaughlin Green, "The Value of Local History" in Caroline F. Ware, ed., *The Cultural Approach to History* (New York, 1940), 275-286.

8. Lois Green Carr and Lorena S. Walsh, "The Planter's Wife: The Experience of White Women in Seventeenth-Century Maryland," William & Mary Quarterly (forthcoming); see also Maryland Historical Magazine, 69 (1974), devoted to the early findings of the St. Mary's City Commission research.

9. Constance McLaughlin Green, *The Role of Women as Production Workers in War Plants in the Connecticut Valley* (Northampton, Mass., 1946).

10. Constance McLaughlin Green, *Eli Whitney and the Birth of American Technology* (Boston, 1956).

11. Oscar Handlin, *Al Smith and His America* (Boston, 1958).

12. Constance McLaughlin Green's research on Washington was published in three volumes: *Washington: Village and Capital 1800-1878* (Princeton, N.J., 1962); *Washington: Capital City, 1879-1950* (Princeton, N.J., 1963); and *The Secret City: A History of Race Relations in the Nation's Capital* (Princeton, N.J., 1967).

13. See A. Theodore Brown, *Frontier Community: A History of Kansas City to 1870* (Columbia, Mo., 1964), and Charles N. Glaab, *Kansas City and the Railroads* (Madison, Wisc., 1962).

14. Eric E. Lampard, "American Historians and the Study of Urbanization," American Historical Review, 67 (October 1961), 49-61.

15. For an example of Stephan Thernstrom's writing, see his *Poverty and Progress: Social Mobility in a Nineteenth Century City* (Cambridge, Mass., 1964; New York, 1969), and *The Other Bostonians: Poverty and Progress in the American Metropolis, 1880-1970* (Cambridge, Mass., 1973).

16. Peter R. Knights, *The Plain People of Boston, 1830-1860: A Study in City Growth* (New York, 1971).

17. Sam Bass Warner, Jr., *The Urban Wilderness: A History of the American City* (New York, 1972).

18. See review of *The Secret City* by Arvarh E. Strickland in the Journal of American History, 65 (December 1967), 682-683.

19. Richard C. Wade, "Historical Analogies and Public Policy: The Black and Immigrant Experience in Urban America" in Morris and West, eds., *Essays on Urban America,* 127-147.

20. Allan Spear, "The Origins of the Urban Ghetto, 1870-1915," in N. I. Huggins, et al., *Key Issues in the Afro-American Experience,* Vol. II (New York, 1971), 153-166.

21. Nathan Glazer, "Blacks and Ethnic Groups: The Difference, and the Political Difference it Makes," in Huggins, et al., *Key Issues . . . ,* 193-211.

22. Constance McLaughlin Green, *The Rise of Urban America* (New York, 1965), and *American Cities in the Growth of the Nation* (London, 1957; New York, 1965).

23. Constance McLaughlin Green was the second in her family to win the Pulitzer Prize. Her father, Andrew Cunningham McLaughlin, won the Prize in 1936 for his *The Constitutional History of the United States* (New York, 1935). Twenty-seven years later, in 1963, she received the award for *Washington: Village and Capital, 1800-1878.*

SELECT BIBLIOGRAPHY OF WORKS BY
CONSTANCE McLAUGHLIN GREEN

Holyoke, Massachusetts: A Case History of the Industrial Revolution in America (New Haven, 1939).

The Role of Women as Production Workers in War Plants in the Connecticut Valley (Northampton, Mass., 1946).

History of Naugatuck, Connecticut (Naugatuck, Conn., 1948).

The Ordinance Department: Planning Munitions for War (Washington, D.C., 1955, with Harry C. Thomson and Peter C. Roots).

Eli Whitney and the Birth of American Technology (Boston, 1956).

American Cities in the Growth of the Nation (London, 1957; New York, 1965).

Washington: Village and Capital, 1800-1878 (Princeton, N.J., 1962).

Washington: Capital City, 1879-1950 (Princeton, N.J., 1963).

The Rise of Urban America (New York, 1965).

The Secret City: A History of Race Relations in the Nation's Capital (Princeton, N.J., 1967).

"The Value of Local History," in Caroline F. Ware, ed., *The Cultural Approach to History* (New York, 1940), 275-286.

"Introduction," in Margaret Francine Morris and Elliott West, eds., *Essays on Urban America* (Austin, Tex., 1975), 13-18.

Oscar Handlin

Oscar Handlin (1915-   ) is the Carl H. Pforzheimer University Professor at Harvard University, where he has taught since 1939. His contributions to the fields of social, urban and especially immigrant history are widely known. In 1951, his book *The Uprooted* won the Pulitzer Prize. Handlin has advised many of the leading urban historians, including several whose interviews appear in this volume.

A CONVERSATION WITH OSCAR HANDLIN

STAVE: I believe you were born in Brooklyn, New York in 1915. Could you tell me something about your youth, your family life, and your early education?

HANDLIN: It'd be a long story. I moved about a great deal, and went to many different schools. It wasn't until my teens that we settled down. As it was, I went to three different high schools. I was born in Brooklyn, and also lived in New Haven and Kingston, New York.

STAVE: Where was your family from originally?

HANDLIN: The Ukraine.

STAVE: Were they immigrants?

HANDLIN: Oh, yes. My father came about 1913, 1914. My mother came maybe ten years earlier.

STAVE: And what kind of work did your father do?

HANDLIN: Well, he drifted from one occupation to another at various times. He had a grocery store, was in the real estate business, ran a steam laundry.

STAVE: Had he had much education himself?

HANDLIN: Well, for that class he had. He'd been to one of the few commercial colleges in Russia. And actually he came in 1913 with no intention of staying. Then the war broke out and he couldn't go back. He'd been in the Russo-Japanese War and wasn't too keen on that experience.

STAVE: Did your mother work at all?

HANDLIN: Yes, she'd been in the garment industry, and various other jobs, before she married.

STAVE: At what point did you determine that you would become an historian?

HANDLIN: Well, maybe when I was eight years old (laughing).

STAVE: Why? Why did you like history?

HANDLIN: Well, it wasn't a question of liking it, I just knew that that's what I wanted to do.

STAVE: Did you read a lot as a child?

HANDLIN: Yes. We had books and then the library I'm sure was the genuine educational institution in my times. I just read promiscuously. There's nothing exceptional about this, my generation read a great deal. I suppose a lot of it was just what was available on the shelves.

STAVE: How did you go about choosing graduate school and what kind of training did you first get at Brooklyn College?

HANDLIN: Well, it was mostly worthless but there was one historian who was very important to me—Jesse Clarkson. He taught Russian history.

STAVE: What kind of approach did Clarkson take? This was in the thirties?

HANDLIN: Yes, about 1934. He was a post-Marxist. I don't remember but I should imagine he got his start in the early twenties and his first books had kind of a class angle approach to them. He also translated a history of Russia which is still a very good one by an early Marxist named Pokrovsky, who then ran into trouble with Stalin and was discredited. And for all I know, that may be the point at which Clarkson also changed. Anyway, the first volume of this thing was published and the second one never appeared. But more than the particular approach he took, it was his kind of critical thinking that really started me.

STAVE: In college did you do any work on immigration? Were there any courses in what we'd call ethnic history?

HANDLIN: I don't think so. It was not a subject then. In fact, I wasn't particularly interested in American history.

STAVE: In going to graduate school and coming to Harvard—why that choice?

HANDLIN: Oh, basically I came to do medieval history and this was the place to do it. Haskins at Harvard got sick and retired. Then I floundered around for a while. To me it was always a matter of whom you worked with. Schlesinger seemed to be the kind of person I wanted to work with.

STAVE: I assumed you took his courses. In the second edition of *The Uprooted*,[1] the recent edition, you talk about the fact that one day you walked into his office and he had a copy of a book on the racial history of Boston.

HANDLIN: He had a thesis that somebody else was doing—a fellow named Herbert Hill who taught at Dartmouth. Schlesinger had this letter from him saying he didn't want to go on with the thesis, so I did. Those were the days they didn't know about "ethnic" or use the word racial precisely.

STAVE: Would this have appealed to you if you were Oscar Handlin who was not the son of an immigrant from the Ukraine?

HANDLIN: I don't see why not, because certainly there was no or very little linkage between my experience and the experience of a family of Irish peasants. And I didn't know anything when I started.

STAVE: Do you think not knowing about the city that you worked on was helpful to you? Could you have written a book about New York as easily or as well?

HANDLIN: I think so. I think in some ways New York would have been more interesting. It would have been more difficult and it would have been a bit more complex as a city; many more materials. For instance, even on Boston I had to depend often on what was in New York newspapers, so that I got reflected images. I had no particular rapport with the city.

STAVE: How did you approach the topic? I mean what kinds of things did you do? How long did it take to write the dissertation, and then to publication? It was published in 1941.

HANDLIN: Well, I didn't waste any time choosing subjects. I came in 1934. I took my general examinations in the early spring of 1936, so I began right away. That's one of the great virtues of not wasting time which I try to tell people about. By June of the next year I cleaned up a lot of the sources here. In the summer I went to Washington to look at census reports. Then '37, '38 I spent in Europe at the British Museum. That was not a period of intense work but anyway then I started writing. So really it's less than five years, maybe four and a half.

STAVE: Was the dissertation changed much for the book? Was there much revision?

HANDLIN: A lot of the apparatus was condensed and some of the text was cleaned up. There was no basic change in the structure.

STAVE: You said that you used census records. Of course, today the use of census records has become a hallmark of the so called new urban history. Here you're doing it in the late thirties. Several questions: what put you on to the census records? Why did you feel that this would be the appropriate source to use for the type of thing you were studying?

HANDLIN: Well, I wasn't altogether the first. Charles Wesley used it some. But I knew I had to get back of the aggregate sums. Of course, we didn't have computers. We had to count on our fingers. It had to be done.

STAVE: You say you knew you had to get behind the aggregates. Was this on the advice of Schlesinger? Was it intuitive on your part? Did someone say, take off to Washington to look at those census manuscripts?

HANDLIN: No, actually I don't think Schlesinger had used material like this himself. And the only people who were using these schedules were genealogists. But, of course, Boston, Massachusetts had had good censuses. As a result, I had published aggregates on the kinds of questions that I was thinking about.

STAVE: In the introduction to *Boston's Immigrants*,[2] you say that you were trying to explain the intimate lives and deepest feelings of humble men and women who never left formal records. Translated into 1960s history, you were writing history from the bottom up, as many of the new left historians claim that they are finding the inarticulate, the anonymous Americans. In a sense, you are the vanguard of this movement.

HANDLIN: Well, I don't know whether I'm the vanguard or not (laughing) but it was something I was looking for early on compared to what other American historians were doing. I think Schlesinger was sensitive to this kind of question. He liked the results but he didn't know how to get at it. He certainly was encouraging and pushing it. The kind of people who had treated this material earlier were sort of folklore types. There were no models to follow. I've had mixed feelings about it since.

STAVE: Can you tell me what these mixed feelings are?

HANDLIN: Well, I think a lot of it involves a projection and romanticization of people. It's a very tricky thing. I don't know the precise formula, but whenever you're dealing with oral materials you have to take into account the changes in the transmission of information and attitudes and then the relationship of the historian to the material. It's much more fragile.

STAVE: Could you explain how you avoided the romaticization of the groups and people that you were dealing with, as opposed to someone who has written in more recent years, in the last decade or so?

HANDLIN: Well, I'm not sure I succeeded but I tried. In the first place you have to keep a distance between yourself and the subject. Avoid the temptation of saying how would I feel if I were in that situation and keep thinking how did they feel in that situation. The most important thing is to have a sense of context of the whole social environment which is a way of controlling impressions that you derive from these odds and ends.

STAVE: Isn't there a necessity to empathize? There's one place in *The Uprooted* where you talk about the boy walking up the dark staircase on Columbia Street, apparently a tenement. You're talking about yourself I presume? And this gave you empathy with the peasant and the kind of world the peasant was from.

HANDLIN: Right. That's where it becomes tricky because there's a line between empathizing and identifying. That's why I said there's not a formula but you have to be careful.

STAVE: Let me ask you about your Pulitzer Prize winning study *The Uprooted.* The form of *The Uprooted,* of course, led to a good deal of reaction in the historical profession—the unfootnoted form, the italicized material, and so on. You obviously still feel that this was the most effective approach to *The Uprooted* because your second edition adheres to this.

HANDLIN: Right.

STAVE: Could you elaborate on this feeling?

HANDLIN: I don't want to read back attitudes of a later period. I have come to believe that a lot of footnoting is an empty ritual anyway because people aren't going to check up on your footnotes and verify them. That doesn't change the estimation of the book or its intrinsic value. I still use footnotes. But it depends on the subject matter. In *The Uprooted,* I could have had a line of footnotes two inches deep on each page, but I don't think it would have persuaded anybody who wasn't persuadable. I think in certain kinds of monographic articles, or in certain kinds of books, it's well to use footnotes. It's a way of exposing kinds of evidence on which the argument rests. I would like to see the footnote rehabilitated to its proper use and made respectable by having people use them. As I said, I'm not convinced that anybody who reviews in the *Journal of American History* or the *American Historical Review* actually checks the footnotes.

STAVE: Do you think there was a time when this was done?

HANDLIN: Yes, it was done when the materials were much narrower and restricted and everybody was using the same sources. Therefore everybody knew what was in them and referred back to the source. I really don't believe it's done very much now and in fact, when it is done, it's regarded as a sort of an unfair labor practice—checking little details.

STAVE: You've done some other books that had urban themes to them. In the late fifties you published *Al Smith and His America.*[3] Did the genesis of that book have anything to do with the fact that a Catholic was on the horizon for president?

HANDLIN: No, that series was planned around 1950 and Kennedy wasn't in the picture. He really wasn't taken very seriously until 1957, 1958.

STAVE: Has your assessment of Smith changed at all in the past fifteen or twenty years, with the new literature that's come out? Have you rethought the whole 1928 situation regarding Smith's career or what he represented?

HANDLIN: I haven't gone very deeply into any of that stuff since I finished the book, but I have read the biography by Josephson.[4] I haven't seen anything I particularly liked, except maybe a suggestion that he had an Italian grandfather. That's interesting. It wasn't anything he was conscious of. But anyway, on the elections, there might be differences of shading and emphasis of different elements in the defeat. I don't know how anyone could have believed that the outcome was entirely anti-Catholic, or even that the anti-Catholic theme could be separated from the prohibition theme. Certainly I didn't believe that had Hoover run against McAdoo, it would have been very different.

STAVE: In *Fire-Bell in the Night,*[5] you made what seems to be an interesting prediction in light of Boston today. This was that the problem of civil rights would affect the urban north and the urban south and not so much the traditional south. If we look around us, I think this is something that has occurred. At the time, what gave you this kind of perspective? Why did you see the urban centers as being the prime place of civil rights conflict?

HANDLIN: (laughing) Well, I don't think it was very difficult to see. There are people who are blind in their ideology and their preconceptions. I think it was perfectly evident right then. In the fifties nobody was thinking about these issues. When I was in the social relations department here, I began by giving courses in urban history and race prejudice and conflict. But everybody thought that they were a historical problem. There wasn't a single significant effort to deal with these questions. The foundations especially were interested in culture and personality and international relations and so on. I don't think there was any important serious student of contemporary society who was thinking of questions of ethnicity in that decade. Well, after the big outburst in the early sixties, a lot of people rushed up to the subject and looked at it. The *Fire-Bell* book was not a particularly historical book, but I had to find a way of keeping up with what was going on because I was interested in what was relevant.

STAVE: In several of the interviews I've done previously, you are mentioned as a formative factor in one way or another. Stephan Thernstrom, Sam Warner, and Sam Hays all talk about your influence. Hays mentioned that he was starting out for a social science degree; you said he'd be better off being a historian and then move into other social sciences. The topics that Warner and Thernstrom perceived were topics of interest to you. You've obviously influenced a great many people in the field of history today—social history, urban history. Was there any kind of philosophy you pursued in working with these people?

HANDLIN: First, you have to have the good raw materials (laughing). I was lucky in having good people come. Second, I let them do what they wanted to do. And third, most of my teaching came from listening. I let them talk and I asked a few questions. I never tried to develop a school, have people who would implement, test or elaborate on anything that I was doing. In Europe, France, Germany, it works differently. I don't think it'd be possible in this country anyway, given the nature of the universities and graduate schools. And I don't think it's desirable, either. There are other people—Bernard Bailyn, Robert Cross, and others—in completely different fields. I told them to do something that would work.

STAVE: So you taught, as you say, by listening. Was there an interplay? Did Harvard students affect your own work?

HANDLIN: Sure. I always learn from my students. It was very important to be stimulated by students.

STAVE: Thernstrom's *The Other Bostonians*[6] seems to answer some of the questions you raised in some of your writings about mobility. In Thernstrom's writing, was there a good deal of interplay on your part?

HANDLIN: Less in that book than in his first.[7] One reason he chose Newburyport was the thinness of the Newburyport survey by social anthropologists. Years ago I had criticized that. That doesn't mean that he was just documenting my criticism. I suggested that here was a place where he would be able to test historical materials to give him some conclusions, in a different way. But how he did it and what he did was his own.

STAVE: With respect to urban history, generally, *The Historian and the City,* which you edited, came out over a dozen years ago.[8] In the preface, it's written that "even now it is difficult to define the subject matter of urban history, to disentangle that which is peculiar to the evolution of the city from that which is characteristic of the culture as a whole. But a growing number of scholars have become aware both of the necessity and the complexity of studying the urban past." Do you think things have changed much in the past dozen years? Have we reached this disentanglement?

HANDLIN: Well, whenever you develop a subspeciality like urban history, it begins to generate its own rules. There is rarely a formal definition; that just emerges from the kinds of books and contributions that are considered urban history. I tend to deplore the development of these subspecialties in general. Ethnic history, urban history, western history—they result in a kind of fragmentation. But that doesn't mean that good books aren't written in those fields. People working in these fields have to be specially sensitive to the artificial character of the boundaries.

STAVE: In your essay in *The Historian and the City*, you wrote about the central problems of urban history in terms of space, in terms of time, in terms of organization of society.[9] Have you gone further in your thinking about this than when you wrote back in the early sixties? Do you see any other problems for urban history?

HANDLIN: I don't know. I have been working on the history of certain large cities in the nineteenth century. That's different from what is more generally considered urban history, in the sense of not being concerned with all cities but just the very large ones. There are special kinds of problems.

STAVE: Could you tell me a little more about that for a minute? Which large cities are you dealing with?

HANDLIN: Well, it's not an altogether arbitrary standard. I'm dealing with the kinds of cities that have a population that is metropolitan in the nineteenth century. I'm dealing with English, French, German as well as American cities, seeing what makes them run.

STAVE: What do you mean, what makes them run? What are the questions that you're asking?

HANDLIN: Well, some of the questions are elaboration on things that I mentioned in the essay, but the central theme that I'm trying to get at—and it's still a long way from being finished—is the development of the habits, conventions, relationships of those who live together. I find that there are cultural and national circumstances of life under these conditions, but more important there are transnational, cross-cultural ones.

STAVE: This is very interesting. This is very much like *The Uprooted*, where you write about the common experience of immigrants and migrants, regardless of where they come from. Now you're saying that the experience of someone who lives in a metropolis is a result of the metropolitan experience.

HANDLIN: That's what I'm asking about this. But I'm not sure how it's going to come out.

STAVE: What sorts of habits, customs, and activities do you see possibly resulting from the fact of living in a metropolis?

HANDLIN: I don't want to state these conclusions prematurely, but the simple fact that people don't kill each other. When you look at the twentieth century—particularly a late-twentieth-century city—and see the problems, it's amazing that it worked as well as it did in the nineteenth century. You imagine the first subway trains and people have never traveled in this fashion before and soon they're all piled in. Why didn't they kill each other? (laughing)

STAVE: It's interesting. Glen Holt has an essay about mass transit in America, in which he suggests that mass transit did create some conflict between classes that met on trolley cars and that there were problems such as pickpockets at the rail stations.[10] Boston is faced with massive problems today—of course Boston's population is not quite the population that you're talking about. Or is it?

HANDLIN: I would deal with the metropolitan area. Boston is an artificial construct.

STAVE: In terms of the racial situation, is there more similarity or difference between this Boston and the Boston of *Boston's Immigrants?* How would you judge the difference over the century?

HANDLIN: Oh, it's very different. I'd say it's different in almost every respect.

STAVE: Does the racial factor make a major difference as opposed, say, to an ethnic factor?

HANDLIN: No, I don't think the racial factor is critical. I think there's been a breakdown in understanding. It's hard to get these answers because I'm not through yet, but that's what I'm trying to find really. Say, if you looked at 1910 there must have been plenty of antagonism in New York. It was not as serious and there was much more acceptance of the city as a kind of hope for the future and its ability to work.

STAVE: Is this a matter of perspective? In a sense, you're living through some very bad conditions. Do you think that the Brahmin who lived in Boston in the 1850s and 1860s—the nineteenth century generally— would havé had the same feeling that the end is approaching, that there has been a breakdown of consensus?

HANDLIN: Well, I don't think so. They didn't say so. There were immigration restrictions, they had more options open to them than people right now and didn't exercise them. And they put their money into the region. They had this tremendous investment, founding a park system because people believed it would help make the city work. They invested in the city which they are reluctant to do now.

STAVE: You mentioned in *The Historian and the City* that we need fewer studies of the city in history than of the history of cities.

HANDLIN: That's a general point of view I have, which applies to cities and other things—that is, that the way you get furthest is by intensive monographic studies and I would like to see more histories of particular places and particular times.

STAVE: You talk about intensive monographic studies and yet *The Uprooted,* which is probably your most famous book, was the antithesis of that.

HANDLIN: Right, that's a very different kind of thing, but I don't think I could have written *The Uprooted* without ever having written *Boston's Immigrants.*

STAVE: Which of your own works is your favorite?

HANDLIN: (laughs) I love them all.

STAVE: Was there any one that you enjoyed doing more than the others?

HANDLIN: No, I hated every one (laughs).

SONDRA STAVE: If they were so difficult to do and you hated every minute, what drove you to do as much work as you did?

HANDLIN: Have to (laughs).

SONDRA STAVE: From one who lives with a historian rather than one who is, it seems that there's a certain amount that one is required to do because one has to, but then there's a certain amount beyond that one does because of some pleasure or compulsion. It's not from outside, it's from inside.

HANDLIN: Yes, it's a compulsion. There are all these things that have to be done and they're not being done by somebody else, so it's up to you. You have to. It isn't always pleasurable.

STAVE: Well, then, in a sense you're saying you like to work. I mean it's hard to work.

HANDLIN: I don't like to work, I have to work (laughs).

STAVE: One of the themes that stands out in your work seems to be the family. But, when *Boston's Immigrants* was reviewed initially by William White, he pointed out that the family was ignored. Was it that sort of criticism which moved you to examine the family? It appears in "Generations" in *The Uprooted* and it appears in *Facing Life.*[11]

HANDLIN: I just didn't know how to handle it. I was, of course, conscious of the review by White, and he was right, but I didn't know how to handle that kind of thing. It was there and it was very difficult. So, it got lost. Some of what I said in *The Uprooted* was based on things that should have been in *Boston's Immigrants.*

STAVE: The *Journal of Urban History* recently had an issue on the urban family. Family history is another one of the subfields in social history. Do you see this as the most significant institution in our society?

HANDLIN: Well, certainly it's a significant institution, but the point is that in the forties and certainly earlier, nobody had done this sort of thing. And if you looked at the old books, like Calhoun[1][2] and others, they were dealing with ideas about the family. I just couldn't write a full book about an institution that wasn't treated adequately.

STAVE: Do you think it's being treated adequately now by younger scholars?

HANDLIN: They are beginning. It's still hard. I mean, for instance, now with computers you can do all kinds of things that would have been extremely difficult twenty-thirty years ago. If you were to count family size, the number of people in a household, and things like that, it'd be murder. And there are people handling that kind of stuff. I expect to see what they can make of it.

STAVE: Finally, in the book *Facing Life,* you were critical of youth, universities, and programs such as black studies. From the perspective of 1975, how do you see your analysis of 1970?

HANDLIN: It's too mild because the full extent of the damage is only beginning to be apparent. The only reason for having a university is this—to advance and transmit learning. That business is very clear.

STAVE: Do you think a black studies program could advance and transmit learning?

HANDLIN: Well, I could conceive abstractly it would. But I don't think that those which have been developed, say the one here, could do that.

STAVE: Take something like urban studies which has become increasingly popular in recent years. Do you see that in the same light?

HANDLIN: Well, I don't object to the interdisciplinary quality of black studies. I object to the fact that it doesn't—or I object to it when it doesn't—have a scholarly base, and when it's disconnected. I object to other kinds of ethnic studies as well. If you had an urban studies program that was somehow designed to be action oriented, or to justify or develop pride in a particular urban place, I would object to that too.

STAVE: With that caveat to the practitioners of black and urban studies, let's conclude. Thanks.

NOTES

1. Oscar Handlin, *The Uprooted* (Boston, 1951; second enlarged edition, 1973).

2. Oscar Handlin, *Boston's Immigrants: A Study in Acculturation* (Cambridge, Mass., 1941; revised edition, 1959).

3. Oscar Handlin, *Al Smith and His America* (Boston, 1958).

4. Matthew Josephson and Hannah Josephson, *Al Smith: Hero of the Cities* (Boston, 1969).

5. Oscar Handlin, *Fire-Bell in the Night: The Crisis in Civil Rights* (Boston, 1964).

6. Stephan Thernstrom, *The Other Bostonians: Poverty and Progress in the American Metropolis, 1880-1970* (Cambridge, Mass., 1973).

7. Stephan Thernstrom, *Poverty and Progress: Social Mobility in a Nineteenth Century City* (Cambridge, Mass., 1964).

8. Oscar Handlin and John Burchard, eds., *The Historian and the City* (Cambridge, Mass., 1963).

9. Oscar Handlin, "The Modern City as a Field of Historical Study," in Handlin and Burchard, eds., *The Historian and the City,* 1-26.

10. Glen E. Holt, "The Changing Perception of Urban Pathology: An Essay on the Development of Mass Transit in the United States," in Kenneth T. Jackson and Stanley K. Schultz, eds., *Cities in American History* (New York, 1972), 324-343.

11. Oscar and Mary F. Handlin, *Facing Life: Youth and Family in American History* (Boston, 1971).

12. Arthur Wallace Calhoun, *A Social History of the American Family from Colonial Times to the Present* (3 vols.; Cleveland, 1917-1919).

SELECT BIBLIOGRAPHY OF WORKS
BY OSCAR HANDLIN

Boston's Immigrants: A Study in Acculturation (Cambridge, Mass., 1941; revised edition, 1959).

This Was America (Cambridge, Mass., 1949).

The Uprooted (Boston, 1951; second enlarged edition, 1973).

Adventure in Freedom: Three Hundred Years of Jewish Life in America (New York, 1954).

The American People in the Twentieth Century (Cambridge, Mass., 1954).

Race and Nationality in American Life (Boston, 1957).

Al Smith and His America (Boston, 1958).

Immigration as a Factor in American History (Englewood Cliffs, N.J., 1959).

The Newcomers: Negroes and Puerto Ricans in a Changing Metropolis (Cambridge, Mass., 1959).

The Americans (Boston, 1963).

The Historian and the City (edited with John Burchard; Cambridge, Mass., 1963).

Fire-Bell in the Night: The Crisis in Civil Rights (Boston, 1964).

Children of the Uprooted (New York, 1966).

Facing Life: Youth and the Family in American History (with Mary F. Handlin; Boston, 1971).

Pictorial History of Immigration (New York, 1972).

"The Modern City as a Field of Historical Study," in Oscar Handlin and John Burchard, eds., *The Historian and the City* (Cambridge, Mass., 1963), 1-26.

"The Capacity of Quantitative History," *Perspectives in American History,* IX (June 1975), 7-26.

Richard C. Wade

Richard C. Wade (1922-   ) is Distinguished Professor of History at the Graduate Center of the City University of New York. Previously he taught at the University of Chicago, where he trained many of the leading young historians in the profession today. His own publications include work on the urban frontier and urban slavery, and he serves as General Editor of the *Urban Life in America* series.

A CONVERSATION WITH
RICHARD C. WADE

STAVE: I'd like to start off with a discussion of your background, youth, and family. I've noticed that you were born in Iowa.

WADE: Yes, that's true, but I was taken, when I was three years old, to Chicago. The family stayed very briefly in the north side of Chicago, an area which was largely Irish at the time, and then moved up to Evanston. Later we moved out to Winnetka. My days in grade school were at a Catholic school, St. Francis Xavier, in Wilmette. So my early life was suburban.

STAVE: What was your father's occupation, what kind of work did he do?

WADE: Well, my father was a lawyer by trade, and he came to Chicago and did very well. Then he was the vice-president of the Eskimo Pie Company.

STAVE: One of my favorites.

WADE: He made that into a big, very successful national operation. We had a lot of money in those days. But about 1929 he got bored with the job, and went into what is now television and radio. He made the first table model radios in America. Those were the Aetnas that sold at Walgreens for $9.95. Then he made the Silvertones for Sears-Roebuck—cheap, but, as he always called them, "democratic" so that everybody could afford one. He was also in television. In 1929 they established what was called the Western Television Corporation and they developed early television. When I was just a kid—I was just four or five years old—I remember seeing boxing fights from Milwaukee which were transmitted over the television system. Later my father went into soft drinks and developed a whole new soft drink line. He was the last of the kind of entrepreneurial buccaneers. Even when he was successful he had an eye to do something more and different. He was in and out of business all the time.

STAVE: Now, when did you develop your interest in studying history?

WADE: Well, I went to a Catholic grammar school, and I never much went for history there, but geography interested me. I learned the state capitols—you learned things by rote in those days—I learned those faster than anybody else in my class. We used to have big geography books on China and India and Africa—Catholicism was the universal church and therefore they taught us about those areas. So I had an immense interest in geography and in capitol cities. I knew where Canton or Shanghai was long before other kids. That was one thing. The second thing was that my father had an intense interest in current affairs. There were four newspapers in Chicago at the time and he'd get them the night before—the morning papers—and he'd bring home at 6:00 the evening papers. So I grew up reading the newspapers and it had a very profound influence on me. When I was nine years old I put out my own newspaper; it was called the *Ho Hum Herald,* and this was a little thing that was distributed on the streets and I charged a nickel for it. It was four pages and I typed it up from the machine and everything. My father always made you believe that the world was a big place and that big things were happening, and interesting things, and that was terribly important. I read newspapers. I think that's where I learned to read.

STAVE: In a sociological sense, you grew up in a cosmopolitan household as opposed to one that emphasized the local?

WADE: Yes. And there was also the news. My dad would stop reading the newspaper and turn on the news. He would never miss a news broadcast, and whenever we were in the room as kids, playing around, my dad would shush us when the news came on. So I grew up with a notion of intense interest in contemporary questions.

STAVE: How large was Winnetka at the time?

WADE: When I went to college I used to say: "I come from Winnetka, a town of 13,000, Greater Winnetka—four and a half million." It was 13,000, very small and very wealthy.

STAVE: Was it all bedroom communities?

WADE: Yes. Well, within six blocks of me lived Harold Ickes, Archibald MacLeish, Donald Nelson, the head of the War Labor Board, the son of Henry Demarest Lloyd—it was remote, but it was also a kind of a haven for some national reform figures.

STAVE: Interesting. Your youth seems somewhat similar to Constance McLaughlin Green's. I talked to her not too long ago; she grew up around the University of Chicago with her father a professor there. Well, was your youth totally in what we would call an elite environment? Did you have contact with the children of the "slums?"

WADE: No, we had no contact. We had a small group of retainers who lived in about a five block square area down in Glencoe, just outside of Winnetka. But that was all there was of poverty. Most of the people that we knew were people who had done well and whose children intended to go to college and whose business focus was on the city and not on the local area.

STAVE: In terms of choice of college . . .

WADE: Well, before we get there. One thing that was important to me happened. When I was a Senior at New Trier High School (I had done very poorly in Freshman and Sophomore years), I took a course in American history with the person who ran my homeroom. I just dared not do well because he was my homeroom leader. And so I memorized history. Looking back, it was a dreadful course in American history, but somehow it all stuck. I always had great regard for him. Everybody else in the class was bored. But I memorized and suddenly when I was all through I had some sense of the factual structure of American history. That's one thing. And the second thing is that when I got to be a Senior, we had a fellow who taught sociology. And the first day he said: "Anyone who will work down at the Northwestern University settlement house will get an A in the course." And so I started going down to the settlement house. It was on Milwaukee Avenue on the North Side of Chicago. There I discovered a world I had never known before. This was real poverty. This was in the late 30s, heavily Polish. Though there were all kinds of groups there, it was mostly Polish immigrants. I just got a notion of poverty that I hadn't known before, and that radiates. I only spent one day a week there, a Saturday afternoon, but that made a big difference in my perspective.

STAVE: Now, to get to the choice of college situation.

WADE: You'll never know how I got into the University of Rochester (laughs). I was a tennis player and I thought I was going to the University of Chicago because they were hiring tennis players. But my father said, "What would happen if you broke your wrist?" And so I got worried about this and . . .

STAVE: You mean what would happen in terms of a scholarship?

WADE: Yes. I could have gotten a scholarship to go to college at Chicago or North Carolina, but my father never liked the idea. And finally one day I was talking about school to my principal and he mentioned Rochester. So I said, "That's a good idea, I think I'll go out to the tea they're having and see what it's like." Well, I went to the tea and I thought Rochester was in Minnesota. I really didn't know where it was. They said they would be interested in me coming. I had a scholarship, a full scholarship, to Rochester. I used to play basketball, football, track, and tennis, and this was sort of an all around scholarship that they gave to people with fairly good grades. I was not an outstanding student at all. I think I graduated from New Trier 60th in a class of about 400. I was in the upper part but I was nothing special in high school. In my senior year I got nearly all As but until that time I was not burning up the school—I was on the wrong Dean's list my Freshman year. So I wasn't making any big headway in that sense. But they offered me the scholarship. I do remember them talking more about athletics than scholarship when they gave it to me. But it was a safe thing for me to do. In going to Rochester, I didn't have to keep up my athletics. I had been a tennis bum. Every summer I had spent playing tennis when I was young. I was in the "Junior Davis Cup" and that sort of thing. But I had lost interest. And this seemed like a good way out of that bind. So that's the reason I took Rochester. I didn't know where it was.

STAVE: Were you a History major at that time?

WADE: When I got to Rochester I did very poorly in my Freshman year. I didn't know if I could keep my scholarship at all. The first grade I got at Rochester was a 67 in Geology and I looked up the train schedule back to Chicago. But then I had a person named Arthur May in an introductory course in Western Civilization and he interested me a lot. I think I only got a B, but that was pretty good compared with the other grades I was getting in those days. And so I sort of came to the conclusion that I wanted to be in History, but it was no burning passion. And as time went on I did everything in college except study. I was on the football team, the basketball team, the track team; I was an officer in my fraternity; I was an editor of the newspaper; I went out for soccer—I did anything but study. But I got along. And I got into the Honors Division there which allows you to get out of normal courses and do a lot of writing. That was very good because I did like to write; that's the reason why I went in for journalism with the school paper—I rather liked that. But I was not a very serious student. Then September 26, 1943 I got hurt playing football at DePauw University in Greencastle, Indiana, and I couldn't walk. I was in a C-7 (in the Navy) at the time waiting to be called up. It was an infection of my leg that they couldn't figure out. And I couldn't get around. So I had to sit in my room in the fraternity house and the first thing that I did was to spend two or three weeks learning how to smoke a pipe. After I finished that I picked up a book and I read something that hadn't been assigned, and it was very good. So I told my roommate when he came in, "You know, I just read this book; I think I'll try another."

STAVE: What was the book?

WADE: The book was Harold Laski's *Faith, Reason and Civilization.* It is a dreadful book. But at the time I thought it was the greatest thing I'd ever read. And that was the beginning. I was so far behind. I was 20 years old and I just read everything I could get my hands on. The war pulled away all the teaching assistants from Rochester, so as a senior I was made a teaching assistant in an elementary course in Western Civilization. There I really got interested in history. When it came time for the final examinations in the Honors Division I did very well.

STAVE: Now, in terms of interest in the city as such, there is nothing to point in that direction. Once you started to read after Laski's book, was there much about the city that you got involved in?

WADE: No. I got an M.A. at Rochester because I knew so little I said I better stick around and get a basic background. And when I went to Harvard, I remember the first seminar with Arthur Schlesinger, Sr. I didn't know anything about American history, much less that the city was an important factor. I didn't even know anything about the frontier thesis at the time. He had a seminar in which he asked the class at the first meeting, "I want you the next time to discuss the differences between American and European history." Well, I didn't know much about that either. But the day after I ran across Frederick Jackson Turner and I was terribly taken with him. I thought, "My God, that explains the whole business." We had this meeting the next week and he went around the table—there were twelve of us—and it got to me and I gave a perfect Turnerian discussion of American history, not knowing what Schlesinger's view was at all. I hadn't the faintest idea, never heard of him. And when it was all through he said, "Well, you're all wrong." So I said jokingly, "Oh, if that's wrong, what's right?" He said, "American history is shorter." There then followed the longest silence in the history of the academic world. And he said, "The second difference. . . . " We all lost our power of speech in the seminar. But in that seminar he handed around ten or twelve names which we were supposed to write a little biography about—they were social figures— and I got Charles Loring Brace and the only reason I got that is because somebody got Arthur. So somebody took the only person I knew on the whole list (he had written *Ten Nights in a Bar Room*). Brace, as you know, founded the Children's Aid Society and wrote *The Dangerous Classes.*[1] He introduced me to urban history. I got so interested that I took my spring vacation in New York and went around to the Children's Aid Societies and looked back at the old records. It was going well beyond what was normally done for a seminar paper. But I went around and saw a lot of the early statistics and manuscript censuses and things of that sort. It was at that time I decided what I was going to do for my thesis. I knew I wanted something on cities. Then I began to read various things written on the history of cities.

STAVE: What kinds of things did you read?

WADE: Well, I've forgotten the formal title of Schlesinger's series—the twelve volume *American Life* series. His book is *The Rise of the City.*[2] Also, the series contained a lot of vagrant material having to do with reformers and cities. And I studied reform groups during one period, reading Frederick Howe,[3] who impressed me a good deal at that time. John Spargo and William English Walling[4] I read very early—things of that kind which had a kind of urban focus even though you couldn't really call them urban history.

STAVE: The urban reformer kind of literature that was coming out in the late nineteenth century.

WADE: Yes. I read a lot of that kind of material.

STAVE: Who were your colleagues and counterparts as students at Harvard while you were there?

WADE: Well, that seminar in 1947-1948 started out with twelve and wound up with four presenting the final paper. One of them was Letitia Brown, who was Letitia Woods at the time, another was Dick Smith, now at Ohio Wesleyan, and Phillips, now at college in Austin, Texas. I was the only one in that particular seminar that wound up in urban history. They were mostly in the history of journalism, the history of science, and the history of women.

STAVE: Once you came back from New York and decided that you were going to write a dissertation on an urban topic, how did you decide on the final dissertation?

WADE: Well, I didn't know yet whether I wanted to be a historian; also, I didn't know whether I could be. I was determined not to take a small topic. I would undertake a big topic and if I could do it I would know I was an historian. If I couldn't do it I'd find something else. I had in mind already that American history could be interpreted from an urban viewpoint. Very early I had the notion that there are three things which distinguish American history. It goes back to the first question which Schlesinger had asked, and to which I had so facetiously responded.

There were three things that seemed to be uniquely American. One was the frontier; the other was the institution of slavery; and the third was the party machine.

STAVE: These all appear in your writing at various points.

WADE: When I started out I thought I was going to do a trilogy. I wanted to do a book on each one of these general topics and then I was going to write a general book of American history, a sort of urban interpretation of American history. So I wanted to see the urban dimension of the frontier, the urban dimension of slavery, and then the urban dimension of the party machine, the boss-reform conflict with which you've done so much. And when I was through I wanted to write the book that I'm working on now called *Concrete Roots*.

STAVE: What is that about?

WADE: That's the urban interpretation book.

STAVE: We'll get back to that later.

WADE: I thought that if I couldn't do the first of this series there's no sense in going on. I was fortunate because when I finished my general oral examinations, the University of Rochester asked me to come back. Jobs were scarce then but I was in a peculiarly strong position because the university knew me; they were going into a doctoral program and were anxious to have another American historian. I remember telling Dexter Perkins that I wouldn't get my degree for six years. The thesis topic meant that I could not do anything at Rochester because there were no books there. That meant that every summer I would go to each one of my cities. Later I would have to take a year off to write my dissertation. I said if you're not willing to wait seven years for me to get my degree, then I can't take this job. He was very generous. He agreed that, if I worked out otherwise, the university would wait for my dissertation for seven years. So every summer I went to Pittsburgh or Cincinnati or Louisville. At the end of that I was able to get an S.S.R.C. grant which allowed me time off for a full year to write my dissertation. Doing comparative history you can't write anything until you've got the comparative parts. Therefore, it took that long.

STAVE: Obviously, *The Urban Frontier*[5] has a meaning to most urban historians, but why did you end up choosing those specific cities? Were there any other alternatives that you could have dealt with that you did not select?

WADE: Yes. Going back to the first summer, I went to Cleveland, which I considered as one of the cities. Then I thought about New Orleans, which I found to be connected with these cities. But the unity was the Ohio River, and also the chronological grouping. And also, having by this time read Turner (laughs), I came to the conclusion that if you wanted to test the Turner thesis what would be a better place than just beyond the mountains, from 1790 to 1830? There you could see, in a sort of laboratory of the Ohio Valley, everything that he was talking about. And if he had trouble there then he would have trouble almost anywhere. This seemed to be a prime urban territory, and that's the reason that I went into the Ohio Valley. I had for a moment thought of doing the lake area, because I had come from Chicago, and when I had been playing tennis I happened to go to all those cities by boat. I had thought of that for a doctorate.

STAVE: Now, you say that you thought of the cities. How much feedback did Schlesinger give you once you had selected the topic?

WADE: Well, he was remarkable in this regard. First of all, when I told him what I had in mind he thought of all the problems. He said, "Are you sure your job is secure enough?" He asked me all the very practical questions. The second thing, he said, "Why don't you just take one or two of these cities?" And I said, "Well, if I do, I still won't know what I want to know, which is whether or not I *can* be an historian, and so I think I'd like to do the whole thing." So after we had a couple of conversations, he said, "Go ahead and do it." But he was wonderful. He used to send me postcards when he'd run across an article in the *Ohio Historical Quarterly* on Cincinnati on the history of printing or something. It would happen four or five times a year. It shows the extraordinary extent of his readings in these obscure state journals. He kept showing me that he was paying attention. The other thing was that I would see him in my political life. We were both active in A.D.A. when I was an instructor at Rochester and he was on the National Board. We would meet once a year at the American Historical Association meeting and once a year at the A.D.A. meetings. The A.D.A. meetings were better because he was always bored by the rhetoric and would mention during the meetings that we should talk a little history. In that sense it was constant encouragement. Then said, "I think you can get some money from S.S.R.C." I never thought about it. I'd been out six years and not done one thing, not written anything on anything. But he was right.

STAVE: You developed several major theses in *The Urban Frontier*, of course the main one being the city as the spearhead of the frontier, which some feel can be found in Schlesinger's writings. Was this the view that you started off with?

WADE: No. The irony is that I assumed the Turnerian thesis that the city would come up in the last stage: that you'd have a pathfinder, then the fur trade, then extensive farming, then the intensive farmer, finally the city. I think I'd been captured so much by that poetry that I assumed it to be true. It was only afterwards I found out that, first of all, you begin with St. Louis—the farthest west but the first town. You have to keep thinking about that all the time and the fact that they all were founded within 25 years well beyond the line of settlement, no matter how you draw the line. Louis Wright in one of the first reviews, in the *William and Mary Quarterly*, accused me of parachuting cities out in front of the pioneers. The book was an attempt to explain how that took place. One of the exciting things that happened was that my whole notion of the West was changed.

STAVE: The whole question of imitating the East is another thesis that comes out of that book—how did you develop this? Again, was this a mind-set? Were you looking for this kind of thing?

WADE: I was looking for just the opposite. I had read Ray Billington's *Westward Expansion*[6] and my assumption was that here you have a fresh country with fresh responses to old problems. But what was suddenly striking was the way they emulated the East. In retrospect I came to believe that Turner wasn't right on these questions but in a sense I was a captive of him.

STAVE: Well, would you say you were more Turnerian than Schlesingerian in the midst of writing this book, if you could measure such an influence in retrospect?

WADE: About Schlesinger—what I always like about him was his skepticism about conventional views. He was, most people thought at the time, *the* establishment, almost a one-man establishment. But it is interesting that he was always quizzical. And the first moment he found that I began to produce things he'd never thought about, then he sort of turned in a friendly way to encourage me some more. And I think that it was not so much that I had a notion that this was Schlesinger versus Merk. It was never that. In fact, they had a very cordial and congenial personal relationship; I never got any sense that there was a big fight between Merk and Schlesinger or Turner and Schlesinger. Most of the things Schlesinger said about Turner in the seminar were quite favorable. Dan Aaron did his thesis on Cincinnati from 1810 to 1850, which is an anti-Turnerian tract,[7] but I didn't read this until after I'd finished my work so I didn't really realize the ideological contest that I had been involved in. I think in that book I only mention Turner once in a footnote and very favorably. All this big controversy was really quite remote from my thinking. I was out there teaching Latin American History and World Communism and American History; they didn't even let me teach urban history until 1956. I was teaching everything but. So I never had any feeling that my dissertation was dropping any bombshells. I wouldn't have been comfortable if I did.

STAVE: You say you taught urban history in 1956 for the first time. I find this interesting; it's an early time to teach urban history, in the context of 1975 at least. What kinds of reading materials did you use in 1956?

WADE: Well, I always used Tunnard and Reed. I alw. ays thought that they gave a kind of overview in *American Skyline.* [8] It gave its own kind of periodization and its own interpretation, limited as it is. Moreover, living in Rochester I had Blake McKelvey's books [9] so the students would have a sense of the town in which they lived. That was always a critical part. Then I used a lot of novels, partly because there was a dearth of good books on the social science side, and also I wasn't quite sure what I wanted to do. My own framework was uncertain, hence I had trouble with my reading lists. I thought it would be hard to get students in urban history so I sugared the pill a bit by putting in a lot of novels that students would like. My introduction of urban history at Rochester was so popular that I could drop off Latin American history. From the beginning I could see that the generation of students coming up were interested in urban history. It was what students wanted. They didn't like frontier courses any more and equated them with cowboys and Indians. A lot of them knew the conventional emphasis on diplomacy, presidential elections, and labor by the time they got to college because they had much better high school textbooks. They were just anxious to get to something else, especially at Rochester where most of the students came from cities or suburbs. I remember I used Turner's essay on the frontier, Louis Wirth's essay on urbanism as a way of life, and O'Henry's "Voice of the City" as an introduction. I used a lot of the University of Chicago sociology—Park, Burgess, Wirth, etc. [10] I used Frederick Howe's *The City: The Hope of Democracy.*

STAVE: You said that you had desired to write a sort of trilogy. Your frontier book was well received in general, then you moved on to the slavery book. Now was this part of your game plan—*Slavery in the Cities?* [11]

WADE: Well, I bumped into that precise topic in Louisville and Lexington and St. Louis. It happened that three of the five cities in *The Urban Frontier* were in slave territory. And I remember talking to Arthur Schlesinger who was then writing a new introduction, a long and a wonderful introduction, to Olmsted's *Cotton Kingdom.* [12] As early as 1957 I told him that it didn't look to me as though slavery in Louisville and Lexington was anything like I presumed it was elsewhere. He replied, "Well, you know I've just been working on it and I don't think there's anything new in there." But I kept it in the back of my mind, and the more I worked on *The Urban Frontier* the more it seemed to me that there was something there. I didn't know whether that was just a border city phenomenon or whether it would appear in other Southern cities as well. So I concluded that I wanted to do something on slavery and cities but I didn't know exactly what. I already had the notion that urban slavery was quite different than rural slavery, and that the urban perimeter of the South (because the cities were always on the edges) minimized its visibility as a Southern institution. In Louisiana, scholars all said, "Well, you know New Orleans is special," and in South Carolina they said, "Well, you know Charleston is different," and in Virginia they said, "Richmond is the state capitol." Everyplace you looked at a city it was said to be "different" from the rest. Well, in a sense, that was true. But the object was to examine the role that the city played in the major themes of American history. It doesn't seem, I suppose, such an obvious encore to *The Urban Frontier* but it was to me. In fact, I began to accumulate some of the notes for *Slavery in the Cities* even before I started the book.

STAVE: There is a connection between the two with some of these themes repeating themselves, as you pointed out. In *Slavery in the Cities* I think one of the major points concerns segregation, why it occurs in these cities, and the concept of fear developing. What was your thinking in developing this notion say, after 1845? Why the difference from the earlier period?

WADE: I began with C. Vann Woodward's notion and assumed that no segregation had occurred in the cities at all.[13] I was simply trying to show that slavery was transformed as an institution by its urban setting. In examining the institution of slavery in the cities, I saw the transformation clearly from 1820 to 1860. The change of status from a question of slavery to one of color was a change which minimized the freedom of the free black and maximized to some degree the independence of slave owner. I had not anticipated that. I always assumed that segregation began with the Jim Crow laws more recently; I had no reason to question that. It's just that it seemed to me when I got into both *The Urban Frontier* and *Slavery in the Cities* and lived in these cities for three or four or five years, that there are certain things about the shapes, the forms, the streets, the layouts, and the houses that give you a feel for the city. This is seldom true for someone who is writing about a more remote time and place—few things are left. In some cases an awful lot is left. I watched race relations in these cities and looked backwards on certain things. That's when I began to isolate architecture and see it as a social setting as well as buildings.

STAVE: The way the house lots are set up?

WADE: Yes. You walk into the yards and find the slave house still there. You can just stand there and turn yourself around and it's a chilling experience. You know what it must have been like with those high walls and endless masonry. The only way out is through the big house. Then there is that sense slaves must have had when they walked outside and into the wider, less constrained world of the city.

STAVE: The physical structure of social control, in a sense.

WADE: Yes, and you just sort of got a feel for it. If all the written documents had been available in Chicago, if I didn't have to go south and live in those cities, I don't think the book would have been the same.

STAVE: So you feel that the historian has to have the presence of the area that you're dealing with?

WADE: I think that means a lot to both those books. You stand at the dock on the waterway at St. Louis and turn around and see the cathedral; just beyond is the court house where Dred Scott was first convicted. There's something about that; you get a sense of the scale of things from this block to that block. It takes some of the abstractness out of history.

STAVE: Do you advise students who are doctoral candidates writing dissertations to go down to where they're writing about? Is this a normal process?

WADE: Yes. In some seminars I even went so far as to say, "One of the things you're going to do in this seminar is write a biography of a block. I want you to go downtown, see what is on it now, go back to see what was on it before, find the critical moments in the life of this block."

STAVE: Now, at the time *Slavery in the Cities* was published you were teaching at Chicago. You developed a large following of students who have gone on to make a new reputation in terms of urban history. Were you brought in there to develop an urban history doctoral program?

WADE: I inherited a tradition. Bessie Pierce had been at Chicago earlier but had been retired for many years. I think that the department hoped to get a kind of extension of the interest that Bessie had developed. But there had been no courses in urban history for some time. Hence, the students there had no training in it. What was attractive about Chicago was the university's historic interest in urban sociology and urban geography.

STAVE: How many doctoral students have you had.

WADE: I never added them up. But when I left Chicago I had 28 students in one phase, either in my seminar, the last seminar, or in the last phases of dissertations. I am just completing the last of the Chicago dissertations. I would guess about 40 and probably 15 books. And there are about five more coming.

STAVE: The topics for these books—how have they been chosen? Could you just name some of the students who have worked with you and published books?

WADE: Well, let's take some of the cases. Ken Jackson had done a study of the Klan at Memphis State and he came to my seminar. I had run across enough material in Chicago and New York to know full well that there had been a Klan in the cities but it had never been put together. So I suggested he try it out in the seminar. The first part of his book came from that seminar.[14] Take a case like Howard Chudacoff. Howard was a Junior in my undergraduate course at Chicago. He got nothing but As in everything. I arranged with the department to find a system whereby an undergraduate student could take my graduate course and see what happened. Chudacoff got an A as a Junior (laughs). He then got all kinds of scholarships to Harvard and every other place. But he was already interested in Omaha. He was born and grew up there. And so I said to him, "You can get your degree two years faster if you stay here. We'll give you one of those NDEA Title Four's and you'll have lots of money. Unless you have some great desire to go to another institution, you ought to stay at Chicago." He stayed and the first chapter of his book was a paper he did in my seminar. He then took that topic right on through.[15] Thomas Philpott, now at the University of Texas, has a book that's coming out in the Oxford series next year on housing in Chicago. It's going to be a stunner. Tom was an ex-bus driver in Chicago, had gone to Loyola University, and didn't have much prospects, except he had very good grades in history and was interested in neighborhoods. So he did a history of housing in Chicago from 1890 to 1940; it's going to upset a lot of views. He understood neighborhoods; he walked them, he knew them, house by house, street by street.

STAVE: What is the thesis about, what is it on?

WADE: It emphasizes the centrality of race in housing development. It goes far back and examines everyone's view on the question of immigrant neighborhoods as well as the ghetto. He finds that you could seldom find an Italian block or a Polish block and that you had a mixture of people all the time. It also demonstrates the interaction of neighborhood change and public policy. Or take Humbert Nelli. Nelli's Italian, obviously, and reads and speaks Italian well. I'd been interested in having somebody look at the question raised by Rudolph Vecoli's attack on Oscar Handlin. I believed that Chicago would be a perfect laboratory for this test. So the first chapter of that book was written in the paper he did for the seminar.[16] This was true of many of the books that we're talking about. What I tried to do in a seminar was to have a student write on what might be his thesis. Now some people will try something and reject it as a dissertation topic. I tried to get John Alexander, who is now at Cincinnati, to try to do a study of the urban roots of the 55 men at the Constitutional Convention in 1787.[17] Well, I got him to Philadelphia but I couldn't get him to stick on the topic of why the document has a centralized theme and why the cities played such a disproportionate role in its ratification. I always believed in getting a student ahead faster by developing a topic in the seminar instead of doing what I did—waiting until I finished my oral examination and then looking around for a topic. I've done the same thing at CUNY. Gene Moehring is going to have a book soon on who got public urban services first between 1840 and 1880 in New York City. He started it in a seminar.

But in the choice of topics I always try to adjust to the interests of the student first. Carl Abbott, who is now at Old Dominion University in Norfolk, Virginia, wanted to do a study of boosterism in the Old Northwest; I wanted a somewhat different approach. Of course, he won. There is another book coming out next year by Howard Rabinowitz, who's at the University of New Mexico.[18] He's doing race relations in Southern cities between 1865 and 1890, taking the capitol cities—the old and the new, big and small, Richmond, Atlanta, Nashville, Montgomery and Raleigh. He started that in a summer project on one city, and then he took John Hope Franklin's seminar the next year and did another city. In other words, I try to find a student's interest and then encourage it as fast as I can. I have a lot of topics that I have been unable to get students to do. For example, the importance of the telephone in reform politics from 1890 through 1910 is something I've pressed and pressed and had paper after paper in my seminars but nobody has taken the bait for the whole thing.

STAVE: Around 1970 you published an article, "An Agenda for Urban History," in which you listed assorted topics that should be covered.[19] Six years later, how much of that do you see having been covered and what do you still think needs to be done?

WADE: I haven't looked at that article for a long time, but I know that a lot of the topics that I raised there have found historians since that time. The studies of Philpott, Moehring, and Rabinowitz which I have already mentioned deal with items on the agenda. Regarding real estate, Barbara Flint is just finishing a study of the racial impact of real estate practices and zoning legislation. The undercurrent of racism was there very early, both North and South. Barbara Berg, in what may be the most remarkable of all these so far, is working on urbanization and the origins of feminism in the first half of the nineteenth century. I always knew there was something in that subject because I kept running across it all the time. But I had no idea of the strength and articulateness of women in that period. These are just some of the new ones investigating certain areas of that agenda. The article called attention to the centrality of race in the development of cities. It also called for more work on neighborhoods and residential mobility. There's been a good deal of attention paid to this topic since that time, although I don't attribute all that to the agenda—it was a logical emphasis in the field. In fact, I think we've pretty much now done about what has to be done on mobility and it is time to go for other things. One of the really big ones is the relationship between the banking community and the financing of municipal goverment. Perhaps I'm a bit more sensitive here in New York to the topic than scholars elsewhere. But it goes way back. The other big area is what Sam Warner began to work on in *Streetcar Suburbs*—not simply the impact of transportation on the growth of the city, but the whole development of the real estate industry with its connections with the savings and loan banks and the ethnic associations—all that kind of thing.[20] As I said before, we don't have a good historian of real estate.

STAVE: One of the things you mentioned in that agenda article is the use of photography, not simply as illustration but as evidence. This seems to be the case in your book, *Chicago: Growth of a Metropolis*.[21] Do you think, beyond your own work in that book, much has been done with photography?

WADE: There have been a few things. I think Judy Gutman's book on Lewis Hine is a beginning in this direction.[22] She was interested in a variety of sides to Hine as a photographer. Since the publication of *Chicago,* a lot of historians told me what they're doing in various cities with the "dumb" pictures. By a dumb picture, I mean one that was taken for a purpose quite extraneous to the historian's use of it. For example, if you bought a house on the west side of Chicago in the 1920s, a professional photographer would go to the newly developed subdivision and take pictures. Then he would try to sell the pictures as postcards which the owner could send to friends showing what a nice house he had in a nice part of Chicago. We ran across the remains of a company which did that. This technique provided a unique housing inventory in new residential areas.

In the 1960s I tried to interest the federal government in developing what I called a visual census. Every time they interviewed on a block, I suggested photographers take a picture of the buildings in which the interviews were going on. A combination of those two things would tell you more about the block than just the cold census material. I got ten very good photographers in Chicago who were willing to give the government virtually free time to do a few square miles as a pilot project. We were unable to do it. At the last minute the census bureau got mail happy and decided to change their system. There isn't any library I know that doesn't have thousands and thousands of pictures taken in the nineteenth century. Chicago is a particularly good city, thanks to the *Chicago Daily News* morgue that was handed over to the historical society. I've asked other historians to go to the leading newspapers in their area and see if they have a space problem, and if they do, to encourage them to give to libraries.

STAVE: Some of the books that you mentioned earlier began as papers in your seminars and ended up in the *Urban Life Series* published by Oxford University Press. The *Urban Life Series* has made a significant impact. What's the origins of that, how did it get started?

WADE: Well, it got started initially with some conversations between David Donald and myself. David was at that time an advisor to one of the major publishers and we were thinking of some kind of urban series. But then nothing came of it. And I think David's publisher had in mind books that would sell a little bit better. The idea interested me, and when Oxford asked if they could have the *Slavery in the Cities,* we also talked of a series. We decided on an open-ended series, that is to say, we were just going to publish so long as the field was relatively untouched. Our first contract, I think, called for ten books. At that point we would reassess our situation. We would discontinue if the volumes were not selling at all, or if the books were not making much of an impact on the profession, or if after that ten we had already made the point and it wasn't necessary to continue a series. At the very beginning, I observed that the trouble is not how to begin a series but how to end a series. I didn't want to get into editing books for the rest of my life just because we had a series. So we will conclude the series in 1977 or 1978, after six or seven more books.

STAVE: That would make about twenty, twenty-five books?

WADE: I think it may be exactly twenty-five. We knew they'd almost all be first books. One of the reasons urban history was so weak in the 1960s was that there were few people and the topic was immense. We knew full well that urban history would depend on the next generation. We wanted to encourage those new scholars by the possibility of publication by a major firm. That was the idea—a first generation of monographic work, significantly different from what had been done before.

STAVE: Now, would you say that series is more in tune with what we call the "new urban history" or the "old urban history," if there are such things?

WADE: In the series we tried to get a broad spectrum of interest among urban historians. So there are two books, Knights and Chudacoff, that are directly quantitative; that is to say, we took them for that precise reason.[23] Other books showed some of the new interest in quantification, but in a much less sophisticated fashion. My own theory about the whole question of urban history is that you don't want to define it. The moment you do, then textbooks appear and people begin to think that urban history is this and it isn't that. I was even opposed, and I still am opposed, to a journal devoted to urban history. I think we should have infiltrated the other journals and not made ourselves into some kind of specialty or some kind of special discipline. I think it's much more important to have a good article on cities in the *American Quarterly* than to have even a good four articles in a journal that's read only by ourselves. The idea of the series was to indicate the breadth and endless richness of urban history. The editors of this journal asked me if I would serve on the board. After years of saying I thought a special urban journal was a mistake, I was hardly in a position to serve. I want to add, however, that I think the quality of the journal is very good. But I still think that what we should be doing is keeping our contacts with other people outside urban history and not become self-centered. I think of what happened to American Studies in the 1950s. More and more the *American Quarterly* attracted a certain kind of article using literary sources. Soon it became a very predictable and less interesting journal. I think we ought to be much more ecumenical and nurture our contacts with other disciplines. I think urban history is too big for a journal. But, back to the point. I don't know what the new urban history is and I don't know what the old urban history is. The only thing I can see that is new is the interest in quantification which is, after all, not history but methodology. To that extent, it is new. But when you look at the writings of the "new" urban historians they are not dealing with topics which are different from a more traditional interest. I don't see any subject that wasn't in Arthur Schlesinger's seminars in the 1940s.

STAVE: Well, with quantification, how valuable a tool do you think it is?

WADE: Well, I'm glad you asked me that after *Time on the Cross*[24] (laughs). In *Time on the Cross* the authors say that they have discovered real estate conveyances in New Orleans. I told them where, since I used 8,000 of them in *Slavery in the Cities;* they used 800. I told them that the same thing happened in Kentucky with quite different outcomes. I also told them if you're going to get into an argument about the decline of urban slavery (at that time they were saying there was no decline in slavery in the cities, now they speak of "the relative decline of slavery in the cities"), that one of the interpretive questions is what led people to sell slaves out of the city when they could have made more money selling them in the city. The price of urban slaves was always higher than the price of other slaves. You could quantify that. And you can quantify some aspects of the crisis in discipline. But you'd have to sit down with the newspapers for forty years in eight cities, look at that mayor's court record every day to see how many cases of blacks were being brought in and why—for lack of papers, for illegal assemblages, for pilfering, for "being out of place," for hiring their own time, for living away from their masters—for all of these things. That's quantifiable. But you have to sit down and do it. And I thought that if they'd just take the proportionate cost of police protection in a city budget and compare it with Northern cities, you'd begin to find some quantifiable evidence of discipline problems. But they had this narrow fix that the only issue was whether slavery was profitable or not profitable. Therefore, even with all the sophisticated (or at least I thought it was sophisticated until I read recent critiques about it) apparatus, I don't think that book does anything that cannot be done without quantifying. That is to say, if you say it was profitable, well L. C. Gray said it was profitable in 1933.[25] He said it in a much more sophisticated fashion; it was profitable where you had good land and good management. Slavery was less profitable in South Carolina than it was up the Red River. To me that was a much more sophisticated way of doing it.

STAVE: What about quantification in terms of mobility studies? You alluded to the fact that you think that perhaps they've gone as far as they can go.

WADE: Well, I don't know. I think now we're just adding city upon city. I think the fascination for mobility as a topic is diminishing; at least I've found that I'm learning less and less while reading more and more.

STAVE: What about quantification and conceptualization in terms of your own work? If the new urban historians are interested in methodology and conceptualization, do you see conceptualization coming out of your work in a broad sense? In *The Urban Frontier,* you talked about an index of urbanization. Has this been carried through in your work?

WADE: Well, that book covered the period to 1830 in an area which started with nothing and began to develop cities. That index was designed to tell when you had a genuine urban phenomenon. I tried to use such things as the appearance of the business directory which suggests that a city is now too big for people to know everyone else, or to be able to shop conveniently without having some kind of help. So I took that as being an almost self-conscious description of urbanization. One of the other indices at that time was the separation of work and residence, something you could also do out of business directories. I also thought that the broad fracture between people who have earned money in one area and put it into another indicates a much broader economic structure than before. But the idea was largely confined to the early period when cities were being born. I made a distinction for a lot of reasons around 1812. The war had some influence on it; the appearance of the directories had another. There was also a good deal of evidence about the separation of work and residence. The residential part, I think, is one of the most important untouched matters for the urban historian. There's been a tendency to emphasize occupation, age, family, ethnicity, or religion. I believe that we need work on residential mobility. I think that if a man has $50,000 and decides to live in Lake Forest, Illinois instead of Hyde Park it tells you an awful lot about that man.

STAVE: But don't you think that residence is determined by all of these other factors? In other words, the reason that they'll live in an area is not simply because they can afford it, but because they're drawn to that area by social and cultural factors. Then you end up with a certain kind of person in Lake Forest, and that residence is a function of sociocultural factors.

WADE: Well, okay. But the choice of a place to live is about the only time we have any freedom of expression left. We have no choice about our age; we have no choice about our sex; we have no choice about skin color; we inherit religion; we don't even have much choice about our job unless you're successful. The only time you express yourself is in the choice of residence, and that is what seems to me to gauge the social and political configuration of most American cities. It also explains why the ghetto is such a confining factor to the blacks. Even when they get everything—education, job, income—they still don't have that most important freedom of choice to live where they wish.

STAVE: Well, this is an important point and I don't want to drop it yet. I see that residence adds up to a manifestation of everything else, that everything focuses in on residence; but residence, I would argue, is determined by all of these other things. If you just look at the residential variable what you're really saying is this is surrogate for the fact that someone is an upper middle class WASP, rather than the fact that they live in this area and this is an upper middle class area, because the WASP would be in one area. . . .

WADE: But the WASPs aren't in one area, nor are the Italians. We're having some suburban studies done on the Italian migration out of New York from 1920 to 1950, and what is interesting is to see the rapid scattering of that Italian community. The same thing is true with the last studies by the Jewish Committee here in New York. The people living in dispersed areas are much larger in numbers than those that live in concentrated areas.

STAVE: Yes, but I'm curious about the question of dispersal. In a sense, are you dispersing to regroup? The model that I see working is the concentration and even when people move out and they move into varied areas, you still, perhaps, within the context of the area would have Jewish people or Italian people living within a few blocks of each other.

WADE: That's not what we're finding. We're finding just the opposite. What would you say would be a concentration?

STAVE: Well, this is what I wanted to ask you. What is a community or a neighborhood? How many people do you need in an area to make it an Italian area?

WADE: I've always asked this question of people who say: "Well, you know that's an Italian neighborhood; that's little Italy." And I ask, "What constitutes an 'ethnic concentration'?" They usually say 50%. I reply that, "In Chicago it's almost impossible to find any blocks that are 50% Italian."

STAVE: Chudacoff to a certain extent found this too in Omaha.[26]

WADE: But the concept of neighborhood was, I think, invented by the Chicago sociologists. They defined a neighborhood as coterminous with primary school districts. The great trouble with the neighborhood concept is its static quality. People define it geographically and then assume that the area is stable, that its people for a long period of time stay around. In fact, people are moving in and out of it all the time. One out of four Americans will have a different address next year. Residential mobility is probably even higher in some cities historically, especially in very young cities.

STAVE: You mentioned the ghetto before, that the ghetto is contained. This is one of the problems as far as blacks are concerned. You wrote an essay on violence in the cities originally done for the National Advisory Commission on Civil Disorders.[27] In that paper you talk about ghetto riots and said that we'd have long hot summers until the ghetto begins to break. Now, long hot summers, the race riots, in that sense, have dissipated; yet the ghetto hasn't broken for black Americans. How would you account for this discrepancy?

WADE: Well, if you were to define a long hot summer as riots, then there are obviously less riots than there were then. If I used the phrase "blacks are frozen" in the ghettos, it would perhaps have been better. The ghettos are quiet now not because there's any larger measure of justice, but because there's a larger sense of resignation. There is little dispersal of blacks into the suburbs and much of what there is can be found in mini-ghettos of the suburb. Brian Berry's recent study found little breaking out of the middle class blacks into white suburban areas.[28] Little has happened since 1960. I'm afraid that the ghetto will fester for a while until a new generation of blacks comes up. Studies indicate rioting is for the young, and they tend to burn themselves out fairly early; it takes some time for another generation to come up. I would take no consolation in the fact that the ghettos seem, from the white perspective, to be tranquil. The other thing that I think has attenuated black urban discontent for a while has been the election of black officials, particularly the mayors of big cities. Even though Ken Gibson hasn't done much to help Newark, there at least is the feeling that City Hall is not just a honky hideout.

STAVE: Earlier you said there's a lot of history to be done on the financial aspect of cities. What's your view of New York City's crisis? You're at the City University which has been affected by it.

WADE: There are more New Yorks down the road unless certain things are done. First is the short-term fiscal crisis. New York had been expanding expenditures by 12 or 13% a year, while increasing revenues by only 6 or 7% a year. You can only do that for a while. It might be said that while the city was doing it the banks never complained one bit; they were prospering by dealing in short-term loans. The second part of the problem is, I hope, also short term. We've got an unemployment rate of around 12%, in fact, some people feel it's really substantially higher, perhaps 18%. That means 24% black unemployment and about 40% young blacks. Well, these are people that are now simply consuming services and money and are producing little for the tax rolls. If we had the fiscal crisis and high employment, my judgment is that we could handle the fiscal crisis fairly simply. But it's the combination that hurts.

But the basic problem of the cities is that they can no longer afford the normal urban services on a shrinking tax base. Tax producers are leaving the city and are pulling industries and commerce to the suburbs. The city became increasingly occupied by tax consumers. Though New York is the most visible case, there are very few cities in the country that can continue to provide what we expect as urban services. That is, I think, the heart of the problem. Even a few places like Houston will face the problem in ten years or more. Generally speaking, three-quarters of the cities over 100,000 are heading toward the same bind. New York's crisis was magnified because, as Veblen would say, of the "penalties of pioneering." New York did a lot of things no other city did—we had municipal health before there was any interest in national health; we had a city university when very few other cities did; we had welfare programs here in the city before there were welfare programs by the national government. We had claims upon our revenue that no other city had. Some cities had one or two of these; Baltimore had welfare, Boston had hospitals, Cincinnati had a city university. But no other place has all of them. When you add those extraordinary burdens onto New York the trouble is very large.

STAVE: These are the causes. What do you see as a possible solution?

WADE: First, the federalization of health and welfare. That would take the biggest burden off New York's back. Then I would say that shifting the burden of education to a combination of state and federal government. A second solution, which I think feasible, is to have the federal government offer bonuses to metropolitan areas which merge city-suburban services. The present revenue sharing undergirds the autonomy of outlying places because they're getting money from the federal government to provide services. If there were genuine bonuses in the areas of water, environment, transportation, and education, the federal government would underwrite efficiencies instead of competition in the metropolitan areas.

STAVE: A few years ago, John Lindsay gave a paper to the NATO conference on cities, talking about the new "national" cities. He came out with the notion of 25 national cities of over 500,000 having a special relationship with the federal government, then within that context having a metropolitan basis for neighborhood systems—sort of a city-state notion.[29] What do you think about that?

WADE: I think it's politically impossible. Hence, I don't care how wonderful the concept might be. As a practical matter, you're having enough trouble getting functional cooperation without asking for much more. But the inner suburbs are now heading for their own crisis, and will have an urgent need for cooperation. The outer ones, of course, will resist it. What is needed now is at least a new formula for revenue sharing which takes into account the larger problems of the bigger and older cities. That's the very least. But so long as you have a system which is basically a per capita system, it's bound to favor the suburbs over the cities because that's where the people now live. And then, lastly, I would want a new housing program which stipulates that whenever a developer of multiunit dwellings gets a subsidy he has to provide 10 or 15% of those units for low and moderate incomes. We now subsidize developers on a large scale. They get less than market mortgages, tax write-offs, or insured loans and a great many other things. In the suburbs, as well as in the cities, the local government puts in the infrastructure at its own cost. Then the developer comes in with almost all the expensive things already done and builds nice houses. This proposal would have to be conditioned on open housing. Hence, I think the ghetto would begin to dissolve in a matter of ten to fifteen years.

What I'm suggesting is a new national strategy for our cities. In the past liberals always shouted for home rule. That made sense up until about 1950 because you had within the city limits all the talent, all the personal wealth, all the commerce, most of the industry. Whenever you had a problem you could put all your resources to bear on it. In that fashion we phased out a good many of our problems from 1900 to 1950. But with the great flight to the suburbs that is no longer possible. Even the very able mayors of the 1950s, probably the best we've ever had, intoned home rule all the time.

STAVE: Any special people you have in mind in talking about the mayors of the 1950s?

WADE: Well, men like Dillworth, Lee, Tucker, West, Morrison, Wagner, Allen, Daley. That was a great set of mayors, but they all ultimately headed toward Washington. When the deeper crisis came, Washington wasn't prepared to accept it and didn't really know what to do. It's first response was simply to throw money at problems. They brought in task forces and formed commissions. They also pumped a lot of money into the obvious running sores—the school systems and the slum neighborhoods. There was no fully developed strategy. It was rather to buy a little time to head off the riots. The Nixon strategy was essentially a suburban strategy. It announced that the urban crisis was over and adopted revenue sharing which favored the suburbs. It was as political a response as Johnson's had been political, except Nixon's constituency was in the suburbs and Johnson's was in the cities. What is needed now is some coherent strategy which understands the long-term crisis of the city and on that analysis begins to develop programs.

STAVE: You mentioned that you were on several task forces, and this raises the question of the academician as public servant, as advisor to politicians, in politics actively. How have you seen your two roles mesh as an academic and someone active in politics on the Democratic side for a number of years?

WADE: I think in some other fields of academic work this would be a perilous thing to be doing. I admire my friends in Literature or Music or Biology who go out of their offices into this foreign world of public affairs and politics. But if you're an urban historian that wrench isn't as much. I learned more about housing as a housing commissioner in Chicago for three years than I did by reading for 20 years. Housing was one of my great interests from the very beginning. But I learned a lot in those three years. I learned enough in the first three weeks to stop saying certain things. But I have always taught in an urban center—in Rochester, St. Louis, Chicago, and New York. I find it complementary rather than contradictory. Of course, there is a drain on your time. And not all meetings are equally productive. I think I've learned a lot about cities by participation. I don't think there's any way to understand that reform-boss antagonism and conflict, for example, without actually having been involved and dealt with it. I mean dealing with it on both sides. The profession tends to be reform oriented. On the whole, I think that the reform bias is a sound one, but unless you have had some contact with the other side in a more fundamental fashion I think it's very hard to get the regular party view without sentimentalizing.

As you know, there's a lot of literature coming out in political science and history about the "good old boss." You wouldn't get that sentimental notion after dealing with him. You might say in the long run he was better than his critics, and maybe the reformers were worse than their own ideals. It's that intersection between the academic world and the public that is enlightening to the scholar. I think it is usually a mistake for academics to hold public office if they want to continue their academic career. I think there are ways of moving in and out of it without totally interrupting scholarship. There are always opportunities for academics to serve in government. I think it's a mistake, however, to get on the payroll. When you are on the payroll you may be asked to do things you don't want to do. That's when the trouble starts—your independence is lost. The minute a scholar loses his detachment he's really of no use to the people who hired him. The independence is essential, it keeps your detachment.

STAVE: You did a review last year on the Moses book—*The Power Broker.*[30] Living in New York now, what impact do you see Moses having had on the city? Do you think it's as broad as Caro laid it out to be?

WADE: The question is to what degree New York's development stemmed from Moses and to what degree from deep historical forces. The trouble with Caro's book is he didn't understand those deep historical forces. He didn't realize that when he was looking at what

Moses was doing in New York the same thing was happening in Chicago without a Moses, or in Atlanta, or in San Francisco. In other words, what happened here was a genuine urban response to the new scale of cities, the impact of the automobile on cities, and the general rise of prosperity over a long period of time. The job of the historian is to find a balance between the individual's shaping of this and the way in which it was shaped by historical forces. Moses always looked like he was shaping things because he was going with the grain of experience, and therefore he was around on top of things. In that sense I think the book overestimates Moses. If Moses had never lived I don't think that New York would look much different. The rubber tire boys were all over the place in every city in the country and in Washington as well. They were basically responsible for the parkways. Moses' invention of public corporations and the undemocratic character and unaccountability is one of the biggest legacies to the city and state and one of the unhappiest. There's room for these corporations but he built into them a secrecy and an authoritarianism that has been picked up by everybody who has sat in one of those plush chairs ever since. The trouble with the book is that Caro doesn't have anything to compare Moses' record with. He doesn't compare it with London or Chicago; he doesn't compare it with earlier New York. He just takes that slice and like a good investigative journalist he finds out a lot about it. Because he has no framework he doesn't distinguish between the important and the merely interesting.

STAVE: With respect to your own writing, is there anything that you would rewrite, anything that you would like to change that you yourself have done?

WADE: I would like to and intend to do more. I think if I were to redo *The Urban Frontier,* I would do more on intercity mobility with city directories. I tried to correct my mistakes on the question of race in *Slavery in the Cities.* In that book I would do more on the question of profitability. I talked about it there for a couple of pages, but since I was assuming the profitability it never occurred to me that I should have, perhaps, developed it a little bit more. I don't differ with Goldin on the point that urban slavery was profitable.[31] I thought I had made that point. And it had been quite flexible—the hiring out system had become in a sense a surrogate wage system. I'm now working on a book entitled *Concrete Roots: Cities in American History.*

STAVE: What will that be looking at?

WADE: That will be from the beginning to the end.

STAVE: Is there any overriding thesis that you can tell us about?

WADE: Well, it has two parts. One is to show how cities actually grow. And the second part of the book, which will continue in a chronological fashion, is what difference this massive urbanization made to American history. It will be, I suppose, an urban interpretation of our historical experience.

STAVE: When do you anticipate completion?

WADE: Well, some time ago (laughs).

STAVE: If you had to choose a half a dozen books in urban history that you most admire, that most influenced you, what would you choose?

WADE: Oh, boy. Well, I would say Schlesinger's *Rise of the City,* Handlin's *The Uprooted,* Handlin's *Boston's Immigrants* (I would say that book had a very great influence). Homer Hoyt's book on land values. This will sound corny—Lincoln Steffens' *Shame of the Cities.* The census of 1880.

STAVE: The census of 1880?

WADE: Yes, I read that like it was a novel. There are a lot of good books recently, but they're not the kind of books that are formative. You're talking about the formative books.

STAVE: Right. Do you have any concluding words for the profession or for younger people in the profession interested in urban history?

WADE: Write on (laughs). One thing I do think is important—and not confined to urban history—is to get rid of this fascination with historiography. History is much richer than anything we think about it. Increasingly, I go to meetings and the papers tell us what so-and-so said and how that was different from what someone else said. You never get what the author thinks. To be sure, it's possible to build a reputation by climbing up some established historian's back. Perhaps it's a fine corrective for the book he's handling, but it doesn't create an alternative way to look at things. When you ask on an oral exam about the origins of the Civil War, for example, the student will give a good review of the literature. Then you ask: "Well, what do you think?" It's often at that time that you discover they thought history was historiography.

STAVE: And not synthesis.

WADE: History is a good deal richer than anything any of us will ever say about it, and I think that's what people ought to know.

STAVE: I think on that note we'll conclude.

NOTES

1. Charles Loring Brace, *The Dangerous Classes of New York, and Twenty Years' Work Among Them* (New York, 1872).

2. Arthur M. Schlesinger, *The Rise of the City, 1878-1898* (New York, 1933).

3. Frederick Howe, *The City: The Hope of Democracy* (New York, 1905).

4. John Spargo, *The Bitter Cry of the Children* (New York, 1906); William English Walling, *Progressivism—And After* (New York, 1914).

5. Richard C. Wade, *The Urban Frontier: The Rise of Western Cities, 1790-1830* (Cambridge, Mass., 1959).

6. Ray Allen Billington, *Westward Expansion* (New York, 1949; 3rd ed., 1967).

7. Daniel Aaron, "Cincinnati, 1818-1838: A Study of Attitudes in the Urban West," Ph.D. thesis, Harvard University (1943).

8. Christopher Tunnard and Henry Hope Reed, *American Skyline: The Growth and Form of our Cities and Towns* (New York, 1956).

9. Blake McKelvey, *Rochester: The Water Power City, 1812-1854* (Cambridge, Mass., 1945); *Rochester: The Flower City, 1855-1890* (Cambridge, Mass., 1949); *Rochester: The Quest for Quality, 1890-1925* (Cambridge, Mass., 1956); *Rochester: An Emerging Metropolis: 1925-1961* (Rochester, N.Y., 1961); summarized in *Rochester on the Genessee: The Growth of a City* (Syracuse, N.Y., 1973). See *Journal of Urban History* (August, 1976) for "A Conversation with Blake McKelvey."

10. Robert E. Park, Ernest W. Burgess, and Roderick D. McKenzie, *The City* (Chicago, 1925); Louis Wirth, *The Ghetto* (Chicago, 1928).

11. Richard C. Wade, *Slavery in the Cities: The South 1820-1860* (New York, 1964).

12. Frederick Law Olmsted, *The Cotton Kingdom* (New York, 1953; originally published New York, 1861).

13. C. Vann Woodward, *The Strange Career of Jim Crow* (3rd rev. ed., New York, 1974).

14. Kenneth T. Jackson, *The Ku Klux Klan in the City, 1915-1930* (New York, 1967).

15. Howard P. Chudacoff, *Mobile Americans: Residential and Social Mobility in Omaha, 1880-1920* (New York, 1972).

16. Humbert S. Nelli, *The Italians in Chicago, 1880-1930: A Study in Ethnic Mobility* (New York, 1970).

17. See John K. Alexander, "The City of Brotherly Fear: The Poor in Late-Eighteenth-Century Philadelphia" in Kenneth T. Jackson and Stanley K. Schultz, eds., *Cities in American History* (New York, 1972).

18. See Howard N. Rabinowitz, "From Reconstruction to Redemption in the Urban South," Journal of Urban History, 2 (February 1976), 169-194, which cites several of Rabinowitz's other articles; also, *Race Relations in the Urban South, 1865-1900* (forthcoming).

19. Richard C. Wade, "An Agenda for Urban History," in Herbert J. Bass, ed., *The State of American History* (Chicago, 1970), 43-65.

20. Sam Bass Warner, Jr., *Streetcar Suburbs: The Progress of Growth in Boston, 1870-1900* (Cambridge, Mass., 1962).

21. Harold M. Mayer and Richard C. Wade, *Chicago: Growth of a Metropolis* (Chicago, 1969).

22. Judith Mara Gutman, *Lewis W. Hine and the American Social Conscience* (New York, 1967).

23. Peter R. Knights, *The Plain People of Boston, 1830-1860: A Study in City Growth* (New York, 1971): Chudacoff, *Mobile Americans*.

24. Robert W. Fogel and Stanley L. Engerman, *Time on the Cross: The Economics of American Negro Slavery* (Boston, 1974).

25. L. C. Gray, *History of Agriculture in the Southern United States to 1860* (Washington, D.C., 1933).

26. Chudacoff, *Mobile Americans;* also see his "A New Look at Ethnic Neighborhoods: Residential Dispersion and the Concept of Visibility in a Medium-Sized City," Journal of American History, 60 (June, 1973), 76-93.

27. Richard C. Wade, "Violence in the Cities: A Historical View," in Jackson and Schultz, eds., *Cities in American History,* 475-491.

28. Brian J.L. Berry, *Race and Housing: The Chicago Experience, 1960-1975* (Cambridge, Mass., 1976).

29. John V. Lindsay, "For New 'National Cities'," New York Times, June 9, 1971.

30. Robert A. Caro, *The Power Broker: Robert Moses and the Fall of New York* (New York, 1974). See review by Richard C. Wade, New York Times Book Review, September 15, 1974.

31. Claudia Dale Goldin, *Urban Slavery in the American South, 1820-1860: A Quantitative History* (Chicago, 1976); also see Goldin, "Urbanization and Slavery: The Issue of Compatibility" in Leo F. Schnore, ed., *The New Urban History: Quantitative Explorations by American Historians* (Princeton, N.J., 1975), 231-246.

SELECT BIBLIOGRAPHY OF WORKS
BY RICHARD C. WADE

The Urban Frontier: The Rise of Western Cities, 1790-1830 (Cambridge, Mass., 1959).

Slavery in the Cities: The South, 1820-1860 (New York, 1964).

Chicago: Growth of a Metropolis (Chicago, 1969), with H. M. Mayer.

"Urban Life in Western America, 1790-1830," *American Historical Review,* 63 (October 1958), 14-30.

"The City in History—Some American Perspectives," in Werner Z. Hirsch, ed., *Urban Life and Form* (New York, 1963), 59-79.

"Urbanization," in C. Vann Woodward, ed., *The Comparative Approach to American History* (New York, 1968), 187-205.

"Violence in the Cities: A Historical View," *Urban Violence* (Chicago, 1969), 7-26. Reprinted in Kenneth T. Jackson and Stanley K. Schultz, eds., *Cities in American History* (New York, 1971), 475-491.

"Historical Analogies and Public Policy: The Black and Immigrant Experience in Urban America," in Margaret F. Morris and Elliott West, eds., *Essays on Urban America* (Austin, 1975), 127-147.

"An Agenda for Urban History," in Herbert J. Bass, ed., *The State of American History* (Chicago, 1970), 43-69.

"The End of the Self-Sufficient City: New York's Fiscal Crisis in History," *Urbanism Past & Present,* (Winter 1976-77), 1-4.

Editor, *Urban Life in America* Series, Oxford University Press.

Editor, *The Rise of Urban America* Series, Arno Press.

Editor, *Metropolitan America* Series, Arno Press.

photo by Rollin Bailey

Sam Bass Warner Jr.

Sam Bass Warner, Jr. (1928-   ) is William Edwards Huntington Professor of History and Social Science at Boston University. His study of urban growth in Boston is basic to the understanding of urban development generally. Warner's other publications also have attempted to establish broad frameworks for the study of urban history and reflect his interest in planning and public policy.

A CONVERSATION WITH
SAM BASS WARNER, Jr.

STAVE: Let's begin by discussing how you got into what we call urban history.

WARNER: O.K. We'll do that. I don't have my vita, so I don't have all the dates. My father was a law professor. After I graduated from Harvard College, I went to law school. I mean, that's what happens. I went a year to Yale Law School. I did O.K., but I really couldn't see being a lawyer. So then I decided to take a try at journalism. I spent a delightful year at Boston University in the School of Journalism. That was just an unbelievable operation. It was a strictly money-making program. I had courses that never met in which I got an "A," but I spent that year essentially courting my wife, who was then studying sociology at Radcliffe. So that was a pleasant year. Then I went into a weekly newspaper in a residential and industrial satellite right outside Boston—Watertown, Massachusetts. My wife and I did that for about a year and a half. We worked night and day, lost a fair amount of money, and decided that that wasn't really going to do it. The problem with weekly newspapers is that you are associated with the merchants; that is, your whole life depends on those local merchants. And the local merchants in a town like Watertown are scattered all over the metropolitan region. They run a series of marginal businesses. Some of them are chains, some of them are not. So it was really a kind of a non-community, a very hard situation. Since I had enjoyed history as an undergraduate, which is just how everybody gets to be a graduate student, I went back to graduate school. I took all the courses that you wouldn't take as an undergraduate because they weren't required then, and they now become required. I took a seminar with Arthur Schlesinger, Sr. That was his last year, and he was what little urban history there was. He was its big promoter. He wrote that book, what's it called?

STAVE: *The Rise of the City?*[1]

WARNER: *The Rise of the City.* It's one decade or two of the series. He had a whole vacuum cleaner approach to history, so it's a very useful series. I still look things up. If you want to know whether there were or weren't weekly newspapers or monthly magazines, or what lengths women's skirts were, or anything, you can just go to that series of volumes and there it is. I don't think he really had a history of the city. What he had was a period and he wrote on the South and the West and he just said the city was the most important event in that time period. Anyway, he was at that time into public health issues, and he had me write a seminar paper on public health, which I enjoyed.

The other seminar I took was with Frederick Merk, who wrote about the West, and I did an extraordinarily primitive quantitative study of the Taylor Grazing Act and the problems of the farmers and so forth. But mostly I just did whatever was required. There was this terrible business about having to have a pre-1600 field so I took Helen Maude Cam's course on English constitutional history, which I hated, but I managed to get through, and subsequently found some use for. Arthur Schlesinger, Sr.'s lecture course proved to be very useful. I don't think anyone would ever teach such a course again. He had this theory that American history unfolded from the Revolution to the New Deal and he divided it into a series of progressive events that got you to the New Deal. In the course of that, he had us reading bits and pieces of everything. For each section, like the Jacksonian period, you would read labor, reform, the West, politics, science; so it was kind of like memorizing a tiny encyclopedia. I think that in the end proved to be useful because I have a little sense of what happened when. But the rest of the courses, it seems to me, were in no way useful to me. You just went to lectures, and most of my work was graded by graduate students, and they graded things hurriedly. Like in the final exam in Arthur Schlesinger, Sr.'s course, there was a question on painters. I had a good friend who was a painter then and I had noticed from the hour exam the way this guy graded was by checking off whether you had mentioned the names and events the professor had mentioned. That was sort of a test of competence. It didn't really matter what the structure of the sentence was, whether you said someone was or wasn't a painter. The big thing was to get that name in there. So I put all the names in, plus my friend's and it was fine. I guess what I'm trying to get to is, except for perhaps Arthur Sr.'s course, the rest of it, it seems to me, was an extraordinarily bad education, just did these reading lists. Despite his encyclopedic approach, Schlesinger did carry a real interest in what we would call "popular history." And that was the useful tone to it. He was interested in everything and that really was useful.

STAVE: Could I interrupt for a minute? What years were these and who were some of your contemporary graduate students?

WARNER: '53 to '59. I got the Ph.D. in 1959.

STAVE: Anyone else in urban history as well as . . . ?

WARNER: No, in fact I didn't know any of the graduate students. That was a problem. I had a very good friend who was in American studies at the time. He was one of my buddies. We talked together all the time. He was a Marxist and that really was helpful, and he was very encouraging as fellow graduate students often are. Being married and having children and being a graduate student is a terrible thing. Right? Your wife is in the position of having this student, like "Who are we? Well, I've got this husband who is still studying and still passing things." It's a completely nonstatus situation for the family. We were having many children at that time, and so the family seemed to absorb a whole lot of my time. Also, since I had lived around that area, we had many friends, and there really wasn't any need for being involved in graduate student life. So I don't really know what it's like to be a graduate student with graduate student friends and all that sort of exchange. We were part of the community. While I was a graduate student, I was involved in municipal reform politics and whatever you do as a plain old citizen of Cambridge. So that in a way was a great educational weakness, since whatever I might have learned from my fellow graduate students, I didn't except for this one friend whose name I mentioned in *Streetcar Suburbs.*[2]

STAVE: Who is that?

WARNER: His name is Lee Halprin. He has been writing a great Marxist interpretation of American literature ever since, and he's never finished it. Nor has he ever got the degree, but he teaches at the New England Conservatory and is presumably still writing this epic. So anyway, I just spent time taking the courses, and the Harvard system was that you take courses to match each field. I took Mrs. Cam to do medieval, and I took Morison to do colonial—he was a very entertaining lecturer. I guess the kind of picture I'm trying to give is that I got an extremely poor education because of the extremely bad teaching and disorganization of the Harvard History Department, and partly because of my own isolation which came from being in the community. I did such unbelievable things. For instance, to prepare for the orals in English history, I read the Oxford histories. Of course, I didn't know any better; I didn't have any other way of dealing with this and so that was my approach. I got the impression that what you were supposed to do was have this sort of general mastery and I suppose that was reinforced by studying with Arthur Sr. And so the Oxford history looked just about perfect to me. I also had to pass a language requirement, and I'm terrible at languages. I literally spent a year doing the languages. It took me a summer to get the French, and then I hired a tutor in Spanish, started in Spanish, by those cards, and on the eve of the exam, I think I knew 5,000 Spanish words. I could not speak Spanish. I could hardly read it, but in any case I passed the exam. But that was a whole year out of my graduate training.

Between this sort of poor approach to graduate education and teaching, I think I did rather poorly on the oral exam. I really didn't have any kind of sense of what history was about. I liked it, seemed to do all right in it, and I could get "A's" in all these courses, but I didn't have any formed sense of it except from a series of conversations that were developing with this fellow graduate student. He had a notion that there was an American tradition and that it was capitalist and that it was destructive, and that looked like one way of organizing the material. Anyhow, once I passed the exam, the question became one of what I was going to do for a thesis. Arthur Schlesinger, Sr. had retired, and obviously Merk was not the thing, although I have always respected him. Handlin was on leave, or had just come back, so I had never studied with him. I had never taken any of his courses, though I had audited one.

As a college student or as a high school kid, I had read Siegfried Giedion's *Space, Time and Architecture,*[3] which is just a fascinating book. You can just look at the pictures, or you can read it, or you can do anything you want with it. And that had led me to read his book called, *Mechanization Takes Command.*[4] These are very confused books. It's very hard to know the historical sequence, what the rationales behind the sequences are, but he had a notion that American Technology unfolded in a democratic climate, so that sort of fit with Schlesinger—and I was also fascinated by architecture. This period of the fifties was the time when architecture was very fashionable, and urban renewal was coming in. There was a lot going on. I just went over to the Design School Library, because I felt I liked those sorts of things, and these were the kinds of books that people were reading in the School of Architecture. I had several friends who were graduate students in the School of Architecture. A particular one, a close family friend, was a guy named Norman Hoberman, who now practices in New York very successfully and who won the Roosevelt War Memorial Prize. So I was kind of hanging around the architecture school. I was reading three or four books. I read Mumford's *The Culture of Cities,*[5] and that just seemed ... wow ... that just seemed like so many exciting ideas. And also he had this mode of organizing society into these periods, and for each one there was a culture that came from the technology. So that looked better than anything I had heard up until then and sort of fit with what I had been discussing with my colleague. Then I read, in addition to the Giedion, Lynd's *Middletown,*[6] and that seemed just right. Those were the kinds of things I really would like to talk about, I thought, everyday life. There seemed to be some link between that and Mumford in my mind, whether there is a logical link or not; you know how these things go, it's really much more how you respond than maybe what's in the book. Then I went on to read an old urban sociology reader. I mean, it was just being used in all the planning courses at the time. It was Paul Hatt and Albert Reis.[7] Reis had put together a reader in urban sociology and it had Whyte's *Streetcorner Society,*[8] and a piece of *Middletown* in it, and Park and Burgess and their ring theories,[9] so that all seemed pretty interesting. And then I was reading Lloyd Rodwin's book,[10] which was just then out. It's a history of middle-income housing in Boston, and it was written around the issue of whether rent control was or wasn't helpful. It's a historical work that begins in the 1880s and comes forward trying to trace the rents and costs of middle-income housing. So you see that really looks like something urban.

As I was reading Rodwin, I came across a sentence that said something about a vast area of middle-class housing in Dorchester and that sounded right to me. Well, I lived around Boston all my life, and there's this huge area that I know nothing about. It was built as a middle-class area, and how inner parts of it are falling down. I'd like to know how it got that way. After all, Lloyd was just writing about general pricing of rents, so there was the simple question of how it got built. Also, I guess I should tell you, I was always a big sidewalk superintendent, home carpenter, and so forth. So, it seemed like these would be interesting things at many levels. I just hit upon this idea: I will write about the development of this area. And somehow in reading about it, I guess in Rodwin, I learned that building permits started around 1870, so that looked like a way to study it. I went with this little description to Oscar Handlin, who was the logical person, and I told him I wanted to study this, that would be my thesis. He said, "That would be very interesting, but it would take a long time. Why don't you do the Back Bay?" Because the Back Bay is defined, it comes on in a moment and it's planned, and so forth and so on. I think that was good professional advice, but I didn't want to do that especially because of the whole class nature of the Back Bay. I wanted to do something that had to do with a mass phenomenon.

The thesis took me six years altogether—three years to get to it and three years to complete it. I hit upon this plan of using the building permits, and I got into the City Hall Annex and looked through these huge, old books of building permits. I started to copy them off onto cards and that obviously wasn't going to work. So I hired a secretarial service that was down the street to type them up, take the ledger entries and just type them on a card, and they made an original and a carbon. I used to come every morning with a kind of cocktail tray that I had purchased, you know, one of those tin things on wheels. I would come in and get these big books from the city hall, take them down the elevator and wheel them through the streets of Boston, with wheels falling off. And these ladies typed them all up.

Now, you see, Oscar Handlin did one very good thing for me. When this was going on, I said wouldn't it be nice if I could get some sort of fellowship or something, and at that time the New York Metropolitan Region study was opening up. You know, the Vernon and Hoover series.[11] Well, Harvard was then doing that and so Oscar got me a one-year Ford Fellowship which meant that I became part of that seminar, although what I was doing had no relevance to them. I did begin to get a little sense of what was going on in urban economics, at that time. And that was very helpful. But there weren't enough linkages then; I wasn't well linked to the institution, and Harvard was a very diffuse place. So, although the computing sciences were really taking off, no one in history was in any way connected with them. I suspect even if they had been, I wouldn't have found out about it. So I could only do what a commonsense person would do, which was to arrange these building permits in geographical order, into subregions, and then I arranged them by the names of the builders and looked up the builders in the street directories.

So that was a very slow process and in the course of what was essentially a year's filing, I took a course in creative writing and wrote a piece of a novel, but that proved to be very useful. Actually, when I was trying to get out of the language requirement initially, I applied to the chairman of the history department to get excused from either French or Spanish and to substitute English as a foreign language and to take a writing course. Of course, that didn't catch on. But I really think it was an immensely useful thing, because the problem in writing fiction is that the data are whatever you want, but now how do you organize them? How do you say whatever it is you want to say? The kind of criticism that I got from Theodore Morrison was just very useful; I didn't become by any means a polished writer, but that really was the beginning of my making some progress in my writing.

STAVE: We were discussing the origins of *Streetcar Suburbs.*

WARNER: I guess we did the origins, right? And it might be important to add one other thing. At that time, I knew from Schlesinger that there was the *Urban History Newsletter,* [1 2] that comes out of the University of Wisconsin—Milwaukee, although then I think it was being put out by Blake McKelvey. But I really didn't know there were other urban historians. I just knew there was this newsletter, and I subscribed to it, and it came very infrequently. That was my first kind of tie with that. When I was a graduate student, Dick Wade's book, *The Urban Frontier,* [1 3] was just then going through the Harvard Press. I went to a very snooty Harvard meeting in which they discussed that book and thought of it as a not particularly interesting book, but still they were going to accept it. They couldn't see that it had any potential as part of a whole lot of things that people were interested in. I want to get across the idea that I think it was not just my own isolation, but there were very few urban history courses being taught anywhere, and the newsletter represented a very small group of people. I think Arthur Schlesinger, Sr., Dick Wade, Constance Green, and Blake McKelvey really were whatever urban history was.

STAVE: Do you see any difference between the history that they were practicing and the so-called new urban history today?

WARNER: Are you going to tell me what the new urban history is?

STAVE: This is what I would like you to tell me. Do you think there is such a thing?

WARNER: I think there could be, but I don't think it's come about yet. Steve Thernstrom's book which talks about the new urban history—the Thernstrom and Sennett *Nineteenth-Century Cities*[14]—it seems to be is not urban history, by and large. It's about cities, but it's really largely social history in which the impact of whatever is cityness is not measured or talked about or really dealt with. There are things that take place in cities, like Frisch's elite,[15] or Steve's and Knights' social mobility,[16] or maybe Sennett;[17] Sennett's thing, in which I think the interpretation is interesting but doesn't fit with the data, purports to say there is an urban phenomenon here. But most of the material there is not urban history. So I think our subspecialty is really in deep trouble, because the most active things that are being done are the social mobility studies, in which there isn't much urban content as yet, although Steve's new book does try to deal with this a little bit, especially in the last chapter.[18] And then somebody like Chudacoff has the idea that he's in a city, and that there is some city contribution to what's going on, although there's no analysis of the city in a region or what's special about the city.[19] That's the thing that disappointed me.

STAVE: Well, you're indicating that perhaps it's really not urban history. Now about Sam Bass Warner's books? Are they urban history?

WARNER: Well, I hope so. But as I tried to explain to you, I came into what later became a field. I didn't try to start a field or anything. I just came into it out of the sort of simple question of how did something, some part of the city, come to be? In *The Private City*,[20] I originally wanted to do a comparison of several cities, and that was really more than I could manage, so I started with Philadelphia, which was the oldest. I was much influenced by my experience at trying to teach urban history at Washington University. Essentially, I was trying to teach the American side of what Mumford was talking about in his *The Culture of Cities,* and I just couldn't get the material. The most abundant material was in architectural history. I guess I had read some for *Streetcar Suburbs,* and I was teaching with half the class architecture students, so I started that way, but I wanted to talk about all these social issues that were in *Middletown* and so forth. There were no data. A guy would ask what was the eighteenth-century situation, what was the early nineteenth-century situation of workers and residential distribution and so forth; there was no place to find out. So I really did the Philadelphia book just to have some comparable data between the twentieth century and the eighteenth.

STAVE: One thing that puzzles me somewhat is that you have your article, "If All the World Were Philadelphia: A Scaffolding for Urban History,"[21] and then you have *The Private City,* in which I assume much of the data are the same. But it seems to me you're setting up two different scaffoldings in the article and in the book. The article is dealing with the organization of work, with population, with different variables, sort of on a purist basis. The book is tying it into privatism. Do you think there is any difference here? Do you think these are two different themes? Do you think you've reached the same themes in the book and the article, and can you explain what privatism is? I've often wondered, is it capitalism, or is it many individual decisions?

WARNER: Well, it's capitalism, but the reason why I didn't use the word capitalism is that I wanted to talk about the internalizing of the value, which is capitalism. I don't think most people think of themselves as capitalists, right, but they do have that sort of individualistic, looking out for their family orientation, as opposed to some more communitarian focus. I wanted some word that would suggest that this isn't necessarily simply a political or general large-scale ideology, but it's carried within each individual, and it affects individual psychology. In the sixties, the way classrooms behaved, there was that little break when people got interested in groups and each other as part of a group; that all seemed so strange to us. It seems to me a kind of a proof that that was not natural for Americans. It may be natural for Chinese, but it wasn't natural to us. So there really was a psychology that went with a kind of individual behavior, that went with what you in general could call capitalism. Now people have said, "How are you going to tell your privatism from Swedish privatism or British privatism" and so forth. I don't have an answer for that. I've always had trouble with the cultural dimensions, because in *Streetcar Suburbs* there is this sort of romantic view of suburbs—I've forgotten what I called it, "rural ideal" or something. It's not well worked out, and it's not completely satisfactory, but to explain what's going on you have to have some cultural input onto which you put a label, and that was the best I could do. I certainly think someone like J. B. Jackson unfolds the ingredients that go into that kind of culture much better than I do. And I think someone could explore the values of capitalism and the psychology of privatism and how it changed and developed. I would suspect that it's a general cultural set, which is enduring as adequate for the private city kind of issues, but if one wants to explore it in its own right, it would have many more subtleties. I just never worked on that.

STAVE: This is answering my question about privatism and capitalism. How about the scaffolding article and the book? How much difference, if any, do you see between these two?

WARNER: The book was essentially to say that there's this general tradition; it's laid down early and, as the city develops, has certain consequences, political, social, and so forth. But the notion of the article was—look at these systematic structural relationships that exist. And I guess I never considered whether they would exist under a different value structure. They might very well, because what's talked about in the article is very gross and very large scale and might very well be applied to a whole mess of things. I mean, I'm trying to deal with modern urbanization. There's a better version, really, a much better version of that kind of thinking. Eric Lampard has just now written a survey in this big book, the two-volume thing, *The Victorian City*, that was published by Dyos and Wolff in England.[22] He's written just a marvelous chapter which is a survey of urbanization from the late eighteenth century to the present. He says this is a whole period. It's a whole set of relationships, of structure, demography, attitudes, and institutions, and it's come to an end. His is really a much better version. I was just trying to call people's attention to these systematic relationships, which it seems to me are still ignored. I mean, nobody does anything; everybody reads the article and they think, "yeah, that's a good article," but it didn't seem to tell people what to do. I've done things because I'm curious about them. They've developed out of my own intellectual life. But they don't seem to help other people to know what to do.

STAVE: Aside from privatism and some of the points you raised in the scaffolding article, in a general sense, of your three major books, what do you see as the main interpretive theme? Would there be any other themes beside these?

WARNER: I have a focus on the way people sit in the world, which may be inconsistent with some of these themes. In any case, I'm interested in and see people as enmeshed in and trapped in and as victims of modern institutions and environments and maybe also values. So, I see the residents of Roxbury and Dorchester, whether they be the original builders who are trying to make a buck, or the later people that lived there, as being maybe not powerless, but having very low increments of power in these large-scale situations. That's a theme that runs through everything that I've been doing. That's why I think a lot of people come away with a sort of bad taste from my books. They don't like them. The books are not upbeat. They don't suggest that good things are going to happen. But my central notion is of the ordinary person being largely powerless. It's very much a notion that you get in the mid-twentieth century, and I'm trying to look at what the forces are that constrain people. It's just like the Puritans—they want to study the Devil to know what he does to people and what the boundaries of moral action are. Well, this is really the same kind of inquiry. You ask what the general trends are, the major forces and so forth which confine actions of individuals, and then you know what the boundaries of moral action are. That's my kick.

STAVE: If that's your kick—your most recent book, *The Urban Wilderness,*[23] has had several reviews, one of which has seen it as a fine book, but also as a polemic.[24] What's your reaction to this?

WARNER: When you call something a polemic, then you say it's an argument and you don't like its politics. Actually, I wrote Dick Wade and I said I thought it was quite a generous review, in the sense that he gave a lot of space, said a lot of nice things about it, and said there's a lot going on there that someone should pay attention to. But he and I just don't have the same politics. I mean, if he had the same material in his hands, I think he would interpret it very differently. So, then, what becomes the argument? If you call the book a polemic, and not an argument, then I suppose you say that it has transcended some proper bounds for history. For instance, if you say, "Professor Warner makes the following argument," and you see the unfolding of capitalism or something in this urban situation as being disastrous, etc., etc., then you say it's an acceptable history; it just has this theme and argument to it. If you say it's a polemic, you really imply that it has passed over some boundary, that it's too argumentative. I think there is a tendency in that book to be somewhat preachy. I didn't want anybody to miss anything. So it has that quality, but I don't think that's what Dick principally objected to, although maybe in part. I don't see why history shouldn't make arguments as strongly as possible. It's perfectly clear I'm not trying to slip something over on anybody. It's not a research book, so if it has any merit, it has the merit of being a strong argument, saying let's look at urban history, it has this trend to it, and making the argument as strongly as possible. But I think it's just a matter of politics. If you view the American tradition as one in which the large and growing middle class runs the country for its own benefit, then you write about it one way. If you think of it as Arthur Schlesinger, Sr. and maybe Dick Wade did, as some sort of unfolding of a political society that becomes ever more inclusive, then you would say mine is a wrongheaded way to do it.

STAVE: All right, the book itself includes your suggestions for how to avoid a society that you indicate is rotten from the top down, not from the bottom up. You've been criticized for being utopian in those suggestions, for instance about government housing—what it has been in the past, what it is today; would this be an improvement? Could you indicate your reaction to this? Do you feel you're being utopian?

WARNER: That's a very hard question, because I've never done any systematic studies of politics, and I have a feeling that the political system is only partially connected to the social and economic system. They do intersect at important points, and I think the way they intersect depends a lot on the time period. I get in big fights with my students now, who have this impression that General Motors is down there in City Hall all the time beating on the Mayor. It seems to me that General Motors doesn't give a damn about City Hall, most of the time.

Every once in a while there is some issue, and it does have a lot of clout. But for a historian, it makes it very complicated to trace the influences through media. You have to look at who's doing what, and maybe that's what Samuel Lubell is into. But, in any case, if you think that the economic and political system don't run smoothly together, that both have partly a life of their own, then it's very hard as a historian. If you've not been doing very careful studies of this kind, to come up with prescriptive statements that say if you did that then the following would happen. I think historians could do that.

I think that the sort of historical political scientists—people like Jerry Clubb and so forth—who are doing voting analysis feel if they really get to understand it they'll be able to make predictive statements. I do feel a weakness in this respect. The thing that drives me bananas is that in every period in time, when you look back, it's perfectly clear that there were choices that the society turned down that would have made a difference. These things that some people call utopian may not be the most practical suggestions to what the political system can do at this moment. But it seems to me we are in the position of people who know what could be done to make important changes that would make this society better. There's a common kind of academic discourse which says that the society is so complicated that we don't know what to do, and I guess I'm really addressing myself to that. I think that's nonsense.

There is a whole series of things that would work, and in this case government housing is such an issue. Anthony Downs will tell you—and his is not the same politics as mine at all—that public housing would solve the racial and class distributions of the United States in about twenty years' time if the society wanted to do it.[25] So we have the knowledge, we have a way of moving toward that goal. Now, if you add what is possible within the political situation, you get a more complicated answer. So does that help you?

STAVE: If you take public housing in the past, for example, in my view at least, it's added up in the cities to a ghettoization of the poor, an institutionalized ghetto. Now you talk about scattered site housing, I believe. Do you think this would be much of an improvement if the institution of government is essentially run by people, and people have run these institutions for such a long time before?

WARNER: I don't know quite how to answer that. By and large, nationally, public housing is popular; there are waiting lists. So, given the bad situation that people are in, they're trying to tell us something as consumers. Although you and I would find all sorts of things wrong with public housing, in its design and location and so forth, still it represents for a whole mess of people a positive choice. As to the scattered site issue, that's my politics, right? It seems to me very simple as a government to move in two directions at once—that is, to build some of what we're going to call ghetto public housing which is decent, and some scattered site and see which direction consumers go. I guess the utopian thing maybe does bother me a bit in that I can't come up with, because I haven't really studied it, what would be the most likely political choice at any given moment. I would answer it this way—there is something very peculiar about our society: we are not in the position, let's say, of the eighteenth century, where you could have an economic problem, if you think of those eighteenth-century money fights where economics was poorly understood, and the outcome of any one policy was quite uncertain. We're not in that situation. I mean, we really know if we build so many housing units, what will happen, at some levels. I guess I'm very persuaded by Heilbroner's whole approach—that once economics comes on as an intellectual discipline and gets developed, a whole lot of things are now known to you and are predictable. And a whole mess of our urban problems, it seems to me, are at that very simple level. These are only utopian statements in the sense that they are unlikely for our political system to undertake, which is like saying that bad boys are unlikely to leave the candy on the shelf, right? And it seems to me it's like that. People ought to know that they're making those choices and their institutions are making those choices over and over. We'll get into the energy crisis in a moment.

STAVE: You also talk about the democratization of work and what has to be done with corporate structure and the way work is organized. It seems to me, you didn't emphasize that work is a major theme of your studies. In the scaffolding article, you talk about it and you're doing it now and you talk about it in *The Urban Wilderness*. Could you tell us why you think this is so important, perhaps something about the current research you're doing?

WARNER: I began to pick this up in the Philadelphia book because in the eighteenth and early nineteenth centuries you run into that whole change in artisan life and it seems to have such an impact on everybody. And then in the twentieth century there are these little empirical studies done by the Wharton School of people finding jobs and working conditions and so forth. It just made sense to me, both from this historical data and also from thinking that if people spend eight to ten hours a day at something, it probably has some effect on them. So the issue is not only how much money some people make but how they make it.

There's been a complaint about the Philadelphia book, and I think it might apply to *The Urban Wilderness,* that I don't tell people how to study this and that I don't know really how to study this. On the prescriptive side, I spent a long time talking to Heilbroner, and I've done some talking to people at Michigan who've done studies of the sociology of work. Unlike housing, it is a field in which people are very unclear. It's not known, it seems to me, what to do. Certainly what to do with large corporations is a very troubling problem. You notice I just say they should be socialized. There's no detail as to what that would mean or how it would be done. There's some speculation about structures of corporations, but I just can't do any better than that and I don't know anybody who has. One of the whole weaknesses of radical thought in this country is that they haven't been working on this problem. If you look around the world, there's this corporate problem everywhere, either in the state form or in a private form. It's just a very troubled subject, and I didn't mean to lay down any rules about what should be done. On the work field, it is not at all clear. There are productive workers who are happy, and there are productive workers who are unhappy. There are little firms in this country that run on a completely Yugoslav model; there's a company in Michigan which makes mirrors for automobiles where they don't buy a broom without consulting the workers. And then there are other firms that are run on a totally chickenshit basis. So what I'm trying to do now is ultimately select a sample of cities and industries and talk to people of various ages and see if I can detect the impacts on their family life and their careers caused by the kinds of work that they've done.

STAVE: Will this be done through oral history?

WARNER: To prepare a good oral history, you read as much as you can, but in the end I can only get these data from people. I think the idea would be a systematic random sample of some kind, some industry population in a particular place, and then the source will just have to be the informants.

STAVE: Will this make you more of a sociologist or a historian? Do you see any difference?

WARNER: No. The thing about a historian is he works with change over time—that's all. The only thing that makes you a historian is a long time scale and bad data. In fact, in this project I'm thinking of teaming up. One possibility is to team up with Marc Fried of Boston College and for him to do a current survey and for me to try to find as much historical background as I can.

STAVE: Do you have any second thoughts about any of your work, any of the points you've made in your publications in the past?

WARNER: Well, I mean, each one of these things has its really central limitations, and we talked about some of them. *Streetcar Suburbs* is very weak on the specifying of what this rural ideal is, how it came together, and how it changes.

STAVE: Do you think that there's been much elaboration, say, in the works of Jackson, Schmitt, or Tarr[26] on this in some of the recent essays that have been coming out?

WARNER: I don't know. I really haven't been following what they've been doing, and I've just been out of that field. I don't see any reason why it couldn't be done better. I think the landscape architect J. B. Jackson writes the best about this I've read.[27] But *Streetcar Suburbs* is also weak because it is not a systematic study of land. That is, I picked up when the builder comes on the scene. To make it a complete story, there should be a study of subdivision practices in that period. I had some data that I picked up about that, but the transferring of ownership and the marketing of land would have been essential to complete that story. And it seems to me the Philadelphia history, aside from the fact that it has the breaks in the time period, would have to have more political and institutional history to build that out.

STAVE: With respect to the Philadelphia study, it's been suggested that if you chose other decades or other time periods, you might have come up with another book. Do you think you would have ended up with the same conclusions, if, for example, you chose another decade in the eighteenth century, another three decades in the nineteenth century, etc.?

WARNER: Oh, yes. I'm very confident about the structure of that one. I mean, I think I got the structure right. Again, if you did more institutional history and more political history, it would become a more complicated story. But, for instance, you'll notice that the sort of basic outlines of the political sequences there are the same as Robert Dahl's from New Haven,[28] and I keep meeting other local stories that fit into that model very well. I think that Dahl has got it right, and I regard my study as confirming that. That sort of succession of elites. I mean, it just seems right. And so I don't think you could have mixed up the time period. That's why I pushed the idea that people must look at these underlying structures, because they are moving in a fairly regular way through U.S. history. And so, whenever you pick up the story you should be aware of where you are on that structural process. In fact, I'm now doing a very exciting piece of research to find the cities that I want to sample for the oral history. I am handling the entire population of the United States from 1820 to the present in a series of urban regions and watching how the whole system of cities unfolds over time.[29] This is a simple computer study using basic census variables, but I think the kinds of patterns that I've been discovering will show up very clearly, and it will be very easy for other people doing case studies to place themselves now in these systematic relationships. I've been going around muttering at Steve's [Thernstrom] conferences and the like that people have to place their studies carefully. For instance, I have a student at Michigan who has just submitted her thesis to Thernstrom and Tilly's series, and she took the trouble to do systematic work—the study of Irish, German, and native Americans in that mid-nineteenth-century period in Detroit.[30]

STAVE: Who is that?

WARNER: Her name is Jo Ellen Vinyard. The story is just totally different from Boston and has very high rates of mobility for the Irish. She took the trouble to do a study of the general growth and economic condition of midwestern cities and port cities during the nineteenth century. She shows opportunities were opening up more rapidly in the Midwest. I think we should just get into the habit of doing such systematic work. It doesn't take that long, and it has a lot to do with what you're reading when you read the local situation.

STAVE: We were talking about second thoughts with respect to your first two books. Any second thoughts with respect to *The Urban Wilderness?*

WARNER: Well, for instance, now I'm doing this national urban system research. I could do those three chapters on Chicago, New York, and L.A.—I could do that sort of basic structural part better now. I could place those more clearly for you and talk about the development of manufacturing cities, small manufacturing cities in the nineteenth century and so forth. I could just do that now more systematically. Maybe if there was ever another edition of the book I might redo that. It's always been missing political studies. That always seemed like a field of its own.

STAVE: I was intrigued with your view of Los Angeles, especially from personal experience, as this place of great potential and great freedom. Could you elaborate on this?

WARNER: It seems like America itself, in a way. I guess I have that old vision that America was a special place, that it had all those qualities—wealth, freedom, choice—and then it produces the things you object to in L.A.—racism, ugliness, disorder, and bad politics, all that sort of thing. But it seems to me that it is a place people like and we shouldn't throw that away. People probably feel about L.A. now the way they used to feel about Chicago at the end of the nineteenth century. It had a sort of upbeat quality to it because it was an embodiment of the possibilities of the moment. Chicago suffered from the same kind of Eastern snobbism that L.A. suffers from now. I think there are probably more painters now in L.A. than there are in New York; it certainly is an artistic center. And a lot of what we don't like about it—and for perfectly good reasons—is the sort of thing we don't like about the rest of the country. You must have seen "An American Family," that long series on Santa Barbara. Those people really are American, right? And you don't like it.

STAVE: We often hear of the notion of an anti-urban feeling in America and yet our whole demographic trend has been toward the city, voting with our feet. Do you see Los Angeles as an example of voting with our feet, in the attraction that it has for Americans running to the mecca?

WARNER: I don't have this hangup that cities come in a certain way. I don't understand why people back here say that the area similar to Los Angeles in the New York region, which would go well into Connecticut and New Jersey, is a real city. Whereas if you put the same area down in California, it's not a city. All we've said is that Los Angeles doesn't have the old core and the old satellite remnants that we have here in the East. But most of the New York region is on the L.A. plan. You drive down the Long Island Expressway, and except for the fact that it doesn't have any ivy and it's dirty, it's like any thruway anywhere. So it seems to me that Los Angeles is a city. These spread-out American cities are cities by any classified definitions; it's a heavy concentration of social overhead capital; there is a high degree of political and institutional integration, a very high level of interaction among the citizens, and very heavy concentrations of business and commerce, etc., etc. So it seems to me incontrovertibly a city. It just doesn't have some of those old packages in it, that's all. Now there is this interesting mystery that one of the most persistent differences among cities comes in a somewhat mysterious way from their age. New York, for instance, has that small establishment size in identical industries compared to Los Angeles or Chicago. That must come about, it's the only way I can figure it, although it's just a guess, when a city reaches a certain size, and it develops a whole series of institutions and networks and habits and so forth; then it grows continually in that pattern. Whereas when you start afresh you start with whatever the logic of that time period is. That may not be an adequate explanation, but the fact remains that Leo Schnore's studies show that habits do get laid down as seed and do persist.[31] But I don't see because you have an old pattern that that should be a pattern of rightness by which to judge all later patterns.

STAVE: Speaking of old patterns and new patterns, you mentioned the energy crisis before. What effect do you see on the city of the energy crisis or the alleged energy crisis?

WARNER: A lot depends on what you call a crisis. Let's say when the smoke is all cleared, we have dollar-a-gallon gasoline. If that's the only thing that happens, then one would suspect the cars will get smaller. Just by changing the automobile we could get the equivalent of fifty cent gas by making a car that went thirty miles to the gallon, which is called a Volkswagen, right? Now I suspect that other things will happen beside that; as that trend will set in, I suspect there will be some transit subsidies and so forth. You see, the transit thing worries me a lot because the people with the leverage in transit are some combination of the middle class and the merchants, and they can make a big noise. After all, a lot of them were very much supportive of highways and cars, and so they're apt to get the new transit. You know, we'll get really nice train service into New York and things like that. I would think of what you would call rolling adjustments, more condominiums. Actually, if I were to build a new city, the Sam Warner utopian city would be largely a high-density, low-rise city, I think. That would be my preference, with getting the green space by having a high density. But that is my aesthetic and you can make more money on presumably a combination of single-family houses and then condominiums and high-rise brought together. You can put those on the spines, just as in the late nineteenth and early twentieth centuries they put the apartment houses on the transit lines and the single- and two-family houses filling in. I suspect you'll get something to look a little more like that.

STAVE: But you don't see the return to the classical industrial city?

WARNER: No. There doesn't seem to be any need to organize people at a center, to such a degree. Since that city came together everybody now has a telephone, which wasn't true then. And everybody has a car now, even if they're going to wind up with a little one. Well, not everybody, but about 85% of the population. So these things have happened, and that stuff is in place and that affects land values. It will be a long time before land values and the need for concentrated access grow high enough to justify a single, centered city. There is a terrible problem that I only mutter about, and allude to over and over again in *The Urban Wilderness* and still worry about—which is who gets what land, the trickle-down housing phenomenon, and class and racial segregation. There's every reason to believe that the new environmental movement will just pack these people in a more segregated form. The ecologists have perfectly justifiable complaints about builders and development, but it seems to me they are adding a political force to the containment of class in this country, which bothers me.

STAVE: Do you see it as a bourgeois movement?

WARNER: Well, yes. But you see, I regard it as the same thing as the ghetto black, pushing black culture, who says, "This is our turf and our culture." I mean I think there's a lot of bullshit mixed in with that, but I think it's a genuine emotion: "It's our place and we're entitled to preserve it." Or the working-class ethnic people—they also have some universal truths that they are pushing, self-determination and sense of self and place. Well, it seems to be the environmental movement is saying that there is a popular middle class and upper-middle class culture which is no longer Protestant, Catholic, or Jewish. It's an integrated class culture which likes to have a certain type of amenity. It has to do with bird watching and climbing mountains and driving on scenic drives and mowing lawns and all this sort of thing; it's as though the suburban turf had come to suddenly include the summer place. And so now we not only defend our suburb, but we defend our recreation place, keep out the snowmobiles and the power companies. And it's a kind of life I live, so I'm very sympathetic with this statement as to what constitutes the good life in America. But it seems to me they are pushing, just as a black group or a Polish group pushes for its own turf, only there are a lot of us. It's a big space we're after.

STAVE: This is interesting, because you talk about a black group or a Polish group pushing for space. I found myself somewhat in disagreement with your view that ethnicity is less of an important variable than class and religion. I think ethnocultural issues are certainly important in the sense of the ethnic group and the religion, but you seem to downplay ethnicity. I found this in most of your work, or at least in *Streetcar Suburbs* and *The Urban Wilderness.* Can you elaborate on this?[32]

WARNER: Well, I'm just not into ethnicity. I felt out of it, and I represent an old WASP culture myself. I married a Jewish girl from Brooklyn, so we represent this other kind of culture which is class and education and not ethnicity. Relatives are our problem, not our answer. I think peoples' values are related to their experiences and it's well worth keeping that in mind. Oscar Handlin writes about the Jewish experience and the immigrant experience.[33] I should write about from where I come. I think what I have given is a perfectly respectable body of research and evidence. I have some friends who are sociologists who think the current ethnic revival won't last.

STAVE: Why not?

WARNER: Because it seems to me if you ask the question in a future way you can see why it won't last. You can say, what should the Poles do to define Polishness in 1972 such that they will have something to pass on to their children and their grandchildren? And so you say, all right, the way we'll answer that question is to look at what happened to Polishness between 1890 and 1972. You'll see loss of language, decay in the national church and parishes, some segregation, but also wide scattering, lack of support for the Polish Catholic colleges, a general watering down of whatever it means to be Polish. And I don't see there's much they can do to stop that. I think you could look at any ethnic group . . . in fact, there was one really good thing that Chudacoff missed in his book *Mobile Americans.* When he was talking about segregation in Omaha, he pointed out that he had very mixed neighborhoods, that neighborhoods were thought to be Italian or German or whatever depending on the stores. And it seemed to me that was an excellent point. I think a lot of what goes for ethnic is sort of a little cluster of some remaining merchants and maybe symbolic institutions.

STAVE: It seems to me, as one who is interested in urban politics, that perhaps your avoidance of political issues is something that would lead you to this view, because ethnicity has persisted greatly in politics. You can isolate voting returns frequently on the basis of ethnic or ethnocultural groups.

WARNER: That's a good point, and it might well be if I was doing a political study there would be these political traditions. But politics itself then takes the role of an institution, which perpetuates a series of behaviors. You might say, aha, well I'm looking at an institution that has an ability to make a Pole out of a Polish son or a Polish grandson, because it's going to keep after him and try to do things for him and try to connect him. Just as a church has this function. So you have an institution that is working to preserve and make ethnicity in the future. And you might be quite right that more should be done if you're doing a political study than if you were doing sort of general social attitudes toward the city and housing. I guess that really was my focus. It's that I just didn't see in ethnicity any really big cleavages in the society that would stand in the way of taking on capitalism.

STAVE: What do you conceive of as the impact of your work on the work of other scholars, of graduate students? In other words, your major contribution to the field of urban history?

WARNER: I'm in Boston now, so everyone knows me because I wrote *Streetcar Suburbs,* which is a kind of odd thing because it's a long time ago since I did it. I'm not really dealing with physical and architectural issues anymore, and people keep wanting me to do that. I figure the reason why you go into academics as a profession is that at the end of each day you can say you learned something and that's really the pleasure of it, and it's really not much fun to go back. In fact, I've never given lectures from the past. All my courses have been in a shambles because I keep changing the lectures and I'm talking about things I don't know much about a lot of the time. And that's really not for the student, it's for me, it's the way I stay alive. So I don't know. There was a fellow, Roger Simon, a student of Eric Lampard, who replicated *Streetcar Suburbs* in Milwaukee and really did a better job than I did.[34] He went into the building process and land better than I did; really, he did a better job. He knew what I knew. He sent me his thesis. It was excellent.

STAVE: But anyway, so your contribution . . . ?

WARNER: I really don't think I've had much impact at all. I think my principal impact has been providing materials which people use in urban history courses. Because of forces that are much larger than I am, urban history has been multiplying, and I appear on reading lists. When I finished my thesis, I went to work at the Joint Center for Urban Studies and there I was very much involved with city planners, and then at Washington University with architects and planners, so I had a kind of funny training. I had a city planning focus, which I am just now giving up to move into the work field. And I'm starting to work with labor economists and manpower economists, hoping they will provide me with the same kind of intellectual stimulation that the planners did—people with the current data and the current issues so that I can then work on the historical background. And I just don't think there are many historians who had this experience or have that point of view.

STAVE:, I am interested that your chief stimulus seems not to come from history or from historians; it comes from people outside.

WARNER: I tried to tell you that at Harvard I was very badly trained as a historian, and I guess Mumford is the principal one that turns me on.

STAVE: I was going to ask you if you had to name a half a dozen books that you think are the key books today in urban history, off the top of your head . . . ?

WARNER: That Lampard article, in fact, the two Lampard articles—the one he did on urbanization in advanced countries that appeared in *Economic Development and Cultural Change*. It's called "The History of Cities in the Economically Advanced Areas."[35] Lampard goes back to Marshall, the economist. He applies Marshall's ideas. It's a long article and it's really marvelous. It's about how cities grow and why they grow and so forth. Now, this one he's done on the Victorian city I think is just fabulous. And then Mumford seems to be essential. He may be wrong about things, although I'm not sure about that. His prediction of a necropolis for New York—the kinds of things he was talking about like crime and destruction of property are coming about. He just seems like someone who works entirely differently from the way I do, but he's tremendously talented and exciting. The other book I've used a great deal for my own intellectual development is the Paul and Percival Goodman book, *Communitas*,[36] which seems to me to be really crucial. Now if you want some books in urban history. . . .

STAVE: Just books that have influenced you.

WARNER: The book that's currently interesting to me, and I'm working off, is Brian Berry's text on urban geography, which I'm studying and learning from.[37] I think it's a way of handling the urbanization of all cities and comparing nations. It's a geography text, and it's therefore abstract at times, but it's very good.

STAVE: Well, do you think you could teach an urban history course without borrowing from other disciplines?

WARNER: I don't think so. I guess my idea is that there are a lot of social science hypotheses that help us to understand the city and that what's missing are the historical data to tell you whether those hypotheses are accurate or inaccurate or in what way they need to be molded or changed. I did have a little lucky break. There's this argument that cities lead to innovation, and I wrote a little article about Philadelphia showing that in some areas it does not always happen. It doesn't mean the hypothesis—

STAVE: Was that in *The Historian and the City*, Handlin's book?[38]

WARNER: Yes. That little thing on innovation in Philadelphia. It just means that it's more complicated. But I see myself working with current problems and modern social science and looking at the past. I guess I get a lot of ideas that way, but it doesn't make you a very good citizen, as a historian. I'm associated now with Jerry Clubb and the Consortium people who do the voting analysis thing. I don't know how that's going to be linked to institutional and political history. And politically these people tend to be very conservative, but in any case they just have a lot to say about voting that fits with Lubell's ideas much better than conventional history. It just wipes out a whole mess of political history. It seems to me when history flowered in the days of Parkman, historians knew the best social science and philosophic thought of the day, and they applied it. And I think that's just essential.

STAVE: What do you see as the future of urban history?

WARNE: It's very hard to say. It's popular now, because people figure they live in cities and they want to know about them. That seems to be a really good impulse and that will generate courses. But they can become terribly dull courses if people don't ask good questions.

STAVE: What about in terms of research?

WARNER: I think there is just a series of very serious breaks in the profession which somehow people have to figure out how to bridge. The ethnic people are doing their little ethnic thing, without any good way of sorting out the issues of class and the impacts upon ethnicity or class of urban growth. Somehow they've got to fit their people into urbanization, which I think could be done, but I don't know who's doing it. Then the great weakness in the sort of urban geography planning kind of thing that I've been involved in is that it doesn't connect well with the political and institutional history. And it needs to. I mean people do make decisions, and groups do have power. Aside from the music of the spheres or the development of the economy, there are important decisions made, and we haven't hooked onto them. There's really a very bad break in my own work and that kind of stuff somehow just has to be worked on. And then on the political side there's that terrible break between the concerns, let's say, of Sam Hays or the people who are studying particular cities and the networks of elites, and economic structure, the state as a whole, the national government. All those interrelationships are not well spelled out and developed, and we really can't write any impressive urban histories until these links are made.

STAVE: A final question: I have noticed that you were a candidate for the Vice President of the American Historical Association. Why did you choose to do this?

WARNER: That's a different kind of career issue. But that comes about from being involved in various radical educational schemes at Michigan. Since then, I have been involved in an attempt to see whether something couldn't be done about what is going on in the profession and in most of the institutions in which historians work. For instance, most of what we've been talking about is not in any form that can be taught in high schools. Or it's not what Sturbridge Village people want to know about. So there's a real disjunction between what we see as the sort of logic of history and what people can teach. I saw, for instance, a New York City curriculum on urban history for the eighth grade. They had put together whatever there was, and as researchers or as college types we just hadn't provided what they needed. The problem wasn't that they hadn't been conscientious with the bibliography. So I was very concerned with what historians studied, which is not what most practicing historians—namely, high school teachers and community college teachers—need. Somehow that should be bridged. And I really don't know quite how to bridge it except to open it up and have groups hammer at each other. And then there's the other issue, which has to do with the whole job crisis and who controls the profession and all the fights about blacks and women and so forth, in which the officers of the association, it seems to me, have either been reluctantly responsive or outright hostile. The notion was, this is my block, it's the history profession, so I should be active. Although none of the dissident candidates were elected, I got 38% of the vote and twice as many people voted as ever before. So we did make the point that there are a lot of people out there who think you're not doing the right thing. It comes back to the notion that history really is a useful and natural thing and that if the whole profession sank beneath the sea, it seems to me it would hardly be missed.

STAVE: Thank you very much.

NOTES

1. Arthur M. Schlesinger, Sr., *The Rise of the City, 1878-1898* (New York 1933).

2. Sam Bass Warner, Jr., *Streetcar Suburbs: The Process of Growth in Boston, 1870-1900* (Cambridge, Mass., 1962).

3. Siegfried Giedion, *Space, Time and Architecture: The Growth of a New Tradition* (Cambridge, Mass., 1941, 1967).

4. Siegfried Giedion, *Mechanization Takes Command: A Contribution to Anonymous History* (New York, 1948).

5. Lewis Mumford, *The Culture of Cities* (New York, 1938).

6. Robert and Helen Lynd, *Middletown: A Study in Contemporary American Culture* (New York, 1929).

7. Paul Hatt and Albert Reis, *Cities and Society: The Revised Reader in Urban Sociology* (Glencoe, Ill., 1957).

8. William Whyte, *Street Corner Society: The Social Structure of an Italian Slum* (Chicago, 1943, 1955).

9. Robert Park and Ernest Burgess, *The City* (Chicago, 1925, 1967).

10. Lloyd Rodwin, *Housing and Economic Progress: A Study of the Housing Experiences of Boston's Middle-Income Families* (Cambridge, Mass., 1961).

11. Raymond Vernon and Edgar Hoover, *Anatomy of a Metropolis: The Changing Distribution of People and Jobs Within the New York Metropolitan Region* (Cambridge, Mass., 1959).

12. Beginning with the winter 1975-1976 issue the *Urban History Group Newsletter* published in a new format and was retitled, *Urbanism Past and Present*. The journal dedicated itself to the exchange of theories and techniques for uncovering the history and the social organization of cities.

13. Richard C. Wade, *The Urban Frontier: Pioneer Life in Early Pittsburgh, Cincinnati, Lexington, Louisville, and St. Louis* (Cambridge, Mass., 1959, Chicago 1964).

14. Stephan Thernstrom and Richard Sennett, *Nineteenth-Century Cities* (New Haven, Conn., 1969).

15. Michael Frisch, *Town into City: Springfield Massachusetts, and the Meaning of Community, 1840-1880* (Cambridge, Mass., 1972).

16. Stephan Thernstrom, and Peter Knights, *Men in Motion: Some Data and Speculation about Urban Population Mobility in Nineteenth-Century America* (Los Angeles, 1970), reprinted in Tamara K. Hareven, ed., *Anonymous Americans: Explorations in Nineteenth-Century Social History* (Englewood Cliffs, New Jersey, 1971) 17-47.

17. Richard Sennett, *Families Against the City: Middle Class Homes of Industrial Chicago, 1872-1890* (Cambridge, Mass., 1970).

18. Stephan Thernstrom, *The Other Bostonians: Poverty and Progress in the American Metropolis, 1880-1970* (Cambridge, Mass., 1973), 220-261.

19. Howard Chudacoff, *Mobile Americans: Residential and Social Mobility in Omaha, 1880-1920* (New York, 1972).

20. Sam Bass Warner, Jr., *The Private City: Philadelphia in Three Periods of Its Growth* (Philadelphia, 1968).

21. Sam Bass Warner, Jr., "If All the World Were Philadelphia: A Scaffolding for Urban History, 1774-1930," *American Historical Review* 74 (October 1968), 26-43.

22. Eric Lampard, "The Urbanizing World," in H. J. Dyos and Michael Wolff, eds., *The Victorian City: Images and Realities,* (2 vols. London, Boston, 1973), 1, 3-57.

23. Sam Bass Warner, Jr., *The Urban Wilderness: A History of the American City* (New York, 1972).

24. See Richard C. Wade's review of *The Urban Wilderness* in The Journal of American History, LX (September 1973), 471-474.

25. See Anthony Downs, *Federal Housing Subsidies: How Are They Working?* (Lexington, Mass., 1973), and *Opening Up The Suburbs: An Urban Strategy For America* (New Haven, Conn., 1973).

26. For an example of Kenneth T. Jackson's work, see his essay, "The Crabgrass Frontier: 150 Years of Suburban Growth in America," in Raymond A. Mohl and James F. Richardson, eds., *The Urban Experience: Themes in American History* (Belmont, Calif., 1973), 196-221; also see, Joel A. Tarr, "From City to Suburb: The 'Moral' Influence of Transporation Technology," in Alexander B. Callow, Jr., ed., *American Urban History* (New York, 1973), 202-212; also see Peter J. Schmitt, *Back to Nature: The Arcadian Myth in Urban America* (New York, 1969).

27. J. B. Jackson, *Landscapes: Selected Writings of J. B. Jackson* (Amherst, Mass., 1970).

28. Robert Dahl, *Who Governs?: Democracy and Power in an American City* (New Haven, Conn., 1961).

29. For an aspect of this work, see Sam Bass Warner, Jr., and Sylvia Fleisch, "The Past of Today's Present: A Social History of America's Metropolises, 1960-1860," Journal of Urban History, 3 (November 1976), 3-118.

30. Jo Ellen Vinyard, "The Irish on the Urban Frontier: Detroit, 1850-1880" (Ph.D. dissertation, University of Michigan, 1972).

31. For an example of Leo Schnore's work, see Leo F. Schnore, *The Urban Scene: Human Ecology and Demography* (New York, 1965).

32. In Chapter 7 of *The Private City: Philadelphia in Three Periods of Its Growth* (Philadelphia, 1968, 1971), Professor Warner does emphasize ethnic and racial conflict as well as politics, ethnicity, and race generally.

33. Oscar Handlin, *The Uprooted* (Boston, 1951, 1973).

34. Roger Simon, "The Expansion of An Industrial City: Milwaukee, 1880-1910" (Ph.D. dissertation, University of Wisconsin, 1971), also see his article, "Housing And Services in an Immigrant Neighborhood: Milwaukee's Ward 14," in the Journal of Urban History, 2 (August 1976), 435-458.

35. Eric Lampard, "The History of Cities in the Economically Advanced Areas," Economic Development and Cultural Change, 3 (January 1955), 86-136.

36. Paul and Percival Goodman, *Communitas: Means of Livelihood and Ways of Life* (Chicago, 1947, 1960).

37. For an example of Brian Berry's texts, see *Spatial Analysis: A Reader in Statistical Geography* (Englewood Cliffs, N.J., 1968, edited with Duane Marble); *Geographic Perspectives on Urban Systems* (Englewood Cliffs, N.J., 1970, with Frank Horton); *The Human Consequences of Urbanization: Divergent Paths in The Urban Experience of the Twentieth Century* (London, New York, 1973); *The Geography of Economic Systems* (Englewood Cliffs, N.J., 1976, with E. C. Conkling and M. Ray); and *Contemporary Urban Ecology* (New York, 1977, with J. Kasarda).

38. Sam Bass Warner, Jr., "Innovation and the Industrialization of Philadelphia, 1800-1850," in Oscar Handlin and John Buchard, eds., *The Historian and the City* (Cambridge, Mass., 1963), 63-69.

SELECT BIBLIOGRAPHY OF WORKS
BY SAM BASS WARNER, Jr.

Streetcar Suburbs: The Process of Growth in Boston, 1870-1900 (Cambridge, Mass., 1962; New York, 1973).

Planning for a Nation of Cities (Cambridge, Mass., 1966).

The Private City: Philadelphia in Three Periods of its Growth (Philadelphia, 1968, 1971).

The Urban Wilderness: A History of the American City (New York, 1972).

The American Experiment: Perspectives on Two Hundred Years (Boston, 1976).

Measurements for Social History: Metropolitan America 1860-1960 (Beverly Hills, Calif., 1977 with Sylvia Fleish).

"Innovation and the Industrilization of Philadelphia, 1800-1850," in Oscar Handlin and Burchard, eds., *The Historian and the City* (Cambridge, Mass., 1963), 63-69.

"A Selection of Works Relating to the History of Cities," in Oscar Handlin and John Burchard, eds., *The Historian and the City* (Cambridge, Mass., 1963), 270-290 (with Philip Dawson).

"If All the World Were Philadelphia: A Scaffolding for Urban History, 1774-1930 " American Historical Review, 74 (October 1968), 26-43.

"Cultural Change and the Ghetto," Journal of Contemporary History, 4 (October 1969), 173-188 (with Colin B. Burke).

"A Census Probe into Nineteenth Century Family History: Southern Michigan, 1850-1900," Journal of Social History, 5 (Fall 1971), 26-45 (with Susan E., Bloomberg, et al.).

"The Past of Today's Present: A Social History of America's Metropolises 1960-1860," Journal of Urban History, 3 (November 1976), 3-118 (with Sylvia Fleish).

Stephan Thernstrom

Stephan Thernstrom (1934-   ), the youngest historian
interviewed for this volume, is Professor of History at
Harvard. His investigations of social mobility shaped the
study of that subject during the past decade and led to the
development of the new urban history. Thernstrom's *The
Other Bostonians* received the Bancroft Prize.

A CONVERSATION WITH
STEPHAN THERNSTROM

STAVE: The first thing I wanted to ask you was how much mobility has there been in the Thernstrom family? Could you give us a little of your own background in that area: upbringing, education, and so on.

THERNSTROM: Well, I suppose it is a kind of classic case of midwestern social mobility and it has something to do with my interest in the subject. My grandfather was a day-laborer, a Swedish immigrant. My father left school at fourteen, worked for the railroad as a telegraph boy, and eventually ended up as division superintendent of a small Michigan railroad. His own career mobility and intragenerational mobility was reasonably dramatic. I'm not sure whether any further mobility is going on in my generation; not at least by the crude occupational classification schemes I use in my work. In terms of geographic mobility, the family was a deviant case. It never struck me before, but now I see it as unusual that we were so rooted in one place, Port Huron, Michigan, where my grandfather settled. My father was born in Pennsylvania, but moved to Port Huron at a very early age. He lived there most of his life and turned down more attractive jobs to stay in the town. In fact we lived next door to my grandparents. He built the house next door. In that sense, it's something of a deviant case, long-time persisters in a small town. Then we moved, finally, for his career reasons, to Battle Creek, Michigan when I was fourteen. I went to college at Northwestern, then to graduate school at Harvard.

STAVE: Again, what was your father's exact occupational history?

THERNSTROM: He was initially a petty white-collar worker, that is, a telegraph boy, then clerk, and eventually division superintendent. So he worked for one employer his whole working life, fifty-plus years. Fifty-plus years rising within the organization.

STAVE: And your grandfather, you say, was a Swedish immigrant? What year did he come over?

THERNSTROM: Oh, mid-eighties.

STAVE: Did he work on the railroad, too?

THERNSTROM: Hmm. I'm not very clear about that, although he did live next door. He didn't die till I was, oh, what, ten years old. I suppose at that point he was doing mainly odd jobs. He would have been a very old man then, I guess. My father was forty when I was born and I think his father must have been relatively old when he was born. I never checked it out. It seems to me he must have been born around 1860, and my memories of him are, at the earliest, the very late thirties, early forties. He already was pushing eighty.

STAVE: You say you went off to college. Were you a history major there? Did you have any interest in mobility at the time?

THERNSTROM: No, in fact I was a public-speaking major, of all things. Just to retreat a little bit, as I think about what was important in my education, two great things happened to me: first, I was always a very difficult student, a tremendous disciplinary problem. Then, in the ninth grade, I first took up Latin, which thrilled me. I developed an interest in the English language and literature through the study of Latin. The second thing immediately after that was that I became a fanatic debater in high school. I was on the debating team, traveled around the state, and really, chose my college in terms of its debating curriculum and strength rather than anything else. And Northwestern had a very distinguished school of speech with a well-financed fellowship program for college debaters. During my four years there, the football team lost 39 games and tied 1. But the debating team was spectacularly successful. I was a major in the school of speech, so I took such courses as principles of group dynamics, elements of persuasion, rhetoric, the history of public address; it seems odd in retrospect, but in fact it provided a general social science-humanities education. I took a fair number of history courses under other labels like the History of American Public Address, in which you would read a speech by Henry George, a speech by Teddy Roosevelt, and one got into basic American history in that way. And then I did take, oh, I suppose, five or six formal history courses as well, some sociology, some political science, some economics. My greatest interest, as I was moving toward graduate school, was economics. It's a little ironic, since I've become a quantitative historian of sorts, but my economics teacher said, "Well, if you want to go into economics, you had better get busy and do some math." I had no college math whatsoever. So I began to take the freshman algebra course as a fifth course, at eight o'clock in the morning or something. On the first midterm I got a C minus. I wasn't used to getting anything but As. So I decided that perhaps I had no real talent for math and should drop any plans to become an economist. So I dropped the math course, abandoned the notion of becoming an economist, and applied to graduate school in political science. And, in fact, I came to Harvard as a first-year graduate student in the government department with a special interest in American government, not a very strong historical interest. Then I moved into history my first year, I think, mainly through contact with Louis Hartz, who happened to be in the government department, but was, of course, an important American historian. I ended up transferring into a small interdisciplinary program that Louis was the chairman of, the History of American Civilization program, which is sort of the Harvard version of American studies. So I worked in that program ending up working only with historians. But the degree is not technically a Ph.D. in history, but in the History of American Civilization.

STAVE: Well, you were in an interdisciplinary program, came from another discipline of study. How did you find graduate study here, and were there any contemporaries of yours who are now urbanists?

THERNSTROM: Well, I found my graduate years absolutely glorious, an altogether wonderful time. Harvard was a wonderful place. None of my contemporaries who come to mind really developed particular urban interests. Sam Warner was a bit ahead of me. I came to know him towards the end of my graduate career here. I had a fellowship at the Joint Center for Urban Studies, and Sam was on the staff there then. Some of my strongest interests were political at the time—a social democratic variant of Marxism. And in a way, much of my intellectual life was in Marxist study groups. Michael Walzer, the historian of Puritanism, was a very close friend in the same study group. Gordon Levin, Norman Pollack, and Gabriel Kolko were also involved. Of the intellectual influences aside from that, one would be Barrington Moore with whom I worked; of course, he has a strong interest in social class and social theory and is sharply critical of quantitative approaches to the study of social phenomena. Oscar Handlin, whom I worked with primarily and whose interests obviously were sociological approaches to historical phenomena, was very important. In a way, the main question my work began with was the Hartzian question, "Why no socialism in America? What is distinctive about the American political system, the American social ethos?"[1] And I resolved to try to explore the Hartzian question not through further study of ideology, but through study of the social fabric.

STAVE: Now, in taking a different approach, the social analysis approach was opposed to the ideological approach, was this your own idea or was it Hartz who suggested you move in this direction? Was it Handlin who suggested that you move in this direction?

THERNSTROM: It was pretty clear that I wanted to work on some question that would illuminate the Hartzian question, the question of American exceptionalism, and I think it was fairly clear in my mind that I would be interested in looking at behavior rather than ideology. It was really Handlin who suggested that social mobility might be a handle on this topic. I read a fair amount of sociological work about social mobility but I didn't really begin to think of doing a study to examine social mobility until Handlin threw that out as a possible theme. And then I took it from there.

STAVE: The Newburyport study was your dissertation, right?[2]

THERNSTROM: Yes.

STAVE: Were you aware of the census material? How did you go about discovering the manuscript census? Did Handlin suggest it?

THERNSTROM: That's hard for me to remember. I was, of course, very familiar with *Boston's Immigrants,* and in fact had gone back to the dissertation version of that as well, which has more detail on some matters. So I think that it was probably clear to me from reading *Boston's Immigrants* that that would be a way of getting a listing of the common people that could be used for this sort of analysis. As far as I can remember, although things do blur, I certainly had no a priori interest in doing a quantitative study, in getting together information about large numbers of people and pioneering in the use of quantitative techniques. I think that Lee Benson, for example, in a quite deliberate, self-conscious way, resolved that when he went into the New York study, he would demonstrate something general about the utility of these methods. But, as I've said, I had no knowledge whatsoever of mathematics or statistics, no previous experience with quantification, and some of Barry Moore's scepticism about it had certainly rubbed off on me. I had simply an interest in dealing with the common people. The subsequent decision to work in a quantitative way was really forced on me by the nature of the evidence. That is, there were few bits of information about any one individual, but such bits of information were available for large numbers, so that there was virtually no other way of dealing with that material except by counting it, putting it under categories, analyzing the material in a quantitative fashion.

STAVE: When did you start your Newburyport study?

THERNSTROM: I passed my generals in the fall of '58. And I guess I'd say around the beginning of '59 I began reading, trying to formulate a problem. I know I was into the census material at that point. I left the country in August of '59 on a traveling followship. I went to Europe and the Middle East, and I know before I left, I had written up a fifty-page paper that presented some preliminary tabulations of mobility patterns. So I had done that much by then, and I came back and spent about another year on research and a year on the writing. It was a finished dissertation in the spring of '62.

STAVE: And the book was published in '64.

THERNSTROM: '64, right.

STAVE: Was there much revision?

THERNSTROM: Well, I would say relatively little. I changed the order of a couple of chapters and worked out some of the comparative analysis in the last chapter of that book more fully; but I would say that perhaps ten percent of the stuff in the published version is fundamentally different from the dissertation.

STAVE: Now, did you use a computer?

THERNSTROM: No, no. All was done purely by hand—not even a counter-sorter.

STAVE: O.K., if you were writing that book today, would you do it differently? You've given some indication in some of your subsequent writings about this.

THERNSTROM: I certainly would do the last chapter differently, and I might want to come back to this later, in that I'm now less impressed with the generalizability of Newburyport in that period than I was at the time. I would say that it is certainly silly in this day and age, when it's so easy and inexpensive to get material processed through a computer, to rely on manual tabulation. If you're dealing with more than a few dozen cases, it's absurd not to punch cards and to process them with SPSS or some simple language of that sort. And given that fact, I suppose I would have dealt with, let's say, the entire working class of Newburyport, and that would be pretty simple to do. I'm not certain it would be a notably better book; I think that much of its appeal is precisely in showing that one can do a very modest little trial-boring with very little effort and open up some interesting kind of questions.

STAVE: Do you think the conclusions would be the same?

THERNSTROM: Yes, I would think so.

STAVE: Why did you choose Newburyport? I think you talked about this someplace—was it simply out of convenience? Why not another town?

THERNSTROM: Well, the reasons for doing a place like Newburyport—you know, Salem, Newburyport, Andover, Worcester, communities that were more than tiny towns, and yet not overwhelmingly large, and within an hour or so of Boston—are fairly obvious. Newburyport in particular, of course, because Lloyd Warner had been there, and I did have this interest in providing a kind of historical critique of the Warner methodology.[3] I was hesitant about it, in fact, and suggested it to Handlin half-jokingly, and he said, "Why not?"

STAVE: With respect to that book, it made a major impact, obviously. What do you conceive of as the major impact of your work? At least your early work, on reshaping the field, on other historians, on graduate students.

THERNSTROM: Well, one, it provided, I think, a kind of formula or model which could be very readily applied to other communities, so that there is a small, but not absolutely infinitesimal literature on nineteenth-century mobility. People have categorized the data in much the same way, have looked at other cities, and have looked into the question of differential immigrant mobility, that sort of thing. More generally, I think it was one example, again very simple, concrete, modest, of how one could deal with grass-roots social behavior in the past in a more scientific way. I think that some investigators who are not interested in mobility, per se, nonetheless found some drama in the basic method of finding everybody in the unit that you're looking at and following them over time. Now that was by no means my invention. James Malin was doing it in the 1930s,[4] the Owsley school did a little but unfortunately only a very little of it—they mainly concerned themselves with cross-sectional analyses;[5] and of course, outstandingly, Merle Curti did it in the late '50s.[6] I've often wondered why the Curti book had such a limited impact on the profession. One reason, quite simply, is that it isn't very well written, and I do think that literary values are extremely important, that the quality of one's prose style is going to affect the reception of one's work in this profession for a long time to come, and it should. There are some people who would say that's unfortunate. Also the fact that Curti centered his whole project around an issue that was really passé, the Turner thesis, didn't help. And then I think more generally that in the '60s, the society as a whole had a new concern that poverty, race, ethnicity, and urban problems were important. It was an interesting coincidence that *Poverty and Progress* came out the same year that the War on Poverty was announced; that doubtless made it seem a sexier book than *The Making of an American Community*.

STAVE: Well, you talk about the book as being history from the bottom up, and you have your essay in *Towards a New Past.*[7] Do you consider yourself, in this respect, a New-Left historian?

THERNSTROM: No, I consider myself an Old-Left historian (laughing). That is, I'm a Social Democrat, a democratic socialist. I think the questions I've asked about the past definitely reflect my early involvement in Marxism. Marx, after all, is first and foremost a theorist of class, a student of class relationships. That's what I've tried to be too. The New Left, however, would seem to me to be something very different from the Old Left. If you look at those pieces in the Bernstein collection, for example, not many of them have very much to do with class relations. Gene Genovese's certainly does, but most of the rest don't. I feel some ideological affinity with those people in the simple sense that I became a vehement critic of the war in Vietnam, when most people never heard of Vietnam in this country. I have been involved in peace politics, generally in the McGovern style of politics if you want to call that New Left; but in the more narrow meaning of the New Left, SDS-style politics, say, I don't find myself very sympathetic.

STAVE: O.K. Now, you've mentioned the War on Poverty, the Newburyport book coming out at the time, and that this probably didn't hurt the book. You've also done a book that I don't think is very well-known, *Poverty, Planning, and Politics;* at least among the historians it's not well-known.[8]

THERNSTROM: No, it's not very well-known, nor does it deserve to be. It's a very minor little thing. I wrote it in two months.

STAVE: This is *Poverty, Planning and Politics in the New Boston?*

THERNSTROM: That's right, yes.

STAVE: You say you wrote it in two months?

THERNSTROM: Yes, it was something I did initially for the U.S. Department of Labor, which commissioned studies of these projects in various cities. I was hired at a generous rate to spend a couple of months rummaging through the Boston files and writing up a report. I wrote the report very, very quickly, with no intention of making a book. But when it was done, it seemed to be an interesting little venture, really in narrative history. It's not highly analytical at all. I know some people have read it and said, "It's a nice little book, but it's not the kind of book I'd expect you to write." I found it great fun to do, and I think it was worth getting it out between hard covers, but it's not an important book.

STAVE: Well, do you see it tying into your other work? Does it tie in to *The Other Bostonians,* for example?[9]

THERNSTROM: No, I don't think it does, except in the very general sense that I'm interested in cities, I'm interested in poor people, I'm interested in class relations and the power structure, and it deals with some of those issues, in a very different, quite superficial way. It's instant history.

STAVE: When you meet people, are they aware of this effort?

THERNSTROM: Not if the sales figures are any guide. In the last couple of years I've gotten the royalty statement from Basic Books and have been very puzzled by it. There seemed to be something crazy about the figures, until I discovered that the reason they were debiting me rather than crediting me was that the net sales were minus three one year, minus one another year. More copies were returned than purchased. It's now remaindered around Harvard Square for 98 cents.

STAVE: How about *Nineteenth Century Cities,* a book you edited? The origin of that was a Yale Conference on this subject?[10]

THERNSTROM: That's right, yes. Dick Sennett was at Yale at the time, and they were interested in doing a little something on the urban front, as it were, and so put up the money for this small, and I thought very worthwhile, conference. In fact, Yale press at that point did a very amusing thing. If you look at the volume you'll see it's identified as Yale Studies in the City, Number One.

STAVE: Right.

THERNSTROM: There's never been a number two! (Laughs)

STAVE: Now, had you, when you went to that conference, intended or planned to be the editor of the volume, or was this something that came afterwards?

THERNSTROM: I don't recall us thinking of a volume in particular. I may be wrong there. I suspect it was more that the Yale sponsor Joel Fleishmann, who was the head of their whole urban program, was interested in some larger exposure. You know it often happens with conferences that the people who organize them really would like to get together with their fellow co-workers and exchange papers, and chew them up without really thinking that you're necessarily going to have a decent book out of it. But sponsors feel, "Let's have a book, so more people will know about this."

STAVE: Well, you know, the title *New Urban History* has been criticized by several reviewers, who claim that. it's really not the new urban history. It's social history, and this whole mobility business is social history. Is there such a thing as the new urban history?

THERNSTROM: Well, it would be more lively for me to present some brilliant rebuttal, but in fact I've come pretty much to feel that myself and have largely given up the term; in fact, I've stopped labeling myself an urban historian at all.

STAVE: What do you see yourself as?

THERNSTROM: A social historian. Perhaps a new social historian. I think there's still some utility in some sort of label like "new," or "behavioral," or whatever you want to call it, to call attention to methodological differences. I think there is still a real methodological divide in the scholarly world, in the literature, and it's certainly true that in general I tend to be particularly interested in seeing behavioral work. I read it with greater interest. I find more I can use in it than I can with other kinds of nonbehavioral work. I most certainly accept the criticism—Bob Swierenga made it, for example—that there's an unfortunate implication in the slogan, "the new urban history," that one isn't interested in rural social processes. Swierenga has now written a piece "towards the new rural history," and I, in fact, prefer that we get them together and just make a new social history.[11]

STAVE: Do you think there's any future for what's called urban history?

THERNSTROM: Well, I don't know. Maybe I've got a very peculiar kind of mind. There are people who very much like to categorize and to define with precision. I like to define the social phenomenon that I write about as precisely as possible, but I've never had any very strong feeling about the importance of defining what is social history or urban history or rural history. If I were giving a lecture course, it wouldn't matter very much if it were called urban history, social history, or even just American history. I would tend to do much the same thing. So I guess I find it hard to see that there will emerge a well-defined, subdiscipline "urban history" which is as distinctive as, say, demographic history. Do I think that the label will be used, and perhaps used with increasing frequency? I don't know. What I'm more concerned with is whether people in fact treat the processes of urbanization, industrialization, changing class structure, and the like. Whatever label they happen to use doesn't matter terribly much to me.

STAVE: What's the name of the course that you teach here at Harvard?

THERNSTROM: The Central Themes in American History is the main lecture course that I give, and that's a version of the basic survey. But in a rather heavily sociological kind of way, obviously.

STAVE: And do you teach a seminar?

THERNSTROM: Yes, I teach a conference course, a limited enrollment discussion course, ten undergraduates, ten graduate students. At the moment I'm calling it the Shaping of the American Class Structure, but I think in different years I might do different themes; I might do it on immigration, race, education. And then I have a social history research seminar in which students do intensive work on topics of their choosing. A lot of it happens to be work along the lines that I work in.

STAVE: What kinds of studies are coming out of that?

THERNSTROM: While I was at UCLA, a number of things got underway on Los Angeles history that were quite interesting. Here at Harvard this last year, topics ranged from a social analysis of Masonic lodges in Boston to a study of patients in the New England Hospital for Women in the late nineteenth century, an analysis of their changing social characteristics, and the changing practice of hysterectomy. What else? An interesting study along Michael Katz's lines of the school system of Needham, Massachusetts in the nineteenth century.[12] An intriguing look at sentencing in Boston criminal courts from the mid-1840s down to the early twentieth century, looking at the relationship between the ethnic and class characteristics of the defendants and the length of sentences they got. So many of them dealt with Boston since it's here; none were mobility studies, but all tried to get down to the level of individual behavior, to reconstruct past society. Oh, and another interesting one on the Washington Temperance Society's home for alcoholics—who was there, for how long, and for what reasons, and so on.

STAVE: There are a couple of things that I want to follow up on. One is *Nineteenth Century Cities,* let's go back to that for a minute. Do you think that that book, as it has been published, is even? Do you find any of the essays there more useful to your own thinking than some of the others?

THERNSTROM: I have to refresh my memory. I would say in general about the book that it's obviously quite limited. These are very preliminary reports of people just in the early stages of a particular project, and it's probably of lesser use with every passing year. Perhaps I shouldn't say that. I think we need more books of this kind that take the whole question further. I don't know if there are any essays I would want to single out. Some of them are better than others, some have broader, more interesting implications than others. But it's hard for me to say that one or two changed my mind much more than others did. Did you have something in mind?

STAVE: No, I was just wondering if there was anything there that you wouldn't include now, or any that you feel were more appropriate than others. O.K. We'll leave that. You wrote a piece when you were out at UCLA, on Los Angeles, which was a study of the growth of Los Angeles from a historical perspective, a short little thing.[13] And I assume some of this is used in *The Other Bostonians* in terms of comparison, in that last chapter.

THERNSTROM: Well, yes, that's true. Yes.

STAVE: Can you give your view of a city like Los Angeles compared to a city such as Boston? The findings, I guess, have not been overly publicized on Los Angeles. You seem to find it not quite as different as people suspect.

THERNSTROM: Yes, the essay was written with a polemic intent. It was intended to challenge what I thought was a much too common, a much too extreme view of Southern California as quite unlike any place else. I found that if you actually looked at the hard data on the question of how often people moved from place to place, for example, Los Angeles wasn't very special. It wasn't even quite as special as one thought with respect to the dominance of white Anglo-Saxon midwestern migrants and the relative absence of other groups. There are a lot of other groups there, a fairly substantial immigrant population. It was not an attempt at a really full-blown comparison of Los Angeles with any eastern city, but more a warning to anybody doing this job—you better be aware of the fact that, on these counts at least, the differences are not very striking.

STAVE: So it's the warning that it's not that different. Why do you think that it has this stereotype, and that the evidence doesn't seem to uphold it.

THERNSTROM: I don't know. You know the feeling of life there is certainly remarkably different in all kinds of ways. It's still fairly fresh in my mind now. For example—and I don't know how you square this with the statistics—in our neighborhood in Los Angeles I would say that in spring, at least, roughly one out of every three houses in the neighborhood would have a FOR SALE sign out in front of it. It may be even higher. In Lexington where I live now, a very comparable community in terms of income level, maybe one house out of fifty is on the market! Now, nonetheless, people change residence about as often in Boston as they do in Los Angeles. But that aspect of Los Angeles life somehow is much, much more visible. Differences in attitudes toward consumption are certainly intense there. The way people dress in Lexington compared to West Los Angeles. Or take cars. In our neighborhood in Los Angeles, half of the cars were Mercedes, and most of the rest were Cadillacs. In Lexington, in a very similar sort of income area, they're battered old Valiants, and VWs. So there are many crucial differences in living patterns there. Now, of course, I came into this, into the comparative problem, through the mobility route, and I've been comparing rates of migration, population turnover, and social mobility. And you can have tremendous differences in many other aspects of life without their necessarily producing differences in those demographic patterns. I'm not sure what else I can say on that question. I've toyed with the idea of doing some kind of book someday on a Tale of Two Cities, Boston and Los Angeles, and other people have talked about comparative studies of that sort, but very few people have done them, and the reason is apparent. It's a nice idea, but it may be impossible for many, many, many years.

STAVE: *The Other Bostonians* . . . a lot of questions in some of the reviews are beginning to appear. First of all, when you write a book such as this, do you expect that it is going to be a Bancroft Prize-winning book?

THERNSTROM: Well, you know, you can only hope! But, prizes are very funny things, and I think they're particularly delightful because they come as manna from heaven. Who can write a book planning for any particular prize? So if a prize comes, it is totally unanticipated as well as tax-free.

STAVE: Did you think this was really going to be a good one, that *Poverty and Progress* made an impact, but here I'm really working on stuff that the profession is going to look at and say "Wow, he's really done it this time." I assume that one of the reasons for doing this is the time dimension that you use, what is it, 1870 to—

THERNSTROM: 1880.

STAVE: 1880 to 1970. And one of the things in *Poverty and Progress,* as some of the critics have said, "He's criticizing Warner." How about your own time dimension? What happens if you had gone back into the eighteenth century? What kind of changes would you be finding there?

THERNSTROM: Well, I think that if I had only had good Newburyport data on the 1840s, it's possible that that would have given me a different impression of the place. I did what I could, it's a dissertation, but that's certainly a valid question to raise. On the general question of what I expected of *The Other Bostonians,* I don't know. I find it hard to answer. I certainly hoped that this would be a book that really would have a large impact. I can say candidly that during the long years in which it was written, I very often worried that it would have much less impact than *Poverty and Progress* and would on occasion pick up *Poverty and Progress* and look through it and think, "Hmm. . . . That's a hard one to beat." I mean, I felt pleased. I felt that that one was good, and I wasn't so sure about this. And one reason, of course, is that *Poverty and Progress* has much more in the way of descriptive material; in a way it's a broader book in terms of its treatment of the community context. Whereas this is a much more narrowly focused book, many more tables, much harder going, so that I wasn't sure, and I'm still not sure, for that matter.

STAVE: You seem to move away from the use of what some people call impressionistic data, or rhetorical data; in other words, you don't have much manuscript material, much newspaper material, or newspaper clippings; it's an analysis of the tables, essentially, You know, you could read the narrative, look at the tables, or do both.

THERNSTROM: Right.

STAVE: When did you start working on this, was it immediately after the other book? How did you get into it, and why?

THERNSTROM: Well, I got into it pretty shortly after I finished revising *Poverty and Progress*. I think I first must have started reading general material about Boston history going back to Robert A. Woods, settlement house studies, and things like that, around '63-64;[14] I think the first batch of census data was gathered in the summer of '65, if I'm not mistaken. It may even have been the summer of '64. The notion was to do a much bigger study, treating the whole population of a much bigger city over a much longer time span, down to the present. When I started it certainly was my plan to make it much more like *Poverty and Progress* in being rooted in a full reading of newspaper files, some manuscript collections, and the like. But as it worked out, it took all my energy to do justice to the quantitative material I had, and indeed, I think I've barely done justice to that, in that many sorts of things that might be fruitful could still be done. I hope that some future investigators will take my computer tapes sometime and play other games with them. It simply took so darn long to get that material into shape, to begin to work it into something readable, that I didn't want to spend twenty years on the book, ten was enough. Now, I'm sure it would be a stronger book if it had both sides rather than one, but I may still write more general social history of Boston. I expected to when I first gave up the notion of putting off one book, and I decided I would do a second, more general, perhaps more popular book without tables. At the moment I'm not clear when or if I'm going to do that. And one more thing I might say: the time wasn't taken up so much by just getting the right tables and working out what they meant. It was that there really wasn't a model for handling a lot of these problems, so that an awful lot of time went into figuring out how to categorize the material, how to set up the tables so that they'd be most meaningful. I'm not sure how to describe it, but there's really a kind of agonizing feeling that there must be useful important material here, I've got to make sense of it. I found it really very hard to get it into shape so that it did cohere. I think it finally shaped up.

STAVE: You thank several assistants for gathering data. How much of the data-gathering did you do yourself, how much did you have done for you?

THERNSTROM: I really didn't gather any of it, in the sense of going into the tax records, the census schedules, the city directory. I was close enough to the process so that I was confident about the fact that it was done with reasonable accuracy. I learned to delegate responsibility for people in terms of going out and taking every xth name and copying down this and giving it to me or even coding that material once the coding scheme was worked out. But I never wanted, as most social scientists have, to delegate greater responsibility, and say, you know, read this book for me, and sort of digest it or at least call my attention to what I would want. I've tried that a bit, but it never seemed to work. In that sense I'm a very old-fashioned, individualistic historian. I've certainly never asked an assistant to write up some preliminary thoughts on what those tables mean. I can't do it.

STAVE: So the analysis is paramount.

THERNSTROM: Yes. You may get a lot more work done through such teamwork, and you can train students to be useful, but it's not my style, for better or for worse.

STAVE: Now, in the book itself, one of the reviews that I've seen is the one by Berthoff.[15]

THERNSTROM: Oh, yes.

STAVE: It came out in *History,* and talks about the . . .

THERNSTROM: Berthoff reviewed *Poverty and Progress,* too.

STAVE: Right.

THERNSTROM: He said that I certainly established that I was well-qualified to write a more general social history of Newburyport. We have some differences.

STAVE: How about this notion that he's saying, well, now that Thernstrom concludes that from comparison of the Boston case with similar studies elsewhere, that transiency itself was what "nationally integrated" American society. Now, in other words, there's this great paradox here. How do you feel about this kind of criticism?

THERNSTROM: I don't think I concluded that. I think the remark that he's referring to is the observation that we had a nationally integrated labor market, as it were, with a flexible flow of labor from place to place, as suggested by this material going back to roughly 1800. I don't recall my making a suggestion so paradoxical as that—that an incessant flow of people from place to place knits the society together in a social way, though I think that one could indeed argue that the fact of people moving around so much suggests that probably most Americans have a broader range of social contact, encountering in the course of their wanderings a wide variety of ethnic groups, people born in the different regions of the country, different social class groups, than would be the case in a less geographically mobile society; but whether that produces integration, or greater conflict and disintegration, I don't think I'd want to say.

STAVE: All right, another point that's made is while demonstrating that intergenerational mobility worked better in Boston than Newburyport, you never asked whether child labor's "stultifying effect was in greater demand in a pre-1880 milltown, than in a later metropolis." Is this a question that if you were writing it now, you would go back and deal with?

THERNSTROM: It might be worth it—a passing comment; it doesn't strike me as terribly central, particularly since so many of the communities whole mobility patterns I draw together in the last chapter, using the work of other investigators, are places where child labor in fact was reasonably widespread. But it might be something I'd want to think about more. You know, I think there is a fundamental difference between Berthoff's style of doing history and mine, and it's become more accentuated over the years.[16] That is, I think he does raise interesting, very general questions about the meaning of it all, and I think what's happened to me is that I have become more interested in settling what I think I can settle with this material at hand and drawing fairly limited conclusions about demographic processes, in large measure, and less willing to speculate more broadly as I grow older. That may be terrible, it may be good, but that's the way it is. In a way, and to put it in an extreme form, *Poverty and Progress* is certainly a broader book and a more speculative book. I had always planned, when I was writing *The Other Bostonians,* for the conclusion to have some grand wrap-up that went well beyond *Poverty and Progress* in talking about the meaning of it all, in terms of class relationships in America, the disability of the political system, and so on. What I finally produced in that final section of the last chapter, "The Significance of the American Mobility Pattern," or whatever it's called, is quite brief, and cautious. It's just where I am, mentally, right now.

STAVE: This is an interesting point. What does it tell us about mobility studies? What is the future of mobility studies, if there is a future? Are they all going to be repeating the same conclusions? Your last chapter makes some comparisons. It's one of the few attempts to try to generalize what's being found. There seems to be a basic unity with respect to mobility, persistence, this kind of thing. Where do mobility studies go from here? And, you mentioned *Poverty and Progress* as being a thing which in a sense had more theory in it. By using more data, by becoming more sophisticated in methodology, does this really tie you down because you can't make the intuitive leaps that you're supposed to make?

THERNSTROM: Let me take the first one first, on the future of mobility studies. I don't think there is, nor do I think there should be, an incredibly glowing future for mobility studies per se; that is, I do think that we've gone a fair way toward blocking out the patterns, as conventionally measured. I think there will definitely be a literature which challenges the general thrust of that last chapter, and tries to show—well I've got a paper here, as a matter of fact, that I'm reading for some journal, showing that there's more mobility in San Jose, and there's a manuscript on Detroit, showing the Detroit Irish have done much better than the Boston Irish. And you know there are empirical questions there that will be worth exploring. It may be that in time, what I couldn't find from the present data, general patterns, in which newer cities look different than older ones—cities with a heavy industrial base look different than a commercial base—maybe in time we'll develop a sort of typology that for particular periods will indicate substantial differences. What I'm more concerned about is that I very much hope that we don't have a huge literature of mobility studies which simply uses the same categories that I've been using, and adds another city or another ethnic group. An example of that is the work of Barr on San Antonio, published in the *Social Science Quarterly*,[17] where in an utterly mechanical fashion the man takes Richard Hopkins' tables for Atlanta,[18] prints exactly the same tables with the San Antonio data. The only distinctive thing is that San Antonio has Mexican Americans, so there's another group added. But I shudder to think that in time, journals might be filled with mobility in Peoria, mobility in Madison, and so on. I do think there is a future, if you define the concern more broadly—that is, a systematic analysis of class, ethnicity, sex, other social characteristics in the American past. Most closely related to mobility studies, I would put very great priority on more direct analysis of economic differences in past society. We have some literature now by economic historians on the distribution of wealth in 1860. Fogel and Engerman have some tantalizing things there; that's one thing in particular I would like to do more of.[19] And wealth mobility can be studied directly out of these things. In a way, Chapter 5 of *Poverty and Progress* seems to be stronger than much of the rest of it.

STAVE: Is that the one on the property? Yes, that's an interesting finding. You indicate in *The Other Bostonians,* I think, or someplace, that you don't have that much on wealth, which is another direction that you might want to go.

THERNSTROM: That's right. Boston lacked a large home-owning class through most of my period, and that's mainly what the real estate tax records allow you to treat. But there are ways of going further. For example, Civil War income tax returns were printed in the newspapers in many communities—the richest 25% of taxpayers for Milwaukee, for example, and all of them for Poughkeepsie, Clyde Griffen has found.[20] I think it may have been a very common practice, and it would be really worth digging into.

STAVE: What about Berthoff's criticism, and I hate to keep going back to him, but the notion that your book is a retrogression in method. You imply, he says, quantifiable evidence is the only empirical or even historical data, and mobility itself is the one central social process mechanism with a structure.

THERNSTROM: A lot of the charge is very funny to me, and it seems to me that's what Berthoff said to the world some twelve, fourteen years ago, in his famous essay. I make no such claims. I think mobility is important enough for me to want to write a book about it, two books, actually, but no more books about mobility, incidentally; but I certainly wouldn't want to claim that. I think it's a fundamental thing in American society. In a way, I do think it may be unfortunate that I've given so much attention to mobility, and other people working in my tradition have; perhaps greater attention might have been given to the structure itself within which mobility proceeds.

STAVE: I wanted to ask you about this, because Sam Hays has a paper,[21] I don't know if you've seen it, I think it's still unpublished, on structure in the new urban history, in which he makes some very interesting points. He says O.K., let's look at the structure of things. In a sense, you have persistence in patterns and movement of people. Now, you have family, you have kinship groups, you have this kind of thing, which is of significance; and then you can ask if you have voluntary associations, associational activity, trying to, say bind things together in light of the flux. What's the structure of the associational kind of thing? You know, who is in it? And I guess he's talking perhaps about Glazer's findings and similar work.[22]

THERNSTROM: Yes. And this point comes through beautifully in Michael Katz's new manuscript, which I hope will be coming out in the *Harvard Studies in Urban History* in another year.[23] That's mainly an analysis of structure in Hamilton, Ontario in the 1850s, with only one chapter on mobility, and what Katz does with mobility rests on a much more thorough and sophisticated analysis of structure. It's certainly quite different than what everybody else has done. As for displaying a retrogression in method, tastes vary here. As I've grown older, I have retained a great respect for traditional history. I find it immensely illuminating to read a great biography, or an account of the mind of the South, even, however wildly impressionistic Wilbur Cash was.[24] But it is true that in my writing and increasingly in my teaching as well, I find myself constantly raising the question, "How do we really know that these words have real resonance in the culture? What does this utterance represent?" And I find myself increasingly concerned with statistical representativeness, and willing, I suppose, to say, "I don't know how representative that is." Here I can say some fairly solid things about some things that are measurable. For example, I find, to take an example, Perry Miller wrote a paper on Virginia after his work on Puritanism, in which he suggested that the Virginia experiment, too, was profoundly formed by Puritan conceptions of meaning, that Virginia was really a Puritan colony.[25] Well, it depends on what you mean by that. I find far more telling than Miller's few literary documents the fact that there was one church per 385 settlers in Massachusetts Bay Colony in 1650, and one per 4,000 in Virginia. So that whatever the intent of the literary few whose writings Perry Miller analyzed, religion as an experience for ordinary people was very different in those two places.

STAVE: Another point from the Hays paper, he says that "those who think in terms of structure are beginning to argue that what heretofore has been described as social disorganization may not be a characteristic of society in general, but of life cycle. It may well be, for example, that much of the simple phenomenon of geographic mobility, which has impressed historians of the nineteenth century, is a phenomena of youth. Current census data bears out the notion that migration rates decline from birth to age 17, rise rapidly to age 24, then fall sharply to age 65, and then they level off. That it's not irrelevant that much of the written record about social disorganization has a strong element of the older generation writing about the younger, and doing so in the same way, again and again with each new generation. It may be that the concept of social disorganization, as a long-range change concept represents a perspective of a particular stage of life-cycle, as much of objective social data." What do you think of that?

THERNSTROM: Oh, I think that's a very good suggestion. It's certainly surprising (I guess it reflects the newness of these concerns) that the published analyses that we have so far of persistence in turnover in nineteenth-century America have done so little with the simple age variable, which any demographer immediately would say is crucial. I think that people certainly recognize that an awful lot of this movement is accounted for by people very early in their life cycle. Now, on this social disorganization point, I find it provocative, plausible; I don't find it disturbing to me in that I don't think I've ever gotten deeply committed to social disorganization, the Chicago school of sociology sort of conceptions, although I guess maybe in some of the early part of *Poverty and Progress.*

STAVE: Sam Warner reviewed your book in *Political Science Quarterly* . . . [26]

THERNSTROM: Really, no, I didn't see it!

STAVE: Yes, that just came out, I got it last week. And he's very kind toward it. But at the very end . . .

THERNSTROM: It stinks? (laughter)

STAVE: He notes that, he's talking about the time to "design a systematic, organized national history, which would employ an adequate research design, and adequate samples to deal with the structural and cultural variables, from which they, and all of us wish to reason." Your last chapter mentioned this. You know, this is the closest attempt to do this. Do you think that you really are touching on some sort of a systematization of mobility?

THERNSTROM: It's certainly very sketchy, and shaky. I mean, just simple matters of different coding procedures, differences in the sample design, things like that, you know, very strange, and entirely ad hoc kinds of cases that have come to scholarly attention. We happen to know a fair amount about Poughkeepsie because Clyde Griffen teaches at Vassar. No, I think we'll be able to do something more in the reasonably near future, in that there are some tentative plans afoot to bring together all existing historical mobility data in machine-readable form, to bring them together in some archive, and possible get a team of people working them together in some archive, and possibly get a team of people working for summers, maybe, to compare and in a much more strictly comparable way, retabulate all the material. That would not, however, get at the limitation that we presently have a strange sample of the American urban population, with the South and the West highly underrepresented. No way of getting at that until people gather a lot more information.

STAVE: Ray Mohl wrote to me the other day that Peter Knights has an article out, or a review, with respect to *The Other Bostonians*. It is very critical.[27]

THERNSTROM: I haven't seen it. I've heard that he has attacked my sampling or something, and I'm eager to see it, but he hasn't sent it to me.

STAVE: Thought you might have seen it, I was wondering if there's any reaction to it . . . (laughing) . . . preemptive strike, or something.

THERNSTROM: (laughing): No, I feel ready to defend my sampling against any and all comers.

STAVE: Let's see, what did you do? You chose "x" out of . . . what was the sampling method, you had about 8,000 or so in the sample?

THERNSTROM: Yes, right, it was simply every "x" name, I've forgotten the interval. You know, there is a real problem after 1880, although now you have the 1900 U.S. Census manuscript available. The other sources are considerably less adequate. I used marriage license records for one of them, which have been used conventionally by sociologists working on this, but of course that's not really the adult male population, it's only those adults who got married. Then the other sample—there's one small sample from a city directory, just to wrap up some things—the other main one was the birth certificates when I found that the marriage license sample was suffering such extreme attrition rates; it appeared that people were coming to Boston to marry and then disappearing. It certainly would have been more symmetrical if I had had the same source, but I don't see that as a devastating attack on the main conclusions.

STAVE: Do you think that some historians who are involved in, well, either social mobility, or econometrics, become too tied up in the methodology as opposed to the substance? We hear the expression "barefoot empiricism" sometimes. You have not been accused of this; others have. Is there a division among quantifiers, actually?

THERNSTROM: I would say certainly quantifiers could be arranged along a continuum from sort of an extreme enthusiasm in a belief of the absolutely revolutionary nature of the implications for history of the quantitative revolution toward much more chastened pluralistic uses of them. And I would like to think that I'm somewhere over toward the middle, over toward the more chastened variety. The interest in method itself may also be good. I don't know enough about the history of science, but I wouldn't be surprised if many of the innovations in chemistry, physics, and the like, came, not in situations where someone always asks the ultimate cosmic question, "What is the nature of the universe?" but came, rather, out of a deep absorption in a much narrower and more technical problem. I do think that solving these technical problems can often really help a lot. But beyond that, it's probably just a difference in temperament and personal styles. Some people will write books like Berthoff's general book on American society. I couldn't write that kind of book. Berthoff apparently finds the sort of work that I do terribly narrow, cautious, timid, retrogressive. We'll see . . . (laughing) . . . how the future evaluates these things.

STAVE: (laughing): We'll leave it to history on that one. O.K., which of your own writings do you prefer? Which is your favorite?

THERNSTROM: I don't know. My children are at the stage where they're always saying, "What's your favorite color?" "What's your favorite name?" And I respond awkwardly, "I like a lot of colors." I don't know. If I meet people and I'd like to give them a book, I'd give them *Poverty and Progress* because it's a lot more accessible.

STAVE: It's in paperback. (laughing)

THERNSTROM: (laughing): It's cheaper for me, yes! I think there are some things in *The Other Bostonians:* the chapter on blacks I'm really fond of. I think that has in a way greater weight and scope and ingenuity, maybe, than anything in *Poverty and Progress.*

STAVE: Outside of your own works, if you would choose a half-dozen or so history books in any field, what would be your favorites there?

THERNSTROM: All of history, including Thucydides?

STAVE: Since we're interested in urban history, or social history, why don't we keep it down to that field? The things that have influenced you, or that you just think that are good.

THERNSTROM: I would say that one certainly is *Middletown,* [28] which I think is a stunning book. So many problems with their uses of history, so many ways in which it would have been much, much better if they had really looked at the 1890s in detail, but in its basic conception and method of compiling data, it's certainly one of the most influential things I've ever read. I'd put *Boston's Immigrants* in that category, too. [29] I think Marx's economic writings, the Marx who's read now, the early Marx of the philosophical manuscripts, the theorist of alienation, I'm quite impatient with. I don't really like the Hegelian aspects of Marx very much. But *Kapital,* the *German Ideology,* the applied historical works, like the *18th Brumaire* made a terrific impression on me at the time. Barrington Moore's *Soviet Politics: The Dilemma of Power* is a historical analysis of the evolution of the Soviet system that I really think is a magnificent model; in a way, to me more challenging than Moore's more grand later work that he's received so much more attention for. [30] James Sterling Young's *The Washington Community,* [31] Charles Tilly's *The Vendee,* [32] Michael Katz's *The Irony of Early School Reform* [33] and just about everything ever written by Eric Hobsbawm seem to me exciting and illuminating. [34] Of course, not many of these titles would ordinarily be labeled "urban history," would they? That may be a telling fact about the state of the field today.

STAVE: What are you doing now? The classic question asked of historians after they've finished a book that wins a prize is "What are you doing now?"

THERNSTROM: I'm writing a history of the United States, from beginning to present, a history of America. I mentioned this basic survey course that I'm giving currently, and I'm trying to write that up into a relatively brief, basic, introductory book; much more emphasis on social structure, economic change, class, ethnicity, than you'd get in a normal, basic book.

STAVE: Will this be a text?

THERNSTROM: It's supposed to be a text for the introductory course.

STAVE: Let's see if there's anything else I wanted to tie in here. A final thing is the idea of what you see as—maybe we touched on this in the beginning—as the key interpretive themes of your work.

THERNSTROM: Oh. Wow! (laughing)

STAVE: 25 words, or 25 hundred.

THERNSTROM: Hmm . . . I may duck that one. I've stated a lot of themes in my work; some of them with much more emphasis than others. The particular balance I would strike between the larger ones and the minor ones, I have struck such as it is; and I feel it would be doing violence to try to do anything more in pulling them out.

STAVE: Putting this in a somewhat slightly different way, do you see any distinctive characteristics of your way of "doing history"? Anything distinctive that you feel that you do, and others don't? Or that few people would do . . .

THERNSTROM: Not very much. There is one thing, a thing that I sounded before, but I would just mention it again for people who are working in considerable part in the behavioral or quantitative mode. I would really want to emphasize that for people who teach students to work in this way, I believe that a fine piece of historical analysis has to be written with crisp, pungent, absolutely lucid, graceful prose. And that ain't easy. I'm very distressed with the notion that some students, it would appear from what I read, are being taught that a historical article is like an article in a medical journal, let's say. There's a theory you state in a clumsy way, and here's a sample, and here are the findings, and ergo . . . Now, I think that this sort of history is becoming more important, and it will continue to do so. Thus the plans now underway to form a new social science history association. Clearly there is going to be an increasing audience which will digest articles like that, just as research physicians do, because they're interested in the material, and the prose be damned. But I very strongly feel that one ought to write up these findings, these analyses, in such a way that an historian untrained in statistics or social theory, can understand them. I think Fogel and Engerman's *Time On the Cross* raises that problem much more dramatically than anything I've done, or any others in social science history. That book proposes absolutely immense revisions in much of the conventional wisdom on the subject—but relatively fewer revisions than they claim. And I don't think, much as I admire the book, that they have very successfully addressed this problem of how you provide the untrained "lay" historian, as it were, with enough knowledge so that they can critically evaluate what it was they did that led to these conclusions. The whole device of a separate, second volume doesn't help, but much more important, the contents of the second volume—they haven't made the effort, it would take them years, I suppose, to do it properly, to really explain the economic models, lay out all the assumptions, so someone untrained in economic history can still think, "Gee, is that plausible? Does it really make sense?" I hope that social science historians will feel that obligation to continue to talk with their colleagues, and continue to write for them, even colleagues who don't speak this lingo.

STAVE: Fine. I think I'm done. So we'll terminate and I hope that graduate students hear the clarion call.

NOTES

1. See Louis Hartz, *The Liberal Tradition in America: An Interpretation of American Political Thought Since the Revolution* (New York, 1955).

2. Stephan Thernstrom, *Poverty and Progress: Social Mobility in a Nineteenth-Century City* (Cambridge, Mass., 1964; New York 1969).

3. See W. Lloyd Warner and Paul S. Lunt, *Yankee City Series*, Vols. I & II, *The Social Life of a Modern Community* (New Haven, 1941); and *The Status System of a Modern Community* (New Haven, 1942); and W. Lloyd Warner, et al., *Yankee City* (one volume, abridged, New Haven, 1963).

4. See James C. Malin, "The Turnover of Farm Population in Kansas," Kansas Historical Quarterly, IV (1935), 339-372.

5. See F. L. Owsley, *Plain Folk of the Old South* (Baton Rouge, 1949).

6. Merle Curti, *The Making of an American Frontier Community* (Stanford, Cal., 1959).

7. Stephan Thernstrom, "Urbanization, Migration and Social Mobility in Late Nineteenth-Century America," in Barton J. Bernstein, ed., *Toward a New Past: Dissenting Essays in American History* (New York, 1968), 158-175.

8. Stephan Thernstrom, *Poverty, Planning, and Politics in the New Boston: The Origins of ABCD* (New York, 1969).

9. Stephan A. Thernstrom, *The Other Bostonians: Poverty and Progress in the American Metropolis, 1880-1970* (Cambridge, Mass., 1973).

10. Stephan Thernstrom and Richard Sennett, eds., *Nineteenth-Century Cities: Essays in the New Urban History* (New Haven, 1969).

11. Robert Swierenga, "Toward a New Rural History," Historical Methods Newsletter, 6 (June 1973), 111-121.

12. Michael Katz, *The Irony of Early School Reform: Educational Innovation in Mid-Nineteenth Century Massachusetts* (Cambridge, Mass., 1968).

13. Stephan Thernstrom, *The Growth of Los Angeles in Historical Perspective: Myth and Reality* (Los Angeles, 1970).

14. Robert A. Woods, *The City Wilderness: A Settlement Study by Residents and Associates of the South End House* (Boston, 1898), and *Americans in Progress: A Settlement Study by Residents and Associates of the South End House* (Boston, 1903).

15. Rowland Berthoff, review of *The Other Bostonians* in History 2 (January 1974), 59-60.

16. For example, see Rowland Berthoff, *An Unsettled People: Social Order and Disorder in American History* (New York, 1971).

17. Alwyn Barr, "Occupational and Geographical Mobility in San Antonio, 1870-1900," Social Science Quarterly, 51 (September 1970), 396-403.

18. Richard J. Hopkins, "Status, Mobility, and the Dimensions of Change in a Southern City: Atlanta, 1870-1910" in Kenneth T. Jackson and Stanley K. Schultz, eds., *Cities in American History* (New York, 1972), 216-231.

19. Robert Fogel and Stanley Engerman, *Time on the Cross: The Economics of American Negro Slavery* (Boston, 1974).

20. For example, see Clyde Griffen, "Workers Divided: The Effect of Craft and Ethnic Differences in Poughkeepsie, New York, 1850-1880," in Thernstrom and Sennett, *Nineteenth-Century Cities*, 49-97.

21. Samuel P. Hays, "Social Structure in the New Urban History," (unpublished mimeo, Pittsburgh, January, 1973).

22. Walter S. Glazer, "Participation and Power: Voluntary Associations and the Functional Organization of Cincinnati in 1840," *Historical Methods Newsletter*, 5 (September 1972), 151-168.

23. Subsequent to the interview, Michael Katz's study was published as *The People of Hamilton, Canada West: Family and Class in a Mid-Nineteenth Century City* (Cambridge, Mass., 1975).

24. Wilbur Cash, *The Mind of the South* (New York 1941, 1960).

25. Perry Miller, "Religious Impulse in the Founding of Virginia: Religion and Society in the Early Literature," *William & Mary Quarterly*, 5 (October 1948), 492-522, and 6 (January 1949), 24-41.

26. Sam Bass Warner, Jr., review of *The Other Bostonians* in *Political Science Quarterly*, 89 (June 1974), 413-414.

27. See Richard S. Alcorn and Peter R. Knights, "Most Uncommon Bostonians: A Critique of Stephan Thernstrom's *The Other Bostonians*" in *Historical Methods Newsletter*, 8 (June 1975), 98-114, and the rejoinder by Thernstrom, 115-120.

28. Robert and Helen M. Lynd, *Middletown: A Study in Acculturation* (New York, 1929).

29. Oscar Handlin, *Boston's Immigrants: A Study in Acculturation* (Cambridge, Mass., 1941, 1959; New York, 1972).

30. Barrington Moore, *Soviet Politics: The Dilemma of Power–the Role of Ideas in Social Change* (Cambridge, Mass., 1950, New York, 1965).

31. James Sterling Young, *The Washington Community, 1800-1828* (New York, 1966).

32. Charles Tilly, *The Vendee* (Cambridge, Mass., 1964).

33. Katz, op. cit.

34. The works of Eric Hobsbawm include: *The Age of Capital, 1848-1875* (London, 1975); *The Age of Revolution: Europe, 1789-1848* (New York, 1962, 1969); *Bandits* (New York, 1969); *Captain Swing* (New York, 1968 with George Rude); *Industry and Empire: An Economic History of Britain Since 1750* (London, 1968); *Primitive Rebels, Studies in Archaic Forms of Social Movement in the Nineteenth and Twentieth Centuries* (New York, 1959, 1963, 1965).

SELECT BIBLIOGRAPHY OF WORKS
BY STEPHAN THERNSTROM

Poverty and Progress: Social Mobility in a Nineteenth-Century City (Cambridge, Mass., 1964; New York, 1969).

Poverty, Planning, and Politics in the New Boston: The Origins of ABCD (New York, 1969).

Nineteenth-Century Cities: Essays in the New Urban History (New Haven, 1969, ed. with Richard Sennett).

The Other Bostonians: Poverty and Progress in the American Metropolis, 1880-1970 (Cambridge, Mass., 1973).

The Growth of Los Angeles in Historical Perspective: Myth and Reality (Los Angeles, 1970).

"Quantitative Methods in History: Some Notes," in S. M. Lipset and R. Hofstadter, eds., *Sociology and History: Methods* (New York, 1968), 59-78.

"Urbanization, Migration, and Social Mobility in Late Nineteenth-Century America," in Barton J. Bernstein, ed., *Towards a New Past: Dissenting Essays in American History:* (New York, 1968), 158-175.

"Immigrants and WASPS: Ethnic Differences in Occupational Mobility in Boston, 1890-1940," in Thernstrom and Sennett, *Nineteenth-Century Cities,* 125-164.

"Men in Motion: Some Data and Speculations about Urban Population Mobility in Ninteenth-Century America," Journal of Interdisciplinary History, 1 (Autumn 1970), 7-35, reprinted in Tamara K. Hareven, ed., *Anonymous Americans: Explorations in Nineteenth-Century Social History* (Englewood Cliffs, N.J., 1971), 17-47.

"Reflections on the New Urban History," Daedalus, 100 (Spring, 1971), 359-375, reprinted in Alexander B. Callow, ed., *American Urban History* (2nd. ed., New York, 1973), 672-684.

"The New Urban History," in Charles F. Delzell, ed., The *Future of History* (Nashville, Tenn., 1977), 43-52.

Co-editor, Harvard Studies in Urban History.

Eric E. Lampard

Eric E. Lampard (1922-   ) is Professor of History at the State University of New York at Stony Brook. He was formerly Professor of Economic History and Adjunct Professor of Urban and Regional Planning at the University of Wisconsin. He has long advocated that the study of urban history should be the study of the *process* of urbanization, and his publications have been influential in moving the field in that direction.

A CONVERSATION WITH
ERIC E. LAMPARD

STAVE: This is a nice place for an interview with someone interested in urbanization—Chesterfield, Massachusetts. Is the population two hundred?

LAMPARD: Something like that—unfeathered bipeds.

STAVE: Before I ask you about why or whether you're an urban historian, I'd like to get some background about your family, your education, and how you became interested in history. Could we start there?

LAMPARD: Well, I certainly am not much of an historian, nor for that matter an urban historian. Most of my original training in England was in economic history and demographic history. My work at Wisconsin was in economic history again and in land economics, and it's very obvious that my knowledge of history is quite limited [laughs]. So that is the kind of formal training I brought to the study of urban phenomena. And my interest in urban phenomena has largely been in connection with something else—namely, economics. Nevertheless, when reading about economic developments, one simply cannot avoid problems of population distribution and changes over time and the significance of these matters for economic development. Then one starts to look for normative population concentration, gets into cities. When I first got involved in this, around 1950 or thereabouts, I discovered there wasn't all that much to learn of interest to economic historians in what had been written about cities, American cities, up to that point. So I dabbled in urban history and got more and more interested in its possibilities while keeping my own narrow focus on economic questions.

STAVE: Were you brought up in an urban area?

LAMPARD: Yes, a very ancient urban area—Southampton in England. As a high school boy, I worked on medieval town records.

STAVE: How did you get involved in that?

LAMPARD: Through the school. There were school masters who were very interested, encouraging local boys to make good. One in particular got me interested in the local record of the Doomsday Book and later on I got on to town records.

STAVE: Did you have an interest in history from the earliest time?

LAMPARD: Yes, it must have been quite early. At the age of five or six, I was going through Cassel's many-volumed *History of England* and such bilge as Harmsworth's *With the Flag to Pretoria* and *Sixty Years a Queen.*

STAVE: What about your family? What kind of work did your father do?

LAMPARD: Oh, my father left school at the age of twelve and was an apprentice to a grocer, became a baker. My mother was a schoolteacher, which in the American sense sounds as if she must have had some formal education and mobility. But in the days when she became a teacher, in fact—as was true in the United States for a long time in many places—she was a pupil teacher; she learned the job in classrooms of infants and never really had any formal education other than Saturday mornings at the local Hartley Institute. Now it's the University of Southampton.

STAVE: What prompted you to go on to higher education?

LAMPARD: Well, I suppose it seemed much easier to me than the hard work that all my relatives and family had experienced. In fact, I was the first member of my family to complete secondary school and nearly the first to go to secondary school; there was my brother, but he dropped out after a short while and went to work.

STAVE: Where did you go to university?

LAMPARD: London University, School of Economics—*rerum cognoscere causas.*

STAVE: Now, while you were there, were there many people who today are considered urbanists? Any that you can think of, any of your contemporaries?

LAMPARD: No, I think any connection with cities in my education at LSE, if you can call it an education, came through public administration and the work of William A. Robson in municipal government and administrative law. Of course, in constitutional history one has to learn about the boroughs and reform of the boroughs and political administrative law. In economics and economic history not much attention was paid to urban phenomena.

STAVE: You said, "If you can call it an education." In talking to people, I've been finding some dissatisfaction with education, with what one learned in college and graduate school. Do you have any of this feeling?

LAMPARD: I think one has to take what people say with a pinch of salt. Reflecting back on one's education is a very distorting process. Maybe for what I could cope with at the time, I was getting a very good education. But, in retrospect, one would like to have done otherwise.

STAVE: Well, is there anything that stands out in your mind as needing improvement?

LAMPARD: Well, LSE generally, in my day—early in the second World War (I went back again after the war)—certainly needed a lot of improvement. It was one of the few places in England where there was, I suppose, some effort at mass education. The School, of course, had a very distinctive ideological tradition about education and no boarding and no living in; they thought it was very good for people to have to live out in the city, as a matter of fact. One can't really separate the ideology of the founders of the School of Economics from the fact of London and the kinds of people who wanted to study in social sciences. Those who would introduce Fabian utopias should in fact live in the city and, of course, the School of Economics always had a big evening program for working people, for professional people, and made a point of not providing any cosy intramural residential collegiate atmosphere.

STAVE: Do you think living in London at the time influenced you greatly?

LAMPARD: Well, I didn't get to live much in London because the school was promptly evacuated to Cambridge during the war. I didn't really get to live in London until after the war. But then, with the large numbers of ex-servicemen and so on, the school was greatly overcrowded. The London facilities were very small, and it was always mass education in contrast to some of the smaller or older richer universities; they were working, essentially, with smaller numbers, or at least the numbers were organized in smaller aggregations, and they could attempt different kinds of education. On the other hand, at the School of Economics one was exposed, if one took the trouble, to a remarkable group of men and women who were very often working in the war or who had work to do other than their academic work and were very much involved in public affairs and so forth, and being in London afterwards it was possible for many people to come visit.

STAVE: When did you come to the United States, and what prompted your coming?

LAMPARD: Well, I hadn't really determined when I finally graduated in 1948 what I was going to do. I was very interested in some of the new industrial developments in England, particularly the nationalized industries, but I wasn't quite ready to commit myself to that and I certainly must have had some kind of hankering for "further education," as they say in England. To the extent that I was going to specialize in economic history or economic development, I was most probably going to work in Anglo-Argentine economic relations and the development of the meat industry in Argentina and the connection with the British market. I had grown up with that in my home town—one of the prime targets of German bombing during the war was to knock out the cold storage facilities, where the boats brought the meat in from Argentina [laughs]. I doubt whether that interested me in the subject, but at least I'd known about this connection all my life, and relatives and other people in the town had worked on the boats going to Buenos Aires. To the extent that I had any focus, that was the direction in which I was going; but then Harold Laski asked me if I would like to spend a year in the United States. He had recently been in the United States and someone had said, "Do you know a young person who could come across for a year and teach—more or less any topic in economic history or policy would do." That was at Cornell College in Iowa. My first physical confrontation with the United States was Port Huron, Michigan, where—as Herbert Heaton used to say—many of the best immigrants had come into the United States.

STAVE: This is interesting—this is Steve Thernstrom's home town.

LAMPARD: Is that so? I don't recall what Heaton said about the natives! Well, that was where I got my official number and moved on to experience the joys of Parmalee transportation, crossing from one Chicago station to the other. I went out on the Northwestern local and arrived early in the morning at this little depot, as they call it, Mount Vernon, Iowa, and there, in this little "small town," I had my American baptism. I suppose it would be appropriate to say, "You know I couldn't have chosen a better place."

STAVE: [laughing] Why?

LAMPARD: [laughing] Rather than come into Boston or New York or one of those places where everybody comes in.

STAVE: How long did you stay there?

LAMPARD: That was only a year, 1948. I got to know many friends in Iowa City, and that was really my first confrontation with a state university. Cornell was an old Methodist college with an extremely interesting group of students at that time, since many in the student body were G.I.s. They had a very small college and an extremely good faculty. Later on when I got to Wisconsin, another of these big mills, I could at least appreciate the fact that there was a wide range of educational facilities in the United States. By no means was the big university necessarily better than the small college as a place to get one's liberal education. Different kinds of people need different things—unlike the situation in England, where we got more or less channeled or pushed from the word "go" as soon as we could breathe, in the old days anyway for my kind; I don't know what it's like now. But even between Cornell College and the State University of Iowa, there were enormous differences. I also got to know some of the other colleges—Grinnell, Coe, Ames, places of that sort. I think what impressed me the most about the American educational scene was its comparative diversity. It ranged so widely, both in the quality and quantity of the institutions.

STAVE: Now, you stayed there for a year.

LAMPARD: Yes, and in the course of that year I lost my interest in Argentine steers and became more interested in middle-western cows. I became very interested in the agricultural development of Iowa and that part of the upper Mississippi valley, and I even knew what I wanted to do: I wanted to work on the dairy industry in Wisconsin or in that area. Of course, the only way I could do that was, in effect, to sign up for a Ph.D. [laughs]. I had no more idea of getting involved in that business than of jumping over the moon when landing that morning at Cornell College in Mount Vernon, Iowa. And, I was extremely fortunate, for at the time I was admitted to Wisconsin, not only was Vernon Carstensen there beginning to develop specialized studies in agricultural history, but Abbott Usher, who had just retired from Harvard, had come there in the Economics Department. So there was a very fine opportunity for me to get to know the two men—a "Schleswiger" and a "Yankee"—who probably influenced me most in my subsequent work on the development of the dairy industry.

STAVE: So you took your Ph.D. at Wisconsin and the thesis was the rise of the dairy industry?[1]

LAMPARD: Yes. I'm trying to think now how this all happened. Of course, in studying agricultural developments the effects of urbanization and the development of urban markets were inescapable—particularly in that kind of agricultural development. In contrast to the earlier frontier grain cultivation, the livestock industries and the dairy industry in particular were inescapably bound up with urbanization, the growth of urban populations. Tom Cochran wrote around at some point and wanted to know whether anyone wanted to conduct an exploratory study for the Committee on Research in Economic History, which was interested in exploring the relationship between urbanization and economic growth. I went to see Tom Cochran and Dorothy Thomas, the demographer, and Simon Kuznets, the economist, who were involved in this study at the University of Pennsylvania. And I eventually got what was, in effect, a postdoctoral fellowship at Penn. I think that was probably the most productive single year of my life in the sense that it was an extremely able group of people focusing on related topics. The population redistribution and economic growth studies that Everett Lee and Dick Easterlin[2] were producing, squired by Dorothy Thomas and Simon Kuznets—that work was going on. There was another group, the Norristown group, working there—Sid Goldstein and others on the development of Norristown.[3] And, so between these two groups I was able to get a great deal of help and assistance.

STAVE: So it was very exciting.

LAMPARD: Yes, it was indeed.

STAVE: How do you think it affected your own thinking and your own work?

LAMPARD: Well, in a sense, it was the first time I'd had any time to stop and think. And not being under the pressures of graduate school anymore or the burdens of teaching, for the moment one could really stop and think—engage in reading and writing in ways where one explored the possibilities of one's own thinking.

STAVE: Well, you mentioned the dairy industry, the effect of urbanization on agriculture, this mix, this tie-in. In a sense, people might say, "Well, he started off looking at the dairy industry—very much an agricultural topic. What does it have to do with urbanization, and why would Eric Lampard move in this direction?" What were the ties? How do you bring these together?

LAMPARD: Well, I don't think in terms of this kind of dichotomy. I think this grew partly out of my reading in those years. It certainly goes back much earlier to my work at LSE, and my work with Abbott Usher was precisely along questions of social systems and economic systems and location, innovation, transformation—questions which were at a level of abstraction above simple dichotomies between rural and urban, agriculture and industry, or things of that sort. So, I guess somewhere along the line in there I began reading in geographical and ecological studies. I went back and read some of the old work of Friedrich Ratzel,[4] some of the French geographers, some of the Chicago human ecology school, which was empirically devoted to the local Chicago scene. Nevertheless, to the extent that there was a theoretical core underlying ecological thinking, it was precisely in terms of settlement patterns, distribution, redistributions, and densities and these kinds of things.

STAVE: Now, what brought you to reading in ecology? Because it seems to me, at least, with much of what you've written about urban history and how it should be approached, you look at it from the ecological point of view, the systems point of view. Was this your own doing, out of your other interests, or did someone suggest, "Why don't you take a look at this Chicago school; why don't you look at these ecologists?"

LAMPARD: No, no. I think this was my own bent. At this point, undoubtedly, the most immediate mentor I had had in this direction would have been Abbott Usher—both in the history of invention and in the phenomenon of location and particularly his interest in population distributions. And somehow all of these things sort of came together, if not clearly—I still don't see these things clearly—but the relationship between agriculture, cities, change—all this fits very nicely into this kind of spatial thinking.

STAVE: Speaking of clarity, you're very much aware of the essay by Charles Glaab, "The Historian and the American City."[5] Glaab talks about your call for a conceptualization of urban history, and he makes the comment: "How much effect has this kind of exhortation had on the actual procedures of urban historians? Probably very little." And he talks about the 1961 meeting of the AHA; most of the active scholars were gathered there to discuss your now famous 1961 *American Historical Review* article.[6] The questioning, he says, "revealed limited understanding of his position and less sympathy for it. The role of precise definition and logically constructed theory in historical work has traditionally been minor, and so it is likely to remain." Do you think this assessment in 1965 was (a) valid in 1965 [laughs], and (b) what do you make of it in 1974—do you think things have changed?

LAMPARD: Well, I think it was valid. In effect, it's been almost decades because those few ideas that I put in the '61 article were really ideas that I developed back in 1954-55 at Pennsylvania. They were implied in my original piece in *Economic Development and Cultural Change* and in the report that I did for the Committee on Research in Economic History.[7] In the departmental sense of urban history, I don't think anyone had yet paid a great deal of attention to it. This is not to say that what I was saying was very original or very earth-shaking from the point of view of students of geography. And, even much of the economics of it was familiar stuff, although economists really hadn't done much with it, with the exception of the location and land economists up to that point; "regional science" was still at the conception stage. But I think what Charles said was correct and I would attribute this not so much to the churlishness of the audience as to my own inability to state these things very clearly. I only find things out myself as I go along [laughs]. I don't see it all beforehand; it's always sort of through a dark glass, and that is why I have to depend or lean on economic theory. But, I don't think the situation is true now. In fact, people have gone far beyond, I think, the things that I originally suggested; and I would attribute this to the fact that the dissertation scale project is a very convenient format for processing three or four decades of manuscript census data with the aid of computers. Nothing was stopping this work being done decades before and it needed no Banquo to come from the grave and tell people that this material was there. I think Merle Curti's work on Trempealeau County[8] had an important effect here, and certainly one can go back to the work of the agricultural historians and the regional historians in the United States and find plenty of forerunners and prophets of this kind of work. I've always been impressed with the work of James Malin in Kansas[9] —very illuminating—and I, personally, have always found Frederick Jackson Turner's work [laughs] very interesting.[10]

STAVE: Yes, I've come across something that you've written, your "Two Cheers for Quantitative History."[11]

LAMPARD: That's the mathematics committee in history, Bob Fogel's History Advisory Committee. They had a conference in Madison. There were a number of papers given and some of those papers have been collected together by Leo Schnore as *The New Urban History,*[12] and I wrote a kind of soft-sell foreword to it.

STAVE: I think you talk about Turner there, don't you?

LAMPARD: Yes. Well, Turner was, at least by implication, and, indeed, among his graduate and undergraduate students and colleagues, a sort of an early quantifier. And—I think Dick Jensen has often pointed this out—some of the students of Turner and Libby, in the senior theses that they wrote in those days, were doing precisely the kind of local counting that, however modest the operation (and after all they were undergraduates), nevertheless was a forerunner of the work that's been done more recently with the manuscript census data and efforts to use certain kinds of statistical techniques in the analyses of this information.

STAVE: Now, the people you're talking about who have influenced you and might have influenced the field of what's become urban history certainly are not urbanists. And then you're talking about quantification as well. Do you equate urban history with quantification?

LAMPARD: No, no. Quantification is simply one of many tools. Enthusiasts probably overrate it. It hasn't been adequately exploited, certainly not only in urban history, but in economic history, where it has had it's most powerful impact so far. But after all, most other social scientists—certainly many, many sociologists, many economists—have been quantifying a long time with greater or lesser success.

STAVE: Well, you talk about the quantifiers in that piece in the Schnore book, *The New Urban History,* as "historical accountants."

LAMPARD: Yes. Well that's what I think it is really. It's accounting business and statistical manipulation, and, to me, the most interesting part is not all of that so much as the actual model-building and the conceptualization and the sort of setting up things in ways that you can test with this statistical information. Now, what I find the exciting thing about work in economic history is that people can actually tell you what they're going to do and how they're going to do it [laughs]. You can tell how good or how bad it comes out, and one can even know what one would need to know in order to have it come out right, although it rarely does.

STAVE: Well, you indicate as far as urban history is concerned, quantification is in its pioneering stage now.

LAMPARD: I would tend to think it is, yes. It'll be taken for granted after a while. People will stop huffing and puffing about it, and it'll just be taken for granted as almost a necessary tool for certain kinds of historical research. But I certainly would regard it as a very limited kind of tool. I'm not certain that historians have all that number of strong methods to work with. So we sort of have to "quantificate."

STAVE: What do you foresee as being useful in moving out of the pioneer stage into a more sophisticated stage?

LAMPARD: Well, I would think a great deal more can be done with spatial analysis in quantitative terms on the actual functional design of cities, the social structure of cities, the morphological features. The problem there, I think, is with areal units at the moment. We rely too much on ward boundaries, and, of course, a number of scholars are already going down into micro-units analysis—blocks, tracts, and constructing their own grids. I would think a great deal more could be done this way with more sensitive kinds of measures of social-economic status. I'm not very happy with the use of census occupational categories as an indication of anything.

STAVE: Why not?

LAMPARD: Well, they're extremely gross, and they bear very little relationship to people's working lives and experience; and I don't think that census categories—they're very blunt instruments—have the fineness for intensive local historical studies. Certainly there's enough criticism of them in the nineteenth-century census literature, and they are not all that reliable even for macro-studies. And I would think that people working on case studies in particular should do no more than begin with these things: they tell you something; but eventually, presumably, as one gets to know the local scene and the local population, one can begin to make distinctions peculiar to that place or peculiar to certain elements in this population that would make the use of a term like "semi-skilled" or "professional" much different in one city from another, especially when combined with local data, i.e., data which originates locally. And I think that a great deal more will be done with this, and perhaps even dimensions that have not as yet been quantified much will become available for quantification. But, in contrast to economic history, I think that the use of quantitative methods in most other fields that I'm aware of is going to be limited simply because these other focuses—social history, political history— don't have the theoretical structures, and I'm not yet certain that they can. I tend to think that they deal with much more complicated things than economy. Economy, as conceived by an economist is an extremely simple model of the world, and the relationships are so much more specifiable and certain and logical and so forth; whereas, I'm not so certain that in political theory or sociological theory, if that's the right word for it, the theories have this character; or perhaps the problem they are dealing with is much more difficult, complex, obscure. The work will be more empirical.

STAVE: Well, if historians, especially urban historians, move in the direction you are talking about, do you think that there is a danger of the methodology becoming more significant to many than the substance? Or does methodology simply illuminate substance? Here I'm thinking of the criticism, and I've asked some other interviewees about this, of "barefoot empiricism."

LAMPARD: Yes. Well, in a sense that's my point. The lack of theory is a critical factor. This is why, in fact, very little of the work gets beyond accounting, in a sense. It doesn't get to model-building and explanatory operations and testing and so forth even though we know all of the "rigormarole" [sic] of scientific method. I don't really think there is much by way of substance other than what the method reveals. I tend to think of it, most of history, as bunk, or of historiography as a branch of fiction rather than nonfiction. Now, what are we going to do about this? What we come up with will never be any better than the methods that we used to find out—and I'm not arguing this from the point of view of the quantifiers, far from it—there are more things on heaven and on earth than are dreamed of by quantifiers. But, as a problem of knowledge, I don't see that any knowledge is worth having unless you know how you got it—not the data alone, but what you have done to the data. And so the problem of the sort of methodological tail wagging the substantive dog—I don't think that's an adequate formulation of it—is always there. This is not to say that history is nonsense. Historiography is, after all, a letristic art and comes out of literature, out of story-telling, and I find it very akin to journalism—different deadlines but many of the problems of composition, selectivity, organization, and the telling of the story, and the sort of derivation of the plot; these are essentially arts, I think, and I'm certain that this is the long-run value of history—that it has to be communicated, it's essentially something to be communicated. I think those of us who are digging around in quantifying, methodizing, and so forth, all we're really doing is sort of a set of preliminary operations *on* the data, *on* history, and that ultimately the story-teller will have to take such findings into his account, into his writing.

STAVE: I see. In that "Two Cheers for Quantification" piece, I think you conclude by noting all historians best serve their muse by serving best her readers.

LAMPARD: Yes. And I think we are a lay subject. Or rather, I think we deal with lay audiences; our audiences are not necessarily professional, in the way that economists, political scientists, other magicians of that kind are professional. We try and communicate in ordinary language, ultimately, and I see a very grand role and responsibility for the telling of stories [laughs] about the Folk. It's a very ancient role, I think, and it has been terribly perverted and abused and, at the same time, probably we historians are the only people who care. If we don't really care about the past and take the business of, in a sense, inventing and creating a past seriously, no one else will; there are plenty of other operators around (with or without Ph.D.s) who will, for various purposes, invent more convenient ones or more pleasing ones for their audience. So that all of this methodological stuff is very critical, because I don't think what we can really ever know is any better than our methods of finding out. I think one realizes this in, say, anthropological studies, in the use of archaeological data, or in the historical interpretation of archaeological data. Particularly those of us who have worked in modern history haven't taken these problems seriously enough in the past. And, apart from the general admonition that one shouldn't falsify the sources or one should try to make a thorough canvass of sources, we don't really take much responsibility or our graduate schools of history have not shown that much responsibility in the training of historians with these infinitely complicated questions of how one can create knowledge out of remote times and places with limited resources.

May I add that, in the published version of "Two Cheers . . ." that has just come to hand, some kind editor has completely altered the meaning of that last sentence you quoted. It now has my plea for communication coupled with a call for "an end to quantifying," whereas I actually called for "an end to quantificating," or huffing and puffing about quantification. The editor converted me from an agnostic into an atheist, from a 0.66 endorsement to a 0.00 rejection!

STAVE: There are two things I wanted to get to, to ask. One has to do with the origins of the 1961 *AHR* article, because essentially, if you have been preaching at all, you have been preaching conceptualization and methodology. What were the origins? How did you come to write that article, which I think is a very key piece in the historiography of urban history, even though you're not an urban historian [laughs]?

LAMPARD: I wrote that in 1958-59, in there somewhere, for the Social Science Research Council Committee on Urbanization; I was a member at the time. They thought it might be useful to pull this stuff together, and they more or less agreed that I should go ahead and publish that piece and see what reactions we would get to it while the committee was still in existence (it went on until 1965). We got some feedback from that, and part of our response to that feedback, in turn, was to commission Charles Glaab to do that more elaborate and comprehensive survey on the historical profession and the study of U.S. cities that came out in the committee's volume, *The Study of Urbanization,* edited by Hauser and Schnore.

STAVE: So, in a sense, this was prompted by the committee and, as I said, I think it has had a great influence on the direction of urban history. What influence do you think it's had? Do you have any direct indicators of this?

LAMPARD: No, I don't think I do really. I'm much more aware of the influence of my earlier paper, "The History of Cities in the Economically Advanced Areas," in *Economic Development and Cultural Change.* A lot of work has gone on in urban economics, as the field is now called, as well as in development studies and a lot of references are made and criticisms are made, or expansions and qualifications are made, and a lot of research has been focused from that article. But I really think that the kinds of work that I had in mind in the American History article really have only been coming to the fore in very recent years, and, as I say, it's mainly in the form of the case study which, to me, is fine. It is a natural scale of subject for Ph.D.-type research and, of course, people like Sam Warner and Steve Thernstrom have gone far beyond local case studies.[13] But I still think that a lot of useful research can be done by graduate students on the scale of the particular city and some particular time span, an analysis of populations. Certainly I have learned enormously from my former students—people like Bill Derby, Peter Knights, Kathleen Neils Conzen, Roger Simon, Joe Garonzik, and so forth. In fact, I would think that, perhaps since Abbott Usher, my most important teachers have been students [laughs]. That's what I've learned of urban history. And, of course, reading the work, in effect, of other people's students when they've published their stuff.

STAVE: Now, Knights' material has been published—*The Plain People of Boston,* "Men in Motion"[14]—this kind of thing. Simon has, actually here in your bookcases, a dissertation on Milwaukee,[15] and I guess, Kathleen Neils Conzen has also written on Milwaukee in *The New Urban History.*[16]

LAMPARD: Yes. They will make Milwaukee famous.

STAVE: Are there any special trademarks—anything that distinguishes this kind of dissertation—that you'd like to see graduate students doing, aside from simply case studies.

LAMPARD: Well, I think that most of my students established some kind of *modus vivendi* with quantification. Very few of the students either in economic history or urban studies that I worked with ever went very far beyond quantitative studies. But most of their quantitative cases involve big general questions.

STAVE: Well, what kinds of dissertations would you like to see? What kinds of studies would you like to see being done? Any specific kinds of studies that you have in mind?

LAMPARD: I would tend to think a lot more of the same and better. I would like to see more micro-studies of histories of blocks, and the histories of parts of towns, very intense—almost brick by brick; bricks add up and fit into frameworks.

STAVE: I find this brick-by-brick point interesting because of one of your most recent pieces, "The Urbanizing World" in *The Victorian City,* edited by Dyos and Wolff.[17] It's masterful piece in the sense that it's so broad and you cover so much territory, rather than covering brick by brick. Do you have anything to say to this [laughs]?

LAMPARD: [laughing] Yes. Well, if I'm going to keep going with my windy generalizations, somebody has to be doing the brick-by-brick work, so I'm a sort of scavenger for these intensive studies. I see things in them that I think affect larger patterns. The edifice may not be sound, but the bricks are. But fundamentally, no matter how grand and pretentious the scale on which I sometimes write, in fact, I never really try to handle more than two or three ideas at a time. That's how I keep sane.

STAVE: In that article, while you covered a wide geographic range, you were limited to questions of population and . . .

LAMPARD: I'm really getting at certain kinds of population change. I make some grand assumptions about the economic and demographic relations going on and then try to see what the emotional and visual reactions to those changes were, and then I sort of play the same game with the problem of developing areas today. All of the breast-beating and introspection that went on at the end of the nineteenth century—I find much of that paralleled and echoed in relation to what's happening in the great variety of developing countries today.

STAVE: Well, do you think that this is a legitimate kind of operation? Does the past teach us? Does it set up an analogy for these developing countries. I know you've made some differentiations.

LAMPARD: Yes. Well, I think in terms of demographic possibilities and economic possibilities—formally identical, as I see them. You have to update for knowledge and technology and financial institutions. But conceptually, the problems are almost identical in demographic terms and economic terms; the terms merely have different numbers; but there are infinitely variable cultural, social, and political terms and so forth. But this is what I was saying earlier. I think that when you have powerful theory you can sort of take on the world; but as your theory gets weaker and weaker—or is unable to incorporate more exogenous variables—you have to get back into more concrete, circumstantial cases. In some ways that's a harder kind of knowledge to get at, but in some ways it's perhaps more useful—more useful knowledge, more akin to practical wisdom. And I think economic theory and demographic frameworks do enable us to conceptualize for vast, varied situations and, I suppose, that's the charm and fascination of theory. But, I think that is where the quantifier comes in; the theory without the operational tests is as vapid and useless as anything else, but the two have to go together. Theorizing without the operational testing can be rather a vain exercise, while the numbers without the theory can be as deceptive probably as any other kind of empiricism, as you pointed out earlier.

STAVE: So this is where the conceptualization is so significant in what you have been saying all along. Several questions with the *Victorian City* article. One is that you end with the Geddes quote about moving from Polis to Necropolis,[18] and you mention that the city today is already a megalopolis, and I think you say, "It's still too early to say whether it will have even a surviving monument." What do you see as the future of the Victorian or the industrial city or whatever you want to call it?

LAMPARD: Well, there I put on my historian's hat and say: "I don't deal with the future." No. In the sense of extrapolating and interpreting what will be called "city" in the future, I think that we tend to use language as a very flexible and adjustable animal and almost chameleon-like in its ability to fit itself into situations. There's also a strong inertia in language and heaven only knows what they will be calling "city" in the year 2000 or the year 3000! But clearly, I think, historically we can see that what we call "city" today and what they called "city" in the mid-nineteenth century and what they called "city" in the fifteenth century or the twelfth century are very different social fruits; and yet the language enables students to compare these apples, pears, and bananas and really think they are talking about the same thing. And I suppose there's a kind of romanticism or symbolism in the word "city." Now they're no longer there, they've been found, and when people had them they didn't really care all that much about them. But now that we've got into this kind of urbanized region pattern—as Geddes would call it, "the megalopolis stage"—there's almost a kind of nostalgia, an urban romanticism, and I'm not certain that these places were all that they're cracked up to be in the past. The particular kind of central city and the daily routines and movements that we associate with the late nineteenth century, early twentieth century, were very different from eighteenth and seventeenth century patterns. I see no reason why late twentieth and twenty-first century patterns should not be equally remote from those of the mid-nineteenth century.

STAVE: Let's look at the United States for a minute—the ecosystem, the patterns that might develop. What relationship do you think these might have to the whole question of ecology today and the question of energy systems? A very colloquial way of asking this is: do you think the "energy crisis" is going to make a big difference for our cities?

LAMPARD: Well, it will certainly place a great emphasis on the need to develop alternatives if conventional, traditional forms of energy conversion and consumption are going to be relatively high-priced. There will be a very strong incentive to find other means of communication and transportation that will be less energy-intensive than the old petroleum pattern. I would think that would certainly have some kind of impact on the overall pattern of urban settlements, on metropolitan areas; but I wouldn't see any return to nineteenth century conditions, even cleaned-up nineteenth conditions. I sort of see them as specific to their time and place and part of the unfolding. I don't see us going back, short of some total disruption of human systems which, presumably now, is intellectually inconceivable other than as an act of God—His or Her judgment [laughs]. So that apart from the extreme unthinkable situation, I would expect change to occur, not simply the continuation of, say, the tendencies of the last fifty or one hundred years, but some modification of them, gradually on to something different—parameters change, possibly new variables.

STAVE: Do you think communication systems have made a big difference so that you cannot return to the cleaned-up nineteenth century conditions?

LAMPARD: I would tend to think so, yes—electrical, electronic, etc., as Allan Pred suggests[19] —also new forms of organizations.

STAVE: In your "Urbanizing World" piece, you use 20,000 population as what you see today as urban population. You know, it's always a question—"What's a city?"—and you were saying that it's apples, oranges, and pears. Why do you settle on something like 20,000?

LAMPARD: Largely because the United Nations serves up the data in that bracket.

STAVE: Do you think that this is a valid breaking point?

LAMPARD: It's valid for identifying some kind of gross notion of urban population, I would tend to think. Although, as they point out in their publications, the range of administrative, political, and legal situations in countries is such that fairly many places of less than that population are "urban." In some countries, many places considerably larger than that would not be "urban" as in other countries. So it's an approximation, and I don't think one takes that kind of thing too seriously. Of course, that's part of the problem, I think, when one comes into making larger studies of urbanization. One gets to take the figure somewhat more seriously and attach too much weight to it. I don't think it makes much difference really whether you take 2,500, 8,000, 10,000, 100,000. At times there's a greater or lesser array; cities of different sizes are growing faster than others. But the whole measurement of urban population is so gross that I don't find that it makes much difference where the cut-off point is. But in some ways we greatly exaggerate the amount of urban population in the United States; in other ways we underestimate it simply by using the old, conventional 2,500 plus or even the 8,000-plus definition. And to suggest somehow that there is a homogeneous population in some "urban" sense that differentiates it from population settlements of less than whatever the number is—this is an absurd fantasy; size is a continuous variable.

STAVE: Well, here we're sitting in a summer home in a town of 200. Are we rural? Are the people who live here all year round rural?

LAMPARD: I wouldn't know what the word meant. They're different from people in New York City in certain observable ways. They're different from people in Springfield in certain observable ways. But I would doubt whether New York or Springfield or Chesterfield is urban or adequately represents urban or rural at either end of some spectrum. Urban and rural has never seemed to me a very useful distinction. Local people here are rural nonfarm commuters nowadays. People and space—they're my fundamental categories, and everything else sort of has to be invented, is a human creation. Culture, societies, artificial terms like "region," "urban"—we lose a lot when we use these terms too rigidly. We gain something presumably, or we hope we do; but fundamentally you've got people and space and hence different kinds of settlements, different cultures, different technologies, different environmental tensions, and that's our old ecological complex. The conditions of life and livelihood in Chesterfield also depend on energy!

STAVE: Exactly. All right. Culture, space, people—what about ideas in urban history?

LAMPARD: Oh, I fight shy of ideas, of course. I really don't know how to deal with ideas—that's pretty obvious. They seem to me the most difficult things to handle and the most difficult things to measure and interpret. I can well believe that this is perhaps going to be one of the great areas of quantitative exploration. Intellectual history may well become the quantitative field par excellence.

STAVE: How do you see that?

LAMPARD: Well, with man's infinite capacity to deceive himself, he can start categorizing ideas and codifying them and putting them on tapes and juggling them around, tabulating them, factoring them, cross-tabulating them, correlating them. So that we could very well find out that the Enlightenment wasn't very enlightened at all. Conventional notions, as these things exist and get packaged in literary form, are rather overly discreet, limited things—semantic traps.

STAVE: Within the context of urbanization, there is one place I think ideas seem to play a role and that's in what we've come to call "suburbanization," for want of a better word. You might be familiar with some of the work on the "moral imperatives" of suburbanization and I think you yourself, in the *Victorian City* piece, talk about Garden Cities and this kind of thing. In a sense, these are ideas—where people belong and how they belong to places. How do you react to these kind of things in urban history?

LAMPARD: I tend to think they're probably the most important—not necessarily as urban history, but in the sense of how human beings see themselves as individuals and their families, and how they see their relationships toward other people and their environments. As these things become formalized and structured or packaged, I would think that they're enormously important. This is how *we* live. This is who *we* are. And, in effect, this is the area of human communication—how people learn to relate to each other. This is a critical part of our environment that I personally have very few resources to deal with. I think one senses the gravity of this in the efforts of historians to create images of the past and to create worlds in the past—the idea of communities and community, the idea of the frontier and frontier society, and the effort to characterize these situations or periods as having some generic quality, some all-pervasive essence. This is the human imagination at work. Of course it operates in many areas, but it is particularly noticeable in the idea of the design for human communities. It must undoubtedly come out of the religious and traditional elements in the development of culture. The term "suburb," for instance, is a metaphor to me: the varieties of suburbs in history, over time, and even in the present are so great that you can use that word "suburb" and convey something which isn't really there; and yet that word is so evocative and powerful. Howard's Garden Cities, however, were anti-suburb.

STAVE: Well, can you separate suburbanization from urbanization?

LAMPARD: No, I don't think so, except as conceptual conveniences. I think all we're really talking about there is some variations in the forms of local concentration, the differential rates between peripheral and central growth, and perhaps some changes in overall density within the urbanized area—things of that sort, which I find enormously interesting, but the significance of which I don't always see. But clearly an enormous amount of fantasy has developed in our twentieth-century communications about the suburb, which is largely the result of gross census categories and crude census measurement and not just of real-estate promotion. I was struck just sometime this spring by an article in the *New York Times* which began: "Since the end of World War II the American population has been moving to the suburbs." It was a lead-in to a story. What the guy wanted was to get on to something else, some specific situation, and report it; but the fact that he could condense all that human experience into this grossly misleading historical statement! And what was it meant to imply anyhow? The words sort of take on a currency of their own, a weight, which they don't really have. I feel this about "city." "City" has an enormous metaphorical weight. But "suburbs"—Henry VIII was complaining about suburbs as well as wives, and suburbs in Rome were a horror. They've always been there, I would think, as long as there have been cities.

STAVE: Do you think the American suburb is different?

LAMPARD: Well, of course, the thing that I said earlier about cities—the same applies to suburbs. They're not the same animal. I think the work of Ken Jackson has shown this.

STAVE: Yes, he has a nice essay in Mohl and Richardson's *The Urban Experience*.[20]

LAMPARD: Yes, and also in Schnore's *The New Urban History*.[21] In a sense they've always been there and what I hope he'll do, if he continues in this line of work, is—having established the fact that they are there, always have been, and we're stuck with them—that he will actually get around to differentiate more about their character over time. At the moment he is sort of using a variety of gross longitudinal measures rather like a sociologist in order to establish that the animal is there. Once he's established the animal is there, then I would like to see Jackson or his students really go deeper into the varieties of suburbs and, perhaps, changes in their nature. I wish Bridenbaugh had done more of this for colonial cities instead of just differentiating them from rural or frontier populations.[22]

STAVE: I wanted to ask this with respect to urbanization and your 1970 article in the *Pacific Historical Review*, "The Dimensions of Urban History."[23] You wrote that

> the study of urbanization is reducible to three basic questions: (1) How do cities grow and how does a population, to a greater or lesser degree, become resident in the cities? This is the study of urbanization as dependent variable. (2) What difference does it make (and to whom) that some activity or other aspect of population is "urban". This is the study of urbanization as independent variable. (3) What are the consequences for cities and citizens of *continuing* urbanization? This is the study of urbanization of society or, more specifically, of urban transformation of society.

Can you elaborate on this at all? Have you extended beyond this? Do you see any other questions involved in the study of urbanization or do you think that these are the basics?

LAMPARD: There I was letting it all hang out [laughs]. No, it's my sort of grand construction of the thing. But I don't even begin to see what's involved in those very things that I'm saying.

STAVE: Have any studies touched on these satisfactorily, answered some of these questions for you?

LAMPARD: Well, I think we know a considerable amount about the social changes that create cities. I tend to think that we know much less exactly about the effects that cities have on society—in other words, the cumulative feedback on social change as these phenomena become more and more the characteristic human habitat. I would see this as almost the modern human predicament and thus approachable by an infinite variety of disciplines and approaches and not exclusively the responsibility of the historian, let alone the urban historian. I always thought our contribution was going to be comparatively limited; but I think that there's so much that we don't know about the past that might be interesting and informative instead of the kind of pasts that get created in some introductory paragraphs by sociologists when they get down to some contemporary project, or in some fantasy being purveyed by the Supreme Court as it leads into some new judgment accommodating ourselves to the present. As human beings we're constantly reinventing these past things to meet the needs of the present. But, generally, I don't see the study of history by historians as being related to the present in that way. I see the study of the past as something that exists in its own right—a sort of disinterested virtuous activity [laughs].

We as historians, or should I say modern historians (because certainly ancient historians and medievalists have been doing this all their lives), are now beginning to focus on cities. And if we're trying to get at the nature of our contemporary urban situation and how it evolved (which may or may not be useful to others), and if our historical work is to have implications for the present and our future and so forth, I think that those three are the fundamental questions that we have to keep in mind. How and why in some comparatively discreet period of human history did this phenomenon of urbanization gather momentum and take on such force? What difference did that make to us as human beings, as members of groups, societies, and so forth? And as this situation, this condition, becomes more characteristic of human populations everywhere, what does this do to their societies? So it's really coming back to my old interest in transformations and the people-in-space situation, recognizing that everything else is more or less affected by the way people are arranged in space.

STAVE: Which of your own writings do you like best?

LAMPARD: Well, of course, one goes through periods when one can't bear to look at them. There are other times when they're the only things in the world you can look at [laughs]. At times when you're utterly ashamed, you want to repudiate them; at other times, you really think that there isn't much else worth reading. I don't think that I have any great interest in any *one*. I'm always aware of their shortcomings, the inability to say what I want to get at, the inability to marshal enough evidence of a particular kind that would convince me that what I'm saying is so. I'm always aware of the limitations of what I'm saying or doing. I do have a tendency to repeat myself. But I think that by persisting in a rather narrow area or in a rather narrow focus, particularly one which has such grandiose implications as I've been suggesting all along, any clarification and any accumulation of knowledge in this area can be important. This is why I've learned so much from what my former students do because, in a sense, they are solving their own problems, and they are also providing me with data which I can relate to my problems.

STAVE: But again on this question: you have written a large number of articles on urbanization. Does anything stand out as a favorite—one thing that you would stand by and feel truly proud of?

LAMPARD: No, I don't think so. I think I would be almost apologetic. I would think my piece on "The History of Cities in the Economically Advanced Areas," with all the warts on it—it's something that I sweated out—treats or broaches the first two of the three questions you mentioned. It was written in 1953-54 and published in 1955 in *Economic Development and Cultural Change*. That's the one that, I think, I live with most and I constantly go back to it and marvel [laughs].

STAVE: [laughing] At how you did it twenty years ago?

LAMPARD: [laughing] Yes. How did I know that? Even though I know that it's not true. But, by and large, I'm not a promoter of my own work, although I often quote myself! I'm always happy when other people pick it up.

STAVE: What about other people's work? If you had to choose six of your favorite works in the field.

LAMPARD: Ouch! [laughs] The field of urban history?

STAVE: Well, how about trying both: in general, your favorite history books and then if there's anything in urban history that is of great interest to you.

LAMPARD: [long pause] No, I don't think I could name six off hand. From the point of view of books that are very useful in teaching, I think Sam Warner's *Streetcar Suburbs*[24] is the one that I've found students respond to most. This book makes them think in ways they've never thought before; they're changed after they've read that. Whether they like it or don't like it ultimately is beside the point, but they're different people after they've read that book.

STAVE: In what way?

LAMPARD: Well, I think they've got some sense of cities changing and they've got some sense of physical environment and some sense of transportation and accordingly some sense of the way in which city residents change. And it's all so concrete and so specific, something that they can respond to. I'm not certain that there is much historical writing that really creates this sense of time and place, that has a historical concreteness. Very few historians that I find, and I think it's particularly noticeable in urban history, can take the reader out of *his* time and place and put him in that time and place; the use of the literary method in historical writing does not guarantee a great literature. As students respond to books, naturally they're always talking out of their own experience and their own concerns and they can deal, say, with the American revolution and the problems of constitution-making as though it were a question in their own lives—which, perhaps, is some people's idea of what the study of history should be, but it isn't mine. My idea would be precisely the opposite—that students would realize the great difference between themselves and the founding fathers or the constitution-makers. Similarly, in dealing with cities, they would realize that the mid-nineteenth century and later nineteenth-century experience of Boston and its spreading communities were very different from their own experience, say, of living on Long Island or of living around a metropolis in the later twentieth century. I think I am being consistent here with my earlier notions about historical study—that it is, so to speak, to transport us from our own limitations, our own personal experience, into something that is very different, or partly different. In that sense, it can tell us indirectly more about ourselves than if we simply assume that the founding fathers and their problems were analogous or similar, that they were the same kind of people we are, and so forth.

One of the problems that interests me in teaching urban history is to somehow create the idea that, or get the student to appreciate that, cities did not provide services and that city governments weren't there to service the population—that they were little sovereignties, little body politics, that had a police power. To make students understand that the legal and political meaning of the term "police power" is something other than "cops" or "support your local police." Precisely the problem students face is the conversion of these rather exclusive and highly structured legal corporations, and the settlements that they controlled, into our contemporary all-knowing, all-seeing, all-providing, omni-competent, big city governments—that is, a kind of transporting them into another world.

I would far sooner be critical than laudatory of books. Precisely what is lacking, I think, is a good political history of American cities. I mean political in the larger sense—not just elections and running for office, who governs, but the nature of local government and community self-definition, community organization, community order, and the extension of these ancient, inherited instruments into the nineteenth century, and the transformation worked by the twentieth century. I think there's something of that, of course, in this old book by Ernest Griffith on *American City Government: The Colonial Period*.[25] But this, I think, is where lies the creativity of the historian—the capacity to project a different sense of person and place and social structure and social direction—and I would certainly welcome some more general books on the political history. One picks up hints in the writing of, say, Wade[26] or McKelvey[27] of all these things happening, but not of the way they happened. There the changes are almost obvious and taken for granted. What I want to do is to say: stop, look how marvelous this transformation is, for better or for worse, how great the changes that have occurred, and don't take anything for granted, but regard it all as a marvel the way the thing unfolds—the changes. Warner does this again in the middle of *The Private City*,[28] and Sam Hays is trying it for a later period.[29]

I suppose ultimately I would like to see much more work done in the area of intellectual history, the history of ideas, in terms of urban consciousness and urban self-consciousness. I, myself, am not very convinced about what I hear of the urban mind or the rural mind. I've done enough work in American history sources where I don't find urban minds and rural minds very obviously at work. But I'm certain something can be done with this; I sense the need for it, but perhaps because of my own lack of experience in this area.

STAVE: Well this is helpful, I think, because you answered the question about potential kinds of things that you'd like to see done. If we go back to books that you appreciate, I'm glad that you mentioned Sam Warner because he mentioned you [laughs] and your *Victorian City* article in his interview as one which he thought an excellent piece. So it's a good mutual admiration society [laughs]. Is there anyone else?

LAMPARD: Well, I also learned a lot from Roy Lubove's works, not only in the housing field, but his general work on the development of social work and planning.[30] I found these very interesting. There again, I don't necessarily always agree with him, but I find his work extremely valuable as a teaching medium. It's readable, clear, informed, and always provocative, and students react to that. I don't find political work yet, or even work in social structure, that affects me in the same way as some of these other works. I think the political field is still wide open, from the point of view of urban history. Much is going on, of course, and I'm certain that all of these studies contribute to our understanding of American history. I think I agree with Michael Frisch's argument that urban history at some point has to become or merge into mainstream history.[31] I have never really disagreed with that, but I also have to be interested in urban history and cities as human settlements and so forth in and for itself. I don't find the treatments of social structure and political history that I need; perhaps this is because of the legacy of the Progressive tradition in political historical writing. One mustn't just knock the Progressives. I'm certain that if I were alive at that time I would have been a Progressive—and probably for the same wrong reasons [laughs]. Just because I've found out about them since doesn't allow me to presume that I would have seen through them at the time.

I find one of the great illusions is the study of social mobility. This is a peculiar field; it studies movements through structures, without really relating the movements to the processes that create and transform the structures; it takes too much for granted.

STAVE: You say illusion—why do you feel this way?

LAMPARD: I don't think it's very real. I think it's sort of the imposition of crude measures on extremely crude sociological concepts; and then projecting this on to the historical past isn't yet subtle enough. I think that in Steve Thernstrom's latest book, it is much more subtle than he's made it before or than many other scholars have made it before. I think he's getting beyond these rather gross measures of frequencies and so forth, getting beyond the "escalator" notion. I don't find the notion of social mobility very interesting, except perhaps as an ideological statement. I prefer the term social structure, circulation, or simply change which is going on all the time. But the field is only just beginning and Thernstrom's *The Other Bostonians*[32] is really a more interesting book than the earlier one, more important substantively, whatever the conceptual weakness of the mobility framework or the methodological problems of the samples and their subsets. He's getting beyond the limitations here and has added a lot more qualification. All the world wasn't Newburyport.

STAVE: Anything special he has added? In talking to him there are certain aspects of *Poverty and Progress* he thinks more favorably of than *The Other Bostonians.* Is there anything that you see in this book that you really think is a contribution to the field?

LAMPARD: Well, he's brought it all together in the last chapter. But I think he's getting to the notion that all people, classes of persons, so-called groups—however you categorize people: job, nationality, sect, parentage—are not all running in the same rat race. They don't necessarily conform to the homogenization of an industrial job structure or accept a status contest view of life as their end. People live with their personal and affiliational characteristics, as it were, as well as those of the structure. It is kind of ironic too, Steve seems to take a milder view of American capitalism because it appears to have delivered more "upward" mobility than he once thought. But a lot of good research possibilities emerge in his *ad hoc* speculations about this or the other group's performance—the possibility that some people had more or less other evaluations of themselves, other areas of motivation and achievement than status as indicated by census-type sociological measures. Maybe we need to get inside group self-definitions, more like anthropologists.

STAVE: You mentioned that the field is just opening. Some people feel that the usefulness of social mobility studies has ended.

LAMPARD: Oh, I think yes, in a way. I think some sociologists, like S. M. Miller, have given up on social mobility studies, and it will be a good idea when historians do too. I still think, even with the limited technical apparatus, that there is a lot of variety to be found in the local American experience and that this will contribute something. But I think the study of social change and the way individuals and groups of people fit into the changing structure as it unfolds is something which is beginning. This is what I was after in the piece on social change that I did for Handlin's volume, *The Historian and the City*,[33] and I wouldn't call it social mobility. I've never been attracted to that; it's a kind of ideological construction: "upward" is good, more "upward" is better, etc.

STAVE: Yes, but in several of your articles—the 1961 *AHR* article—don't you use the term "social mobility?"

LAMPARD: Yes, I regret to say I do.

STAVE: You do. Yes, and you encourage people to go on and do this.

LAMPARD: Oh yes, indeed, guilty. Well, what I had in mind there was that social mobility seemed a useful way of categorizing the notion of the social structural and behavioral dimension of economic change. I had in mind there particularly the work done since the 1940s—Elbridge Sibley, Gladys Palmer,[34] and others on labor mobility. The framework was heavily sociological because I didn't really want to burden that AHR communication with a lot of ecological jargon. Ecologists can talk about the unfolding of structures and niches, and functional and affiliational relationships, adaptation, and employ a different language from that of social stratification. Ecology and morphology were dirty words in those days.

STAVE: By the time you picked it up the sociologists were sort of . . .

LAMPARD: Through. Yes. Well, ecology had been dropped in sociology and had not yet come in through the environmental "crisis" area. So that there was a period there when human ecology was reduced almost to a small sect, and I think that perhaps the person who did most to revive it and rehabilitate it and certainly to expand on the old Chicago notion was Amos Hawley and people such as Dudley Duncan and Leo Schnore, who were affected by Hawley.[35] And now, in a sense, ecology has gone far beyond human beings and it's almost back to its biological state, which may not be the most useful way of looking at human ecology. Human eco-systems are human organizations, more or less consciously adapting. Unless the social-cultural aspects of human beings are brought in, I don't think that there's any particular sort of natural ecological system for humans such as what may well exist in nature, but there are always changing environmental constraints or "costs"—hence, my ecological approach to regional development in the *Regions, Resources and Economic Growth* book.[36]

STAVE: What kinds of things are you working on now yourself? The usual question that historians ask someone after they've finished one thing and gone on to another.

LAMPARD: Well, as a matter of fact, I'm very interested in comparative urban studies. In particular, I'm interested in the development of urban populations in nineteenth-century Europe and North America in comparison with situations of urban populations in developing countries today. I'm pursuing that continuously and, in a sense, trying to get beyond the economic framework—the so-called economic growth framework which I regard as a particularly narrow post World War II construction of human activities. I think this has already led to a great deal of misunderstanding of what is happening in developing countries.

STAVE: Well, get beyond the economic framework to what?

LAMPARD: To a more social framework for economic development in different cultural contexts. For example, to see the populations, the growing urban populations, in underdeveloped countries—much as I think they were in nineteenth-century Europe and North America—as extremely dynamic and creative social arrangements shaping economic development. And although in retrospect one can look back and see the misery and the shortage and the suffering, the dark side of our urban development, one is also aware of the enormous creativity and, almost, multiplication of human powers, human achievements, that came out of this development—Durkheim's "dynamic density" notion. I see this differentiation as going on in many parts of the world today. It's not simply crowds of people coming out of some rural environment into some urban environment and waiting for something to happen to them. The fact that they are migrants means something. They are doing something for themselves and they're not waiting for bureaucrats and technocrats to arrange to raise the amount of capital investment to 10% of Gross National Product, whereupon they will duly "take-off." I doubt whether human experience is ever that way. I'm not trying to ignore the problems of human suffering or the problems of "overpopulation" or all of the other woe that goes with social change as it did in our own experience in town *and* country, but to explore those possibilities at least in a number of countries. Some work I'm doing with the Asia Foundation at the moment is directly related to that. We're interested in Southeast Asia's urban developments and I'm particularly getting data and information from them which will be useful for this kind of comparison of situations. To be sure, it's very artificial. I tend to think that comparative history at any time is a work of art; and to compare more recent situations with more remote situations over time, rather than simply comparing cross-sectionally at one time, is even a greater work of art. But, nevertheless, I think it's illuminating.

STAVE: I guess a preliminary to this is "The Urbanizing World" piece?

LAMPARD: Well that's an example of some of the initial kinds of considerations in a "contemporary history" framework. I've gone beyond that by now. I've got much more data and so forth, and I'm aware of a lot more. In fact, I've remembered things that I'd forgotten were already there in the 1950s with the kind of data I had then. So that's one area in which I'm continuing to work, and it's really getting at the social changes that, in fact, can be conceived of and later measured as economic growth rather than the other way around. Instead of saying economic growth is the great engine that makes the world happen—quite the reverse, how the world, how the society, how the population is the engine that makes economic growth happen. And so, in a sense, I'm a kind of social-cultural determinist rather than an economic determinist. I tend to treat American history in this way. I don't accept economic explanations for things that happen. I guess I still continue to be very interested in these related questions of spatial and social organization and the utilization of space—how space gets divided up and classified and utilized, and I think this may very well become an important area of urban study. It's partly there in some of the social mobility studies; it's there in the studies of ethnic distributions; clearly it's very germane to the present discussions of national land utilization policies which necessarily involve some departure from traditional local determination of land use. That's an area of politics I'm still pushing into. I think that perhaps legal history and, to a lesser extent, constitutional history will have a lot to say in this area. Perhaps we have become too familiar with economic and social and political dimensions from our freshman courses and we sort of take them for granted. In our thinking and writing, a lot of the consciousness that all these matters take place in a system of law has gone out of our historical writing. I'm certain that a lot of people are aware of this, of course. One couldn't be around Willard Hurst very long at Wisconsin without finding this aspect a central feature. Harry Scheiber and others are working on legal aspects of American economic development. I think legal aspects of American urban development will provide clues to power relationships as well as structures.

STAVE: This is very interesting. You mention land use. It seems to me, and I might be wrong, that one of the major future issues of this country—well, I don't know if it's a future issue because it's so present—is the question of growth, and of course it ties in to the whole notion of land use and whether individuals can prevent other individuals from living in certain places. History is sometimes "trendy"—at least, the writing of history is "trendy." Do you foresee a time when the "in" thing is going to be the study of land use, growth, no-growth policies, and here's where the law of zoning will play a role?

LAMPARD: Yes, I think that just as the Supreme Court follows election returns, historians imitate yesterday's headlines. So I can well believe we will be pushing studies in that direction. On the question of communities trying to limit growth of population, in a sense this is one of the historic functions of city government—if one is really thinking in historical terms—to determine who's to be in the "self" of self-government. There is just a brief period in the late eighteenth and nineteenth centuries when things open up, when cities become almost *the* place for the migrant. There's a connection between liberalism and population growth, but it didn't last long. Historically, one of the primary concerns of city government was to keep most people out.

STAVE: It's always been that way.

LAMPARD: To warn them off, chase them away, prohibit them from doing business or performing their trades in the city, or from becoming a tax burden. The exclusiveness of the city is one of its historical points of definition, and there's a marvelous period in the nineteenth century when the whole thing becomes wide open and the city becomes the ultimate destination almost of everyone—even in the land-rich settler societies of North America, Australia, Argentina. I'm not surprised after 150 years of this growth and movement that, probably for the same kinds of exclusive, self-preserving, self-regarding, and self-governing motivations as in the past, neither the world nor the community can any longer stand, so to speak, this enormous turnover—the scale of it all.

STAVE: So the wall is going to surround the city again.

LAMPARD: Yes, yes. Walls of sorts will come back, and within the urban areas too, perhaps. Obviously we're not going back to the eighteenth, let alone the fifteenth century, but it's almost inherent in the nature of government as the world rushes in, the areal base for social organization changes. For those who look to governmental solutions, one of the most obvious solutions for politicians is some kind of exclusion or controlled access. If you can't expand, you retreat, you draw the lines differently. Of course, they have to invent a new vocabulary, a rhetoric, and legal stratagems. And one way would be new land use controls. It's implicit in zoning, in building codes, even in the old law of nuisance, and it was always inherent in looking at the environment as property rights. If one now brings a whole new weight of public environmental factors into the language and into law—well, maybe you've just run out of "progress," and your society will now have to change the subject. It would be a very different picture from what we've thought of cities, especially nineteenth-century cities and urban areas.

STAVE: Well, in the United States, especially, we're supposed to be, according to our mobility studies, such a residentially mobile area. It would seem that this could change the whole direction of our history—the notion of the closed society, physically closed, geographically closed.

LAMPARD: Yes, it more or less has to happen and I can think Americans in the past perhaps have exaggerated their psychological capacity for absorbing or tolerating more and different, at greater rates. Presumably, there was a simpler, physical, spatial solution to these things in the past, if we're to believe Turner. We don't have to believe the whole interpretation—we can just see the continent was there to be ripped off; it was obviously attractive to many people. But I think it is implicit in Turner's writing: this enormous kind of change, the magnitudes, the diverse outcomes of the change were managed either through changing social-economic organization or, expressly, through political, administrative organization; there was no longer a physical or "natural" solution to American problems as in the past, when there was always open space. I suppose industrialization and urbanization was one kind of solution, an alternative to going West and starting over, although both were organizational features of the westward movement too, inherent in transport and communications. But growth and expansion brought new problems, or forms of problems; the city may have been a frontier or way out in the 1830s and 40s, but it was itself the problem by the 1890s. Some people thought a more specialized residential suburb was a way out of the city, but business and industry followed even beyond the city limits and merged in suburban/satellite rings; the walls were going up against this, that, or the other. Just like the old frontier, the urban process repeats itself, most recently in the sunny Southwest. Maybe things are already slowing down in California and Florida, but now there's no "where" left to go, no natural spaces, and the only spatial solutions have to be social solutions *in* urbanized areas. So our urban spaces will probably have to be organized along lines different from the late nineteenth and early twentieth centuries: smaller, more variegated areas perhaps rather than larger, more specialized ones. All this will involve great social reorganization, presumably more rather than less public spending and possibly much political-administrative forethought, not to mention psychological stress. I hate to stigmatize this by calling it planning because that in my vocabulary is rather a dirty word. Not for ideological reasons but . . .

STAVE: Why is it a dirty word?

LAMPARD: I don't think human beings are really capable of much long-run planning. The more comprehensive, the more disastrous it would likely turn out to be; "master" plans are too inflexible unless kept utterly vague, while piecemeal "pragmatic" planning, budgetary planning, collapses in "shortfalls" and bureaucratic in-fighting. How on earth do we get the notion, other than through some kind of despotic delusion or collective fantasy, that it is possible to plan the lives of other people? We cannot know enough to run other people's lives; plans only appear to work at all because human beings adjust, they can be bribed or otherwise coerced into conformity. I see almost the impossibility of planning, of controlling change in the large for very long. What I'm suggesting here, nevertheless, is the necessity for forethought and whatever unconventional wisdom is available, since most conventional wisdoms are pretty obsolete by the time they are built into decisions affecting the future. Think, for example, of the expertise in the federal housing programs of the 1930s—the notion of "filtration," that as better-off people could be moved up and out into the new housing, everybody else would sort of move up one into housing vacated by their social betters. Filtration didn't begin to take into account the bundle of concerns affecting residential decisions other than the price of housing—a host of only partly "rational" environmental values, as well as jobs, schools, and transport, that were not fully reflected in relative prices. One difficulty I see in manipulating market models, or even the welfare accounting framework, is just their meagerness for allowing a variety of urban situations to develop. Planning that simulates markets, especially at high governmental levels, is essentially a narrowing or homogenizing process, just as it is in big business, even when it claims to be maximizing "benefits" in relation to "costs" and not "profits." Some of my misgiving on this comes out in the later part of my *Victorian City* chapter. But, like big business, we can't leave our urban planning to unstable market forces, particularly as change involves scarce physical space. So, I imagine we are stuck with urbanology and the urban management focus in our academic studies, as in real life, for a long time. As a historian of sorts, however, I should hate for people to get the idea that our urban past has been a kind of single unfolding strand of rural-to-urban-to-suburban movement, explainable by the automatic simplicities of price mechanism and social escalator models, without a lot of help from friendly politicians and pundits. Again, without being a doomsdayer, I wouldn't want people to conclude that social improvement is tied to the existing composition of GNP. I wouldn't want to leave the impression that the structure and form of eighteenth or nineteenth-century cities were *the* city, and that we no longer live in real cities. Adaptation is the name of the ecological game, but in human ecology all of the conditions aren't given; there are learning and choice as well as environmental constraints. Urban history can contribute to our knowledge of human settlements and, I would think, to the education of those who are to be our masters—namely, those experts and functionaries who will make our urban "critical choices."

STAVE: Are you suggesting that urban history is really a policy science, as they call it?

LAMPARD: No. It is almost an anti-policy science, notwithstanding the predicament that makes some kind of policy science inevitable. Our primary responsibility would be to the public, the laity, our readers. So far from reinforcing and confirming the policy scientists of whatever think-tank hired for the occasion, some historians might be critics of their pronouncements, not just in technical ways—although we have to get some mastery of the methods—but by holding up "scientific" findings and rhetoric, especially when they contain generalizations about the past, to broader standards of historical experience; by bringing in more varied and less systematic considerations that any good policy science might want to allow—if we were good enough at it, not just even more piously reckless. They might even hire some of our Ph.D.s. The more historical experience we can persuade policy science to include in the parameters of its models, the more likely its predictions would end up as tentative and confused as the exogenous world it presumes to straighten out.

STAVE: Okay, as you pass this mantle on to urban historians, perhaps we'll conclude on that point.

NOTES

1. Eric E. Lampard, "The Rise of the Dairy Industry in Wisconsin: A Study of Agricultural Change in The Midwest, 1820-1920" (Ph.D. dissertation, University of Wisconsin, 1955); also see *The Rise of the Dairy Industry in Wisconsin, 1820-1920* (Madison Wisc., 1963).

2. For examples of works by Everett S. Lee and Richard A. Easterlin, see Abbott L. Ferris, ed., *Research and the 1970 Census* (Oak Ridge, Tenn., 1971); Richard A. Easterlin, *The American Baby Boom in Historical Perspective* (New York, 1962); *Population, Labor Force, and Long Swings in Economic Growth: The American Experience* (New York, 1968); also see Easterlin's recent "Factors in the Decline of Farm Family Fertility in the United States: Some Preliminary Research Results," *Journal of American History*, LXIII (December 1976), 600-614.

3. Sidney Goldstein, *The Norristown Study: An Experiment in Interdisciplinary Research Training* (Philadelphia, 1961).

4. Friedrich Ratzel, *The History of Mankind* (New York, 1896-1898); Volkerkunde (Leipzig and Wien, 1885); *Kleine Schriften* (Berlin, 1906); *Anthropogeographis...* (Stuttgart, 1912-1921).

5. Charles N. Glaab, "The Historian and the American City," in Philip Hauser and Leo Schnore, eds., *The Study of Urbanization* (New York, 1965), 53-80.

6. Eric E. Lampard, "American Historians and the Study of Urbanization," American Historical Review, 67 (October 1961), 49-61.

7. Eric E. Lampard, "The History of Cities in the Economically Advanced Areas," Economic Development and Cultural Change, 3 (January 1955), 86-136.

8. Merle Curti, *The Making of an American Community: A Case Study of Democracy in a Frontier County* (Stanford Cal., 1959).

9. For example, see: James C. Malin, "The Turnover of Farm Population in Kansas," Kansas Historical Quarterly, IV (1935), 339-372.

10. Frederick Jackson Turner, *The Frontier in American History* (New York, 1921, 1923).

11. Eric E. Lampard, "Two Cheers for Quantitative History: An Agnostic Foreward," in Leo F. Schnore, ed., *The New Urban History* (Princeton. N.J., 1975), 12-48.

12. Leo F. Schnore, ed., *The New Urban History: Quantitative Explorations by American Historians* (Princeton, N.J., 1975).

13. For examples of their work, see Sam Bass Warner, Jr., *Streetcar Suburbs: The Process of Growth in Boston, 1870-1900* (Cambridge, Mass., 1962), *The Private City: Philadelphia in Three Periods of It's Growth* (Philadelphia, 1968), *The Urban Wilderness: A History of the American City* (New York, 1972); Stephan Thernstrom, *Poverty and Progress: Social Mobility in a Nineteenth Century City* (New York, 1969) and *The Other Bostonians: Poverty and Progress in the American Metropolis, 1880-1970* (Cambridge, Mass., 1973).

14. Peter Knights, *The Plain People of Boston, 1830-1860: A Study in City Growth* (New York, 1971) and Stephan Thernstrom and Peter Knights, *Men in Motion: Some Data and Speculation About Urban Population Mobility in Nineteenth-Century America* (Los Angeles, 1970), reprinted in Tamera Hareven, ed., *Anonymous Americans* (Englewood Cliffs, N.J., 1971), 17-47.

15. Roger Simon, "The Expansion of An Industrial City: Milwaukee, 1880-1900" (Ph.D. dissertation, University of Wisconsin, 1971); also see his article,

SELECT BIBLIOGRAPHY OF WORKS
BY ERIC E. LAMPARD

"The History of Cities in the Economically Advanced Areas," Economic Development and Cultural Change, 3 (January 1955), 86-136.

Industrial Revolution: Interpretations and Perspectives (AHA Service Center pamphlet, Washington, D.C., 1957).

With Harvey S. Perloff et al., *Regions, Resources, and Economic Growth* (Baltimore, 1960).

"American Historians and the Study of Urbanization," *American Historical Review,* 67 (October 1961), 49-61.

The Rise of the Dairy Industry in Wisconsin, 1820-1920 (Madison, Wisc., 1963).

"Urbanization and Social Change; on Broadening the Scope and Relevance of Urban History," in Oscar Handlin and John Burchard, eds., *The Historian and the City* (Cambridge, Mass., 1963), 225-247.

"Historical Aspects of Urbanization," in Philip M. Hauser and Leo F. Schnore, eds., *The Study of Urbanization* (New York, 1965), 519-554.

"The Evolving System of Cities in the United States: Urbanization and Economic Development," in Harvey Perloff and Loudon Wingo, Jr., eds., *Issues in Urban Economics* (Baltimore, 1968), 81-139.

"Historical Contours of Contemporary Urban Society: A Comparative View," Journal of Contemporary History, 4 (July 1969), 3-25.

"The Dimensions of Urban History: A Footnote to the 'Urban Crisis,' " Pacific Historical Review, 39 (August 1970), 261-278.

"The Urbanizing World," in H. J. Dyos and Michael Wolff, eds., *The Victorian City: Images and Realities,* 2 vols. (London and Boston, 1973), I, 3-57.

"The Pursuit of Happiness in the City: Changing Opportunities and Options in America," Transactions of the Royal Historical Society, 5th Series, Vol. 23 (1973), 175-220.

"Two Cheers for Quantitative History: An Agnostic Foreword," in Leo F. Schnore, ed., *The New Urban History* (Princeton, N.J., 1975), 12-48.

"Housing And Services in an Immigrant Neighborhood: Milwaukee's Ward 14," Journal of Urban History, 2 (August 1976), 435-458.

16. Kathleen Neils Conzen, "Patterns of Residence in Early Milwaukee," in Schnore, ed., *The New Urban History*, 145-183; also see Kathleen Neils Conzen *Immigrant Milwaukee, 1836-1860* (Cambridge, Mass., 1976).

17. Eric E. Lampard, "The Urbanizing World," in H. J. Dyos and Michael Wolff, eds., *The Victorian City: Images and Realities*, 2 vols. (London, Boston, 1973), 1, 3-57.

18. For the work of Patrick Geddes, see *City Development: A Study of Parks, Gardens, and Culture Institutes* (Edinburgh, 1904), and *Cities in Evolution: An Introduction to the Town Planning Movement and to the Study of Civics* (London, 1915, 1949).

19. Allan R. Pred, *Urban Growth and the Circulation of Information: The United States System of Cities, 1790-1840* (Cambridge, Mass., 1973).

20. Kenneth T. Jackson, "The Crabgrass Frontier: 150 Years of Suburban Growth in America," in Raymond A. Mohl and James F. Richardson, eds., *The Urban Experience: Themes in American History* (Belmont, California, 1973), 196-221.

21. Kenneth T. Jackson, "Urban Deconcentration in the Nineteenth Century: A Statistical Inquiry," in Schnore, ed., *The New Urban History*, 110-142.

22. See Carl Bridenbaugh, *Cities in the Wilderness: The First Century of Urban Life in America, 1625-1742* (New York, 1938. 1964), *Cities in Revolt: Urban Life in America, 1743-1776* (New York, 1955).

23. Eric E. Lampard, "The Dimensions of Urban History: A Footnote to the 'Urban Crisis,' " Pacific Historical Review, 39 (August 1970), 261-278.

24. Sam Bass Warner, Jr., *Streetcar Suburbs* (Cambridge, Mass., 1962).

25. Ernest Griffith, *History of American City Government: The Colonial Period, Vol. 2* (New York, 1938, 1972).

26. See Richard C. Wade, *The Urban Frontier: Pioneer Life in Early Pittsburgh, Cincinnati, Lexington, Louisville, and St. Louis* (Cambridge, Mass., 1959), and *Slavery in the Cities: The South, 1820-1860* (New York, 1964).

27. For an example of Blake McKelvey's work see his four volume study, *Rochester: The Water Power City, 1812-1854* (Cambridge, Mass., 1945), *Rochester: The Flower City, 1855-1890* (Cambridge, Mass., 1949), *Rochester: The Quest for Quality, 1890-1925* (Cambridge, Mass., 1956), *Rochester: An Emerging Metropolis, 1925-1961* (Rochester, N.Y., 1961); also see *The Urbanization of America, 1860-1915* (New Brunswick, N.J., 1963) and *The Emergence of Metropolitan America, 1915-1966* (New Brunswick, N.J., 1968).

28. Sam Bass Warner, Jr., *The Private City* (Philadelphia, 1968).

29. Samuel P. Hays, "The Politics of Reform in Municipal Government in the Progressive Era," Pacific Northwest Quarterly, 55 (October 1964), 157-169, and "The Changing Political Structure of the City in Industrial America " Journal of Urban History, 1 (November 1974), 6-38.

30. For the works of Roy Lubove, see *Community Planning in the 1920's: The Contribution of the Regional Planning Association of America* (Pittsburgh, 1963, 1964); *The Professional Altruist: The Emergence of Social Work as a Career, 1880-1930* (Cambridge, Mass., 1965); *The Progressives and the Slums: Tenement House Reform in New York City, 1890-1917* (Pittsburgh, 1962, 1963); *Social*

Welfare in Transition: Selected English Documents, 1834-1909 (Pittsburgh, 1966); *The Struggle for Social Security, 1900-1935* (Cambridge, Mass., 1968); *Twentieth-Century Pittsburgh: Government, Business, and Environmental Change* (New York, 1969); *The Urban Community: Housing and Planning in the Progressive Era* (Englewood Cliffs, N.J., 1967); "The Urbanization Process: An Approach to Historical Research," Journal of the American Institute of Planners, XXXIII (January 1967), 33-39.

31. See Michael H. Frisch, *Town Into City: Springfield, Massachusetts, and the Meaning of Community, 1840-1880* (Cambridge, Mass., 1972).

32. Stephan A. Thernstrom, *The Other Bostonians* (Cambridge, Mass., 1973).

33. Eric E. Lampard, "Urbanization and Social Change: On Broadening the Scope and Relevance of Urban History," in Oscal Handlin and John Burchard, eds., *The Historian and the City* (Cambridge, Mass., 1963), 225-247.

34. See: Gladys L. Palmer, *Labor Mobility in Six Cities: A Report on the Survey of Patterns and Factors in Labor Mobility, 1940-1950* (New York, 1954); *The Philadelphia Labor Market in 1944* (Philadelphia, 1944); *The Reluctant Job Changer, Studies in Work Attachments and Aspirations* (Philadephia, 1962, 1963); *Research Planning Memorandum on Labor Mobility, Prepared for the Committee on Labor Market Research* (New York, 1947).

35. See Amos H. Hawley's works: *The Changing Shape of Metropolitan America: Deconcentration Since 1920* (Glencoe, Ill., 1956); *Human Ecology: A Theory of Community Structure* (New York, 1950); *The Metropolitan Community: Its People and Government* (Beverly Hills, Cal., 1970); *Urban Society: An Ecological Approach* (New York, 1971); *Metropolitan American in Contemporary Perspective* (New York, Beverly Hills, Cal., 1975).

36. Eric E. Lampard with Harvey S. Perloff, et al., *Regions, Resources, and Economic Growth* (Baltimore, 1960).

Samuel P. Hays

Samuel P. Hays (1921-   ) is Professor of History at the University of Pittsburgh, where he headed the department during the 1960s and early 1970s. He is a leading advocate of a systematic social history and has influenced many younger scholars in their behavioral approach to historical studies.

A CONVERSATION WITH
SAMUEL P. HAYS

STAVE: Let us begin at the beginning. Can you indicate some of your background, including your education and your family, and how you got into the field of history?

HAYS: I grew up in southern Indiana and graduated from a small town high school and Swarthmore College. I had no idea I would go into history and was a philosophy major for a while. I was a conscientious objector in World War II and as a junior I entered an alternative program that we thought was going to lead to relief work in Europe. I took a concentration in Europe, and in that we had a European history course taught by Dan Boorstin. He was an excellent teacher and interested me in history. Actually, I majored in psychology, and had a considerable dose of Gestalt psychology as a result. So history was the minor, and I was a psychology major, but with the definite idea that I would go on in history. Another part of the background has had some influence in a subtle way. I grew up in a county where most of my great-great-grandparents had lived, and I was deeply steeped in family tradition. I was very interested in family genealogy, and I suppose the first real historical research I ever did was with tombstone inscriptions in cemeteries. It was actually through genealogy that I later got interested in the census, the manuscript population census. I did not know anything about it then as a historical resource, but several times going through Washington I used the census at the National Archives for genealogical research before it was available on microfilm.

STAVE: At what age was this?

HAYS: This was in the 1940s when I was an undergraduate.

STAVE: So this was not when you were in high school?

HAYS: The genealogical interest began when I was in high school and has continued ever since.

STAVE: What about your family—what did your parents do?

HAYS: My father was a lawyer, a country lawyer, primarily involved in probate work, and my mother was a housewife, who had got an M.A. degree at Wellesley, taught Greek, Latin, French, and German in high school, quit, married, had three children, and taught piano lessons throughout her life. In terms of cultural background, both were Protestant, and my father was a fairly typical waspish-type midwesterner. He was a Methodist, a staunch prohibitionist before the 1930s. My mother was a little bit more secularized. As a matter of fact, her father and her grandfather both had been admirers of James B. Weaver, and I have some interesting and laudatory things they said about Weaver and the Populists. They were both pro-Bryan and prohibitionist. My grandfather ran on the prohibitionist ticket one time for Congress. My background was heavily laden with the "soft" side of evangelical Protestantism, concerned with ethical matters and reforms in an evangelical Protestant tradition. Perhaps there were some effects of this when I decided in the thirties that I was a pacifist and would be a conscientious objector to the war. It was no problem as far as my mother was concerned. In fact she sort of preceded me in thinking that way. But my father was more skeptical; being a lawyer he would say, "Okay, but don't decide you're going to go to jail." It was that kind of a background. I grew up in a small town with overtones of the entire syndrome of WASP attitudes, such as anti-Catholic sentiment. There was a lot of the waspish type of politics that I write about today, and I can feel the background.

STAVE: Are you talking from retrospect or did you feel this at the time? Were you very conscious of this type of thing?

HAYS: In the first grade, 1928, in the middle of the Hoover-Smith campaign, there was another kid behind me who was an ardent Catholic Smith advocate. I was a Hoover supporter, and I remember very clearly that we were called down by the teacher three or four times for throwing epithets back and forth. That was real. Of course to me then it was just that Al Smith, being a wet from New York and Tammany Hall, was, as we used to say in southern Indiana, "no-count." And, on the other hand, Hoover was a real straight and honest fellow—good, upright, and moral. It was sort of good and evil. There was real morality in being a Republican then. I remember sporting a Landon button—sunflower—in 1936, but I think in 1944, the first time I had a chance to vote, I did not vote at all, or else I voted all over the ticket.

STAVE: With respect to schooling, you mentioned you were at Swarthmore and Boorstin was teaching you. Did you take many courses with him?

HAYS: Just the one, a European history course. It was an excellent course in terms of just excitement. Plus the fact that he spent a lot of time with students on their writing. I would bring a paper back and then it would be just all cut up, and he would explain how it should be done differently. That was extremely helpful. I liked to write papers. I was in the seminar program at Swarthmore where the main job was to write one paper a week, and I really enjoyed reading a lot of secondary works and mulling over what they meant, coming up with a paper which essentially was my idea about the assigned topic. So the people in college helped me to perfect my writing. I did not get any of this in high school. The first paper I wrote in a philosophy course at college I got a D on. But I soon learned to write papers and really enjoyed that part of the seminar program.

STAVE: Why did you go to Swarthmore in the first place?

HAYS: It is one of those accidental things. My mother had very high ambitions for her children, and it seemed to spill over on me an awful lot as the last child. My brother and sister had gone to Grinnell, and my mother wanted me to go to Swarthmore. It was largely a matter of where I got the scholarship. At that time college expenses were $1,000 a year, and I got a $300 scholarship. But there was another wrinkle too, and that is that my grandfather had moved to Bloomington, Indiana when my mother and her brother were ready for college so that they could have the benefits of going to Indiana University, and while there he had met a man by the name of Pittenger. They ran the bookstore at the university together, and then Pittenger went off to Swarthmore with Frank Aydelotte as controller—treasurer—of the college. My mother knew the Pittenger family, and in this way knew about Swarthmore. This was the time that Swarthmore was becoming quite well known with Frank Aydelotte there.

STAVE: What year did you graduate?

HAYS: 1948. Actually, in between there is another pre-graduate school thing. I started Swarthmore in 1940, and when the plan to go abroad and do alternative service work folded because General Hershey decided against it, then I was drafted and went into Civilian Public Service. For three years I was out in Oregon working in a branch of what is now the Bureau of Land Management, but was then called the Oregon and California Revested Lands Administration. It was a large tract of forest land, the only land grant of any size given to the railroads that was actually taken back by the federal government. And it was put into the old Bureau of Public Lands in 1916 when it was taken back and became managed by the Department of the Interior. We were in a camp of about 130 to 150 people who were employed fighting forest fires in the summertime, planting trees in the winter, felling timbers, building roads. I spent about three months as a cook after I got appendicitis, several months sharpening jackhammer bits, three months working as a truck mechanic. All these things connected with forestry. That was really where I got my first interest in conservation.

STAVE: After serving as a CO, you went back to Swarthmore, and then did you go directly to Harvard?

HAYS: Yes, I went directly to Harvard. I married in June 1948, and both of us went to graduate school, Barbara to Radcliffe and I to Harvard.

STAVE: Was she an undergraduate?

HAYS: She was an undergraduate at Swarthmore and graduated the same year I did; she started out in biology at Radcliffe.

STAVE: Why Harvard, and what did you intend to do when you got there? Had you made a determination to go into history at that time?

HAYS: Yes, I had already decided to go into history. I was briefly tempted to go into psychology which was my undergraduate major. We had outside examiners at Swarthmore, and one was Jerome Bruner from Harvard. I did very well on my psychology exams and very poorly on my history exams. As a matter of fact, the psychology people wanted to give me highest honors and the history people wanted to flunk me. They compromised. Bruner offered me a fellowship on the spot if I would go on in psychology. Well, I really was not interested in a career in psychology. I had been searching, I think, for a field with a lot of range and flexibility to it. At first it was philosophy and then later history. History was as comprehensive as philosophy, but it was a little bit more concrete—that concreteness was always quite important. I liked the abstract thinking in philosophy, but I always wanted some concreteness. History was a kind of alternative to philosophy, you might say, but interest in psychology was closely connected because I always felt that history was about people and how they thought and acted and I wanted to have that slant. So Bruner's attempt to interest me in psychology did not take hold, and I went on in history. Barbara and I both applied to Chicago and Harvard, and we agreed we would go where the most scholarship money was. That is why we ended up at Radcliffe and Harvard.

STAVE: Did the decision to go into history come when you were at Swarthmore?

HAYS: Yes. As a freshman in college I had no interest in history. High school history was very dull—very factual, very workbookish, filling in the blanks for dates. This turned me off. I do not recall history being even a possible option until I had this course with Boorstin.

STAVE: So this was, in a sense, a turning point. Now, when you got to Harvard you were going to study history. What kind of graduate program did you go through?

HAYS: Well, now here is another interesting thing. Because of the combination of social science and history and psychology at Swarthmore I was attracted to a degree that they offered at Harvard then called the social science Ph.D. It was, frankly, a smattering of many things. Largely as a part of that I took a course in statistics with Samuel Stauffer the first term, and I really enjoyed that. But the other courses were history. I had gone to Frederick Merk as an adviser, largely because Frederick Tolles of the Swarthmore history department had told me he was personally very helpful and likable, a sympathetic adviser for students, and in addition my interest in conservation fitted with Merk's field in the history of the West. During the first term I also had a seminar with Oscar Handlin which got me into a lot of things that I had not been into before and found quite interesting.

STAVE: What kinds of things?

HAYS: Well, I did a paper on the Socialist Labor Party, for example, the ethnic and immigrant composition, and Daniel DeLeon's role in relating to a lot of ethnics that were not involved in the standard trade unions, the Cuban Cigarmakers as distinct from the Germans, for example. And, as a result of that, I had several meetings with Handlin. One time I remember in his office he said, "You don't really want to take a social science degree, that's just nonsense." He talked me out of it, and I think very sensibly so. He said if you are interested in that sort of thing get your degree first so you can sell yourself as an historian, and then read social science on your own. And that was, I think, very sensible advice.

STAVE: Which you followed apparently.

HAYS: Which I followed, yes.

STAVE: The choice of your dissertation topic, which became the book *Conservation and the Gospel of Efficiency*, would seem to tie in with your earlier experience.

HAYS: Right, that plus one of these other fortunate things—a fellowship had been given to Harvard, known as the Theodore Roosevelt Fellowship, and I think the first recipient of it was Wallace Chessman who did a study of Roosevelt as governor of New York.

STAVE: May I ask, to interrupt for a minute, who were your contemporaries at Harvard?

HAYS: Chessman was just a little ahead of me. I remember Arthur Mann was a year or two ahead; and John Blum, Bernard Bailyn, and Rowland Berthoff. There really are not very many professional historians today who were in that same year and who were in the same seminars and classes as I was. Ted Fenton was. Ted went to Carnegie-Mellon and became involved in curriculum development for secondary education. I knew Ted very well; he was working on a dissertation on Italian immigrants for Handlin and we talked a lot about immigrants and ethnics. Bob Fear did a study of Shays's rebellion. He was there at the same time. But I do not really remember offhand any others from that particular year who have become professional historians.

STAVE: Did you have any special friends there? Anyone who influenced you other than faculty that you dealt with?

HAYS: I do not think so. I think that the main intellectual influence, perhaps, was Handlin in getting me exposed to a lot of things that generally today are called social history. Mr. Merk was very good in exposing me to the history of the West and things that pertained to conservation, but Handlin was the one who was responsible for introducing me to new areas of history that I found attractive.

STAVE: You were starting to give the origins of your dissertation, and you mentioned the Theodore Roosevelt Fellowhip.

HAYS: Yes. Mr. Merk came to me one day and told me about this fellowship and asked if I wanted to apply for it. I agreed, and that sort of jelled the subject—Roosevelt, the Progressive Era, and conservation. So I applied for it, got it, and that shaped the final decision. But I do not think that before then I had in my mind very much of a concrete notion about a topic. None of the rationale that I might have today for choosing a topic in social or urban history was there.

STAVE: The development of the thesis of *Conservation and the Gospel of Efficiency*, was this your own idea working with the materials? Did you see where you were going, did your materials lead you there, or what?

HAYS: I have often thought of that and the best that I can reconstruct is that it really evolved as I began to look at the materials. I had done one paper in Mr. Merk's seminar on the Taylor Grazing Act in the 1930s, but I do not think it began to shape ideas; it continued the interest in the content. The notion that the innovative impulses in the whole conservation field were among scientists and the focus on the impact of science and technology on American politics, that really was not there at the start as far as I can remember; it emerged as time went on. I was probably sold on the traditional notion of Progressive politics—conservation being simply a kind of popular mass movement against corporations, for example. I remember these new ideas coming in and taking over, so to speak, but I cannot really pinpoint when it happened. It really was not as a result of conversations with anyone, but just the development of my thinking as the research progressed.

STAVE: I see. How long did it take you to do the thesis, and how much revision was there before it became a book?

HAYS: I am not sure just when I took my comps. I went to Harvard in fall 1948 and I certainly was starting the dissertation in the early part of 1951. As I recall, I took my comps in the latter part of 1950, and so it had been all of 1951 and much of 1952. The summer of 1951 I spent in the Library of Congress working largely in the Pinchot papers, forestry papers, and the Department of the Interior papers, and then for a little time at Yale in the Newlands papers. I spent a lot of time with the Roosevelt papers themselves, and I recall writing in the spring and summer of 1952. So I would say that I was working on the dissertation slightly less than two years—all of 1951, and in 1952 down to September, and perhaps starting on it a little before the end of 1950. As I recall I took my comprehensives somewhere in the early fall of 1950.

STAVE: So it took two years to do. When did you end up defending it, and when did you go into your first job?

HAYS: I got a job at the University of Illinois in fall 1952 before I defended it, but after I had finished it. I had finished the whole thesis. In fact, I remember having it bound before I left Cambridge, but there was not time to schedule a defense and so I actually came back in the latter part, I think in November, of 1952 and had the defense. So I got my degree formally in the following spring, 1953.

STAVE: I find this, in a sense, interesting—your working on conservation history. Eric Lampard had worked in agricultural history, and of course he has had some major impact on urban history. Well, first of all, do you see yourself as an urban historian or as a social historian? Then let us go back to what happened when you were at Illinois.

HAYS: It is hard to define, but I call it the social analysis of politics because the interest in politics is there as a basic interest, but the close relationship between politics and society is also there. And so I keep coming back, for example, to the kind of problem that the conservation book represents in terms of national politics and how the whole national political scene is organized in terms of the balance of forces, but I am also trying constantly to plug in a lot of social phenomena. So I really do not see myself primarily as an urban historian in the sense that one's interest might be confined to the city. But I see myself as concerned with certain political and social processes and structures which can be observed in the city and in many other contexts as well.

STAVE: Did you see yourself this way in 1952 when you were first getting out of graduate school? What did you see yourself as?

HAYS: I am not sure again. I recall in the summer or spring of 1952 I wrote a considerable number of letters to ask if various schools and agricultural colleges would be interested in having somebody teach the history of conservation and got a completely blank response. So that clearly was out. Later these other interests began to jell. I cannot explain it all too specifically. I do remember that while I was at Illinois I did a lot of fooling around with election statistics for some reason or another and began to take Illinois county data and to make charts and graphs of the distribution of Taft and Roosevelt votes in 1912 and primary votes involving LaFollette and so on. I did a lot of just fiddling around with the data. I am not sure that involved much more at the time because at that point I was revising the dissertation and actually during the Christmas vacation in 1952 went back to Washington and spent two weeks in the Library of Congress and the Archives on research I had missed before and wanted to do to revise the manuscript. I was not thinking much about other research at that time.

STAVE: You stayed at Illinois for a year and then you moved to Iowa?

HAYS: That's right, in fall 1953.

STAVE: You were there for how many years?

HAYS: Seven years—until fall 1960.

STAVE: While you were at Iowa, you published *The Response to Industrialism?*

HAYS: Yes, that actually was published before the conservation book, largely because of the slowness of the process of making decisions about manuscripts at Harvard. From the time the manuscript was submitted until it was published probably took four years.

STAVE: In the interim you wrote *The Response to Industrialism*. Who were your associates at Iowa and what impact, if any, did they have on you or did you have on them?

HAYS: Well, let's see. Al Bogue was there; he had come the year before and we shared an office the first year. Bill Aydelotte was there. I think these would be the two most obvious people that I had an interest with at that time. I'm not sure there were any other people in either American or European history who had similar interests, in social history for example. But I know that we felt a common interest in quantitative research and in developing resources for more. Al and I were very much involved in trying to get the university historical archives going—going out and getting manuscript collections and so on.

STAVE: You say that you three people had an interest in quantitative history and you yourself have never used a computer, although when people mention Sam Hays they immediately think of quantification and computers. I think at a recent OAH meeting someone from the audience talked about "mathematical masturbation." Why is this the case?

HAYS: At that point the technology one talked about was the calculating machine. Our major step forward technologically was being able to have a departmental calculating machine that could be wheeled around from office to office, and having a graduate student calculate, perhaps, percentages of the vote. I do not recall that we even thought of computerizing the vote to calculate it more easily. This was before that became possible. And as far as the larger question goes of statistical techniques and the use of computers, I obviously have no aversion to using the computer and most of my students do. Most of my work since Iowa has been concerned with method and conceptualization rather than with technique, and especially with trying to work out conceptual frameworks for putting American history in the nineteenth and twentieth centuries together. That has taken my time to the exclusion of other matters. I suppose there is some aversion to committing one's time and energy to using a computer, although I do not think that would take very much time at all. The statistics course that I had was very useful; I profited enormously from that.

STAVE: In your article "A Systematic Social History," you talk about concepts and data, and it seems to me that you work more with the concepts than with the data. Now, one of the criticisms of your work has been that you have not gone out, except for the books and the "Municipal Reform" article, and gathered this hard data to test your concepts. Another criticism that I have heard is that Sam Hays really has written a whole series of essays, sometimes published, sometimes unpublished, hasn't done that many books, and they are not reviewed or criticized. How do you feel about this? There are two parts here: what about the concepts first, and what about this criticism?

HAYS: I have felt as I have taught and also tried to get students involved in research that the basic problems are largely conceptual; that is, that one needs to organize research around more meaningful problems. In trying to direct graduate research I have felt that one of the major contributions I could make was to provide some sorts of ideas that people could take up in defining research projects more precisely, and to do it within a framework of a set of ideas about social structure and social change. Very early in my teaching I began to feel dissatisfied with the way that textbooks organized American history. The framework did not make sense to me, and, as a result, I have spent a lot of time trying to reconstruct ideas around which courses could be built and larger thinking about American history could be carried out. Most of the articles I have written have been preoccupied with that. And I think that will continue for some time, since there are many aspects of such conceptual frameworks which are still kicking around in my mind and in my files and have not been developed yet on paper.

STAVE: Are you trying to put it all together in one frame of reference?

HAYS: Yes, that's quite right.

STAVE: What kind of book will it be?

HAYS: Well, it could be called a textbook—I will use it that way, but I do not know how many other people will do so. Others might look on it as an interpretive essay. It will be built around concepts of social structure and social change and focused on the intersection of politics and society. In some cases I have done more research than meets the eye, but do not put it all down because I get more interested in the larger implications and write about that. Or others do so. I did a lot of work on voting patterns in Iowa, and as time went on felt that it was not essential for me to write anything about it because others have gone ahead and done far more than I could have. I think that Sam McSeveney and Paul Kleppner have said as much as I could possibly ever say about voting patterns in the last half of the nineteenth century, so why should I just repeat it. One of the most stimulating aspects of being an historian has been the interaction with graduate students. There is hardly a seminar paper or dissertation which has not shaped my thinking in some way and, in turn, my own ideas have shaped the thinking of graduate students. It has been a heavily interactive process and if one were to understand the whole thing one would have to look at both what my students have done and I have done as very closely related. If you were cynical about this you could say that we exploit each other, but from a more benign vantage point we are stimulated enormously by each other. To get back to the article writing, when you've got an idea that you think will be useful, largely because you find people thinking along with you about it, then it makes sense to spend time working it out and especially when you are convinced that the development of new concepts is the most crucial aspect of historical reconstruction today—that sensible research depends on it. Until I get these out of my system, much of what I will write will be in essay, rather than book, form.

STAVE: You mentioned the concepts of social change and social structure. What do you see as the main themes of your work that have been outlined in the books and the essays? Could you tie this together? And what impact do you see them having?

HAYS: I think themes evolve. I can give some idea as to where I think they're at right now, but certainly they have changed over the years. I tend now to think of two rather broad headings under which patterns of both structure and change can be organized. One has to deal with the problem of the constant reorganization of society into larger and larger units of human activity and relationships. I think that what I have written—this is really implicit in the conservation book, in what I have written about systematization, in the "Municipal Reform" article, and in the local-cosmopolitan article—are attempts to put together a great amount of economic, social, and political phenomena in terms of this persistent historical increase in the scale of organization. The other large set of ideas has to do more with the decisions, choices, and values of people in the context of primary group relationships. I have been especially interested in the transformation of the more traditional patterns, which I think the voting data made very clear, into a set of more mobile options, where one starts being concerned with mobility of various kinds, both vertical and horizontal, and with a process I feel is crucial which I call "psychological mobility." The idea is drawn from

Dan Lerner's study of Turkey, but still I think it also applies in an important way to the United States. Lerner's book, *The Passing of Traditional Society,* contains the notion that there is a direction of social change involving shifts in human perception, particularly the imaginative capability of placing oneself in a different context and role, seeing different options for oneself. Around this theme are the choices that people make in their own lives toward greater differentiation, toward being different from one's past, moving to a different place, being a different kind of person, thinking different things, all of which bring about constant transformation in things such as ethnic ties, religion, family and primary group relationships, and community patterns. Right now many of the historical questions that I am concerned with can be subsumed under these two very broad categories.

STAVE: Where, under these categories, and this is a question of system change and social change, does the city come in, since we are interested in things that are urban?

HAYS: I tend to look on these processes as being rather general throughout the whole society. You can describe the entire social order in terms of them. But they can also be conceived of in different geographical contexts. The way I approach it is first to talk about these processes generally and then to have a series of different geographical contexts where they are worked out in more detail: the community, the city, the region, the nation. These are different geographical expressions of similar social structures and processes. The things I have just mentioned here about system and individual mobility can be examined within the context of the city, and so I would tend to draw these together as urban history. But, at the same time, I would want to do the same thing in the context of a larger region. As a matter of fact, I feel that one of the deficiencies of urban history is that we have confined ourselves too much to the people within the city limits, or within the given metropolitan area, whereas the city, from any kind of network theory, is the center of regional interaction. One can examine these broad social processes in the context of the relationship between the center and the periphery of the region. So I tend to give a two-part sequence to all this: focusing first on the processes generally, and then on the different geographical contexts in which they work themselves out.

STAVE: Perhaps this should be clear, but is there any sort of difference in the way they work out in the city from these other areas? There's a spillover, an interrelationship, but is there a difference? Is there a different working out of these things?

HAYS: I should think so. Take, for example, the question of migration within the city and migration within the region. It has always seemed to me that this is an interesting thing to compare and contrast. When you migrate within a city it revolves around residence, not entirely, but let's say that much of the flow of population is to find a new home, to establish a set of institutions focused on the home—community, religion, education, leisure, and so forth. But this did not necessarily divorce one from place of work. So in intraurban migration one is involved in two sets of processes, one focused on residence and the other focused on work. Migration within the region, on the other hand, involves a transfer of both residence and work from the periphery to the center and breaks the sustained linkages which exist in the city between place of work and place of residence.

Another comparison involves the role of organizational forces. Certain forces in the city organize the city itself, but these same forces reach out to organize the larger region. In each case these forces try to penetrate peripheral areas for a variety of reasons, e.g., markets. How it is done for the near urban population differs from that for the more scattered regional population. But in both cases the centralizing tendencies, the organizing tendencies, that I have argued are physically represented in the central part of the center city, could be conceived of as organizing both the city and the larger region. Another comparison is the difference in the impact of urbanizing influences on ethnicity and ethnic groups when they are residentially located in the rural parts of the region as contrasted to location within the city itself. In the latter case one might argue that traditional ethnic patterns would be eroded much more rapidly. So even though the processes are the same generally, they work out differently depending on the setting.

STAVE: I have heard you speak of yourself as a humanist. You said you were interested in the philosophical approach to things, and you are dealing with broad problems, conceptualization of problems. How do these concepts fit with the data that have to be used to prove them?

HAYS: I think that the concepts have a very strong relationship to data. Almost every point that I find to be crucial in the concepts have roots in some sort of data alternative. For example, analysis of municipal reform was a product of trying to get data about who the reformers were. There is hardly a single idea in my articles which is not rooted in some hard data, and in fact, it is usually a detailed case study with important data distinctions in it that usually sets me off to thinking about the larger conceptual picture. Many of the ideas I have included in the essays have been very much influenced by what graduate students have done both at Pitt and elsewhere, and by specific case studies in social research carried out by historians or nonhistorical social scientists. For example, the language information that has been developed by Joshua Fishman and Vladimir Nahirny in their article on immigrant generations has been very influential in shaping my view of what the second generation immigrant is all about.[1] They look on that generation as not being free to rebel, but being emotionally involved with the first generation; they could not share the old-country community experience and memory of their parents, but they were not divorced completely from them either. The result was a sense of ethnic nationalism peculiar to the second generation. This idea influenced me, of course, but more important was the information distinguishing the memories and experiences of three generations. The case of voting data is very striking. Almost everything I now think about religious values in the nineteenth century has evolved from initial observations in the hard data about how different ethnocultural groups voted.

STAVE: Let us go back for a minute to the hard data you collected for your "Municipal Reform" article. Here is an article where you did go out and you did get data on people, you counted them, and then you made certain assumptions from this data. What is the origin of that article? Why did you even bother doing that?

HAYS: This was the product of some research I had under way in Iowa, trying to reconstruct the political structure of a state, and in the process I got into city politics. It grew out of the voting data, collecting precinct data from about 1880 down to 1940 for all the cities and most of the counties in Iowa and analyzing it. Some elections that dealt with things like city commission voting in Des Moines and Cedar Rapids struck my eye and from this I went to newspaper accounts and found out how the movement for the city commission in Des Moines actually worked out. I observed that it seemed to be operated by people who were at the very highest levels of the business community in Des Moines. They met in the Chamber of Commerce building. They consisted of a select committee of 300 that made the proposals and were very reluctant to let other people come in, and I examined who the 300 were. To that I added data on Pittsburgh, did some research on Seattle, and worked in some observations from studies done earlier on city manager government by political scientists. It all seemed to fit together.

STAVE: It might fit together too with *Conservation and the Gospel of Efficiency,* in a sense of experts tying things together, bringing things together. Is there anything that serves as the nexus for this? I mean, why is Sam Hays thinking about this when some other people are not?

HAYS: I am not sure that there was any connection between the concepts in the conservation analysis and those in the municipal reform analysis originally. I think really it was the data that I saw. I think that grew out of the voting analysis, which I was doing back in the 1950s in Iowa which was a different thing. Originally, I had been dealing with national system building you might say. Now I was looking at the grass roots. In fact, I think these two perspectives are quite different, arose from two unrelated research interests. Since then I have been trying to fit them together, but at that time I was really working primarily from the grass-roots level. It was out of the voting analysis that I began to see some of these votes in Polk County, Iowa and in Cedar Rapids, Iowa and in several other places, and to examine the details, to examine the patterns of voting for commission government, and trying to get a handle on it by seeing who really proposed and who opposed. The really frustrating part of the analysis is that the amount of information available for people who proposed the rationalization of the system is always greater than the amount for those who opposed. Several students have made attempts to do this for Pittsburgh, but it has been very hard to ferret out. In some cases, like in Dayton, Ohio, the Socialists took up the opposition to municipal reform. They actually published tracts against the proposals. But in some places it is very hard to get this potential opposition pinned down. Maybe it just did not exist; perhaps most people were indifferent to the change because it was so remote from the daily lives of newer immigrant communities within the city.

STAVE: Some of these things were outlined in *The Response to Industrialism.* What are the origins of that, and would you suggest themes in that book that have continued in your work? What is new since that time?

HAYS: Well, I would say I have had a very peculiar kind of approach. I feel that book is rather lopsided because there is very little in it that deals with the positive creation of a new social order. I was thinking primarily in terms of reaction and that is why the response idea was there. I think that part of it was the urge to define much in Populism and labor reform as a defensive reaction against change, as a conservative effort to retain past institutions. I think that is probably where I first began to think of many of the things we call reform as being conservative reactions against change. And certainly this perspective has remained in my thinking, that one can conveniently divide social processes in history between those making for change and those protecting the past against change. I tend to apply the terms "radical" and "conservative" to these processes. In this sense science, technology, the business community, and administrative systems are innovations which are radical, and many movements are conservative attempts to prevent older institutions—economic, ethnic, cultural, educational—and values from being modified by these rather persistent and revolutionary changes. The *Response* book was far more concerned with the reaction rather than with the innovation, and that makes it conceptually somewhat limited.

There are several lesser themes in the *Response* book that have been important. One was about voting and political party change in the 1890s. I have a paragraph on the voting patterns of 1894; this was the result of all this work I had done on the old Northwest. The Michigan data were the most spectacular. Between 1892 and 1896 the northern counties shifted heavily Republican and the southern went heavily toward Bryan. It is a very dramatic shift. What I had to say about that was a result of county voting analysis in about five states. Another was the notion of trade organization and interest group organization. I am not sure just where that came from, although in the fifties I spent a lot of time on the politics of agricultural policy from about 1933 on and began to work out the way in which farm cooperatives played a role very similar to the trade unions and the trade associations. I began to develop the idea of the organizational revolution by examining the farm cooperatives; I began to feel that they represented an effort to control supply and demand, to control agricultural economic life, very much in the way the trade union or the trade association did. That idea began to jell in the fifties, and it clearly comes out in this "organize or perish" concept. It is sort of a primitive statement of it, but I think that is where it began.

Another idea in the articles, the local-cosmopolitan framework, is not in *The Response* but came later. I think this really came first from reading Robert Merton's article, as far as I can remember; it seemed to pull a lot of separate things together.[2] I am sure it did not come out of the blue, that there were many loose strings lying around arising from a variety of observations and the Merton article just put it together. This has happened to me a great number of times—pieces of data and ideas picked up here and there, not fitting in very well and a vague uneasiness because of it, and then suddenly an article that puts it together. In this case I felt that much more could go into that conceptual context and so I wrote the local-cosmopolitan article.[3] In fact, it has far wider implications than even in that article—for example, Van Beck Hall's book on Massachusetts in the 1780s, which I thought was a first-rate application of the concept.[4] The concept will play a very important role in the book I am writing now.

STAVE: Any other ideas that have evolved over this approximately a decade and a half now—almost two decades actually—since the publication of that book? It seems to me that I first met you in 1961 and a lot of what you said back then seems new to a lot of people today. Much has not been accepted even today. Has your thinking undergone much change? By the time of the "Municipal Reform" article it was there in place. What new ideas have evolved? The religion, the ethnopietism, in a sense—it is not a new idea although it is not accepted by a lot of people and they are not interested in it or they cast it off. What new ideas came, and do you think your ideas have made much of an impact on the profession as a whole?

HAYS: My thinking on how to put American history together is constantly evolving, not changing willy-nilly, but evolving. As I write essays and chapters in this book, I come back six or twelve months later and want to state it in a different way. Usually this is because of some conversation I have had with a student or faculty member, or an article or seminar paper I have read. *The Response to Industrialism* had this element of response, but now I will put into this a lot more about the evolution of modern society that grows out of technology and science, urbanization, industrialization. Certainly the effort to describe system-atization is an effort to do that and so I think that side of it—development to which there has been a reaction—was weak in that book and has constantly been evolving more in my thinking. I have also added a lot more to defining the institutions that continue the past and become the focal points of tradition, for example, in religion, ethnicity, and the family. I do not think that I was aware of the conservative implications in all this—as well as the innovative—until recently.

STAVE: And why is this?

HAYS: A matter of new awareness. In the past few years, I have become very interested in the family in terms of whether particular families have traditional or more modernized values. I think that certainly if I had been reading the right kind of literature and it hit me the right way

I could have found it back in the fifties. But, on the other hand, you become aware of new things as time goes on simply because other people are talking about them—that is a large part of it. I think I am much more involved with trying to work out aspects of ethnicity than I was before, largely in terms of trying to understand the internal evolution of ethnic groups. I do not remember thinking of that very much ten years ago. Now I think that when I am talking about ethnicity the thing I am really focusing on is the internal structure of ethnic groups. You could call them subcultures. There are the subcultures that come because of different degrees of involvement with modernizing processes on the part of particular groups before they came here, or the different styles of religion developed within the United States, such as German Methodism of the nineteenth century, or the evolution of internal class and value subcultures within specific groups in the United States.

STAVE: Internal evolution—what do you mean by that? What do you mean when you say you are interested in studying the interrelationship of humans or the interaction of human relationships. This is a phrase that you often use. What do you mean by the internal evolution of ethnic groups?

HAYS: It seems to me that any ethnic group comes to America with a certain subcultural pattern which undergoes change in the United States. I have felt that much of that change is erroneously described as a relatively uniform change. The word "assimilation" seems to imply this—a relatively uniform impact of American society on an ethnic group. I have been more impressed with the way in which that impact is not uniform, but produces differentiation within the ethnic group so that you begin to get, for example, a developed class system. That is why Milton Gordon's concept of "ethclass" was very appealing to me. It seemed to focus on variation within each ethnic group depending on the degree to which it had become involved in mobility, in education, had moved up the occupational ladder, had become more cosmopolitan than local. It strikes me that to understand any ethnic group you must first understand that internal variation.

STAVE: Is this at all levels of political space you are talking about now?

HAYS: Yes. I think you can see it best on the community level, but I think this would be true for other levels as well. A number of questions emerge, for example, what subcultural variations are a product of changes in the community of origin—where immigrants came from—and what are a product of the community of destination in the United States.

Several of my students now are dealing with problems such as these and so my mind is working along this line. For example, one student, Peter Rusos, is working on Greeks; he has discovered information about village of origin from church records in Pittsburgh and from it he hopes to relate variations in that background with variations in residence, occupation, and attitudes—Greek subcultures—in Pittsburgh. He might be able to distinguish between the Greeks who came from the islands and the seacoast versus those who came from inland. They migrated to the same place in Pittsburgh, but it appears that they soon separated in a second migration within Pittsburgh and even had different attitudes toward things like political issues in Greece. So this is the notion that emerges—subcultures as they evolved in the United States might well have been due to some evolution of subcultures in Europe. Another student, Victor Walsh, is working on Irish subcultures, by focusing on the Irish middle class in nineteenth-century Pittsburgh. Most of them he finds came over as middle class and were far different in origin than the mass of Irish migrants. I have been particularly interested in the Germans because, it seems to me, the Germans have the most varied subculture of almost any ethnic group. Particularly striking are the many Germans who became converted to Methodism after they came to the United States, or became Masons. Both seem foreign to German culture. Where does all this come from? Is it something that evolves after migration or is it some predisposition in the German setting? Another student, Nora Faires, is exploring this problem of German subcultures in the United States by an intensive analysis of the nineteenth-century Pittsburgh German community. All this I find very exciting. Most of it has actually come from the graduate students who have come up with ideas for seminar papers, and it all begins to add up to some very important historical questions that foster a new line of inquiry.

STAVE: What do you mean by this term—"the interaction of human relationships"—which appears in several of your articles?

HAYS: I do not really think that this refers to anything esoteric. I do not mean anything other than the connections people have with each other, the degree to which they share common values or the degree to which they have an interactive set of relationships. If you have people who at one stage of history have primary group relationships with certain people or common ethnic or religious origins in a certain community and they begin to move out of that into relationships with other people that are more extensive geographically and more heterogeneous culturally, then this is a new pattern of human relationships. Our theory and concepts about patterns of human life—values, inter-actions—arise from the fact that human activity has to be sorted out into manageable categories and when you do this you get a sense of patterns. This is what statistical variation is all about—a set of patterns that vary.

STAVE: While you are talking about patterns, you are very concerned with the episodic and historians taking a very small view of things. What caused you to be concerned with the notion of pattern and change over time as opposed to the very narrow view?

HAYS: Again, I cannot really say. Probably it is implicit in the original social science bent. I did look on psychology not as something to explain individual behavior but social behavior. I think that concern for social behavior, social attitudes, social phenomenon has been there from the start. I do not think that has changed very much. The presidential synthesis article that Cochran wrote clicked right away.[5] So I think it was something built into my way of thinking from a fairly early time, and it just continued. It is a matter of what you are interested in, and my interest seems to run toward trying to understand society as it changes over time. If someone else is not interested in that but in the individual biography and event, then that is their thing.

STAVE: There seems to be some antagonism, I think, to some of the things that you have talked about, that many historians are not willing to accept. Why would this be? Why do you think it is?

HAYS: I think this is a bit hard to assess at this point. For example, I think that the ethnocultural analysis of voting patterns in the nineteenth century is here to stay. I think you can see that in a lot of literature. You can see it in the book reviews. This has had to compete with a very heavy dose of economic motivation, economic causation. Any assertion of the importance of ethnocultural values is going to have hard sledding. And yet it seems to me that the data have been so massive, put together by so many different people—we now have a half dozen books, let alone articles, that focus on this—that even though people may disagree, they now have come to the position that they cannot ignore it. Many people do not know how to deal with it except to say that it is as important as something else or must be taken into account. Now, again, how do you really understand the impact of ideas in a piece of research or writing? The "Municipal Reform" article—that has been reprinted now about twenty times, and it is in the Bobbs-Merrill reprint series and I think last year sold about 1,500 copies. This means that people are interested in that. Sometimes not for the reasons that I think it is important, but nevertheless, it has had some impact.

STAVE: What is the difference here—why do you think they sometimes might be interested for different reasons?

HAYS: Many people will say that the argument there is a class argument, and this means that the article appeals to people who have a class theory. As a matter of fact, Students for a Democratic Society reprinted it obviously because they thought it supported their particular point of view. On the other hand, I tend to be more interested in what I would call system variables. I was not concerned with class and municipal reform. I was concerned with the way people were reorganizing the social order, and I was trying to link people who were reorganizing the economic side of the social order and the social side to a common interest in reorganizing the political side as well. I wanted to argue that there was a relationship, a correlation, among all three, that those who want to organize society on a larger scale in one realm want to do it in another realm. Now that argument has not been taken up by very many people and most of the introductions to the reprintings do not even mention it, even though I think the point is fairly clear and explicit. It was like the conservation book. There I focused—it was very explicit in the introduction and the conclusion—on the political processes implicit in science and technology. Yet that book has been typed for many years as concerned with the subject matter of conservation and most people talk about it in these terms. All this reflects the fact that historians have definite mind-sets that exercise a controlling influence on how they see things. It is often hard to break through that mind-set and to generate a new perspective.

STAVE: Modernization has become a very popular concept. Were you dealing with modernization in that book and the "Municipal Reform" article before a lot of historians had started doing it in the last half decade or so?

HAYS: Well, I would think so, but only in a very loose sense. When we talk about modernization, very frequently what people have in mind is the transfer of a set of ideas that comes from analysis of the non-Western world to the West, and I think it results in a lot of transfer that is not applicable. I never have really been concerned, for example, with the element of modernization theory that seems to put a normative value on stability and order. That has never seemed to me to be too valuable a concept to use. On the other hand, I think we have been in American history very sorely in need of concepts that will somehow or other bring all of these vast changes in society into some sort of conceptual system. The changes are very simple—urbanization, industrialization. But I think we have to add to these some of the variables like systematization, which seems to me to be a terribly important concept, or like psychological mobility, that there are many value changes that go along with this. As a result, terms like urbanization and industrialization are not enough. Other terms describe changes in values, changes in perspective, changes in the way in which people begin to think about possibilities for themselves to create something bigger that is more universal, more national—the sorts of perspectives that describe the "new men" of the American Revolution, for example. How do you talk about all this? These are not economic matters; they are changes in perspective and psychological outlook. They have this element of a great variety of options, greater possibilities, and imagination of one in different circumstances. The term modernization seems to me to incorporate these things. Now it is one of those words which is absolutely ridiculous to use because it is so ambiguous, and yet I am sure that any other word that might be substituted for it would be equally ambiguous. Perhaps ambiguity is necessary in order to have a term that is loose and has some capability of imagination about it. So I do not know what else to use now. I would say that the things I have talked about really involve the creation of a modernization theory of American history, but I would not want that to mean at all the simple transfer of ideas from an understanding of non-Western political development to American history.

STAVE: In desiring this kind of concept that gives you flexibility, going back to what we were talking about before, in a sense does this make you "softer" than some of the individuals who are looking at data in a much "harder" sense, who are interested in making sure that it fits on punchcards and goes into the computer and comes out with certain kinds of answers? Is this the difference that you see between yourself and practitioners of a more scientific history?

HAYS: Well, there is certainly a difference. I do not think that the difference lies at all in the concern for data because I am always trying to find hard data that will tell us something; I am unsatisfied if it has to remain just speculative. On the other hand, I certainly do agree, as, for example, I wrote in a recent review in the *Journal of Interdisciplinary History,* that many, many of the studies that use quantification do not produce effective results. They do not use data to demonstrate an important conceptual distinction and, as a result, are often futile and meaningless. My point of reference always seems to be the construction of a set of ideas and concepts that put history together. I see these evolving in a certain way, and I am looking always for research that will help to clear up an ambiguous point in an evolving set of ideas. I really am not at all happy with seeing simply a lot of data put together and manipulated if it does not seem to be getting anywhere. There is a major difference in approach here which some are describing as a difference between hard quantifiers and soft quantifiers. This difference emerged very early, as early as the summer conference on the use of the voting data which was held at the Inter-University Consortium for Political Research at Ann Arbor in the mid-1960s. The purpose of the conference was to stimulate use of the data that were being computerized. One obvious thing about those data was that they were county-level data. And, as a result, the only way in which you could design research was through county-level aggregations. Now the work I had done in Iowa convinced me that that would not get anyone anywhere, or it would not get anyone far enough, that ward and precinct data were essential to examine the social patterns which they reflected. Now it may well be that through the examination of county-level data and the association of census variables with the voting variables one can find something, but I had been so intrigued with the kinds of patterns that grew out of township and ward analysis, particularly the ethnic and the religious, and was so convinced that the closer one could get to a homogeneous ward the more one could say something fairly important. For example, do you remember the article that George Daniels did when he picked out the German townships in Iowa and examined how they voted?[6] I thought he had something really solid there, and I was doing the same sort of thing, either picking out the strong Republican, the strong Democratic, or the heavily German. I made lists of Scandinavian, Norwegian, Danish, and Swedish districts and examined how they voted. Now you cannot do that with the county-level data. The thing that you clearly cannot do at all is any urban analysis. You cannot analyze any unit smaller than the county the city is in. Now many of the technical people at the conference and particularly the political scientists and some of the historians were convinced that one could still say a lot that was terribly important with the county-level data. Well, I obviously was not satisfied with that, and I think you can actually see the results. In every significant historical book or article on voting analysis to appear recently, the author has relied heavily on minor civil division data, or even individualized data. That is the way insight and analysis have proceeded. An excellent example of this is David Brye's recent doctoral dissertation at

Harvard—Brye was at the Ann Arbor conference—in which he focuses on minor civil division data to examine voting in Wisconsin from the late nineteenth century on.[7] There is more insight in that manuscript than in all the county-level analysis that has been done to date. Another example is the recent Indiana study that Mel Hammarberg did in the *Journal of American History* where he used a lot of individualized data.[8]

So you see here again I have a preference which many people disagree with, for zeroing in on a limited case study where it seems to me the issues are really relevant, rather than developing a statistical analysis on a larger level that may be technically more comprehensive, but does not tell you very much. Now the case study approach does not necessarily mean that any old case study will do. It is one where you really have a possibility of seeing some sort of a major distinction that has conceptual importance. So I think case studies are excellent so long as the issue involved is really relevant. Now to be relevant you always mean relevance within your frame of reference as to what an evolving theory is. If there is any way in which I think you can understand this whole sequence, it is in terms of an evolving set of ideas about how you put history together and then a desire either to find what somebody else has done that really hits a point and helps you to make a choice or to help your students to define research that could be crucial. One thing now that has intrigued me very much is the fact that many of our phenomena may well be phenomena of the life cycle. Certainly now we have a lot of ideas about how migration is deeply involved with life cycle. Contemporary migration data—they are very clearly closely associated with age. All right, now I would be extremely interested in some research somebody has done or some research a student wanted to do which would pin that down and make migration age specific. That is the kind of thing that I would say you ought to go into, and a limited case study that does that I think would make a big contribution. On the other hand, you will find people who will say, "Well, you can't generalize from that; you don't know how representative your case study is." Consider the problem of where people migrate after they leave—this is not a question you can solve by waiting until you get the desired data for the entire county. You have to go out and to find some data that will tell you where people go. One student at Pitt, Dave Pistolessi, working with Bob Doherty, is doing a study of Civil War veterans in Pittsburgh. Why? Because the Civil War pension records give you data on where they went. So for this group we will know how many moves they made in their later life and how far they moved. Now, it is only one group, but it is more than I know of being done on this problem. And so I am quite willing, so long as the issue seems to be important, to zero in with whatever design you can really carry out, to bring out the crucial problems.

STAVE: The notion of age-specific data is in an unpublished essay that you have done called "Social Structure and the New Urban History." First of all, do you think there is such a thing as the "new urban history," and second, what do you mean by "social structure and the new urban history?"

HAYS: Yes, I think there is something called the new urban history in the sense that people are doing things now that they were not doing ten years ago. Certainly almost all of the work that is represented by the Yale conference and the book that came out of it is a new style of research in history, both in terms of problems and also data.

STAVE: Is that *Nineteenth Century Cities,* edited by Thernstrom and Sennett?

HAYS: Yes. So I think that that does represent something new. Now, of course, the "new urban history" becomes a rather well-worn term and does not make any sense after a while. This is why I have tended to zero in on the term "social research." It has a little bit more content to it. It seems to me that we are trying to describe the populations of cities more broadly. Whatever we deal with in the city, we say it has to take into account a far greater number of people and more aspects of their lives. We describe extensive social characteristics of the city, what people do and think, the way they are changing their lives; it seems to me that is really what is new about urban history. I do not see this in any of the older books about the city. Now it is true that a lot of the new urban history is still a single city approach. There is very little comparative research, but there is some being done, and I think that the more that can be done the better. I think that we just have to come to a conclusion sometime about whether or not the patterns we are observing in one city are typical or atypical, and what kind of a scale of variation they stand on. I think it can be done. I think it is fascinating that the five people who are doing the large-scale urban demographic studies—Hershberg, Katz, Glasco, Griffin, and Blumin—are finding that their cities are much alike. They brought this out at their joint meeting at the OAH recently, for example, in terms of occupational structure. Now, I am not sure this makes very clear just how cities are alike and how they are different. One of the problems here is that our data are not as developed as we would like and the indices are not so clear. You could probably arrange cities on a continuum in many different ways and . . .

STAVE: In what ways?

HAYS: Well, industrial types, types of industry, types of population mix, ethnic background, age of city, rates of growth. I think the problem is that we do not yet have a systematic way for selecting cities for comparison according to certain common characteristics which then you control for and sort out similarities and differences. But I do think that cross-city research is one of the aspirations of the new urban history.

STAVE: This is for the future ledger. This is what people should go out and do. Now, a case study itself is very time consuming. A case study of many cities is even more time consuming. What new problems do you foresee for, say, graduate students who undertake this kind of work and are working a longer number of years than someone who does not? Do you actually foresee people doing this on a large scale?

HAYS: I think so, but I also think it will not come until we can facilitate it.

STAVE: How would you go about facilitating it?

HAYS: Well, for example, if we had the census data for 1850 through 1880 and hopefully 1900 some day computerized for ten different cities, then any graduate student could do a lot of comparative research pretty quickly. It would really facilitate it. That has to be done for just that one basic kind of datum bank.

STAVE: But comparative research now on the basis of the quantifiable data, this raises a question.

HAYS: I think you are quite right. But, on the other hand, if you had at least this much done, so that you could compare cities with reference to some phenomenon through the demographic data, through the census data, at least you would have a major start, and I think that a student could afford to invest time, let's say, in picking up two or three cities. Another way, I think, that it might be done is to put every city, large and small, in the United States in the pot, in the computer, with reference to a few variables, maybe ten, the more obvious easy ones to do. I think this really would be quite simple. Then students could at least have a much better rationale for selection. They could select one or two cities of different sizes, of different ages, different rates of growth, different industrial mixes, and this would enable them to design a research problem systematically. We could assist students enormously and move comparative research ahead significantly. I feel we can facilitate this by some just basic innovations like this. At Pitt, for example, we had about six students who were drawing samples from the census, and after about the sixth one of these it became obvious—what was the use of spending all this time? So we embarked on this project of computerizing the census, the entire census for the city. It has taken a long time, but we have 1860 and 1870 done now—all the variables in the manuscript census—have the punching for 1850 done, and are half through 1880. So we now see our way through the woods on this one. By the time we are done it will have been an eight-year project. But the fact is that now not only graduate students, but others also, can use it as well. We have a class of juniors and seniors who are using it, as a way of introducing them to the analysis of demographic data with the computer. The data are there and all they have to do is manipulate them; they do not have to spend time coding or punching.

STAVE: I think this raises another significant question. This is being done at Pittsburgh. It is being done at Pittsburgh because you came there at a point in time, in 1960?

HAYS: Yes.

STAVE: The department at Pittsburgh is an interesting one. Some people see it as a community of scholars, at least more so than other history departments. Could you talk a little about the shaping of the department and how you went about building it in this direction?

HAYS: Well, again, there was no real plan; it sort of grew. I think certainly that my own strong interest in urban history and social phenomena had a considerable influence. On the other hand, it is very clear that from the start this was not very well developed in any sense, and I would not say that until about 1966 or 1967 a clear philosophy had begun to emerge. It had many elements, but one of the most important was the comparative study of similar problems; that is, we began to think of the possibility of bringing together clusters of people not around the traditional country and time period focus, but around kinds of phenomena that cut across countries, and ideally we were thinking in terms of how this could be done on a whole set of problems. I remember one time we made a list of about twenty different types of phenomena that it would be great to have two or three people working on. Well, that was a pipe dream, but at the same time it did guide us so that we began to build up some of them. We have several people now working on ethnicity in different countries, on the city in different countries; the ones that emerged were the ones where specialists were available. I remember one type of problem that we were always looking for somebody to deal with but never found was legal institutions. We began to think that one of the sets of institutions in which people are involved anywhere at any time is the legal system, and by this we meant not just the law, but the courts, the police, everything that comes in a life cycle—birth, marriage and divorce, death, crime and police, probate, buying and selling—the whole thing. Somebody with some imagination could get this into shape so that it could be a window into social history that would be enormously valuable. But we never could find anybody. It happened that the people being trained at that time were into things like urbanization and ethnicity, but we found some others. Bob Doherty's interest in religion was relatively unique and this, I think, has helped to stir interest in this in a number of people. I think that Jon Levine's interest in rural life was relatively unique; most of American rural history is the history of the West, and yet it is a focus on the impact of urbanization on the rural community, I think, that is needed. This fits in with a major interest in the department in peasant societies that brought together a half dozen people and led to the establishment of the *Peasant Studies Newsletter,* edited by David Sabean.

STAVE: You keep talking about "we." Is it we or you?

HAYS: Well, again, I do not think one can really know. I am quite willing to say that probably I had a lot of influence on it. Yet, at the time, it was a matter of working things out. Appointments were made largely as a result of people being exposed to other people, and we would go to a history meeting and sit and talk to maybe ten people a day, an hour for each one, and probe their minds pretty deeply. And there would be several history faculty there. Some we would bring to Pittsburgh and they would give a lecture and be exposed to the whole department; these were departmental decisions. I know that in some cases I had very strong opinions about candidates and succeeded in persuading others. At other times I lost out. So its very hard to sort it out. One thing that was clear, however, was that there was a real premium on candidates having a good set of ideas as to where they were going in making a contribution to historical thinking, and another was the high level of intellectual interchange and mutual respect that developed and cut across countries and time periods and focused on problems.

STAVE: What effect did being chairman for thirteen years have on your own work? Do you think that this had an adverse effect or not?

HAYS: Yes. It prevented me from focusing on a single large-scale research project. Clearly one of the reasons why I could not do that was because of the commitments required of a chairman. Yet, looking back, a lot of the ideas which I have developed, which have come out in a variety of articles—and there are a lot more to come that are simmering on the back burner—are to a great extent a product of the intellectual ferment of the department, among students as well as faculty. I just found that the people who came were terribly stimulating. Take, for example, a person like Julius Rubin, who has an enormous range of knowledge and clear thinking about economic development from a very broad-ranging point of view. He has made an enormous contribution to both students and faculty. I should place special stress on the students. Almost every turn of mind I have had students have made a significant contribution to. Their seminar papers, dissertations, and constant conversations have produced a climate that is difficult to pin down, but has played an important role in the evolution of my own historical thinking.

STAVE: Was there room for someone who did not follow the party line?

HAYS: Yes, the history faculty at Pitt are a diverse group, and some do not share the approach to social history which most take. Most—not all—are interested in social history and interact with each other on that basis. I think we began to define the department primarily—not exclusively—in terms of a concern for social history very broadly conceived. And we found that there are very different approaches to social history. These do not really come out until you get a critical mass of people working on similar kinds of problems, but from different vantage points. The advantages of this cannot be realized if all you have are one or two people working in social history. I would say, however, that social history has been so sufficiently broad in our conception of things that it tends to infuse almost every aspect of history, even foreign relations.

STAVE: In your "Systematic Social History" article you talk about urban history as a branch of social history, essentially a spinoff of social history.

HAYS: Yes, like I was saying a while ago, that is, it is a context in which you can see many social processes.

STAVE: The *Historical Methods Newsletter* emanates out of Pittsburgh and has had an influence, I think, in terms of the methodology that historians use who are interested in quantification. What are the origins of that?

HAYS: That grew out of the summer seminar we had at Ann Arbor in the mid-1960s where clearly something was beginning to jell. I am not sure of the steps. I would have to go back again and see if I couldn't reconstruct that more concretely. But clearly it was felt that there was a need for some exchange of ideas, and so it was started on a shoestring basis. Actually, Paul Kleppner did it on his own time and he kept it for a few years, two, three maybe, and then Jon Levine came along. Jon is a very broad-ranging person; he is interested in a lot of kinds of social research, and he kept it up. So I think it did grow out of that situation, out of a feeling on the part of a number of people involved that this kind of interchange would be very useful. It has always been run as a network kind of thing where you do not have pretensions to being a full-scale scholarly journal, but try to keep it on a communications level.

STAVE: But why at Pitt again?

HAYS: Well, again, I suppose to some extent because of our interest, to some extent because we were able to find a person to do it and a few resources available for it. I do not recall the circumstances. I think there were a few alternatives where other people could not come up with either the time or the money.

STAVE: We are taping now in Brockport, New York, and there is a conference that has been held for seven years on social-political history here which you have been influential in. What are the origins of this, and do you see this as something which deals with the kind of history that you yourself have tried to proselytize?

HAYS: The first meeting of this conference, I think, was at Cortland; it was devoted almost entirely to historical political behavior—popular and legislative voting. Then it went up to Brockport for a year, then back to Cortland, and it has been in Brockport since. I really did not get involved in it at the start, and I think I have been coming only for the last four years. Certainly, there is a great interest in this conference by people who use quantitative data to try to describe social patterns, and I think there is a great interest in the intersection between social and political phenomena, although at times economic phenomena as well. It is this sort of intersection that I find interesting and useful, and this is why I have been involved in it. I felt here that things were being talked about that I found very important. There is also a very different setting than at most meetings. There are only three sessions. Papers are dealt with in depth with a lot of audience participation, and there is a lot of opportunity for informal discussion in the common bar, at meals, and so forth. So it is extremely useful in terms of dealing with things in depth. Part of that is in terms of the people who come, part is the subjects that are dealt with. I also like the very experimental and unsophisticated climate. There are fewer status pretensions than in many meetings, and good work done by people in social research no matter what institution they are in is well recognized. There is little overweight of establishment flavor that one often finds oppressive in many historical meetings. But I have seen it as just a very rewarding, pleasant place to be, plus being a very nice physical setting—the rural setting outside Brockport, always in the fall when the leaves are turning.

STAVE: Which of your own writings do you like the best? Is there any article or book that you really think is the best?

HAYS: No, I do not think I could say that. I think I probably would have to include a number of things. It is particularly difficult to do because I see it as evolving, where everything sort of builds on everything else. Of the articles, I think the "Community-Society" article, the "Municipal Reform" article, the "Systematic Social History" article, the introduction to the Israel book, and then the article on urban history in the first issue of *The Journal of Urban History* may well be the most important—largely because I see them as making conceptual contributions. Again, coming back to the notion that what I am really after is developing a set of ideas to put history together. There may be a subtle but important way of looking at it. I do not see history as a science which proceeds by traditional scientific steps. To me history is always a kind of jigsaw puzzle. You get a sense of what the whole picture is and you have only a few pieces; you try to make these pieces as precise as possible, but then you fill in the gaps to create the whole picture. Often those gaps, in among the "hard data," can be dealt with only through intuitions and speculations; they are better for being "informed by," consistent with, the "hard data." I am not sure that this is a very sensible or sophisticated way of looking at it, but I always come back to that kind of image. And this jigsaw puzzle you are trying to put together is a social order as it changes over long periods of time.

STAVE: Is there anything you have written which you would not write again if you had the opportunity?

HAYS: Well, that is interesting. I am not sure, again, because I see each one of these articles as part of an evolution. Perhaps I feel that *The Response to Industrialism* is the weakest.

STAVE: It is a weak book?

HAYS: Yes, I would certainly do it very differently now, largely because it does not deal with the evolution of American society in terms of positive social institutional development, and what I write next will be a major revision of that, not basically of what is there but of putting more in that ought to be put in. I think it is a rather weak book. I think the conservation book I would not do any differently. I think that is still a sound argument. Of the articles I just mentioned, I think every one of them I would agree with still. Again, I have changed over the years. I would not continue to assign, for example, the article I did in the *Political Science Quarterly* or the article I did which appeared in the Hofstadter-Lipset reader. I think the "Systematic Social History" really supersedes those. I would see that as something I now introduce students to instead of earlier articles.

STAVE: How about other people's works? If you would not assign *The Response to Industrialism,* which a lot of people use, what about other works? If you had to choose a half dozen in, say, social or urban history, which ones would you have on your bookshelf?

HAYS: Well, I suppose the best way of thinking about it is which ones would you assign to students. I have a problem here in that I can never remember my reading lists. One of the problems, I think, is that 70% of what I assign is not really by historians.

STAVE: Well, you are not the only one. In the other interviews I have been doing, I keep getting this; there are very few books pointed to that are by historians.

HAYS: I want students to read something on ethnocultural politics, and this is perhaps a bias on my part, but I think that Kleppner's book is the best one in this whole field,[9] although I think that Ron Formisano's book deals with early stages of this in a very important way.[10] The books are too long for a class to read, so I usually settle for the article that Kleppner wrote in the reader by Silbey and Mc-Seveney.[11] On ethnic development the work I use first is the Nahirny and Fishman article—a sociologist and anthropologist—"Immigration and the Problem of Generations" in the *Sociological Review* I think. Again, I am always fuzzy on sources. I never remember the precise location. I have them read Daniel Lerner's chapter in his book *The Passing of Traditional Society.* That deals with psychological mobility. I have them always read *The Transportation Revolution* by George Rogers Taylor, which is crucial in terms of the reorganization of society through transportation in the nineteenth century. One of the early chapters of Lloyd Warner's book on corporate America in the twentieth century has some very good sense about the reorganization of American society along corporate lines; I assign that. I usually have students read Lubell's, *The Future of American Politics.* I have them read Warner's *Streetcar Suburbs* and Gans's *The Urban Villagers,* Vidich and Bensman, *Small Town in Mass Society,* and Thernstrom's book on Newburyport as well as a chapter from his book on Boston. The Boston book is tighter and more technically advanced, but I do not think it gives the students as much to think about as the Newburyport book except for the chapter on ethnic comparisons. I am sure there are a lot more readings that I cannot remember.

STAVE: Well, what does this say for the state of history if at least half of the books and articles you just mentioned are not by historians, and the fact that this seems to be more common than less among the people who are being interviewed?

HAYS: Well, let's put it this way. I think that certainly historians have a long way to go in social research, and if you are interested in the reconstruction of social patterns you just will not find that much there. On the other hand, I do think that if one looks at the doctoral dissertations over the last four or five years, there has been considerable progress. Now it is true that some of it, in fact quite a bit of it, is written by geographers or sociologists. There is a very interesting dissertation—I wish I could have my students read it, but it would have to be condensed considerably in order to be read in a short time—on the ethnic penetration of elites in Detroit.[12] It is by a sociologist and compares the degree to which ethnics moved into the labor elite, the economic elite, the political elite, and the social elite. There are a number of dissertations in social history, and they are a bit of a problem to assign to students because they are too long for undergraduates. But they do have a good approach. You are right. Many are written by people other than historians. There is a very good dissertation that distinguishes between Federalists and anti-Federalists in 1787, written in 1973 by James Pierson in political science at Michigan State. It deals with the local-cosmopolitan distinction in a very sensible way, and I think is the best I have seen for that whole period. But, again, that is by a political scientist.

STAVE: By the way, you are talking about students now. Do you think that the teaching and ideas you advocate can be assimilated by the average undergraduate in, say, a four-year college, not in a university structure?

HAYS: There is absolutely no question about that. I taught a survey course a couple of years ago for freshmen and sophomores and used the same ideas and the same material that I used for a junior-senior course. It is more difficult, but it works. In other words, the ideas we are talking about are not difficult ideas to comprehend. As a matter of fact, oftentimes they are easy to comprehend, particularly those that grow out of a personal human setting, almost any idea dealing with ethnicity and ethnic change. One thing that interests me very much is the way in which you examine changing values and changing social systems through education as a system. A lot of things you can bring to bear on this that students know about. They experience it personally—family, family history, a lot of these things, and so I am convinced it can be done. Now, the things that are more difficult to deal with are those that are more remote and more abstract, and there is no question that when you try to develop concepts that relate to larger regions or the nation as a whole, and deal with organizational and system phenomena in these larger contexts, they are harder to grasp because they are difficult to personalize. And yet, you can make some approach to them.

STAVE: You talked before about future research on what we could call the variable of age as something to look at. Any other ideas that you think should be looked at for the future?

HAYS: Well, one thing I am extremely interested in is the whole idea of psychological mobility. It seems to me that there are changes in human perception which involve not the conscious assumptions that people have, but the degree to which people conceive of their lives and their future as having alternatives, the degree to which the outside world involves acceptable alternatives. I would like to take that idea, in Lerner's book, and operationalize it for history. This is one of the most intriguing things right now in my mind. With all the problems we talked about, for example, immigration and ethnicity, well, yes, I have students concerned with this; they are especially exploring subcultures and comparative ethnicity. I mentioned the way the region has been neglected; people concentrate on the city as city rather than on the city as region, and several of my students are interested in that. But in terms of questions that would make a major difference in historical thinking, the problem of psychological mobility might be the most rewarding— very difficult to work out, but rewarding.

STAVE: Do you have ideas on how it can be done?

HAYS: Some, but not many. For example, I think given names might be a way of looking at it, particularly in families where you can assume that a given name may well represent something symbolically for the parents. I think this has some possibilities, I do not know what—I would like to fiddle with this. I know it works in several cases. I ran across one where a family of Scotch Highlanders continued to name their children for one generation in America with the old names— Murdock, Findla, Alexander, John, Duncan—and then in the 1790s appeared such names as Hamilton and Franklin and Calvin, and by the 1840s one branch of the family had names like Robert Dale Owen and John Van Buren. This tells quite a bit about changes in the lives of this particular family. But how widespread it is, I do not know. Another place to experiment with it is in religion, and especially the impact of modernization on religious values. We could talk about that change in terms of perceived options. Take a group of Lutherans in the nineteenth century. Some were extremely traditional in their attitudes and others were increasingly secularized in their values. One might do some content analysis of Lutheran magazines and other writings and look for these variations. To what extent does the content reflect an effort to reinforce the traditional and limited perspective and to what extent does it constantly present options. For example, in the role of women; I was struck by this several years ago when I was going through the attic of an old house that used to be a post office. Up in the attic were all sorts of magazines and newspapers from the nineteenth century. There was a religious journal that seemed to convey an image of a narrowly circumscribed life with little breadth, and then there were the family magazines or newspapers that circulated in the nineteenth century which were altogether different—all sorts of information about the wider world, cities "out there," and so on with a mixture of enticement into them and admonishment to avoid them. I think some imaginative use of varieties of literature like that might help in exploring psychological mobility. I am not really sure what can be done with this kind of thing, but it seems to me that there are possibilities.

STAVE: With that note, optimistic for the future, let us conclude this interview. Thank you.

NOTES

1. Vladimir C. Nahirny and Joshua A. Fishman, "American Immigrant Groups: Ethnic Identification and the Problem of Generations," Sociological Review, 13 (1965), 311-326.

2. Robert K. Merton, "Patterns of Influence: Local and Cosmopolitan Influentials," in Merton, *Social Theory and Social Structure* (Glencoe, 1957), 387-420.

3. Samuel P. Hays, "The Politics of Reform in Municipal Government in the Progressive Era," Pacific Northwest Quarterly, 55 (1964), 157-169. The local-cosmopolitan scheme appears throughout Hays's writings.

4. Van Beck Hall, *Politics Without Parties: Massachusetts, 1780-1791* (Pittsburgh, 1972).

5. Thomas C. Cochran, "The Presidential Synthesis in American History," American Historical Review, 53 (1948), 748-759.

6. George H. Daniels, "The Immigrant Vote in the 1860 Election: The Case of Iowa," Mid-America, 44 (1963), 142-162.

7. David Brye, "Wisconsin Voting Patterns in the Twentieth Century, 1900-1950" (Ph.D. dissertation, Harvard University, 1973).

8. Melvin Hammarberg, "Indiana Farmers and the Group Basis of the Late Nineteenth-Century Political Parties," Journal of American History, 61 (1974), 91-115.

9. Paul Kleppner, *The Cross of Culture: A Social Analysis of Midwestern Politics, 1850-1900* (New York, 1970).

10. Ronald P. Formisano, *The Birth of Mass Political Parties: Michigan, 1827-1861* (Princeton, 1971).

11. Paul Kleppner, "The Political Revolution of the 1890s: A Behavioral Interpretation," in Joel H. Silbey and Samuel T. McSeveney, eds., *Voters, Parties, and Elections: Quantitative Essays in the History of American Popular Voting Behavior* (Lexington, Massachusetts, 1972), 184-194.

12. Martin Marger, "Ethnic Penetration of the Elite Structure of Detroit" (Ph.D. dissertation, Michigan State University, 1973).

SELECT BIBLIOGRAPHY OF WORKS
BY SAMUEL P. HAYS

The Response to Industrialism, 1885-1914 (Chicago, 1957).

Conservation and the Gospel of Efficiency: The Progressive Conservation Movement, 1890-1920 (Cambridge, Massachusetts, 1959).

"History as Human Behavior," Iowa Journal of History (July 1960), 193-206.

"The Politics of Reform in Municipal Government in the Progressive Era," Pacific Northwest Quarterly, 55 (October 1964), 157-169.

"The Social Analysis of American Political History, 1880-1920," Political Science Quarterly, 80 (September 1965), 373-394.

"Political Parties and the Community-Society Continuum," in William N. Chambers and Walter Dean Burnham, eds., *The American Party Systems: Stages of Political Development* (New York, 1967), 152-181.

"New Possibilities for American Political History: The Social Analysis of Political Life," in Seymour Martin Lipset and Richard Hofstadter, eds., *Sociology and History: Methods* (New York, 1968), 181-227.

"Right Face, Left Face: The Columbia Strike," Political Science Quarterly, 84 (June 1969), 311-327.

"A Systematic Social History," in George A. Billias and Gerald N. Grob, eds., *American History: Retrospect and Prospect* (New York, 1971), 315-366.

"Introduction—The New Organizational Society," in Jerry Israel, ed., *Building the Organizational Society* (New York, 1972), 1-15.

"The Ebb and Flow of Ethnicity in American History," Pitt Magazine, 29 (Summer 1973), 8-15.

"Historical Social Research: Concept, Method, and Technique," Journal of Interdisciplinary History, 4 (Winter 1974), 475-482.

"The Development of Pittsburgh as a Social Order," Western Pennsylvania Historical Magazine, 57 (October 1974).

"The Changing Political Structure of the City in Industrial America," Journal of Urban History, 1 (November 1974), 6-38.

INDEX